Militarism and Social Revolution
in the Third World

Militarism and Social Revolution in the Third World

MILES D. WOLPIN

LandMark Studies
ALLANHELD, OSMUN

ALLANHELD, OSMUN & CO. PUBLISHERS, INC.

Published in the United States of America in 1981
by Allanheld, Osmun & Co. Publishers, Inc.
81 Adams Drive, Totowa, N.J. 07512
(A Division of Littlefield, Adams & Co.)

Library of Congress Cataloging in Publication Data

Wolpin, Miles D.
  Militarism and social revolution in the Third World.

  (LandMark studies)
  Bibliography: p.
  Includes index.
  1. Underdeveloped areas—Politics and government.
2. Civil supremacy over the military. 3. Underdeveloped
areas—Armed Forces—Political activity. I. Title.
JF60.W63   322'.5'091724   81-65014
ISBN 0-86598-021-7   AACR2

Printed in the United States of America

To
Robyn and Seth

Contents

List of Tables

Tables

Figures

Acknowledgments

Research and writing this book was carried out over a lengthy period of seven years. Those who have encouraged or directly assisted my work during that period deserve more than the brief mention they receive here. None of course can be held responsible for my interpretations, errors, or inconsistencies. My greatest debt is owed to Jim Petras, who provoked me to begin writing in the first place and ever since has been an abiding source of inspiration. Others to whom I am particularly grateful include Martin Needler, David Brown, Jon Kraus, Jayne Werner, Morris Janowitz, Herbert Wulf, Pat Mulvey, Peter Lock, Richard E. Hutcheson, Jan Black, Rosalind Boyd, John Saxe Fernandez, Pat McGuire, George DeBaise, and especially Ellen Stern. I also wish to express my appreciation to the University of New Mexico and the Research Foundation of the State University of New York for their generous financial support, and to my editor Jim Mohoney of Allanheld, Osmun & Co., for his many helpful suggestions. The responsibility for errors of facts and interpretation is mine alone.

Chapter 2 is an abridged and revised version of an article that appeared in Social Praxis II (3–4): 277–308. Chapter 3 is a revised version of an article that appeared in *Studies in Comparative International Development* VIII (Spring 1973): 3–23. Chapter 4 is a revised version of an article that appeared in *The Journal of Peace Research* as "Egalitarian Reformism in the Third World vs. the Military: A Profile of Failure," XV, 2 (1978): 89–114. Chapter 5 is an abridged and revised version of "Conservative Militarism and the Communist Military Subordination Model," *Social Praxis* II (3–4): 277–308. Chapter 6 is a revised and abridged version of an article that appeared in *Armed Forces and Society* VI (February 1978): 245–64. Chapter 7 is a revised version of "Militarism, Socialism, and Civilian Rule in the Third World: A Comparison of Development Costs and Benefits," *Instant Research on Peace and Violence* VII (1977): 105–33. Chapter 8 is a revised version of an article that appeared in *Gandhi Marg* I, 3 (June 1979): 149–60. Chapter 9 is a revised version of an article that appeared in *Civilisations* (1980).

1

Introduction

An ominous political phenomenon has emerged in the Third World during recent decades: conservative militarism. The impressive number of reform-oriented governments which have been forcibly deposed includes such notable examples as Iran (1953), Guatemala (1954), Argentina (1955), Congo (1960), Brazil (1964), Indonesia (1966), Ghana (1966), Cambodia (1970), Bolivia (1971), Chile (1973), and Peru (1975). Are we to regard those which survive—Tanzania, Zimbabwe, Libya, South Yemen, Nicaragua, and others—as deviant cases, or as regimes fated to be overrun by armored personnel carriers and tanks in the months and years ahead? More important, is there any set of policies which might contribute to establishing stable patterns of military subordination? Although the military have seized power and overthrown governments in a steadily rising proportion of Third World countries, a major premise of this study holds that viable policies are available for ensuring both civilian political supremacy as well as socio-economic development. Only the simultaneous pursuit of these twin objectives offers the prospect of ensuring institutional control over otherwise coup-prone military factions.

Without doubting the possible existence of other alternatives, it seems odd that virtually all contemporary civil-military relations analysts have eschewed serious consideration of what I shall call the Communist Military Subordination Model. The incongruity of this void in the literature is magnified by several factors which make Marxist experience broadly relevant to the aspirations of developmentally oriented elites in Latin America and the Afro-Asian countries: 1) most Marxist-Leninist regimes were established in technologically backward nations; 2) within a decade or two they had begun to close the gap on advanced capitalist nations; 3) in the process, these regimes introduced significant egalitarian alterations in class structures—an aspiration shared by populists and

1

reformers throughout the underdeveloped areas; 4) and most important, in not one case has tension between military elites and the political class culminated in a successful coup d'etat. Whether civilian elites succeed in "buying off" the military, are replaced by the latter, or simply become increasingly dependent upon them, ever greater proportions of resources needed for development will be diverted to the armed forces, whose relative domestic position is accordingly enhanced. Even in the best of circumstances, "pressure" tends to be transformed into coercive intimidation.

The core assumption of this work—one shared by most civil-military relations analysts—is that officer corps constitute privileged social groups which commonly perceive their corporate interests to be threatened by social reforms of an egalitarian character. This assumption holds whether the mass-supported reformism is the product of *either* populist or Marxist leadership. Hence, I shall argue in succeeding chapters that the overthrow of social reformers is in large part due to *idealistic assumptions* concerning the range of military tolerance. This in turn contributes to faulty policies by reformist governments toward "their" military establishments during periods of incipient military discontent. The converse holds for Communist revolutionaries. While Marx's theoretical work has been necessarily revised in certain economic areas, it seems well suited to predicting the incidence, if not all the sources, of conservative militarism. Hence, on balance, successful Marxist military policies have flowed from a more realistic appraisal of the likelihood of rightist military intervention.

It is becoming apparent that contemporary Third World militarism signifies a "threat" not only to Marxists and social reformers of a populist stripe, but equally to "moderate" civilian leaders. More than a decade ago, Huntington (1968) theorized that encouragement of professionalism by moderates would lead the military to play the role of an interest group in the developing areas. Yet Welch(1978:143) reminds us that

his optimistic views drew numerous rebuttals from Finer, from Stepan, and, most recently, from Perlmutter. Professionalism seems a scant barrier to growing military involvement in politics; professionalization of the armed forces may in fact have the contrary effect of encouraging greater involvement.

Indeed Hobsbawm's (1973: 184) prognosis—one originally published a year before Huntington's—appears the more prescient if less sanguine:

there are very few countries of the Third World at present under civilian administration in which the chances of maintaining it over the next twenty years are as good as even. Admittedly the recent drift towards military government has been by no means entirely spontaneous.

The rise in the proportion of nation states which have been overrun by military regimes during the past three decades underlines the importance of this phenomenon, as does the concurrent process of world militarization and resumption of intense East-West military rivalry.[1]

In an epoch marked by the paramountcy of a democratic ethos, there is no normative basis for civilians—who constitute the vast majority of citizens—to regard domination by an organized gun-toting professional military force as legitimate (i.e., rightful) in the intermediate or long run. Thus, it is not surprising to discover that militarists—regardless of limited civilian co-optation—generally fail (Perlmutter, 1977a: 24, 26) to legitimize their regimes even among most of those who initially backed them. Further, as Welch (1978) has recently noted, "close to two-thirds of governments that assumed power by means of coup d'etat are themselves ousted by the same means; only one in twenty post-coup governments gives way to a civilian government." The tendency is for military governments to rely increasingly upon force. Even when "power" is handed back to civilians, the return to the barracks is often contingent upon civilian policy deferring to military demands and is, as often, brief. During the interim, the legitimacy of such civilian governments is itself quite problematic. Even where civilian supremacy exists, legitimacy cannot be taken for granted. Yet my argument is that civilian rule remains a necessary if not a sufficient condition. Further, that this should be true in an age when democratic values are so widely held among civilians is so self-evident that it cannot be overstated. In our era, only governmental processes which provide more than a facade of democratic self-rule will be regarded by citizens as rightful, and therefore as worthy objects of allegiance rather than of intense distrust and alienation. Armed praetorians in uniform whose primary resource in the seizure of power is coercive weaponry invariably will be regarded by the civilian mass public as an almost alien "they" rather than as citizen political participants like themselves. To acknowledge that militarism is seldom popular and only rarely legitimate in the minds of most civilians is not of course to affirm that officers are necessarily "demons" of one sort or another. As long as they *defend* a state which civilians regard as legitimate, officers will be accorded the honor and prestige their role merits.

The problem is that some civilians and increasing numbers of officers reject the legitimacy of the state—and this is especially true when governments are bent upon structural reform which inevitably threatens vested privileges and existing stratification systems. Thus, scholars like Welch (1976:315-24) who seek to devise strategies to deter intervention offer at best stop-gap counsel stressing respect for autonomy and material payoffs. Such a tack not only assumes the existing socio-economic status quo but fails to come to grips with the fact (Thompson, 1973:48) that almost twice as many coups are motivated by intramilitary grievances as by such corporate interests. Further, it is the existing socio-economic underdevelopment which negates the *desire* to strengthen the legitimacy of civilian institutions in most Third World countries. Hence, the problem is how to restructure the social order and reduce dependency, while simultaneously limiting the socially conservative armed forces to their nonmilitaristic professional mission of defending a society from external attack. Put differently, the struggle for socio-economic development presumes success in constraining domestic militaristic tendencies.

This traditional perspective on proper military roles—one elaborated some years ago by the noted Swiss military historian Alfred Vagts (1959)—is as consonant with the general thrust of "modernization" theory emphasizing functional specialization as it is with socio-economic performance data for military "developmental" regimes. I intend, therefore, to "save" not only the Marxian perspective on the military, but equally that of the dominant "modernization" paradigm—the latter from scholars like Lucien Pye (1962), who inappropriately assumed the viability of a military modernizing societal role. Similarly, it will be necessary to reject the conclusions of those like Nordlinger, McKinlay, Cohan, Jackman et al., who see little difference between the performance of military and civilian governments. Superior performance by the latter in socio-economic and political areas is clear, as is the outstanding record of state socialist regimes, which underscores the relevance of Marxian theory to the modern era.

I shall begin then by examining the Marxian theory of the state, with special emphasis upon the position and class role of the officer corps. Consideration will also be given to non-Marxian scholarship that focuses upon the sources of military conservatism toward structural change and mass aspirations for greater socio-economic equality. Although non-Marxians tend, like Marxists, to avoid use of the term "class" in characterizing such military interests, their term "corporate" is virtually synonomous. Thus, a leading British civil-military relations analyst (Finer, 1975:234–35) stresses that:

This skein of selective induction, professional training and social code along with the organization and often the social self-sufficiency of the military establishment, give rise to the narrower corporate interest of the miliary: a continuing corporation which has acquired or aspires to a certain social status, political significance and material standard. Interestingly, it has been suggested that this, and not so-called "middle-class values," is what results from increasingly middle-class composition of the officer corps

"Probably the most salient result of the fact that so many military officers originate outside the traditional upper class . . . is rather that they cease to identify themselves in terms of their social origins but instead transfer their primary group identification to the military service itself, which has created a new style of life for them, and has made it possible for them to advance socially. . . . This is likely to heighten, more than most observers have seemed to appreciate, the extent to which the political decisions of military officers are dominated by concern for the corporate self-interest of 'the institution' itself." (Needler, 1963:45)

This statement was prompted by a Latin American example: but a fascinating corroboration comes from the Nigeria situation, where the army officers, *c.* 1966, were of relatively lower educational attainment than their civilian peers, and consequently enjoying lower prestige. In compensation these officers, therefore, espoused the "officers are gentlemen" code to the degree of caricature. "Low prestige led them to search for their own differentiated sphere of military honour with which to protect and validate their position in society." (Luckham, 1971:109)

In concrete terms this corporate self-interest reflects itself in demands for bigger budgets and better pay, etc.; in intense and lethal opposition to the constitution of any rival armed forces like workers' militias or presidential guards; and in a determination to have a say in public policy-making.

Thompson (1973:12–13) identifies seven dimensions or aspects of corporate interest: autonomy, hierarchy, monopoly, cohesion, honor, political position, and resources.

In Chapter 3, I examine the dependence of many Third World nations upon Western and particularly U.S. military training for their officers. Careful attention is given to the rightist ideological content and politically conservative behavioral effects of such external socialization. Ten case studies exploring the dynamics of destabilization between 1953 and 1973 are compared in Chapter 4, not only from the standpoint of resource utilization by antiradical forces, but also in terms of the patterns and deficiencies in leftist leadership. Chapter 5 turns to the most reliable method or policy cluster for ensuring that militaries are subordinated during periods of radical socio-economic change. From this I derive an eight variable Communist Military Subordination Model – one which should be functionally replicated if not imitated. Hobsbawm (1973:178) notes that "a great deal of thought has been expended in some countries to ensure [military] subordination, and nowhere more so than in the states deriving most directly from the revolutionary tradition, those under the government of communist parties."

Subsequent chapters address the prospects for Third World regimes that have endeavored to introduce structural changes which, among other things, have reduced in some measure the degree of social inequality. As stressed at the outset of this chapter and in that which follows, the military has *generally* reacted negatively to socio-economic radicalism. In Chapter 6, I examine what might be conceived of as "deviant" military role-playing. The question asked is, how does one reconcile military "radicalism" in a growing number – albeit a small minority – of social systems with both the dominant conservative pattern delineated in Chapter 4 and Marx's materialist conception of history?

The successes and associated costs for three developmentally oriented regime types are compared in Chapter 7. Distinguished by respective degrees of egalitarianism, social ownership, and class relations, these are the state socialist (or communist), state capitalist (or radical reformist), and the open door (monopoly capitalist) models. Because these terms are employed in succeeding chapters, it may be useful to define them here. They refer to distinctive regime types with markedly divergent class relations and "modes" or organization of production. Concomitant development strategies — communist, state capitalist and "free enterprise" — are also referred to by these terms. In fact, one of the basic rationales for each of the modes of production is its presumed efficacy in catalyzing socio-economic development. As will be shown, military leaders have often opted for "free enterprise" or monopoly capitalism and less frequently for state capitalism. A few have even gone so far as to claim they were introducing "scientific socialism" — a code word for the "Marxist Leninist" or state socialist mode of production.

All of the aforementioned variants are characterized by extensive state involvement in economic decision-making at the national level. Under monopoly capitalism, the political and bureaucratic elites "regulate" to enhance the profitability of the private corporate sector. Because the latter is dominated by transnational corporations in most underdeveloped areas, so long as indigenous officials acquiesce in such relations, their domestic and even foreign policy choices tend to depend upon favorable reactions by such corporations and associated international financial institutions. Hence, "dependency" is the reciprocal of monopoly capitalism in the Third World. As Gunder Frank (1967), Jalee (1968), Rhodes (1970), and others make clear, these phenomena are functionally related to declining terms of trade and "under" development.

State capitalism involves attempts to reduce dependency radically (enlarging policy alternatives) and simultaneous promotion of industrial development. Characteristic of such regimes are state ownership of most large economic enterprises and diversification of economic relations so that major transactions occur with Eastern state socialist systems.

State socialist systems may be distinguished from state capitalism in the following ways. First, the residual sector is being reduced rather than tolerated as legitimate. This residual private sector is also sharply circumscribed and generally limited to medium- and more commonly small-scale economic undertakings. Finally, primary elite or Communist Party roles are those of production mobilizers rather than bureaucratic consumers. Their socialist orientation is manifested by a distinctive ideology, ethos, and style of life.

Many societies are obviously on a continuum, and neither steady forward movement nor stability of position are assured. In short, state socialist systems (Yugoslavia) may "degenerate" into state capitalist regimes, while revolutionary elites who seize monopoly capitalist systems (China) can virtually telescope the state capitalism phase by moving quickly on to state socialism. But even this is no guarantee—as recent developments indicate—against reversion. Similarly, state capitalist regimes like Egypt and Ghana may revert in some measure toward monopoly capitalism. Reversion however is seldom total. Chile is exceptional in this regard. Thus the consonance of state capitalist production relations with the neutralization of at least some major "contradictions" in Third World monopoly capitalism explains why the right-wing coups *generally* accept enlarged state sector—disposal of a few enterprises notwithstanding—and limit themselves to adopting a deferential stance to foreign investment only in as yet unexploited areas. Hence the trend in monopoly capitalist systems is an ineluctable if gradual historical one toward what might be termed "creeping state capitalism." The foregoing conceptualization of systems has been employed with similar if not identical empirical referents by Lane (1976:13–43), Petras (1978:84–102), Farsoun and Carroll (1978).

The comparison of selected indicators for each of the developmental regime types in Chapter 7 highlights the uneven performance of the state capitalist variant in the crucial area of "benefits." Although some of the statistical studies summarized at the outset of the chapter conclude that, except in the area of "costs" (i.e., repressiveness), there is little to distinguish civilian- from military-led regimes, my own data reveal considerable civilian superiority in "benefits" as well as lower "costs" to citizens. These findings—especially those with respect to the state socialist variant—underpin the relevance of the dependency theory and arms transfer thesis elaborated in Chapter 8. There, it is postulated that arms transfers affect developmental prospects by promoting particular regime orientations. The key mechanism involved is officer training and concomitant external linkages—examined in Chapter 3—which are often, if not always, associated with such arms transfers. They also, of course, divert resources that could be allocated to productive investment.

On the basis of the foregoing, an admittedly hazardous attempt is made in Chapter 9 to estimate the survival prospects of radical or state capitalist regimes in the 1980s. Considerable weight is placed upon resource mobilization, domestic military policies, and the openness of the systems to external inputs, especially in the military area. Three broad categories of low, medium, and high survival potential are the basis for classifying the dozen or so regimes in question.

The concluding chapter provides an overall assessment of the relationship of the military to aspirations for social change and development in the Third World today. When the officer corps acts as a ruling social class, it can make a positive though limited contribution. This in turn can be reconciled with Marx's theory of historical materialism. The other military patterns seem more in accord with traditional negative Marxist views. And, ironically, the dominant modernization paradigm can be harmonized with both patterns—though more easily with the latter—despite the fact that it was initially developed as a classless antithesis to Marxist viewpoints. Put differently, it is the *functionally specialized* "vanguard" party which in the present era performs the national developmental role that Marx, as well as contemporary "Western" policy-makers and social scientists, ascribed to the transnational corporate bourgeoisie. While Marx reassessed this bourgeoisie's historic mission after his empirical analysis of Irish economic history and Lenin rejected it (Kennedy, 1974:17) "immediately before the Bolshevik seizure of power in 1917," Western analysts evidence a greater propensity to stress the failures of radical military regimes than to acknowledge the shared responsibility by "moderate" or rightist military elites and the transnational bourgeoisie for what Andre Gunder Frank aptly characterizes as the "development of underdevelopment."

Notes

1. Although the term "militarization" commonly is used to denote the extension of military forms, personnel, and practices to civilian institutions, as used in this work it is intended to refer primarily to the increasing amount of societal resources being allocated to the armed forces. Militarism, on the other hand, implies the exaltation of war, the armed forces, martial values, and military ritual over civilian institutions and norms. As Vagts (1959) emphasizes, civilians may be promilitarist and officers at times are antimilitarist. Similarly, while militarism usually promotes militarization, the latter may upon occasion reflect actual defense needs rather than a militaristic ethos. It can, of course, be hypothesized that militarization over time will be associated with a growth of militaristic tendencies.

2

The Military as a Conservative Socio-Political Force: Marxian and Non-Marxian Perspectives

Marx's expressly negative view of standing armies is neither ambivalent nor qualified. Conceivably more so than the police, they epitomized the repressive agencies of a class-biased state. There was no such thing as a purely professional "apolitical" army that served a neutral state regardless of the policies espoused by the government of the day. The army would fight rather than see the bourgeoisie stripped of its privilege by a populist movement. Conversely, a successful insurrection must democratically restructure or completely supplant the armed forces that were supported by and served the ancien regime.[1]

This perspective infused Marx's analysis of the Paris Commune, as did his belief that a new and democratic militia should be organized to defend a socialist revolution. While he viewed the Commune as a populist rather than a socialist uprising, at the close of the Franco-Prussian War, Marx nevertheless came to its defence because of its democratic and egalitarian tendencies. Furthermore, socialist elements were active participants among the encircled insurrectionaries during the several months that Paris was able to hold out. Although Marx, who was in London at the time, failed to play a direct role in leading the historic mass uprising, he nevertheless praised the fact that like other Commune officials, militia officers were elected, subject to recall, and paid "workmen's wages."[2] And he noted with approval that the "bulk" of the Commune's National Guard "consisted of working men." Peasants, too, were to play an im-

9

portant if secondary role, since, for Marx, "the Commune was to be the political form of even the smallest country hamlet, and . . . in the rural districts the standing army was to be replaced by a national militia, with an extremely short term of service." Clearly, his conception of the "proletarian" but not yet socialist "dictatorship" was both egalitarian and antibureaucratic.[3]

Apparently, Marx believed that a decentralized, democratic, ad hoc militia was sufficient to defeat professional standing armies. He stresses that Thiers' government forces were initially driven from Paris and that during the fighting there were very few defections: "out of 300,000 National Guards only 300 responded to this summons to rally round little Thiers against themselves." The defeat of the Commune was attributed to its encirclement by numerically superior professional armies due to transnational bourgeois solidarity when confronted by an egalitarian insurrection.[4] Hence, the Prussians deliberately kept their troops stationed on one side of Paris to block resupply of the capital while they simultaneously released thousands of officers and men who had earlier been taken prisoner. These were massed with the Rurals (provincial troops) by Thiers on the other perimeters of the city for the devastating siege.[5]

As one analyst (Chorley, 1943:28) has pointed out, the failure of the National Guard to attack Thiers' army when it was withdrawn from Paris may well have doomed the Commune, but neither Marx nor Lenin seem to have entertained the idea that militias may be much better suited to defensive than to offensive tactics. Reflecting upon the failure of the Communards, Ellis (1973:247) emphasizes that:

another organisational prerequisite is that the revolutionary leadership be united at the military and political levels. . . . Again such unity was manifestly absent during the Paris Commune. Both the Commune itself and the Central Committee of the National Guard were constantly at odds with one another, each fearful of the possibility of political or military dictatorship by the other. The National Guard was given neither rationale, organisation nor leadership. Perhaps even if all these things had been present the Parisians would still have been unable to carry their revolution beyond the confines of Paris.

The military setbacks suffered by the militia-type Red Guard units during the first weeks of the Russian Civil War finally induced Lenin to join Trotsky in a pragmatic revision of this Marxian hostility to military professionalism under central political control. Despite heated opposition, the Eighth Party Congress endorsed reconstitution of a professional, centralized, and hierarchically disciplined regular army to defend the Bolshevik regime.[6] The fact that old Czarist officers were, for the most part, press-ganged into serving — some 50,000 more or less — did not imply renunciation by Lenin of the orthodox Marxian view that a fundamentally new military had to be organized. According to Chorley (1943:203),

the old personnel [were] used merely as a technical makeshift and every means was employed to render it politically innocuous. . . . It is not so much a matter of translating the theory of the clean sweep from first to last into action, regardless of circumstances, as of working always in the spirit dictated by that theory.

In Chapter 5, I shall have more to say about officer recruitment and the command structure of the ultimately triumphant Red Army. Here it should be emphasized that there has been only one significant advance since 1918 in Marxian thought on the role of armies in the conquest and consolidation of state power. Until it managed to go on to the offensive in 1947, the Chinese People's Liberation Army (PLA) operated under Mao's leadership as a rather decentralized yet highly politicized guerrilla force whose primary mission was to create and defend civilian party committees along with mass organizations in the rural areas being liberated.[7] In East Europe, the Soviet armed presence was regarded as crucial to the establishment of Communist regimes because most of the armies in that region had not yet been restructured.[8] Red Armies of one sort or another seem to have been a necessary if not sufficient condition for the establishment and/or consolidation of most Marxist-Leninist systems.

Such experience must be treated as partial confirmation of Marx's pessimism, especially when set against the domestic counterrevolutionary role of European officer corps earlier in the 20th century. Woddis (1977:248) reminds us that

the closing stages of the First World War and its aftermath saw the top military brass playing a leading counterrevolutionary role—in Russia, Finland, Germany, Hungary, Italy and Poland—to crush the struggles of its own people. While soldiers were expressing their opposition to continuing the war, taking the road of revolution in Russia, Germany and Hungary, deserting the army en masse in Italy, helping to set up Workers' and Soldiers' Councils in Britain, the carrying through the Black Sea Revolt in the French navy in solidarity with the Russian revolution, the military establishment played its traditional role of siding with reaction in order to uphold the existing capitalist system. In the subsequent period, general staffs in Italy, Portugal and Germany actively participated in preparing the way for the fascists to assume power in their respective countries. In Spain, too, the fascist generals were a main instrument of the counterrevolution.

It is no wonder then that, even more than pre-Cold War liberals such as Vagts (1959), Marxists have until recently (Miliband, 1969; Hobsbawm, 1973:181-83, 193; Carranza, 1978) offered almost uniformly negative assessments of this repressive arm of the state. Such a tendency has been reinforced by the military overthrow of not only the reformist governments discussed in Chapter 4 but also many others between 1948 and 1980.

Among non-Marxist analysts of civil-military relations, only one appears to have been preoccupied with the military obstacles to revolutionary success. Nearly four decades ago, in what she described as an "exploratory essay," Katherine Chorley systematically compared the military parameters of revolutionary conflicts from the 17th century to the defeat of the Spanish Republic in 1939. Although Lady Chorley's frame of reference was European and North American, the historical patterns which she identified may, in varying degree, apply to counterrevolutionary military roles in the Third World. While she is in full agreement with Marx that the consolidation of a social revolution requires an essentially new officer corps and army, Chorley adds some detail in explaining why existing officers generally oppose egalitarian mass movements. First, they are generally recruited from propertied social classes and consequently identify with them.[9] In a revolutionary crisis, loyalty to such reference groups will be powerfully reinforced by "caste traditions" of the officers corps.

Even for those officers who are recruited from relatively humble backgrounds or who have but recently entered the military (and thus are not fully socialized to the caste mentality), there remains the fact that, in societies marked by socio-economic scarcity, the officers' corps itself represents a socially privileged class. As a markedly distinct social group, officers enjoy both material amenities and what contemporary analysts would term an elitist style of life:

There are few groups more difficult to re-absorb into a community about to take up again the avocations of peaceful workaday life than the discharged officers with no place of their own and no training for civilian citizenship, and with little prospect of finding jobs which at all square with their conceptions of themselves as ex-officers. (Chorley, 1943)

This is consistent with her somewhat tentative observation (1943:176–77) that technical branch officers tend to be the most conservative, since they were more often recruited from the status-insecure middle classes than were those in prestigious traditional combat branches, such as the cavalry and infantry.[10]

If upward mobility ensures the counterrevolutionary sentiments of the middle class officer and the NCO who has been accorded similar if lesser privileges, it is equally true that new revolutionary armies draw some of their interim officers from this same "vacillating" petit bourgeois class. It is reasonable to infer that the minority who choose to serve the revolution represent disproportionately those whose existing prospects for advancement appear blocked for personal or professional reasons. These, however, are for the most part obvious opportunists who generally desert *after* the local balance of coercive power appears to have altered in favor of the revolution.[11] Lady Chorley (1943:247) concludes, perhaps with excessive pessimism, that:

The long-service standing army with a professional officers' corps is not amenable to influence from the Left in any serious degree, but it does appear markedly amenable to fascist influences coming through Right channels.

Hence, only when the command structure is undermined and/or the army is confronted by militarily superior forces has the left a chance of victory. Put somewhat differently, Chorley's thesis (23) is that nationalist and especially leftist

insurrections cannot be permanently won against a professional army operating its technical resources at full strength. They can be won only when the introduction of some extraneous factor cripples the striking power of the professional fighting forces for one reason or another.[12]

Consolidation of the revolution requires that the new regime's irregular volunteer forces which initially defended it be supplanted by its own regular army. Yet Chorley's distrust of all officers is reflected by her stress (248–60) upon the need for social heterogeneity in recruitment, the use of political officers, and, above all, the active involvement of the conscripts in the political life of the country. Just as the last is the linchpin for undermining the command structure of the ancien regime's armed forces, it is for her the key means of ensuring officer subordination to a progressive or populist government: "the political independence of the rank and file is the strongest guarantee against the use of the army for fascist purposes. But this can never be achieved without first a radical reform of the officers' corps."[13]

The empirical data and more general speculation generated by contemporary military analysts are largely consonant with Chorley's assumptions. Overwhelmingly, they regard professional military men to be committed to elitist, politically conservative, and authoritarian values.[14] Hence, professional officers tend to recoil from mass protests against existing social structures. There are of course variations, so that junior officers and those in ex-colonial societies where traditional upper classes were discredited or nonexistent are held by some to be less socially conservative.[15] Thus, in his analysis of coup grievances, Thompson (1973:44–45) found the largest percentages of "strikingly reformist" coups between 1946 and 1970 to be in Arab (17 percent) and Black African (9 percent) countries. Even so, this should not obscure the fact that these were very small percentages, and that for the world as a whole only 19 out of 229 coups "were judged to be 'strikingly' reformist in nature." Thompson concludes that even if Table 13 understates the "genuine" reform dimension, it still would be necessary to triple the 19 for strikingly reformist motivations to pertain to even a quarter of the coups examined. Although Table 13 indicates a very slight ascending trend at the coup zone level, one is forced to conclude that the desire for societal reform remains fairly atypical of contemporary military coups.

In the Third World, the military profession constitutes a uniquely significant career to facilitate upward social mobility. Although analysts readily note this fact, they seldom analyze its sources or implications.[16] In the first place, closed ownership patterns along with the stagnant and unbalanced character of economic growth in dependent capitalist societies is such that lower middle class offspring have extremely limited prospects for attaining affluence within the private sector.[17] At the same time, for a variety of reasons, the overall size of the armed forces has expanded markedly in these countries, as it did earlier in the industrialized nations. The class divisions of society are frequently reflected at senior/junior officer levels and most commonly by the sharp demarcation between officers and conscripts. Thus, in explaining part of the pre-1974 appeal of the Portuguese junior officer-based MFA (Armed Forces Movement), Porch (1977:42) notes that:

The "directorship craze" was cited as direct proof that generals had sold out to the establishment. Many top generals and admirals served simultaneously on the boards of large companies—Kaulza de Arriaga sat with the directors of Petrangol and the Espitito Santo enterprises, Admiral Tenreiro owned one of Portugal's largest fishing fleets. Admiral Sarmento Rodrigues was president of the Torralta group, General Sottomayor's connections with his family's interests were obvious, and Spinola sat on the board of the Metalurgica Nacional, to name only a few. The generals thus served the interests of fascism and big money, leaving their subordinates to fight on forgotten in the jungle. "Since most of the junior officers were not slotted into the co-optive mechanisms of the system, the close association of the generals with political and economic power favoured an irreconcilable schism within the armed forces," Bandeira concluded.

In underdeveloped countries such as Guatemala, there are opportunities in real estate and landowning (Etchison, 1975) which are not limited to those in senior ranks.

Similarly, a recent analysis of more than 100 coups in the Third World between 1946 and 1970 by Thompson (1973:26) identifies "corporate well-being" as a "significant cause" of these interventions. Here I have used "class" as a synonym for "corporate" because the latter implies such institutional concerns as autonomy and weapons, while the implications of "class" more easily embrace the additional variable of material and social amenities which seem to have been ignored or mentioned only in passing in much of the literature. Yet even in Africa, where several scholars (Janowitz, 1964:28; Nordlinger, 1970; and Levy, 1971:70) correctly stress the radical implications of extremely low levels of development and/or the absence of indigenous bourgeois reference groups and recruitment bases, such materialistic class interests are nevertheless quite salient. Thus, J. M. Lee (1969:125,145) counsels that a "sense of privilege . . . extends throughout all ranks, and is not simply a characteristic of the officer cadre." He adds that "the army looks like a lobby which can secure for itself a large proportion of the state's resources," and notes that "in conditions where wage employment is rare" there is a strong aversion by conscripts, and presumably officers, to return to rural areas to "apply what they had learnt" to the traditional sector.

Also referring to the African armies, Bebler (1972:153) points to

the internal social stratification of the British and French . . . and the more complex multilayer pattern of stratification that was later created in the British and French colonial empires. The present pay structure in African armies, for instance, reflects the latter—with a huge gap between the pay of the officer (i.e., former white officer) and that of the enlisted (i.e., African) man. The same is true of a number of features of internal army life: separate dining and recreation facilities for officers, NCOs, and enlisted soldiers; very different housing conditions; officers' servants; the officer's style of life, which imitates British, and to a lesser extent French, gentlemen. . . . Officers in these armies most often come from families that are socially very close to those of the soldiers. . . . Once commissioned, most African officers feel obliged to help out numerous relatives, to maintain their younger brothers in school, and so forth. They themselves in time become members of the elite, but the difference in income is minimized by a larger number of claimants on higher incomes. In a certain sense, however, the class stratification of the colonial societies spills over into the new independent polity through military hierarchy as privileges, access to secondary and high schools, capital accumulation in the form of savings invested into real estate and business ventures, and so forth are passed on to the next generation.

A similar idea is offered by the Nigerian political scientist F. Bayo Adekson (1978:32) who not only characterizes the military as an anti-populist socio-political force, but also endorses Nun's (1969) and Perlmutter's (1977) view that

whether actual or imputed, the military qua military is a special class-in-itself, not in the orthodox Marxist sense, but in the sense in which a bureaucracy is, and therefore has its interest and motivations often independent of (though they may also coincide with) those of any one of the conventional classes in society.

It seems that a similar materialistic class interest affects officers' perceptions in most underdeveloped societies. Thus, ex-C.I.A. officer Philip Agee (1975:82) notes that "although the Agency usually plays the anti-communist card in order to foster a coup, gold bars and sacks of currency are often equally effective." Analysis of the overthrow of the ten reformist governments in Chapter 4 revealed considerable evidence of military corruption in the form of kickbacks or "commissions," smuggling, black marketeering, and extortion as well as widespread attachment to such material amenities as travel allowances, servants, luxury imports, mistresses, double salaries, fancy clubs, free personal housing, exemption of salaries from civil service austerity measures, top-heavy rank structures, etc. Pertinent sources are listed in note 14 of that chapter.

For senior officers, the style of life is (to say the least) quite comfortable from the standpoint of servants, deference, and material amenities.[18] As Lang (1972:84) has noted in a somewhat broader context:

Military rank and social rank are closely attuned and the military sector does not visibly differentiate itself from the general social system. Only within a more complex division of labor, particularly when standing armies are large and armaments costly, does privilege come to be associated with differences performed within the military. The privileges martial men enjoy in most societies demonstrate how much the distribution of status or wealth is determined by their possession or control of the means of violence.

Perhaps the most vivid illustration of this can be found in Suharto's Indonesia. High-ranking officers have used military coercion to enrich themselves through embezzlement, extortion, bribery, smuggling, conversion, and double salaries. This has resulted in high living by senior officials and their direct investment in many joint ventures with foreign interests that now control dynamic sectors of the economy. In describing this situation, Crouch (1978:273–330) acknowledges that neither "professionals" nor more "nationalistic" officers within the armed forces have been able to challenge effectively the rapacious majority of corrupt high-ranking officers. And, while "technocrats" have made some limited changes in the direction of increasing central budgetary control, this is probably due to heavy external pressure by the United States, International Monetary Fund, and others. It has not, however, affected the ubiquitous military norm that makes it "perfectly natural for officers to exploit their official positions for personal gain."

Coups in the late 1970s against military regimes in such countries as Nigeria and Ghana indicate that corruption at the highest levels may be pervasive. And Maynard's (1978:149) interviews reveal that it permeates all levels in the Philippines. Even when top officers in rightist and (one suspects) some leftist regimes (e.g., Burma, Syria) are relatively immune to graft, Kennedy (1974:58) points out that:

The army which intervenes with relatively clean hands may campaign against corruption, a few offenders may be jailed, and some may even be shot, but the command of resources in "soft" states soon leads inexorably to a diversion of resources. In an atmosphere where status and prestige are bound up with power and wealth, the scarcity of income among the pious is in conflict with the aspirations of the ambitious; either they succumb to the opportunities or they slide down the social scale.

There is another route that does not involve corruption directly, and that is to develop political ambitions exercisable on the basis of support from the corrupted within the military hierarchy. Thus rising political fortune may be a substitute for direct graft; the status of office, with the perks and privileges that this provides, may compensate for abstaining from the lower ranks' opportunities to graft. In these ways the army itself becomes as corrupted as the previous administration, but the leaders may in good conscience be able from time to time to threaten action against the corrupt as a disciplinary tool over lower ranks. The military leaders have authority over lower ranks and they can remove the "licenses" to state position at will. The lower ranks return loyalty for the "license."

The recently desposed Nicaraguan military almost certainly illustrates the more typical pattern of graft at all levels. But in another way it was probably exceptional. Opportunities for graft were complemented by exceptional material benefits in the form of pay and "legal" privileges which had been authorized by Somoza even for recruits. This ensured cohesion and his personal authority as long as the dictator remained in the country—despite major advances by the radical Sandinista insurrectionary movement whose military victory was ensured only by: 1) external aid from Panama, Costa Rica, and Venezuela; 2) rebel unity; 3) the rigidity and unusual brutality of the regime; 4) petit bourgeois support. Either in an immediate or portentous sense, egalitarian movements threaten the share of national resources which is allocated to top-heavy military establishments. The prospect of forced retirements, a reduction in opportunities for promotion, and very possibly institutional austerity measures awaken latent military hatred for social radicalism. Such professional antipathy is aggravated by the general nontransferability of military skills to high status civilian occupations which, as we have stated, are few in any case as far as the underdeveloped countries are concerned. This seems to hold for technical branch specialists even in "developed" nations. According to Lang (1972:97,98)

most men discharged as well as those retired from the armed forces settle in jobs that have little to do with what they did during most of their military career. . . . Even . . . though a military specialty may be by designation identical with a civilian job, the specific knowledge required is often geared to particular equipment and, hence, much narrower than that required to fill an identically designated job in civilian life.

Ironically, a similar phenomenon in perhaps more muted form afflicts communist societies where retired officers also experience a difficult readjustment problem, one exacerbated by some apparent downward mobility in the standard of living.[19]

If, wherever social inequality exists, the officer corps constitutes a privileged social class, this is not tantamount to saying that all upper classes are equally privileged. Some are more affluent or manifestly privileged with respect to the less fortunate — "privilege" being the allocation of scarce values through superior social power rather than need. Others may be less self-serving and/or avoid the more gross aspects of conspicuous consumption. Variation also exists in the degree of interaction and consequential reference group identification between officers and the upper or middle classes of their respective societies. In many countries, linkages are apparent; in others, officers constitute a virtually independent and relatively isolated social class with extensive intramarriage and self-recruitment. Yet upper class wealth has seldom been exporpriated by military regimes. In most cases, the officer class maintains its amenities by taxing lower middle and working class wages, lives far better than the multitude, and consequently reflects its class interests by reacting conservatively to egalitarian challenges to the existing social order. While their social conservatism is also derived, as the case of Portugal indicates (Porch, 1977), from bureaucratic role orientations, professional values such as order, and possibly the military function itself, Perlmutter (1977) argues persuasively that these are distinctly secondary as sources of social conservatism.

Historically, many military men have often subordinated purely professional concerns — even weapons innovations (Lang, 1972) — to the security of a preferred style of life. Careerism, in short, should never be equated with dedication to advancing the profession or the interests of one's fatherland. Thus, in his recent study, Perlmutter (1977:xvi) stresses that his own "major analytical contention is that the concept of 'corporativism' should be extracted from the concept of 'professionalism' and treated as an independent variable." The acute resentment harbored by regular Portuguese junior officers against the award of equal seniority to selected conscript officers "who had proved themselves in combat" (Porch, 1977:65) is a case in point. Social mobility and/or radical sociopolitical goals (Fields, 1976:2–12) were obviously more salient objectives than maximizing "professional" capabilities. This also reflects the fact that, as Thompson (1973) found, the largest proportion of coups are motivated by subcorporate (i.e., intra-military, factional, or personal) rather than corporate interests, though these tended to be less successful than the latter. Discounting ideology as relatively unimportant in most coups — and virtually absent in 60 percent — Thompson concludes that such subcorporate interests are "probably most responsible for the 'musical chairs' quality of coup chains and cycles."

The importance of not equating professionalism with the vast majority of corporate and subcorporate interests is likewise underlined by

Maynard's (1978:131) survey research on senior officers in the Philippines and Indonesia. It reveals that "personality" is an important factor in co-optation to top general officer positions in these highly corrupted militaries, and also that senior officers in Indonesia are relatively indifferent to professionalism, whereas those in the Philippines differ substantially as to its meaning.

Unlike many officers in Indonesia, members of the Philippine military elite admire "professionalism" in their peers. To some this means simply carrying out the instructions of a civilian president and minister of defense. To others, it means discipline, attitude, effectiveness, loyalty, courage, and integrity. The common denominator in all definitions of professionalism appears to be "self-discipline," a watchword of President Marcos' new society.

This is not to say that grievances of a "professional" character never play a role in coups—only that they may be less important than "commonly believed and are often used to mask more materialistic personal or corporate motives."

The conservative societal impact of officer corps is set in relief by recent quantitative research on the potential of military establishments for bringing "modernization" to their societies. In Chapters 6 and 7, the developmental and repressive consequences of military rule are delineated. Notwithstanding a few exceptions, why has the performance been so dismal? Some have convincingly argued for the paucity or non-transferability of managerial and political skill.[20] Others claim that military demands upon national economic resources divert funds required for investment. Thus, after coups, military budgets as a proportion of GNP rise.[21] I would only add that in some instances the ideological approach to economic development, which has been inculcated by foreign training experiences, may be an antiegalitarian one that inhibits the very growth of internal markets and economic nationalism that is vital to a developmental process.[22] The important point, however, is that whether one looks at role transferability on the individual or corporate armed forces level, the officers find that in terms of social prestige alone, long-run egalitarian alternatives to conservative militarism are unappealing. Feld (1968:69) sees no reason why a "high status social class" in the Third World should be motivated to modernize society and thereby reduce itself to a marginal role.[23] This is consistent with my central thesis that when confronted by dedicated populists, the military will intervene to safeguard their societal privileges. Such coups, of course, will be effectuated in the name of the "national interest."[24]

Military subordination in developed capitalist countries has been explained by such factors as tradition, the resources and organizational efficacy of parties or other civilian institutions, civilian pressure for weapons innovations, and the fact that uncompromising egalitarians have seldom led governments.[25] But two other factors must be noted in this context. First, Western prosperity and economic growth rates have been sufficient to provide many alternative channels for upward mobility to middle class youths. Hence, of those American officers who do have college degrees or transferable skills, large numbers leave as quickly as possible (Lang, 1972:39–40), while Academy graduates—a caste with the best prospects for promotion in the armed services—tend to remain. Lang (1972:48–51) has warned that the decline of the military's "heroic" self-image, along with its increasing dependence upon civilian managerial and engineering talents, is creating a grave identity crisis for military professionals. Yet given continued civilian reliance upon the military for the promotion of overseas interests, such military alienation may well lead to much greater political involvement in the more developed capitalist societies where the armed forces have seldom sympathized with the left.[26]

Military support for the political right in advanced capitalism does not seem to have abated despite the broadened social recruitment base for officers during the past century. This social heterogeneity was occasioned initially by the nobility's lack of attraction to such new technical specialties as logistics, engineering, and artillery, and by the enlargement of armies in the 19th and 20th centuries. Some have argued that, because officer corps reflect social structures, the incorporation of middle class sons would affect military political orientations.[27] However, existing evidence suggests that anticipatory socialization or careerist opportunism, selective promotion, and intramilitary indoctrination have co-opted those middle class officers whose values were consonant with if not identical to those of the upper and upper middle classes. In most Western armies, blue collar offspring make up less than 20 percent of the officer corps—and again here there is no reason to doubt that co-optation and socialization would ensure general ideological homogeneity.[28]

Surprisingly, a recent case study (Salaman and Thompson, 1978:283–304) of British army officer recruitment suggests that social class discrimination may be far more pronounced than official regulations and policy declarations imply. This and the previously mentioned sources of promotion bias account—despite broadened recruitment—for the fact "that the Royal Air Force (Boyd, 1973) had a public school contingent of . . . 62 per cent of its Air-Vice-Marshals in 1970 compared with the Army's 86 per cent of Major Generals and above."

This class bias has diminished in recent decades but remains marked. Thus Otley (1978:335) records that, "for the first time in a century, the public schools now (1967) supply only a third of Sandhurst's entrants [and less than half of *all* officers in the army (1969)], although at the highest levels of the army, public school domination is still very strong

(1970 and 1971)." This lingering domination in the upper levels may reflect not only prior recruitment bias but continuing social discrimination in co-opting officers to higher rank. Even in the less socially chauvinistic U.S. Army, both social upper and upper middle classes are grossly overrepresented (Dye, 1976:151–54) at the general officer level to the tune of 70 percent, while in societal terms these high status classes do not exceed 15–20 percent of the population.

Consonant with this pattern is the highly politicized co-optative character of the peace-time promotion process to senior ranks. Moore and Trout (1978:452–68) call this "the visibility theory of promotion." Normal social discrimination may be even greater than Dye's figures imply, since many of the 30 percent may have been co-opted during periods when the army was engaged in combat. A similar process operates in Latin America and Asia, while in the Middle East and Africa the traditional upper classes (where they existed) were discredited by years of imperial conquest. Here, the military elites are purely middle – often lower middle – class in origin. Although there is greater military openness to leftist perspectives in the Middle East and Africa than elsewhere due to more humble recruitment antecedents, antipathy toward Zionism and Western racism, socialization discontinuities, and the predatory legacy of some transnationals, consequential radical propensities more often are manifested by state capitalist rather than state socialist tendencies. It is my contention that bureaucratic authoritarian norms, social origins, and the style of life attributes delineated earlier remain as primary sources of conservative militarism.[29]

The military establishments of most Third World nations do not, of course, exist in total isolation from each other and especially not from those in military aid donor states. In fact, most have been modeled or fashioned along the lines found in the so-called developed nations. This process has often been one involving continuous foreign indoctrination and reinforcing personal ties to counterpart officers – phenomena which significantly reinforce both conservative and militaristic propensities. To this I turn in the next chapter.

Notes

1. The quotations in this, the following paragraph, and notes 2 and 3 are from Karl Marx's 1870–71 addresses on "The Civil War in France," as reprinted in the *Handbook of Marxism* (New York: International Publishers, 1953). His perspective appears similar to that articulated two decades earlier in the *Eighteenth Brumaire*.

2.

Paris could resist only because, in consequence of the siege, it had got rid of the army, and replaced it by a National Guard, the bulk of which consisted of working men. This fact was not to be transformed into an institution. The *first decree of the*

Commune, therefore, was the suppression of the standing army, and the substitution for it of the armed people. . . . Having once got rid of the standing army and the police, the physical force elements of the old Government, the Commune was anxious to break the spiritual force of repression (churches and education). . . . (Italics added.)

3.

The cry of "Social Republic," with which the revolution of February (1870) was ushered in by the Paris proletariat, did but express a vague aspiration after a Republic that was not only to supersede the monarchical form of class-rule, but class-rule itself. . . . The Commune was formed of the municipal councillors, chosen by universal suffrage in various wards of the town, responsible and revocable at short terms. The majority of its members were naturally working men, or acknowledged representatives of the working class. The Commune was to be a working, not a parliamentary body, executive and legislative at the same time. Instead of continuing to be the agent of the Central Government, the police was at once stripped of its political attributes, and turned into the responsible and at all times revocable agent of the Commune. So were the officials of all other branches of the Administration. From the members of the Commune downwards, the public service had to be done at *workmen's wages*. The vested interests and the representation allowances of the high dignitaries of State disappeared along with the high dignitaries themselves. Public functions ceased to be the private property of the tools of the Central Government. Not only municipal administration, but the whole initiative hitherto exercised by the State was laid into the hands of the Commune.

4. In recounting the first measures of the Commune, Engels(1891:163) emphasizes that the Communards did not view their experiment as essentially national and therefore limited to France:

on the 30th the Commune abolished conscription and the standing army, and declared that the National Guard, in which all citizens capable of bearing arms were to be enrolled, was to be the sole armed force. They released the citizens from all payments of rent for dwelling houses from October to April . . . and stopped all sales of articles pledged in the hands of the municipal pawnshops. On the same day the foreigners elected to the Commune were confirmed in office, because "the flag of the Commune is the flag of the World Republic."

Similarly, for Marx(1870-71:150):

when the Paris Commune took the management of the revolution in its own hands; when plain working men for the first time dare to infringe upon the Governmental privilege of their "natural superiors," and, under circumstances of unexampled difficulty, performed their work modestly, conscientiously, and efficiently – performed it at salaries the highest of which barely amounted to one-fifth of what, according to high scientific authority, is the minimum required for a secretary to a certain metropolitan school board – the old world writhed in convulsions of rage at the sight of the Red Flag, the symbol of the Republic of Labour, floating over the Hotel de Ville.

5. In a portentous paragraph, Marx(1870-71:156) highlights the insignificance of nationalism when bourgeois class interests are threatened – a phenomenon which has reappeared in one form or another during the century since the Commune's defeat:

that after the most tremendous war of modern times, the conquering and the conquered hosts should fraternise for the common massacre of the proletariat – this unparalled event does indicate, not, as Bismarck thinks, the final repression of a new society. . . . The highest heroic effort of which old society is still capable is national war; and this is now proved to be a mere governmental humbug, intended to defer the struggle of the classes, and to be thrown aside as soon as that class struggle bursts out in civil war. Class-rule is no longer able to disguise itself in a national uniform; the national Governments are one as against the proletariat.

For the contemporary significance of transnational class interests, see Kolko(1968).

6. Or in the words of the most recent edition of *Marxism-Leninism on War* (1972:239), the "armed intervention of international imperialism and the vast scope assumed by the Civil War made it necessary to revise this proposition." Yet only a few months earlier, Lenin had still believed that "the simple organization of the armed masses (such as the Soviets of Workers' and Soldiers' Deputies . . .)" would be sufficient to safeguard the new, already withering state (Lenin, 1918:747). This compromise with necessity, it should be stressed, was one that did not contravene the fundamental principle that a socialist revolution must create a *new* military rather than rely upon that which served the deposed regime. Lenin (1918:728) in *The State and Revolution* stressed: "A state is formed, a special power is created in the form of special bodies of armed men, and every revolution, by shattering the State apparatus, demonstrates to us how the ruling class aims at the restoration of the special bodies of armed men at its service, and how the oppressed class tries to create a new organization of this kind, capable of serving not the exploiters, but the exploited."

7. In the final stages, mobile offensive tactics — resembling conventional ones — gradually supplanted the guerrilla orientation(Griffith, 1967:67–73). Tucker(1969:160–62) claims that Mao was obsessed with military aspects of the struggle to liberate China from Chiang Kai-Shek's Kuomintang (KMT) while Lenin emphasized the political in his pre-Russian Civil War writings.

8. According to *Marxism-Leninism on War*(1972:264), "the formation of socialist armies . . . was completed after the establishment of the proletarian dictatorship." A similar pattern was found in Mongolia and Korea.

9. "Now it is obvious that where an officers' corps is recruited exclusively, or even mainly, from the propertied ranks of the population, an officers' revolt will only be used in a counterrevolution against a progressive system or in an insurrection of fascist type (98)."

10. Officers "with no place of their own" are presumably non-upper class in origin. (Chorley, 1943:127).

11. Thus it is reported(Chamberlain, 1935:149) that quite a few officers in the Petrograd garrison adorned their uniforms with Red epaulettes. Why did the Imperial officers fight en masse in Moscow and switch sides or flee in Petrograd? In the latter city the rank and file conscripts had been thoroughly proselytized by Marxists and willingly turned on their officers or joined the Bolsheviks in the October uprising. Identical opportunism was manifested in China when, during the last year or two of the Civil War, KMT officers defected with thousands of conscripts to the advancing Red Armies.

12. Either the officers must be sharply at odds with each other — something that she argues rarely occurs in social revolutionary contexts — or the men must refuse to follow their officers. The latter is, according to Chorley(1943:108–10, 244–47), most often associated with the hardships and demoralization that result from a long and (especially) unsuccessful war. It involves replacement of casualties by conscripts and officers who are new to the "caste traditions," and the cumulation of long-standing grievances over conditions of service. Finally, an important variable is the degree to which conscripts intermingle with civilians and thus continue (or come) to identify with the masses. Proselytization by revolutionaries is, of course, a catalyst of exceptional significance.

13. The type of army which most threatens egalitarian movements is one based upon volunteers as opposed to conscripts. This is particularly true when the troops are isolated

from the populace and the officers are self-recruited and/or preponderantly represent privileged classes.

14. This cluster of values, or what some depict as the "military mind," is regarded as consequential to the following: 1) the mortal and hence heroic nature of the military function itself; 2) increasingly complex weapons technology; 3) bureaucratic specialization; 4) the fact that political conservatives often are more sympathetic to military needs and accord the profession greater prestige; 5) the sharing with conservatives of other values, such as pessimism about human nature and alarmism, which are essential to effective performance of the military (preparedness) function; 6) social recruitment of officers from the middle and upper classes. Intra-military socialization is widely regarded as the welder of this normative consensus. Several qualifying observations have also been proffered: a) premilitary "general" socialization may well be more significant given the limited time junior officers have actually spent in the armed forces and in light of the contemporary trend toward less isolation from society; b) answers to survey research questions may signify articulation of reference group ideology rather than the internalization of attitudes affecting behavior; c) there has been very little empirical investigation of actual linkages between verbalized perspectives and overt behavior. On the officers' general political conservativism, see: Vagts(1959:29-30); Abrahamsson(1972:57-58,74-75,99-110,160); McKinlay(1971:253); Lang(1972:48-51,110). Their hostility to egalitarianism is implied or explicitly referred to by the following: Levy(1971:68-69); Bienen(1971:17-19); Kolkowicz(1967:21-22,323); Feld(1971:55,61); Nauta(1971:386-87); Tromp(1971:361-74); Abrahamsson (1972:13,53-57,62,99-100,117,122-24); Lang(1972:38-40,84,97-99,105,110); Nun(1969).

15. On the latter see: Janowitz(1964:28); Huntington(1968); Levy(1971:70).

16. See the anti-egalitarian sources cited in note 14, above.

17. The relationship between stagnant neocolonial economies and military intervention was well stated nearly two decades ago by Kling(1956). For a similar perspective, which traces the decline of reformist coups in Latin America to lagging economic growth but ignores the dependency issue, see Needler(1966).

18. There is admittedly a paucity of documentation for this very important statement. Yet indirect acknowledgement of such life style enjoyment for Kuomintang and Ghanian officers will be found in North(1952) and Price(1971). And the significance of this factor is underlined by Lang's(1972:39) report that most studies of officer career motivation stress life style rather than monetary appeal. In the preface to a study of East European officers, Ithiel de Sola Pool(1955:8) notes that his team's investigation was "predicated upon the assumption that a man's way of life determines to a considerable extent the sort of person he will be and the types of things he will do. . . . [these] more stable factors influence how a person will ultimately respond to situational variations." It is therefore particularly regrettable that most analysts who refer to military careers as channels for upward mobility do not spell out the class meaning of such terms (see the anti-egalitarian sources cited earlier in note 14). Perhaps this was one of the implications of Janowitz's(1968:17) comments on hindrances to sociological research when he admonished that "more important as a barrier than secrecy has been the intellectual posture of sociology. The discipline has failed to develop a realistic understanding of social structure which would include the military establishment and the role of force."

19. In describing army opposition to Khrushchev's proposal to reallocate funds for the modernization and expansion of strategic missiles, Kolkowicz(1967:260) notes that "among other things, it involved a reduction of the armed forces by one-third, which meant the release of a quarter-million officers from their secure and comfortable life into an unpromising future and often an undesirable social environment, and constituted a blow to many vested interests and personal careers." What "undesirable social environment" probably connotes in addition to distance from former colleagues is suggested by the fact that many retired Soviet officers complain that their jobs do not fully utilize their abilities.

Wiatr's(1969:236) report on Polish officers' self-images in the early sixties is consistent with this view: a "junior officer's perception of his own social position puts him close to skilled or white collar workers. The senior officer, on the other hand, usually sees his own position as close to that of professionals and other intelligentsia groups." In this connection, it is noteworthy that following World War II, Polish officers were "encouraged to marry within the workers and poor peasants classes; after 1956 official restrictions to this effect were abolished and the officer's family started to be more heterogeneous socially" (Wiatr, 1968:235).

20. Military deficiencies in such areas as organizational, bargaining, and civilian mobilization capabilities are referred to by: Vagts(1959:299–383); Janowitz(1964:104–5); Iskenderov(1971:152–53); Feld(1971:28); Lang(1972:56–61,97–103). Both Vagts and Lang also discuss traditionalism and historical examples of military opposition to new weapons and technology.

21. For quantitative trend data on Latin America, see Putnam(1967). According to Bienen(1971:16):

> those who argue that the military is suited to undertake economic and social reform and that it provides a vehicle for national integration as it assimilates groups begin with the proposition that the military is at least relatively the most modernized group in society because its own requirements demand that it be rational, universalistic, and industry-oriented; furthermore, it must have contacts with modern forces outside its own society and utilize an advanced technology. They do not show how the military gets to be this way. Ataturk turned the problem around, according to Lerner and Robinson, by making the modernization of the army dependent on the transformation of Turkish society. In Turkey, the portion of the general budget allocated to national defense fell precipitously between 1926 and the early 1930s and did not rise to pre-1926 levels until 1939. This too is an important fact. The nature of the military as an instrument of change varies not only with its place in society as a ruler or interest group but also with its own size and structure. If the military becomes very large compared to civilian elites, it may be taking such a large share of national income that economic development will be precluded.

(Cf. also, pp. 27–28.) For contrary assessments, see: Levy(1971:41–78,70–73); Janowitz (1971:22–23); Lovell and Kim(1971:102–16); Huntington(1968).

22. Wolpin(1973:59–64).

23. In this context, Bienen(1971:17) acknowledges Manfred Halpern's conclusion that "in the Middle East, the capacity of armies for making effective use of men, machines, and organization has been warped by conscpicuous consumption and continued dependence on outside sources of military assistance." Similarly, according to Abrahamsson(1972:144),

> the assumption that the military interferes in politics motivated by a desire to maintain political order or to prepare for "economic break-throughs" is highly questionable. The result of a coup d'etat is often not primarily more order, but simply a different ruling clique, and the successes of the Latin American military governments in achieving economic growth are hardly impressive.

24. So for that matter will most coups since intramilitary socialization imbues the officer with the notion that his is the sacred role of defending the particular society. While the officers are more often than not sincere in holding this self-serving ideology, they have generally been unable to institutionalize their rule because of mass resistance. The coercion (as opposed to authority) that flows from domination perceived to be illegitimate by the citizenry leads to what Huntington (1968) calls "political decay." Hence, whether one defines political development as institutionalization (as Huntington does), or sees it as the enhancement of individual awareness of policy alternatives and one's environment (as

Nyerere does), military rule is dysfunctional if not retrogressive. Only when the rare alternative of actual chaos exists can a wholly defensible case for a coup be made. In a number of other instances, coups by radical officers have admittedly brought short term benefits to the nation as a whole—particularly when the deposed civilian regime was traditionalist, unusually corrupt, or utterly incompetent. The sources and potential of such leftist militarism are more fully explored in Chapters 6 and 7.

25. Janowitz(1971:28); Bobrow(1971:300-304); Abrahamsson(1972:159-62); Lang (1972:110).

26. Evidence of their extensive political activities, at least in the United States, is provided by Fulbright(1970); Barnet(1971); and Melman(1972).

27. Levy(1971:63-64); Iskenderov(1971:150-54); Lieuwen(1964).

28. Abrahamsson(1972:43-58,72-76,99-100). The same author concludes from recent survey research that:

> as recruitment to the military profession has ceased to rely on the nobility or gentry and the recruitment base has become broader and more diversified, military education, professional socialization, internal means of communication, codes of ethic and other means of ensuring cohesiveness now bring about the uniformity of values that during earlier periods was provided by family and class influence. . . . although recruitment to the military profession in many countries has become more socially representative—sometimes making the military the most "democratically" recruited of the professions—the officer corps seem in large measure to have retained their traditionally elitist outlooks. . . . (57,58)

Lang(1972:34) notes that "this leveling effect has been somewhat less apparent in the highest ranks since recruitment into top positions is usually from within the organization." My contention is that the senior officer ranks are most usefully viewed as both a dependent elite and (in varying degree) as a subsector of the upper middle class. The political interests of these classes tend to be reflected directly by such officers when there is a common threat due to an egalitarian movement, and indirectly through pressure for budgetary levels and autonomy which facilitate the maintenance of a privileged life style for officers. Whether or not their social reference groups are ultimately civilian, officers—and especially those on promotion tracks—will seldom sympathize with mass-based movements which seek to undermine the basic distribution of property ownership as this is the source of both upper and upper middle class life styles. This is not to say that the military is averse to acting independently on rare occasions for direct defense of its life style or for long-range security of its society when civilian politicians have clearly demonstrated their incapacity (e.g., Peru in 1968, Egypt in 1952, Germany in 1944).

29. Given the inefficiencies characteristic of intramilitary socialization in underdeveloped nations, as well as some external training by Communist or nonaligned countries, radical factions occasionally appear. The widening gap with advanced societies and the indignities associated with continued economic dependency are relatively stable reinforcing factors. In some African countries no indigenous bourgeois reference groups exist and, unless external ones fill the void, it is possible the officers themselves may constitute the socially privileged "upper" class. Hence while the coup may be "radical," it is seldom highly egalitarian. The sources, constraints, and effects of military radicalism are analyzed at length in chapters 6 and 7.

3

External Political Socialization as a Source of Conservative Military Behavior in the Third World

The term "military aid" generally evokes images of tanks, aircraft, or ammunition. Similarly, "training" is commonly perceived as a process of transferring technical expertise in the management of men or equipment. Less widely known is the fact that Western nations, and particularly the United States, have gradually incorporated political indoctrination into the technical training programs for officers from the Middle East, Africa, and Latin America. This chapter will examine the evolution, purposes, and impact of such directed political socialization. Before doing so, brief mention will be made of several methodological problems relevant to the analysis of these relationships.

A concomitant of the behavioral revolution in political science since World War II has been the emergence of several semiautonomous subdisciplinary areas. Despite the empirical aspirations of many specialists, much effort has been invested in scholastic model-building and conceptual frameworks for analysis. As one experienced scholar (LaPalombara, 1969) observed, the

so-called revolutionary transformations in comparative politics of the last two decades have involved, among other things, a proliferation of macro-theories of politics, political systems and political behavior. Many, perhaps most, such "theories" are of extremely dubious value. . . . There has occurred an alarming neglect of the political process, itself, and of key institutions directly involved in the policy-making process. The need is, therefore, great for a return to a segmented and partial-systems approach to both theory and research.

One of the most productive empirical approaches has been survey research. Hence, systematic correlation of interview replies with other variables is commonly viewed as the scientific method for the study of institutional roles and policy-making processes.

Attitudinal statements derived from such survey designs often are only tenuously related to overt behavioral patterns. Although this linkage problem is affected by a variety of factors such as the analytical capability of the individual respondent, another obstacle is posed by the assumption of respondent veracity. With respect to mass publics, Philip Converse has reported (Schonfeld,1971:571), for example,

that a large proportion, apparently approaching 50 percent of respondents in a sequence of national panel studies are individuals with no real attitudes on the matter in question . . . [who] felt obliged to try a response to the item despite our generous and repeated invitation to disavow any opinion where none was felt. This seems to be explained by the fact that "the attitude questionnaire is approached as though it were an intelligence test, with the 'don't knows' and 'can't decides' confessions of mental incapacity."

If interviews can elicit the articulation of attitudes that have no effect on behavior at the mass level, they are even more likely to inspire deceptive and self-serving expressions of intent by more sophisticated bureaucratic elites. Included in this category are American and foreign military officers who have been involved in the overthrow of civil governments in the Third World. Given their need to secure the acquiescence of attentive publics and/or potential rivals, "any serious claimant to power, regardless of his antecedents, associations, or intentions, will justify his claim by professing profound concern for national independence, for popular aspirations, for social justice and for economic development" (Rustow as quoted by Nordlinger,1970:1134).

To mendacity must be added the ambiguities occasioned by multiple motives and divergent goals of the factions which frequently coalesce (Potash,1969) during a successful military conspiracy. Professional concerns may reinforce or be impeded by personal antipathies, nationalistic or anticommunist sentiments, and a desire to preserve or increase material amenities. Without denying this complexity or the occasional utility of publicly declared goals, the most useful method for ascertaining military intent is to investigate post-coup policies as the point of departure.

One factor which most analysts of military roles in the underdeveloped areas ignore or underestimate is the external reference group identification with the officer corps of a major Western power.[1] Given the generally conservative and authoritarian attitudes of Third World and Western military officers,[2] it is probable that their propensity to intervene against socialists or populist reformers is significantly increased by ideological indoctrination and interface relations in the course of training abroad. "Narrowly conceived, political socialization is the deliberate inculcation of political information, values, and practices by instructional agents who have been formally charged with this responsibility" (Greenstein as quoted by Schonfeld,1971:551). A case study by Price(1971) suggests that both intentional as well as nondirected political socialization in British military academies powerfully reinforced materialistic grievances such as better uniforms, boots, travel allowances, higher pay, etc., in predisposing the military to seize power in Ghana 15 years ago.[3]

This chapter will focus upon directed political socialization at U.S. military installations for officers from Third World countries. The Military Assistance Program (MAP) of the United States has trained almost a million foreign military men between 1950 and 1980; in excess of 50 percent are "officers, the majority from the emerging nations" (Grand Pre,1970:87). Before assessing the validity of my hypothesis that this program has exerted a moderate, though nonetheless significant, influence upon the ideology and behavior of ex-trainee officers, the MAP will be described and set functionally within a broader or systemic framework.

Since the last decade of the 19th century, the United States has sought an open door for its investors in the Far East, Latin America, the Middle East, and, most recently, in Africa.[4] Noncommunist nationalists and social radicals have been actively opposed since the military counterinsurgency campaign against Aguinaldo's Philippine rebels following the war with Spain. This pattern of foreign policy was manifested by opposition to Article 17 of Mexico's 1917 Constitution, by economic sanctions against Cardenas in 1938, by political intervention against Peron in 1946, and through the overthrow of such radical nationalist leaders as Mossadegh, Lumumba, Sukarno, and Sihanouk.[5] During the Cold War era, the option of a neutralist or nonaligned foreign policy has been a sine qua non for expropriating Western investment interests and instituting egalitarian social reforms, since the latter tend to undermine investment incentives.

Although the U.S. foreign aid program was, during the 1960s, rationalized as intended to promote a world safe for freedom and democracy, such goals seldom governed the amounts of aid appropriated by the U.S. Congress for particular countries (Packenham,1966). Nor were they evidenced by the pattern of U.S. support for authoritarian military regimes, this stance having antedated the Cold War. And if one discounts public relations releases, there is abundant evidence in U.S. Congressional testimony by both Executive officials and Congressmen to the effect that America is hostile to noncommunist leftism, exporpriation, revolution, extremist nationalism, and nonalignment. For the purposes of this analysis, ideologically conservative military interventions will be those which are directed against either expropriation or neutralism.[6] As a caveat, it should be added that there are many political decisions regarding regimes in the underdeveloped areas concerning which the United States is either indifferent or assigns a relatively low priority. The MAP is not a tool for securing complete integration into an empire similar to that of ancient Rome. Nor, on the other hand, is it limited to socializing foreign officers against nonalignment and socialism. Distinct complementary objectives include diplomatic support, intelligence facilities, and communications installations and base rights. Naturally, these are incidental to a policy of containing communist social systems which have been particularly effective in closing the door on drainage of development capital by foreign corporate interests.[7]

Since World War II, one of the major threats to American corporate investments has been the rise to power of nationalist regimes pursuing socialistic policies in the Third World. The problem is to assess the effectiveness of training-induced relationships in preventing the emergence of such governments on one hand, and in deposing them or forcing moderation of their policies on the other. Because of data censorship and the multiplicity of variables which are often operative, measuring the effectiveness of this foreign policy instrumentality with any precision is not possible. Even if the vital interpersonal relationships were not systematically concealed, the immensity of the research effort would mandate nothing short of a Defense Department-financed task force.

The conclusions here, therefore, rely upon a number of partial indicators which can support only the most tentative results. They are based upon the classification of interventions in the Middle East, Africa, and Asia during the post-World War II period. Between January 1, 1946 and December 31, 1970, there were 14 radical and 15 conservative coups.[8] Some 44 additional interventions have been excluded. These will not be considered in the following discussion since they were judged to have been primarily motivated by discontent associated with such nonideological matters as budgetary apportionment, personal antagonism, upward mobility aspirations, dominance ambitions, inefficacy or corruption of the civil regime, and ethnic rivalries. While ideological factors were often present, my conclusion from subsequent policies is that they were appreciably less significant than the forementioned motives.[9]

During the decade of the 1960s, Washington's decision to expand and systematize MAP political indoctrination was accompanied by a sharp rise in ideological coups. Thus, of the 29 coups between 1946 and 1970, 20 occurred during the last 10 years of that period. That this marked increase cannot be solely attributed to the emergence of new nations after 1959 is suggested by the fact that all 29 took place in but 20 countries of which at least 16 were independent for part or all of the earlier period(1945–59).

The widening appeal of socialism and nationalism in the underdeveloped areas was also manifested by a substantial shift in the ratio of conservative to radical interventions. During the 1946–59 period, six of the nine ideological coups were conservative, while 11 of the 20 during the decade of the 1960s were radical. Leftist appeal to officers was due in part to the patent inability of their societies to develop under a regime of dependent capitalism. In some cases, it was sparked by an often related desire to be more independent of Western tutelage and chauvinism. Success for nationalistic officers—as transitory as it frequently is—requires balancing the West against the East to obtain external aid with minimal restrictions. A few of these countries received virtually no military aid from the West for a period of several years. Significantly, within three to five years both the Sudan and Algeria experienced radical—but not communist—coups. In such cases and elsewhere, when only Eastern aid is accepted, widespread economic stagnation, poverty, and economic exploitation provide powerful reinforcement for the emergence of radical goal orientations. This is particularly true when the local bourgeoisie is nascent and overshadowed by transnationals.

The limited, medium-term counterrevolutionary effectiveness of Western military assistance is evidenced by the fate of those nonaligned nations which accepted not only Eastern (most often Soviet or Czech) military aid, but also training and equipment from one or more capitalist donors. (See Table 3.1.)

Table 3.1 *Conservative/Radical Interventions in Countries Receiving Eastern and Western Military Aid*

Years of Eastern Military Aid	Interventions	
	Conservative	Radical
0-4	0	2
5-8	4	1
9-12	1	1
Total	5	4

If the comparison is restricted to those Eastern-supplied Third World countries which received U.S. military aid,[10] an equally pronounced medium-term counterrevolutionary trend is evidenced. While all of these countries received U.S. aid, many also maintained similar ties with other Western nations. (See Table 3.2.)

Similar relationships are apparent if we examine those underdeveloped countries which have not received Eastern or neutral military aid prior to the ideological coups. Here, the counterrevolutionary impact of Western ties is modest and slightly longer-range in nature. (See Table 3.3.)

The secular decline in the incidence of ideological coups shown in Tables 3.1, 3.2, 3.3, and 3.4 reflects the long-term receptivity of civilian political sectors to Western and U.S. reinforcing input constraints. These probably reduce radical threats to military values and privileges.[11]

Table 3.2   *Conservative/Radical Interventions in Countries Receiving Eastern and U.S. Military Aid*

Years of Eastern Military Aid	Interventions	
	Conservative	Radical
0-4	1	1
5-8	5	1
9-12	0	1
Total	6	3

Table 3.3   *Conservative/Radical Interventions in Countries Receiving Western Military Aid Only*

Years of Western military aid	Interventions	
	Conservative	Radical
0-4	2	3
5-8	2	4
9-12	4	1
13-22	1	1
Total	9	9

Again, the relationship is somewhat stronger for those states receiving U.S. military assistance. (See Table 3.4.)

In those countries, the conservative/radical ratio for less than nine years is 1/1, while a more favorable 3/1 is associated with the maintenance of such relationships for ten years or longer. Similar essentially long-term effects are manifested by arranging the date by length of Western aid where all have also accepted Eastern and/or neutral assistance. For nine years or longer the C/R ratio is 6/3, while it is only 7/8 for the shorter period. Again, there is slightly greater effectiveness for MAP recipients, and this extends to medium — as well as long — lead times.[12] (See Tables 3.5 and 3.6.)

If it is hypothesized that the stability of or slight decline in the number of conservative interventions is attributable to the simultaneous penetra-

Table 3.4   *Conservative/Radical Interventions in Countries Receiving U.S. but Not Eastern or Neutral Military Aid*

Years of U.S. military aid	Interventions	
	Conservative	Radical
0-4	1	1
5-8	3	3
9-12	2	0
13-20	1	1
Total	7	5

Table 3.5   *Conservative/Radical Interventions in Countries Receiving Western and Eastern or Neutral Military Aid*

Years of Western military aid	Interventions	
	Conservative	Radical
0-4	4	4
5-8	3	4
9-12	5	2
13-22	0	1
Total	12	11

Table 3.6   *Conservative/Radical Interventions in Countries Receiving U.S. and Eastern or Neutral Military Aid*

Years of U.S. military aid	Interventions	
	Conservative	Radical
0-3	2	1
4-7	5	4
8-11	3	1
12-15	1	2
16-22	2	0
Total	13	8

tion of civilian sectors which makes it more difficult for radical political forces to enter the government over time, how can the marked decline in radical military interventions be explained? The relationships created and reinforced by MAP training not only aid conservative officers in suppressing radical conspiracies, but the process of ideological indoctrination progressively denudes radical factions of potential sympathizers within the military establishments. As conservative ideological cohesion, even when weakly internalized on an individual level, is enhanced, the prospects for radicals are appropriately diminished. The declines in Tables 3.3 and 3.4 are more impressive than in Tables 3.5 and 3.6 where competing (though not especially efficacious) Soviet training is operative. More definitive evidence of MAP effectiveness is provided by comparing the proportion of a nation's armed forces trained by the United States with the incidence of ideological interventions. Although somewhat crude as a measure, it does give an indication of relative linkages with armed forces which vary considerably in size. For those nations with less than 1 percent Continental U.S. Command (CONUS) trained men, the ratio of C/R interventions is 6/5, while where it exceeds 1 percent, the corresponding ratio is 6/1. The relationships are almost identical if those trained overseas are added to the CONUS figures for each country. (See Table 3.7.)

I have not dealt with Latin America because of an excellent longitudinal analysis by Martin Needler(1966). Examining an area where a far higher ratio of officers are U.S.-trained than elsewhere in the underdeveloped world, Needler found a pronounced decrease in the percentage of pro-reformist coups. While the definition of reformism used may include some interventions which would not warrant a radical

Table 3.7   *Conservative/Radical Interventions in Countries Having Different Propor-tions of CONUS*[a]-*Trainees: 1950-1969*

| CONUS trainees (1950-69) as | Interventions | |
percent of armed forces manpower (1968)	Conservative	Radical
0.00-0.49	3	2
0.50-0.99	3	3
1.00-1.99	3	0
2.00+	3	1
Total	12	6

[a] Continental U.S. Command.
Source: U.S. Department of Defense (1970:17); Sellers (1968).

designation, his data are consistent with my hypothesis, and they support the conclusion of John J. Johnson(1964:143–44) "that without the military, every government in the Latin American orbit would be further to the left than it is now." Needler's table (to which the above statements refer) and some methodological comments appear in Chapter 7.

Space limitations preclude a survey of statements by advisory committees, congressmen, military writers, and scholars who conclude that the MAP has been effective in terms of increasing the responsiveness of Third World officers to U.S. policy goals.[13] There are a plethora of self-serving though not necessarily misleading statements by Defense Department officials and military officers associated with this external political socialization endeavor. The following assertion by Grand Pre(1970: 87–89) is fairly typical of this genre:

Actions which we take in the future—or choose not to take—will based on their understanding—or misunderstanding—of our society. . . . Lt. General Robert H. Warren, Deputy Assistant Secretary of Defense for Military Assistance and Sales, recently stated that, although he places a high priority on contacting and influencing leaders in foreign societies, "long experience has indicated that *training* is one of the most productive forms of military assistance investment, in that it fosters attitudes on the part of the trainee which lead to better mutual understanding and greater co-operation. . . ."[14]

External political socialization is an imperfect and (as I have found) only moderately effective means (Olorunsola,1977) of mobilizing bias against radical nationalists in underdeveloped countries. An awareness of this limitation may have occasioned the addition of a low-profile "soft sell" on U.S. free enterprise in the late 1960s and 70s to the traditional anticommunism which characterized the indoctrinational aspects of the MAP during the late 1950s and early 60s. A distinction was drawn between progressive U.S. capitalism and the visibly poor performance of national bourgeois elements in most backward lands. As the gap continues to widen between the economic growth of the metropolitan centers and the underdeveloped areas, pro-American military elites may increasingly reject their own nationally oriented bourgeoisie in favor of the modernizing transnational corporate conglomerates. By strenthening their reference-group identifications with the "ideological frontier" orientation of the U.S. officer corps, the United States increases the likelihood that more Third World military elites will contribute to the integration of their economies into a semistable world order whose basic parameters are defined by U.S. developmental needs.

How effective this strategy will be is an open question which is explored further in Chapters 6 and 9. Hobsbawn(1973:188–89) for example acknowledges:

The view, widely held in the United States in recent decades, that soldiers are more reliable as well as stable governments of satellite states from an imperial point of view than civilians, is based partly on the belief that foreign military advisers and training provide not only technical education but effective political indoctrination, but chiefly perhaps on the capacity of imperial states to bribe them with supplies of the kind of modern equipment and know-how which satisfies the self-esteem of armed forces. In fact it is far from justified. Some of the more revolutionary elements in local armed forces have actually emerged, in Latin America, from among the local military elite trained (e.g., as counterinsurgent Rangers) by the North Americans, as in Guatemala in the middle 1960s. In so far as the military is a force for "modernization" and social renovation, it is pro-Western only so long as the Western model appears likely to solve their countries' problems, and this now appears increasingly unlikely in most countries.

Yet the same author concedes (187–88) not only that radical or Nasserist interventions have been "comparatively rare," but that "many a putsch has been due in recent years to the official or unofficial encouragement by outside powers." It is unsurprising, then, as I indicate in Chapter 4 and elsewhere (Wolpin, 1973), that military training is utilized as an important cover for CIA operatives.

These external inputs and their reinforcing effect upon conservative military behavior do not occur in a vaccum. The fact that, in stagnating economies with no colonial dependencies, blue-collar sectors are often mobilized by unintegrated radical elites who have not been suborned or socialized to middle-class identifications, may well signify a genuine threat to the budgetary aspirations of the officer corps. Also supportive of conservative militarism is the recruitment of officers from bourgeois and socially mobile lower middle-class elements. As in other societies, such persons frequently are avid to distinguish themselves from the unkempt lower orders. A study (Portes,1970) of mass attitudes in Chile, for example, found that middle-class psychological identification correlated much more strongly with hostility to political radicalism than such demographic variables as occupation, income, or even education. Given the status insecurity and social privileges (servants, resorts, limousines, clubs, etc.) of military officers in many of these societies, it is little wonder that MAP indoctrination has attained a moderate degree of success. Jose Nun (1969:55) emphasizes

the special vulnerability of the Latin American middle class in the face of the imperialistic strategy of the Cold War. The vulnerability corresponds to the worsening of the relations of this class with the popular sectors and for this reason, systematic anti-Communism appears as the type of rationalization most suited to its interests. Furthermore, the middle class, as a consequence of the lack of hegemonic vocation on the part of its various factions, achieves only a precarious unity on the basis of negative principles. It is opposed to corruption and it is opposed to Communism, without realizing that corruption is a function of the irrationality of the system it is helping to preserve and that Communism is the name that its fears give to the desire of the popular sectors for a better way of life.

An almost identical distinction between ideological perceptions and systemic functions – but one which emphasizes external linkages – was tendered two years before Nun's by Irving Louis Horowitz(1967:179–80):

While each of the Latin American military elites might employ such themes to justify its own behavior . . . basically they represent supposed United States needs in the area. This supposition is in itself the most decisive aspect of the present situation – namely, the breakdown of neocolonialism and its replacement with imperial politics of a more classic vintage. The present turn to counterinsurgency as a style of politics marks a return to military solutions of economic problems, rather than economic solutions to military problems. While the form of colonialism may be classical, the content is quite new. . . .

In arguing for the utility of a class model in assessing certain types of military interventions, I recognize that a majority have been largely devoid of ideological goals. Many coups must be explained by other variables. If for a moment we ignore those which are unique to particular conspiracies (i.e., opportunism, personal antipathy, etc.), the general pattern of military intervention can be explained by two factors which are ubiquitous in underdeveloped areas: (1) Kling's (1956) stress upon the paucity of alternative upward mobility channels in often stagnating neocolonial economies; (2) Nun's emphasis on the failure of civilian elites to assume leadership in modernizing military technology and in imposing professional norms upon officer corps, thus causing officer corps to develop a type of institutional inferiority complex. Nun argues that because such an historic pattern evolved during the 19th century in northern Europe, such a self-image was translated into respect for civilian supremacy, while rapidly expanding economies provided the most socially ambitious officers from middle class backgrounds with ex-tramilitary avenues for upward mobility.

Although I am ignoring national and regional differences, it can be argued that in general this predator model of military establishments helps explain the lack of legitimacy with which Third World officers view civilian supremacy. When one couples de facto military supremacy (not autonomy) with the accretion of material privileges and middle-class identifications, it becomes immediately apparent why these officers find American indoctrination and social hospitality so congenial. The conse-quential reinforcement contributes to a definition of atheistic com-munism that indiscriminately includes all egalitarian elements which can be perceived to threaten officer privileges, military supremacy, the modernizing oligarchic classes, or their capitalist benefactors in the developing North Atlantic community.

Although Congressional restrictions have been imposed upon the Military Assistance Program since the Vietnamese campaign began to appear hopeless, most of these have simply made it easier for liberal Congressmen to criticize exercises of Executive discretion. The Sy-mington Amendment to the Foreign Assistance Act of 1967 directs the President to terminate economic aid if a country is diverting funds "to unnecessary military expenditures, to a degree which materially in-terferes with its development." And the Conte-Long Amendment to the same Act ends grant aid if underdeveloped recipients (with certain excep-tions) purchase "sophisticated weapons without a determination by the President of the United States that such transactions are in the American national interest."

There have been some modest changes in the 1970s. Due to the weakening of the U.S. dollar, the Nixon administration attempted to substitute military credit sales for grant aid. A decade ago, two Defense Department-associated specialists (Hochman and Ratcliffe, 1970) warn-ed that this could be self-defeating and therefore counterproductive: "The substitution then of credit sales for grant aid is no panacea. . . . It exacts a price in terms of reduced economic growth, diplomatic problems of transition, and the reduction of U.S. control of military forces in the recipient countries." The authenticity of such an apprehension is sug-gested by Irving Louis Horowitz's(1967:180) conclusion several years earlier that "what has taken place in increasing degrees is the external or foreign management of internal conflicts in Latin America. . . ." And a considerable body of data which tends to substantiate Horowitz's conclusion has been assembled by his former student John Saxe-Fernandez (1969,1971).

The overcommitment of U.S. resources (Melman, 1974) and "loss" of Vietnam may then result in a slight erosion of American prestige and hegemony within the Western world. As a consequence, U.S. policymakers have intensified their efforts to use allies as proxies for both training and counterinsurgency interventions, while simultaneously adopting what public relations experts call a low profile.[15] This explains the proposal to transfer U.S. Southern Command functions to the Norfolk head-quarters of the North Atlantic Command because

the maintenance of a large military command structure in Latin America, whose commander-in-chief is a frequent visitor to the countries of the region is seen by critics as too conspicuous and implies Washington's total blessings on regimes that may not be based on popular trust and confidence. (U.S. House of Representatives,1970:120–22.)

Along similar lines, the Rockefeller Report advised that Military Groups (MILGRPs) be reduced in size and visibility. Officers should not appear in public wearing uniforms and the missions would not be called permanent. In addition, it counseled a change in name from "Military Assistance Program" to "Western Hemisphere Security Program." The manipulation of symbols to conceal dependent or hierarchical relationships has also been reflected in the attempt to rename the U.S. Army School of the Americas as the Inter-American Defense Academy.

Neither the adoption of sophisticated low profile public relations styles nor the decline in America's economic position following the Vietnamese debacle appear to have reduced the high priority assigned to promoting political responsiveness through the military assistance program. Thus, Section 17 of the Foreign Assistance Act of 1974 stipulated the sense of Congress that the military grant program

should be reexamined in light of changes in world conditions and the economic position of the United States . . . and that the program, *except for military education and training activities,* should be reduced and terminated as rapidly as feasible consistent with the security and foreign policy requirements of the United States. (Italics added.)

Within a year it was proposed by the Ford administration that military education, training, and orientation be separated from other forms of military aid and be incorporated into a permanent program comparable to that provided under the Mutual Educational and Cultural Exchange Act of 1961. Intended to safeguard military political indoctrination programs from liberal attacks upon arms transfer aid, the proposed severance of training was effectuated by the International Security

Assistance and Arms Control Act of 1976. In the late 1970s, a Brooking's study (Farley, Kaplan, and Lewis,1978:30) concluded that:

Training programs continue to be a strong part of security assistance under the 1976 act. A proposed budget of $35.7 million for such purposes in fiscal 1978 called for instruction for 5,267 foreign military and military related personnel, representing 46 countries. The new act permits wide latitude in the planning and provision of training courses.

With respect to the latter, they noted an increased use of "field training teams," though they seem to have been limited to such countries as South Vietnam, Iran, Saudi Arabia, Yemen and more recently El Salvador, which were receiving quantities and ranges of equipment far in excess of what their militaries could absorb. Future research might well assess the effectiveness of such facades upon attentive publics. Of more direct relevance to my hypothesis that external socialization by the West in general and the United States in particular measurably enhances the conservative domestic role played by officer corps in the Third World would be a detailed analysis of the training-engendered personal relationships and the prior socialization of particular coup leaders. Military journals and educational curricula in such countries could be examined, or the academic profession might request that the Defense Department publish the names and tours of duty of all ex-trainees.

Notes

1. Of the 73 studies annotated by Riddleberger(1965), no more than five held that external military training exerted a significant influence upon indigenous political roles. Sixty-five items completely ignored such inputs as do some more recent analyses (Nelkin, 1967; Perlmutter, 1969).

2. "The average military mind is conservative in its relation to the revolutionary processes of history from the Protestant Reformation to our own times (Vagts,1959:29–30)." In the same vein, see: Lieuwen(1964:130–35); Hovey(1965:70–71); Riddleberger(1965:6–7); U.S. Army Signal Center and School (1967:180); Clotfelter(1968); Needler(1969:239–42); Be'eri(1970:464–72); and other sources listed in note 14, Chapter 2.

3. Price (1971) notes that

the individual trainee is isolated from his past reference and membership groups, that is, from the sources of social and psychological support for his previous beliefs. He is enmeshed in a network of new membership groups, characterized by high levels of cohesiveness and a reinforcing ideological homogeneity. . . . The training process undergone by the officer corps of many of the new states is such as to produce reference-group identifications with the officer corps of the ex-colonial power and concomitant commitments to its set of traditions, symbols, and values.

Although Price was concerned with Ghana prior to Nkrumah's overthrow, aspects of Maynard's(1978:130–35) report on Phillipine senior officer role orientations suggest that the absence of a nationalistic outlook and an identification with a U.S. perspective on the meaning of professionalism may be explained by training and concomitant combat tour-induced American reference groups.

4. Historical studies providing substantive bases for this view have been published by LaFeber(1963); Gardner(1964); and Kolko(1969). In the words of two Defense Department-associated scholars,

> the major long-range task in the underdeveloped countries appears to be less that of the development of military capabilities than the promotion of conditions of general material and psychological well-being and satisfaction with Western political approaches to economic development. The latter goal requires . . . internal security, technical development, and political development . . . military personnel influence all three areas as they attempt to provide military assistance. (Vallance and Windle, 1962:62)

Cf.: Furniss(1957:17,29–32); Holcombe and Berg(1957:17); Wolf(1965:22); Gimbel (1968:117–20); Wolpin(1973); Etchinson(1975).

5. Highly useful sources on such U.S. interventions are Smith(1960:152–53); Gardner(1964:50,116–18); Kolko(1969:49–63,83–97,182–92,428–54); D. Horowitz(1967); Barnet(1967); Radosh(1969).

6. As used here, "conservative" does not necessarily imply opposition to all social change or technological modernization. It may be defined as encompassing at least one, though generally several, of the following policy orientations: (1) high priority to the protection of domestic and foreign property holdings in profitable areas; (2) de facto refusal to redistribute existing wealth in favor of the blue-collar worker or peasant sectors; (3) opposition to publicly owned and controlled enterprises when generous tax privileges or other subsidies will induce private investors to assume responsibility for the undertaking; (4) anti-Communist suppression; (5) advocacy of a de facto pro-Western foreign policy.

7. Although the posture of antagonism which dates from the 1917 anti-Bolshevik allied invasion of Russia has often been articulated and perceived in purely ideological terms, the latter have always been operationally defined within a framework characterized by "open door" constraints. The absence of establishment outrage over torture in Brazil is only superficially inconsistent with the numerous denunciations of Cuban revolutionary justice in 1959 and the subsequent elimination of a free press in that country. On the basic class nature of Cold War antipathies as well as the role of foreign investment as a net expropriator, rather than a source of capital for underdeveloping areas, see D. Horowitz(1969); Jalee(1968); and Frank(1970). See also Gordon(1968), and sources cited in Chapters 6 and 8.

8. Algeria R(7/62); Burma R(9/58); Cambodia C(3/70); Congo-Brazzaville R(8/63); Zaire C(9/60); Egypt R(3/54); Ghana C(2/66); Greece C(4/66); Indonesia C(3/66); Iran C(8/53); Iraq R(7/58), C(2/63); Jordan C(4/57); Laos C(1/60), R(8/60), C(4/64); Libya R(9/69); Mali C(11/68); Pakistan C(10/58); Somalia R(10/69); South Yemen R(5/68); Sudan R(10/64), R(5/69); Syria C(3/49), R(2/54), C(9/61), R(2/66); Thailand C(11/51); Zanzibar R(1/64). These were successful coups with a duration of three months. More permissive criteria used by others increases the number of coups. See, e.g., Thompson(1973), Kennedy(1974), Finer(1976), Janowitz(1977), Palmer and Thompson(1978).

9. My classifications were based upon policies pursued or opposed as reported by the *New York Times,* periodicals, and scholarly publications. When clear evidence of such conduct was lacking, statements by coup leaders and deposed politicians were relied upon. "Conservative" is defined in note 6. The converse is "radical" for my classificatory purposes.

10. I am now excluding a small number of countries which were militarily aided by the East and a Western nation other than the United States.

11. The creation or maintenance of a favorable internal power balance is furthered by strengthening political parties, the provision of economic aid, cultural exchange programs, educational modernization, diffusion of propaganda, and organizing peasant unions and cooperatives. A variety of U.S. nongovernmental entities, official agencies, and interna-

tional organizations contribute to this counterrevolutionary institution-building process which parallels the MAP. Within this overall strategic framework, Woddis(1977:61) emphasizes that "special attention is paid by the CIA to both army and police in the given country."

12. In Tables 3.5 and 3.6, several of the countries did not receive any military aid from non-Western or non-U.S. sources.

13. Some of these assessments have been referred to or quoted in preceding sections of this chapter. Others along with a few dissenting views appear in Wolpin(1973, Chapter 7).

14. Grand Pre goes on to note that

nineteen of the countries receiving military assistance are currently governed by military or ex-military officers. Five of them received training in the United States, among them General Yakulu Gowon of Nigeria, General Anastasio Somoza Debayle of Nicaragua, and General Juan Velasco Alvarado of Peru. Others have deputies who have trained here, such as Colonel Ahvaad Juluud of Libya and General Stylianos Pattkos of Greece. Twelve of the 19 countries have cabinet ministers who receieved military training in this country. They include Colonel Babia(Assistant Cabinet Chief) of the Congo and General Francisco Antonio Imaz(Minister of Interior) of Brazil. In Peru, 11 cabinet ministers received military training in the United States.

Nearly 200 U.S.-trained military officers occupy executive or legislative positions in their governments, are presidents of major industrial firms, or are chiefs or deputy chiefs of their respective military departments.

Over 600 others are senior commanders within their military service; and more than 1,200 fill key staff positions in their military departments.

15. U.S.-supported proxy interventions have occurred in Oman(Iran), Ethiopia(Sudan, Saudi Arabia), Zaire(France, Belgium, Morocco), Angola(South Africa), Western Sahara (France, Morocco), Timor(Indonesia), and Lebanon(Israel). Similarly with American encouragement, the German Federal Republic has emerged as a major source of weapons and training in Africa.

4

Civilian and Military Reformism: The Pattern of Destabilization

Given the predominantly conservative political character of contemporary military organization and the previously delineated reinforcing external socialization, there would seem to be little basis for optimism. Indeed, the pattern of leftist — using that term broadly — failure examined in this chapter suggests that systemic rigidity due to intense class antagonism and insufficient economic growth rates preclude the possibility of incremental egalitarian success. From this deterministic viewpoint, the system is closed to meaningful socio-economic reform. And as we have seen in Chapter 2, there is ample basis in Marx's own mature works upon which to ground such a perspective. Here, inferentially in Chapter 6, and more explicitly in Chapter 9, I shall argue that, notwithstanding the forementioned conservative structural parameters, there nevertheless remains a certain "looseness" within these unstable dependent systems. And this admits a certain latitude of choice among alternative policy options. Put differently, mass socialist revolutionary struggles "from below" are one rather than the only viable short run route to mass social mobility and development. This approach may not be Marxist, but it is certainly consonant (when the empirical basis I am about to elaborate is assimilated) with Marx's own "method of successive approximations," as it is with his increased appreciation of the crucial role of leadership efficacy or "voluntaristic" dimensions of socio-political conflict.[1]

My thesis is that most populist leaders have promoted their own defeat by accepting reformist premises rather than radical ones.[2] The "radical" or Marxian position was that privileged classes would sooner violate the "rules of the game" (i.e., resort to naked violence) than concede their wealth when ordinary procedures no longer could be relied upon to safeguard their material interests. Interestingly, while it has become fashionable in certain social science circles to denigrate the mature Marx by implying a hiatus between his later years and a presumably more relevant "young Marx," here we are treating a predictive statement which he adhered to as much in the post-Commune era as in the 1840s.[3]

Similarly, while others have denigrated Marx by identifying specific propositions associated with his theory of capitalist development that have not as yet been vindicated by historical experience, in this chapter I am considering a distinct Marxian prediction that has with one exception stood the test of time.[4] And by "time," I refer specifically to more than a century of contemporary history, from the fall of the Commune to the sanguinary destruction of the Popular Unity Government of Chile in 1973. My first objective consequently is to identify conflictual patterns in 10 well-known episodes of egalitarian failure which culminated in right-wing military coups. If these cases are representative, as I believe they are—at least of civilian efforts—a logical conclusion is that the reformist option is untenable in similar nonindustrialized societies, whose traditional position in recent years has been denoted by the term "dependency."

Does it follow then that successful guerrilla strategy and liberation by a fraternal Red Army are the only alternatives for egalitarians in "tight surplus" societies?[5] I shall argue that in at least several and perhaps a majority of the cases analyzed, the defeat of egalitarian efforts was by no means inevitable. Had the leader heeded the advice of his radical supporters at an earlier stage of the struggle and premised his tactical decisions upon different (i.e., nonreformist) strategic assumptions, the social position of privileged classes might well have been damaged instead of largely restored. At bottom, such success involves an early decision to mobilize and organize armed supporters overtly if possible, covertly if necessary.

Such views may appear romantically subjectivistic to the orthodox Marxist who rigidly holds to Marx's prediction that capitalist maturity was a prerequisite for socialist revolution. Without claiming that sufficient time and capitalist development have occurred to vitiate that proposition, I only want to emphasize: 1) most 20th century social revolutions have occurred in immature capitalist societies; 2) Marx himself did not denounce the struggle of the Communards while it was in progress as utopian for lack of objectively ripe conditions; 3) in the last 15 or so years of his life, Marx began to place greater stress upon leadership, organization, and other voluntaristic concerns; 4) economic dependency relationships and the diffusion of radical consciousness have created conditions which are functional equivalents for the specific contradictions in the monopoly capitalist relations of production that Marx had anticipated.[6]

The case studies essayed here demonstrate that reformist tactical assumptions are untenable because of the intensity of class antagonism in the developing areas. The level of hostility is, of course, itself a function of the high rate of exploitation (i.e., surplus extraction) by several privileged classes—domestic and transnational—which form uneasy defensive coalitions to "destabilize" reform advocates. Because military officers acted as the strike force that liquidated all of these reformist governments, some attention will be focused upon domestic military policies available to the deposed reformer. Critical analysis of policy choices is particularly important because in most cases leftist pro-regime factions not only emerged but were growing among the lower officer ranks of the armed forces as the polarization process intensified. Did the deposed reformers recognize the sources of this intramilitary conflict and make best use of political resources that were or might have become available at the moment of greatest need? Or, on the other hand, did they overestimate the significance of such factions?

The deposed reformist regimes used in this analysis are: Iran's Mossadegh(1953); Guatemala's Arbenz(1954); the Dominican Republic's Bosch(1962); Brazil's Goulart(1964); Indonesia's Sukarno(1965); Ghana's Nkrumah(1966); Mali's Keita(1968); Cambodia's Sihanouk (1970); Bolivia's Torres(1971); and Chile's Allende(1973). These episodes were selected for several reasons. First, all of the regimes survived for at least half a year and therefore presumably had an opportunity to adopt different policies toward those who led the conservative coalition. That this is not always the case is well illustrated by the fate of Major Hashim Mohammed El Atta's leftist 1971 seizure in the Sudan. Although external intervention and overconfidence were important factors in its downfall, the general proposition is well stated by Woddis (1977:124) when he warns that:

If, as Marx said, the defensive is the defeat of every uprising, then one can add that for intended coup victims to wait passively for the final counterrevolutionary blow guarantees their defeat. Yet defeat is sometimes difficult to avoid. If the relationship of forces on the eve of a foreseen coup is unfavourable for effective countermeasures against it, whatever political awareness of the progressive movement and however strong its desire to stop the coup, it may be impossible in a few days or even weeks to effect the necessary political changes and preparations, both political and material, to prevent such a coup taking place, still less to defeat it once it has begun.

Second, these cases were sufficiently prominent to be newsworthy—hence, because of the availability of periodical coverage and reports, they were researchable. Third, their history spans a considerable though contemporary period. The political environments and relationships remain much the same today in the developing areas, especially with the breakdown of detente and intensified East-West hostility. Fourth, with one exception, all were associated with democratic institutions. While democratic practices in underdeveloped areas generally leave even more to be desired than their counterparts in the North Atlantic Community, they can nevertheless be clearly distinguished from the autocratic mode prevailing in such polities as South Korea, Paraguay, and Saudi Arabia. Although Torres' regime was military in origin, he endeavored to respect civil liberties within society and the "rules of the game" within his own armed forces. Furthermore, his experience and that of Jacobo Arbenz offer us insight into the dilemma of professional military officers who opt for a reformist mission.

These military-led regimes and the civilian ones also share the characteristic that virtually all were moving to the left socioeconomically when deposed. Hence, they can be distinguished from cases where "reformers" survived by jettisoning their "radical" programs (e.g., Betancourt) when threatened by the right.

In the following section, empirical patterns emerging from these cases will be discussed. While at times one or two regimes do not fit the pattern, the general tendencies are in fact broadly shared.

Reform as a Prelude to Economic Crisis

The reformers in question generally manifested their egalitarian commitments by introducing directly redistributive socio-economic measures at the expense of wealthy property-owning classes. Many of these governments sought to implement reform by increasing the share of bourgeois surplus which accrued to the state.[7] Hence, greater funds would be available for welfare programs in the short run, and over a longer period industrialization could be encouraged in a manner that would maximize public sector resources. At the risk of some simplification, what seems to be involved in most instances is a movement on a continuum from monopoly capitalist systems of property relations toward what some have characterized as a state capitalist system.[8]

The reformers' initial moves were ad hoc and tended in all cases basically to reflect a policy orientation or bias rather than an a priori plan. And as such, these nationalizations, rent controls, and wage increases initially provoked ad hoc responses by property-owning classes. Their political representatives denounced the measures as irresponsible and "communist," while the owning classes instinctively began a process of capital disinvestment. Tax evasion, capital flight, hoarding, layoffs, and inflation are ubiquitous concomitants to the initiation of serious reform efforts. Hence, while the latter themselves reflect a desire to tackle longstanding structural socio-economic problems, they ironically trigger reactions by the bourgeoisie which create new dislocations that, at least in the short run, neutralize or reduce the anticipated benefits of the reform measures.[9]

Liberty for the Marxist Left

The same bourgeois sectors that were threatened by initial or anticipated reforms attempted to divide and weaken the left not only by denouncing specific measures as either communist or communist-inspired, but also by calling for suppression and rejection of Marxist support.[10] With the exceptions of Nkrumah, Keita, and Allende, who were themselves Marxists of sorts, the remaining reformers seem to have had serious personal reservations or at least ambiguous sentiments when it came to soliciting support from or collaborating with the so-called extreme left—at least in the early phases of struggle for reform. This is comprehensible because most of them had at one time in their political careers associated themselves with anticommunist suppression.[11]

Intensity of Reformist Commitment

The key to understanding why most of these leaders not only transcended their earlier rigid anti-Marxism but, in a substantial number of instances, ended by soliciting or accepting the organizational resources of the far left was their genuine dedication to bringing about greater mass welfare and thus securing an honored place in their nation's history. They came to recognize that the principal opponents of egalitarian reform were also the most vociferous anticommunists. At the same time, the far left was willing to organize a mass constituency and (in a number of instances) already had won leadership within important labor, youth, and peasant sectors.

Hence, at bottom what best explains de facto and formal coalitions with Marxists was the reformers' determination to push through at least some egalitarian alterations in the social structure.[12] This unyielding commitment, even when focused upon a few rather than a broad range of issues, provoked increasingly fierce antagonism by the bourgeoisie, high level civil servants, many officers in the armed forces, transnational corporations, and leading Western powers—the United States, Britain, and France. Gradually and with difficulty, hostile coalitions emerged spontaneously and often with the covert guidance of the CIA. The polarization process was as natural as it was apparent to the increasingly besieged protagonists of reform. When the struggle intensified, considerable pressure was engendered by growing difficulties in obtaining external economic aid, increased smuggling and tax evasion, declines in earnings from principal exports, and (at times) international denunciations which encouraged domestic opponents of social change. While all of this was obviously not a manifestation of imperialist conspiracy, the pattern is too common to be completely fortuitous.

The Irrelevancy of Radical Labels

One of the most striking findings was that similar antireformist conspiracies appeared, regardless of whether the reforms were espoused by self-styled socialists or Marxists (Keita, Nkrumah, Allende), nationalistic populists (Mossadegh, Bosch, Goulart, Sukarno, Sihanouk), or military radicals (Arbenz, Torres). Although Keita, Nkrumah, and Allende were undoubtedly inspired by Marxian ideals and interpretations of contemporary history, little distinguished their style and substantive decisions from the other two categories of deposed reformers. Furthermore, while both Nkrumah and Allende were aficionados of la dolce vita, Keita boasted aristocratic lineage and an affinity for French culture which made it exceptionally easy to establish close working relations with conservative Francophiles like Houphouet Boigny. It goes without saying that all three were often at odds with the revolutionary Marxists within their countries.

It is worth stressing that neither the reformer's customarily moderate political symbols nor his electoral scruples affected in any way the emergence of hostile bourgeois-imperialist conspiracies. If we ignore the labels and divide the ten reformers into two groups, we find that those who were most committed to electoralism and accorded greatest importance to dealing with—rather than circumventing—national legislatures (Arbenz, Bosch, Goulart, Sihanouk, and Allende) were the targets of "destabilization" no less than their slightly less scrupulous coreformers. Nor are there apparent differences in the onset of such conservative coalitions.

Thus, regardless of variations in political labels or commitments to electoralism, the common denominator of all these men was their aspiration for historical prestige by adopting an unflinching dedication to bringing a modicum of egalitarian social emancipation to their impoverished mass constituencies. The assault upon privilege invariably necessitated an independent foreign policy posture, since the comprador-transnational corporate sector represented one of the primary sources of surplus appropriation and opposition to "radical" reform measures.[13]

Patterns of Military Alignment and Division

Whether or not initial moderate reform goals were later supplemented by more extreme ones, rightist military conspiracies tend to be initiated by officers who identify with and are closely related to sectors of the antireform coalition. These individuals are either socially linked with threatened property-owning classes or—to put it euphemistically—value material amenities that would enable them to imitate the life style of their social betters. The latter was especially true in the Dominican Republic, Ghana, Mali, and Indonesia. Upper middle class social recruitment and interaction characterized senior officers in Iran, Chile, and Brazil, while the situation appears more mixed in Cambodia and Guatemala. Notwithstanding these differences, all of the conspirators—and to a lesser degree the majority of officers—probably viewed the maintenance of existing class structures as a function of the armed forces. Although the degree of commitment to such a role orientation varied, and for many—especially at the junior levels—was probably lightly internalized, nevertheless it created an atmosphere in which conspiracies could and did flourish. Whether officers regarded egalitarian reforms as part of a process that would threaten their life style aspirations through austerity measures and/or destruction of the institutional autonomy of the armed forces or simply identified with immediately threatened social reference groups, the outcome was pretty much the same.[14]

A common theme in civil-military relations literature stresses the provocative effects of creating armed militia or similar paramilitary organizations. What is assumed but seldom explicated is that the armed forces (i.e., the senior officer corps) are hegemonic classes domestically and would sooner depose a government than accept civilian sovereignty along with a truly professional external defense function. In most of the case studies, a sector of the left—primarily the incremental reformist sector—accepted this thesis and vigorously argued against such an attempt. The Chilean Communist Party along with many Socialists and Radicals in Allende's Popular Unity Coalition refused to waver from such a position even though these parties had thousands of weapons cached for potential distribution according to one possibly biased source (Evans,1973:248).

Reformist policy elites generally assumed that, in the absence of a provocative move, the moderates and progressives within the armed forces would wield sufficient influence to constrain coup-prone rightist officers. In all of the cases studied, there *were* officers who opposed the coup—and indeed a few were willing to use arms against their military colleagues, particularly in Brazil, Chile, Bolivia, Indonesia, Ghana, and the Dominican Republic. Two facts, however, warrant reflection. First, the percentage of officers who refused to cooperate with the conspirators appears to have been extremely low, while those who were willing to oppose the operation actively was miniscule. Thus, in Brazil less than 150 commissioned officers were purged after the coup, while in Chile "several hundred" were reported to have been "neutralized" on the eve of the intervention. Between 300 and 500 junior officers and NCOs were purged in Iran, while a mere dozen or so senior officers lost their positions in Mali because of their opposition to the coup and the desire by the low-ranking conspirators for upward mobility. In Ghana, a similar number were murdered or arrested for analogous reasons.

A second pattern revealed by the cases is that neither military rank nor branch of service were uniformly associated with pro- or anti-regime sentiments though one suspects that there was greater reformist backing among junior officers. With the exception of the Dominican Republic, some senior officers appear to have been among the small minority who were opposed to the conservative interventions. Exactly how many junior officers identified with them is problematic, although the proportion was probably higher than among privileged and upper middle class-oriented senior ranks. Only in Santo Domingo did a handful of junior officers take the initiative in offering to lead a preventive action to save Bosch. These were army professionals who undoubtedly were antagonistic toward the degenerate air force officers directing the coup. But in other cases, there was either complete absence of interservice conflict (Chile, Brazil, Guatemala, Mali, Iran, Bolivia, Ghana) or the opposing branch (Indonesia's Air Force) surrendered virtually without a fight. Even Sukarno's Palace Guard, which led a preventive coup attempt, failed to engaged in significant combat against rightist-led forces. This held for Sihanouk's Pnom Penh Police which, notwithstanding its loyalty, turned out but a small number of men in an abortive effort to arrest Lon Nol and other plotters. Subsequently, several army battalions did join the Khmer Rouge-led National Union. The only other sustained fighting occurred in Ghana and Bolivia. Interestingly, in both instances, leftist ideological influence existed at the command level. Nkrumah's palace guard, the President's Own Guard Regiment (POGR), was advised by Soviet and East German officers, while part of Torres' Colorados Regiment was commanded by Col. Ruben Sanchez, who had been proselytized by his university student offspring, their friends, and Inti Paredo himself. In neither case, however, did other units come to the aid of these loyalists. [15]

That reformist assumptions exaggerate the importance of noninterventionist factions and traditions becomes even more apparent when one acknowledges that the existence or absence of militia-type units failed to affect the pattern of military response. Thus, in five (Chile, Dominican

Republic, Brazil, Cambodia, and Iran) of the ten cases, coup conspiracies went forward even though no attempt had been made to constitute a people's militia.[16] In the Bolivian case, atrophied militias of the early 1950s were obviously not a motivational factor influencing either the 1964 or 1971 interventions. Hence, we are left with four cases where recently constituted or imminent armed militia-type organizations may have played some role in provoking the conspiracy, or what is more likely brought "swingmen" into it. Yet in Mali, Guatemala, Indonesia, and certainly Ghana, the conspiratorial activities appear to have antedated efforts to create militias.[17] Even though paramilitary formations broadened the base of support for the conspiracies, it is not clear that on balance the militias themselves diminished the survival prospects of the reformist regimes. They enhanced the potential resources of the deposed reformer and consequently necessitated a more broadly based conspiracy. The real problem pertained to militia capabilities. Most were poorly equipped, ill-trained, and ineptly led. In Ghana and Guatemala, the militia units do not seem to have been armed, while most of Mali's were either taken by surprise or their commanders were suborned. Ironically, in that country, virtually all of the senior officers refused to back the coup even after it had become a fait accompli! Obviously, as beneficiaries of high rank, they felt more threatened by junior officer insubordination than by a parallel armed force.[18]

What does catalyze intense antagonism among career officers — even those sympathetic to social change — is the formal organization of radical NCO/enlistee associations. In Bolivia, Iran, and Brazil, leftists carried out independent efforts that within a short time recruited hundreds of enlisted members. Because of the direct threat to hierarchical command structures, this approach appears even more dangerous than the creation of paramilitary trade union, youth, or peasant militias. On the other hand, when radicals informally develop a dialogue with commissioned officers, such as occurred in Chile or Mali, the moderate or centrist officer sector appears to have reacted with substantially greater equanimity. In the latter country, most senior officers seem to have played a spectator role during the ouster of Keita — a coup largely engineered by the CIA, French intelligence, and several officers who had been passed over for promotion. North(1974) argues that, at the time of the abortive June coup attempt in Chile, many "progressive" officers for the first time became willing to accept lower class mobilization against the conservative civil-military coalition. Between August 25th and September 11th, virtually all of these officers were forced into retirement, deprived of troop commands, arrested, or opted to follow the successful conspirators due to disillusionment with Allende's passivity.

Imperialism and Conservative Militarism

Because reformist egalitarianism and its concomitant dynamic tend to move a system along a continuum from monopoly capitalism to state capitalism, the reactive pattern of Western (i.e., U.S., British, and French) imperialism has tended to be negative.[19] Initially, an attempt is made to bargain with the reformer to assure a privileged climate for transnational corporations; and, if not that, at least an open door to foreign investors. From the standpoint of such early negotiations, the carrot and stick are customarily utilized. Offers of conditional aid are made, while simultaneously efforts are intensified to strengthen internal right-wing sectors and to promote disunity within the reform coalition.[20] Despite wavering and back-tracking, in the cases under study, this process was associated with growing distrust and antagonism, especially as the reformer demonstrated his lack of psychological dependency (i.e., "responsiveness" and deference to the Western powers). At some point, a decision seems to have been made to subvert the regime itself, since it was too difficult to deal with such an independently minded Third World upstart.

Disclosures by former CIA officers Victor Marchetti(1974), Philip Agee(1975), and Winslow Peck leave no doubt of the agency's promotion of coups. "Peck, who served the CIA in Turkey, Vietnam, and France, as well as here at home, says the agency is a 'secret criminal police force' that has been responsible for 25 coups since 1964."[21] Interestingly, the 1968 overthrow of Keita appears to have been orchestrated within and/or through France. Most likely it reflected a joint French-American effort. Director of the French-modeled Military Academy, Captain Yoro Diakite was the earliest plotter, while his assistant, Lt. Moussa Troare, who actually led the strike force, had mysteriously traveled to France (from whence he may have been flown by the CIA to "The Farm" a CIA training center in Virginia) eight or ten weeks before the coup.

The use of propaganda to create a climate of uncertainty along with a number of extremely "professional" moves before and during the coup suggest external technical assistance and quite probably direction of the operation.[22] The Malian coup was typical of a minority of the cases, (Cambodia, Bolivia, and the Dominican Republic) in that, while characteristic indicators of foreign intelligence manipulation are present, direct evidence is absent. The weakest grounds for such inferences apply to Bosch's overthrow. Yet even here, American Military Mission personnel appear to have sympathized openly with and encouraged the Wessin clique. Ambassador Martin's predilections notwithstanding, the State and Defense Departments had (at best) "written off" Bosch. The denial of Martin's request for forceful intervention contrasted starkly with the

U.S. role 20 months earlier when one of Wessin's Air Force colleagues had threatened a conservative civilian administration.[23] This and the somewhat stronger inferential cases referred to above must of course be distinguished from the majority (Guatemala, Chile, Ghana, Brazil, Indonesia, and Iran) where explicit documentation of the CIA role is available.[24]

In most of these interventions, the officers who organized the military conspiracy seem to have had some of their moves coordinated with those of right-wing civilian antiregime forces.[25] The organized mass demonstrations associated with the coup itself are ubiquitous, as are shortages of goods, vitriolic anti-Communist propaganda, etc. Civilians who played a major role in fomenting the crisis were, like their military counterparts, usually linked to imperialist institutions. Thus, most of the officers had been trained by the U.S. (Britain or France in three cases), many seem to have been exposed to the domestic introduction of imperialist military educational curricula and generally they were on friendly terms with foreign officers.[26]

Reactive and Conciliatory Reform Styles

While the deposed reformers were determined to bring about social change in limited areas, until the final phase of the crises, they appeared uncertain about the depth and scope of their reformist goals. Frequently ad hoc attempts were made in some areas, while others were ignored. A willingness to compromise often characterized early phases, though as oligarchic and transnational sectors coalesced into a bitterly antagonistic force, the reform position hardened and the regime's rhetoric tended to become more radicalized. Explicit endorsement of sweeping structural change characterized the last weeks of Torres, Goulart, and Allende, as it did the final months of Keita, Nkrumah, and Arbenz. Yet despite the rhetoric, even these radicals maintained ties and illusions about dealing with imperialist/comprador forces—though they had in fact already been written off by the conspiratorial sectors. Particularly tragic figures were cut by leaders like Allende, Sihanouk, and Bosch who appeared congenitally unable even to begin to fathom the ruthless character of those with whom they had previously consorted.

Because of similar bourgeois social origins and (perhaps more significantly) a web of social interaction, the reformers tacitly identified with the culture of their supporters. This social reference group effect was so pronounced that even the reformer (Nkrumah) who managed to come closest to freeing himself from these psychological encumbrances boasted after his ouster that not one of his enemies had been executed! At the other extreme of our continuum, Mossadegh—a large landowner—failed on the eve of his overthrow to heed the call of Iranian radicals to proclaim a republic; this notwithstanding his association with antimonarchist forces and the central role of the Shah in the then ongoing CIA maneuvers to oust him.

The reformers acted out of a sense of noblesse oblige toward beneficiary mass sectors. Given motives of this sort, we can better understand reactive conciliatory styles toward opponents from their own social class on one hand, and, on the other, a dysfunctional paternalism toward the "masses" as well as parties, youth organizations, and trade unions on the left.

Oftimes the impetus to deepen and broaden reform seems to have come more from secondary leaders of these latter sectors than from the soon-to-be-deposed national reform "leader" who was haltingly pushed further left by the cross-pressures from both sides. Radicalization was defensive—almost reluctant—and therefore unaccompanied by the seizure of initiative (let alone mobilization) of more than a small percentage of available mass energy. Woddis(1977:145–46) pinpoints this ubiquitous failure in the context of Sukarno's overthrow, notwithstanding his introduction of "Guided Democracy."

This paternalist idea is a common feature in many Third World countries. Sukarno may have thought up the term, but the concept was to a large extent evident in Egypt under Nasser, in Ghana under Nkrumah, in Uganda under Obote, in Bangla Desh under Sheikh Mujibar, and in a number of other countries. In fact, often where right-wing coups succeed it has been against progressive, anti-imperialist governments following a policy of 'Guided Democracy.' The whole concept is basically one stemming from the national bourgeoisie and petty-bourgeoisie, and is based on a combination of contempt for and fear of the mass of workers and peasants. The consequences are the stifling of the independent initiative of the majority of the people; the State and Government control of the main social organisations; and restrictions on the activity of the Communist Party or whatever other form of revolutionary organisation may exist. As a result, when a coup takes place under these conditions, the people often display a striking indifference or passivity and even the politically conscious forces are not in any easy position to organise mass resistance.

Occasional rallies did not compensate for the leader's fundamental aloofness and elitist paternalism toward his popular constituency.

The reformers were equally distant from—and reactive to—signs of overt officer discontent. Even when its object was material, conciliatory efforts to raise pay and allowances (i.e., in Guatemala, Brazil, Cambodia, and Chile) proved ineffective. In Mali, Bolivia, and Indonesia, no attempt was made to buy off the officers, while in Iran, Ghana, and the Dominican Republic, limited austerity was threatened or imposed. Perhaps most officers in all of the countries anticipated future austerity, intensification of economic dislocations, and adverse effects upon the "internal power balance."

Several other ad hoc responses to the perceived threat of conservative militarism proved equally inefficacious. One involved an attempt in several countries to involve the armed forces in the reform process via direct participation in civilian bureaucratic agencies or public works projects. Considerable resistance to public works activities was encountered in Ghana, Chile, Mali, Cambodia, and the Dominican Republic. And although bureaucratic co-optation occurred in Chile and Indonesia, outcomes in all cases were unaffected. In the Chilean case, North(1974) suggests that more "progressive" officers may have been attracted to such roles while the conservatives retained troop commands!

A second approach involved the creation of an intramilitary informant network by Mossadegh, Nkrumah, Torres, Arbenz, and Sukarno. While less formal sources of intelligence were available to Allende, Bosch, and presumably the remainder of our reformers, once again it does not appear to have been complemented by other vital initiatives for subordinating the military. One such tactic with optimal payoffs as far as the armed forces as a whole are concerned is the diversification of nations from which training is sought. Yet the initiation of such a policy may catalyze discontent among Western-trained officers. Thus Woddis (1977:128) argues that:

It is not only that a colonial-type army has been inherited; the character of the army is largely perpetuated by the continuing military links with the imperialist countries. Officers who have received their military training in Western academies have in fact been specifically selected for such instruction by the former colonial power as being individuals of a sufficiently conservative outlook, or sufficiently opportunist, ambitious and corrupt, as to provide a reasonable guarantee that they would use their positions to act against any far-reaching progressive changes in their country.

The same motivation lies behind the choice which the United States makes when it selects army personnel from the Third World to be trained in U.S. military academies, particularly for counterinsurgency techniques.

Virtually none of the Soviet- or Chinese-trained personnel in Mali, Ghana, Indonesia, or Cambodia appear to have been associated with the conspiracies. And at least some of these elements seem to have been among those prepared to resist the plotters – given dynamic leadership.

Resource Erosion and Confrontational Dilemmas

Although economic sanctions, the reactions of privileged classes, and administrative discontinuities associated with rapid social change made it more difficult to "deliver the goods" in certain respects to mass sectors, most of the reformers seem to have retained considerable popular support as they went into the final stages of their crises. Even Nkrumah, who lost much of his domestic charisma several years after the struggle for formal independence, was sufficiently popular in the aftermath of his ouster to constrain the military from allowing open electoral competition in 1968 when temporary civilian government was restored. Interestingly, when free elections were organized in 1979, Nkrumah's followers won a plurality. While in most cases, some of the "masses" and a larger proportion of the middle classes had become disenchanted, many others among the politically aware probably sensed that, either in material or status terms, they would be decidely worse off under a restorationist military and thus in varying degree continued to back Allende, Mossadegh, Sukarno, and the others. Under all of these leaders, unsuppressed Marxists were of course simultaneously incorporating additional workers and/or peasants into a movement to "deepen" the reform process. Thus, a unifying theme in Woddis'(1977:124–25) recent analysis of this problem is that:

A coup cannot be avoided or, if begun, defeated solely by vigilance, material preparations and physical countermeasures, although such precautions should never be forgotten. Of decisive importance is political preparation, the conducting of political work in such a fashion that conditions are not allowed to develop to a stage in which it becomes possible, and in some cases relatively easy, to initiate a coup. This involves important questions of working-class unity, winning allies for the working class, rural population, urban petty-bourgeoisie, intellectuals, professional and technical personnel, or of neutralising classes and strata which otherwise might actively support the coup. It also involves the question of the relation of parties to governments, and of parties and governments to the people and their organisations. It poses questions of methods of work, of avoiding sectarianism and ensuring that potential allies are not pushed, by mistaken tactics, into the arms of the other side. Conversely, it requires the avoidance of opportunism and tailing behind events, of failing to organise the necessary struggles to advance the movement.

Because of the reformer's elitism and distrust of the masses, such mobilization as occurred developed with little high-level encouragement, almost no coordination, and (in strictly organizational terms) minimal discipline and efficiency.

This was at least partially attributable to the reformer's unwillingness to delegate authority to secondary leaders whose expressive and/or organizational talents were essential to any significant alteration of the internal balance of power. By eschewing the crippling effects of egocentrism and incorporating what Downton(1973:165–76) terms "trust associations" into a self-conscious movement for social change, the reformers could have measurably enhanced their political resources. Shortcomings in this area were underscored by the fact that the political parties closest to the reform leaders tended to be the object of systematic neglect during their tenure in office. The roles assigned them were usually limited to electioneering, plebiscitary mobilizations, and/or legislative support. This perspective was of course consonant with the paternalistic attitudes delineated in the preceding section. All told, they meant that, in a confrontation, the reformer would be on the defensive with only a marginal chance of bettering his externally supported and coordinated adversaries.

What virtually ensured the reformer's demise was his own failure of nerve. This disabled him from assuming a daring stance when only ruthlessness and a revolutionary outlook offered any possibility of survival. As Black(1966:64) observes with respect to populist leaders who emerge from traditionally dominant classes, "this type of reformer is seldom prepared to go all the way." Equally significant is the fact that almost all of the deposed reformers either were apprised of the conspiracy in advance or had general knowledge of active plotting. In most instances, antileftist terrorism, abortive assassinations, or coups had already been attempted by individuals associated with antireform forces.[27] A related factor may have been the influence or intelligence cover provided by the presence of Western military advisors. Thus, in light of Price's(1971) thesis and Agee's(1975:52) contention, it is especially significant that (Aluko,1977:81)

in May 1962, when every American was being suspected as a CIA agent in Accra, the Ghanaian government signed a military technical assistance agreement with Britain under which a British training team consisting of about 200 men was established in Accra to provide training for the Ghanaian armed forces. These men remained till the 1966 "coup" without being subjected to attacks even by the press.

In this context Woddis(1977:124) counsels: "if, as Marx said, the defensive is the defeat of every uprising, then one can add that for intended coup victims to wait passively for the final counterrevolutionary blow guarantees their defeat."

Yet we find three of the deposed leaders—Sihanouk, Nkrumah, and Keita—absenting themselves from their nations during periods of unprecedented polarization. Like the remainder of our leaders, two of these—Sihanouk and Keita—were offered the opportunity of leading loyalist forces well before the conspirators had consolidated their position. If they lacked the requisite courage to risk their lives, so did the other deposed reformers with the notable exception of Allende; yet he preferred martyrdom to seizing the initiative when a magnificent opportunity arose at the end of June.[28] During the Indonesian preventive action of September 30th, Sukarno failed even to broadcast an address to the nation calling upon his military and civilian supporters to join the effort to suppress the Council of Generals' conspiracy. Both Goulart and Bosch committed the travesty of refusing to permit military supporters to shed blood for their Constitutional Government. Arbenz resigned even though he had a loyal Chief of Staff, a hastily formed militia of thousands ready to take to the field, and probably a considerable number of younger officers who would have responded to vigorous leadership — assuming again that Arbenz was willing to provide it in his moment of truth. Torres failed to distribute arms to thousands of willing trade unionists and students even though he possessed sufficient military support to respond to such calls before Banzer's conspiracy got off the ground. Fearing perhaps that he would no longer be indispensable to the left, Torres wound up in exile for a few years before his eventual assassination. And Mossadegh not only failed to accept Tudeh support which might have included substantial NCO and some junior officer military backing on the eve of his overthrow, but he ended his political career disgracefully cowering in his bed. According to Avery(1965:439), "when he heard the rifle fire and the rumble of tanks approaching, he pulled a sheet over his head and snuggled down giggling and saying 'Look what I've done!'"

All of this might warrant a touch of levity were it not for the millions thereby consigned to misery and alienation from the amenities of modern civilization. And it is equally important to take account of the fate of hundreds of thousands of active members of these movements for social change who suffered imprisonment or execution following the overthrow of these regimes. Ultimately, then, one must confront the moral implications of accepting reformist assumptions which have been vitiated by such tragic experience.

The first conclusion to be drawn from these 10 cases is that, in the contemporary era, efforts to implement egalitarian reforms in underdeveloped societies will probably prove abortive unless conservative military factions can somehow be neutralized. These data are of course consistent with Marx's prediction that property-owning classes would forge a general coalition when they perceived a threat to their common class interests. His conviction that the primary role of the state was repressive and that the military would deploy their resources in defense of such privileges also seems to be well founded.[29]

Marx, of course, was dealing with upper class violence when the relations of production or the property-owning system itself were threatened by a self-conscious working class movement. Although he doubted that peasants could somehow have been mobilized, Marx would have predicted a resort to violence by threatened landowning sectors. In six of our cases (Chile, Dominican Republic, Brazil, Guatemala, Indonesia, and Cambodia), peasant organization played a role of some importance in the struggle to alter rural property relations. Elsewhere their level of organization was incipient or marginal at the time when the crises entered their final stages.

There is of course the question of reform itself. Marx did not predict that the privileged classes would unite and use violence against proponents of piecemeal reform. Yet the coalitions initiated conspiratorial activities well in advance of the final or "radical" phases of these regimes — when, at a rhetorical level and less often in practice, a general class offensive could be said to exist. Furthermore, fully five of the reform leaders not only characterized themselves as non-Marxist but were also so recognized by most members of the political elite. Within this category were Arbenz, Goulart, Bosch, Sihanouk, and Mossadegh. Even those who did characterize themselves as socialist, Marxist, or "revolutionary" were quite far removed from the Leninist prototype. Since this distinction — assuming it is real — appears to have little effect upon bourgeois willingness to use violence against social reformers, prospects for serious reform are extremely poor short of violence in the so-called developing areas. Failing to close the per capita income and welfare gaps, the privileged classes in these areas may reasonably sense there is little they can concede without jeopardizing their modern yet insecure lifestyles. It is pertinent to note that neither military officers nor civilian bourgeois sectors in most of the Third World are as well off materially as their counterparts in industrialized societies — exceptions notwithstanding.

Furthermore, because of low wage levels, the rate of profit in these areas tends to be higher. This and the general burden of taxes upon the lower classes in such exploited societies contributes to latent class antagonism, which appears considerably more pronounced than in the industrialized nations.[30] Perception of such hostility by privileged sectors, reinforced by the economic vulnerability of their own lifestyle, may well inspire the fear that initial egalitarian concessions will start a process of increasingly radical demands which could not be met by existing socioeconomic class structures. In short, once the dam of lower class antagonism is breached, it may give way completely. Hence, Ronald Schneider, who served in the State Department's Bureau of Research and Intelligence at the time of Arbenz's overthrow and subsequently published *Communism in Guatemala* to justify the CIA intervention, opined years later that subversion of the Goulart regime was necessary "to keep the lid on."[31]

While this may indeed be an adequate short-run "solution," in the final quarter of the 20th century, it is unlikely that stability can be maintained. For not only is economic dependency and "unequal exchange" a prominent structural dimension of North-South conflict, but consciousness of this inequity and Marxist ideas are both widespread and likely to become more influential. This trend of course is reinforced by the superior socio-cultural and economic progress of most existing socialist systems in the developing areas. Thus, we can expect a minority of dé classé intellectuals and patriotic officers — especially those exposed in some way to Marxian ideas and whose social interactions with the bourgeoisie and Western officers are limited or a source of disillusion — will continue to attempt to move their societies in a state capitalist direction. And a few who disdain a privileged life style and bureaucratic career for themselves will struggle for more fundamental egalitarian change — socialism.

The cases reviewed here (along with less prominent disasters) may be interpreted as implying that in addition to objectively favorable socio-economic conditions, certain political preconditions are mandatory for any serious prospects of success. These include: 1) leadership that is goal-conscious, risk-taking, and anticipatory; 2) coordination and efficient organization; and 3) preparation for armed struggle. If led by civilians, immediate priority must be given to creating an armed militia and/or guerrilla infrastructure combined where possible with continuous purges of traditional officers and replacement by those who have been exposed to socialist or nationalist ideas. Woddis(1977:130) emphasizes

three solutions to the question: how can the armed forces be prevented from staging a counterrevolutionary coup — a purge and change of the officer personnel, the creation of a people's militia, a change in the political outlook and loyalty of the officer corps and of the armed forces as a whole — are not necessarily alternatives. In fact, in many situations what is required is a pressing ahead on all three of these fronts, together with the necessary economic and social measures to tackle the country's problems, and the necessary political measures to increase the democratic political activity and initiative of the people so that their organised and mobilised weight comes fully into play.

In one way or another, the officer corps must be opened to such perspectives.[32] This approach when combined with reliance upon rather than toleration of egalitarian-oriented parties and mass organizations offers some prospect of success against indigenous privileged classes and their external supporters. Thus, real or deliberately exaggerated nationalist issues must be taken advantage of to close the door of penetrated societies to a broad panoply of external inputs (Woddis, 1977:57–63,147–50) that strengthen and often advise conservative elements. Above all, mass sectors must be given immediate, tangible status and material benefits, and educated to the reality that only complete expropriation of the property-owning classes offers an opportunity to further enhance their welfare. They should not be misled into believing that reformist options are viable as even short-run political solutions. And if there is a temporary united front from above, this should never be extended to the bases. Put differently, contemporary experience reaffirms the wisdom of Lenin's tactical writings despite the passage of more than a half century.

Because the armed forces have been strengthened and indoctrinated by imperialism, and particularly the United States, in many underdeveloped societies, few civilian successes can be anticipated in the absence of military defeat in war or substantial material aid across porous border area. For the same reasons and as the fate of the radical military regimes in Portugal and Peru during the mid-1970s suggest, few consolidated radical coups by left-wing nationalist officers—especially in the larger military establishments—are likely to occur. While socialism of one sort or another may well be the wave of the future, its advance will be slow and increasingly difficult in noncontiguous developing areas.

Notes

1. Incisive treatments of these questions can be found in Needleman(1969) and Mc-Quarie(1978).
2. By "too late" I mean at least until—and sometimes into—the final phase of the con-spiratorially induced crises associated with the toppling of their regimes.
3. A comparison of *The Communist Manifesto* with his address "On the Civil War in France" or his 1872 speech in Amsterdam. As quoted by McLellan(1971:209), Marx stated that

> we are aware of the importance that must be accorded to the institutions, customs, and traditions of different countries; and we do not deny that there are countries like America, England (and, if I knew your institutions better, I would add Holland) where the workers can achieve their aims by peaceful means. However true that may be, we ought also to recognise that, in most of the countries on the Continent, it is force that must be the lever of our revolutions; it is to force that it will be necessary to appeal for a time in order to establish a reign of labour.

4. The exception pertains to societies where the politico-military resources and leadership of the left are perceived by the right as likely to lead to the latter's defeat in a showdown. In such cases, privileged classes have accepted significant egalitarian reforms without resorting to violence. And as used here and elsewhere, "egalitarian" refers to policies intended to enhance the relative resources, status, or material benefits of lower class sectors with converse effects upon the large property-owning, professional, and managerial classes.
5. As used here, the term "surplus" refers to production in excess of what is required to maintain and reproduce the labor force. Works by Baran(1957), Gunder Frank(1967), Rhodes(1970), and Baran and Sweezy(1966) utilize the concept to explore the dynamic relationships within and between imperialist and "underdeveloping" societies.
6. It is true of course as Harrington(1972) emphasizes that Marx assumed, in the absence of material abundance, socialism or the first stage of communism would be unviable. Put differently, even if the state controlled most economic resources, in the short run at least, various groups—including the bureaucratic classes—would use available resources to enhance their material welfare at the expense of other groups. This situation is characteristic of regimes which many Marxists define as state capitalist and where the "administrative bourgeoise" commonly appropriates much of the surplus for its own con-

sumption. In such systems, the "private" capitalist sector is of secondary importance and repression is frequently resorted to against those seeking to restore monopoly capitalism on one hand, and others who advocate the introduction of at least some socialist relations of production such as an end to bureaucratic privileges, workers comanagement, elimination of the hiatus between mental and manual work, etc. In a few countries, state socialist systems of this genre have been introduced. The state however cannot begin to "wither" (i.e., lose its repressive character) until production has begun to outstrip demand. Needless to say, whether and how rapidly this is brought about depends upon many external and domestic variables, not the least of which is the quality of leadership provided by the "vanguard" Marxist-Leninist Party. For a stimulating analysis of Marx's concern with the quality of leadership and voluntaristic factors in the struggle to overthrow capitalism—one that he supported well before that system had matured—see Needleman(1969:332–39).

9. The emphasis varies from one case to another. I have listed some of the more important egalitarian measures below. In some cases they were more anticipated—due to impending internal and foreign realignment—than accomplished. Admittedly state ownership of the means of production is at best potentially egalitarian—depending upon how the surplus it generates is utilized.

Mossadegh. According to Cottam(1964:260), Mossadegh was so excessively preoccupied with the oil issue that he neglected vital programs in health, education, and industry until 1953 when the vise had already begun to close. Avery(1965:429,433–44,445) records that during the second half of 1952 his administration secured the reduction of peasant rents on certain estates and the return of a portion thereof to the villages to finance local services. He was also credited with reducing police and other official corruption. By May 1953, Mossadegh was actively campaigning for agrarian reform. His proposals, according to Nirumand(1969:80) required landlords and the Shah "to return the lands illegally seized by [the Shah's] father or to turn them over to the government for redistribution." The same author also observed(95) that "under Mossadegh the army budget had been cut to make money available for education and health, agriculture and industry, and the generals had been relegated to the position accorded them by law and the Constitution."

Arbenz. Although Schneider(1959), Wise and Ross(1964), and others have discussed various reforms associated with his administration, the following list is based upon Melville(1971:40–80). While Arbenz encouraged urban trade union growth and did not oppose Marxist leadership of these and other mass organizations, most of his egalitarian measures responded to the plight of the peasant. Thus, the rural minimum wage was increased while government support was offered to rural unionization. Cheap state bank credit was extended to more than 54,000 small peasants while 387,000 out of United Fruit's half million or so acres were expropriated and valued at $1,000,000 on the basis of declarations for tax assessments. Between January 1953 and June 1954, approximately 1.5 million hectares of privately owned land were distributed to about 100,000 peasant families. Twenty-five year 3 percent bonds were offered landowners, while rents were reduced and unpaid labor services were proscribed upon land that had not been expropriated. Landlords were excluded from membership on the agrarian committees which administered the reform.

Bosch. In the words of a former State Department officer(Barnet, 1968:165), "Bosch imposed what amounted to a tax on sugar profits to finance housing for workers, which cost the South Puerto Rican Sugar Company 25 million dollars." Kurzman (1965:70–72,80–81,93,100–102) refers to other acts which were redistributive: reduction of high government salaries; a maximum of $350 in foreign exchange for Dominicans traveling abroad; a sharp rise in profit and income tax collections; a new Constitution proscribing foreign ownership of land; and active promotion of agrarian reform.

Wiarda(1969:60–61,205–09) stresses Bosch's delivery on agrarian reform, while Martin(1966:354,489–90,510) notes with disapproval the "confiscatory" nature of the land reform, and records elsewhere that in July, Bosch imposed price controls on sugar and medicine. Goff and Locker(1969:138) observe that he was prolabor and view his cancellation of a contract which would have yielded high profits to Esso, Texaco, and Shell as a manifestation of Bosch's mild nationalism. Article 19 of his new constitution mandated profit sharing in agriculture and industry, while Article 23 proscribed large nationally owned land holdings.

Goulart. Skidmore(1967:218,246,249,269–71,280,288–91) records the following: as early as May 1962, Goulart called for agrarian reform and constitutional change that would end the necessity of cash payment; in March 1963, he proposed the use of bonds for the agrarian reform; three months later, he backed large wage settlements, and during the same year supported legislation permitting the organization of rural unions; in January 1964, he implemented earlier legislation restricting profit remittances by foreign corporations, and a month later extended the coffee foreign exchange rate to sugar; in March, he decreed a limited agrarian reform, proposed a progressive tax reform, and extension of the electoral franchise to illiterates and enlisted armed forces personnel. Arraes(1969) notes that he proposed an extension in coverage of the minimum wage and initiated a limited division of rural estates (limited by his constitutional authority). While Stepan(1971:144,153,190–91) acknowledges that conservative forces in Congress blocked most of Goulart's reforms, he notes that organized labor at last acquired a degree of autonomy.

Sukarno. Aside from the subsidization of rice and other basic food necessities, Sukarno in the late 1950s and early 60s supported the growth of urban and rural trade unionism and by mid-1963 gave his active backing to the PKI's (Indonesian Communist Party) struggle for agrarian reform in Java.

Nkrumah. Bretton(1966:106) provides figures on the rapid growth of the state sector of the economy, while Nkrumah(1969:103,115; 1969:377–418) not only admits substantial corruption existed but also records a series of mass beneficiary measures: expansion of free public education (including texts) and health services; introduction of child welfare centers and nurseries; initiation of adult and technical education; promotion of state farms and cooperatives; subsidized resettlement of 30,000 peasants whose lands were flooded by the Volta project; virtual elimination of unemployment.

Keita. Megahed(1970) analyzes the growth of the state sector in the economy, which increased from about 20 enterprises in 1961 to more than 90 by 1969. During the decade, cooperatives were promoted, while many schools and some dispensaries were constructed in the villages, state firms were used to reduce unemployment by taking on excess labor, and in 1966 salary reductions were imposed upon civil servants. In the final months of his administration, the newly constituted People's Militia launched intensive campaigns against official corruption, smuggling, and black marketeering. Even high-level officials became vulnerable to what was called a "cultural revolution."

Sihanouk. The U.S. Army(1968:87,94–95,111,121–22,220–21,238,258) reported the following changes during Sihanouk's rule: slowly rising rural living standards; substantial reduction in illiteracy, an increase in rural education, and community development cadres in the 1960s; rapid expansion of various types of health facilities between 1955 and 1967; an increase from 400 to 1000 in the number of cooperatives during the 1965–67 period alone; provision of additional land to peasants by extending the area under cultivation; a major expansion in access to public schools between 1955 and 1967 (primary: 596,320 to

903,000; vocational: 2,022 to 7,000; secondary: 33,021 to 83,000); direct aid to peasants; and by the mid-1960s "all civil and military servants of the government [were spending] a portion of their time on public construction projects." Hanna(1968) reports the construction of numerous small irrigation dams for peasants. Despite the 1966–69 rightist offensive (Chomsky, 1970:135–36,142,146), Sihanouk(1973:42–43) maintains that in 1969, he intended to let Siri Matak and Lon Nol mismanage the economy and discredit themselves – after which he would return with Soviet and Chinese aid and orient it in a more socialist direction. Allman(1970) regards domestic antiegalitarianism as the primary motive for the March 1970 coup.

Torres. In addition to ending the use of repression against trade unionists, Petras (1971:15) notes that he restored miners' working and living conditions to their pre-1965 level while nationalizing the processing of tin by-products and a sector of the sugar industry. Promising to "deepen" the revolution, Torres backed the People's Assembly and accepted a pledge from a new revolutionary NCO association that was being organized within the army.

Allende. Evans(1974) records a broad range of egalitarian reforms in addition to the virtual confiscation of large-scale foreign-owned copper mining. Trade union organization was encouraged, the agrarian reform was accelerated markedly, free milk was distributed to poor children, mobile literacy teams and health clinics were assigned to the *poblaciones* and rural areas, and general pay increases were authorized for workers – the largest percentages for those lowest in the wage scale.

8. The basic change here is in ownership of the means of production, which is transferred from the private to the public sector. Under state capitalism, the latter is clearly dominant rather than residual (i.e., for ailing or high risk often infrastructural enterprises), as it is under monopoly capitalism.

9. Only Guatemala appears to have been spared from these dislocations. The economy was not adversely affected by the expropriation of uncultivated United Fruit land. Furthermore, enforcement of this and other land decrees had not begun until a few months before the CIA-engineered coup was consumated.

10. Benign tolerance and an absence of efforts to counter organizational growth of Marxist trade unions, youth groups and parties within an underdeveloped political system are a long-run functional equivalent to short-term redistributive measures. Even in the immediate situation, Marxist-led trade unions secured immediate wage and other welfare benefits for their working class and/or peasant constituencies.

11. The socialization impact of these personal experiences may have contributed to the critical delay in attempting to maximize pro-egalitarian political resources.

12. While not even de facto coalitions existed in the Dominican Republic or Iran, both Bosch and Mossadegh rejected denunciations of themselves as "Communist tools" while steadfastly refusing to persecute Marxist sectors. Although the Iranian Premier began his administration at odds with Tudeh, mutual recrimination ended with the imposition of an Anglo-American boycott on Iranian oil in late 1952. Sihanouk had experimented with de facto coalitions in 1963–66, in lesser measure from mid-1967 to mid-1969, and appeared in his last days to contemplate a more formal arrangement to restore peace and promote mass welfare. In his March 31st address, Goulart too appears to have opted for at least a de facto coalition with various Marxist-led sectors in addition to the Brizolistas.

13. Three of the reformers – Keita, Nkrumah and Mossadegh – appear to have stimulated opposition more by their economic nationalism than as a result of redistributive measures.

14. Sources that refer to extensive military corruption (kickbacks, smuggling, black marketeering) and/or attachment to material amenities (travel allowances, servants, luxury

imports, double jobs or exemption of salaries from general civil service austerity measures, a top heavy senior rank structure, luxury clubs, free housing, mistresses, etc.) include: North(1974:18,22); Martin(1966:485,533); Bosch(1965:195-218); Kurzman (1965:86-87,105); Wiarda(1969:62-63,189-91); Goff and Locker(1969); Skidmore(1967: 242-43); Stepan(1971:31,49,50); Jacobs(1966:168-69); Hurewitz(1969:286); Schneider (1959:437); Bretton(1975:16-19); Price(1971); Kraus(1966:17); Nkrumah (1969:69); U.S. Army(1968); Bebler(1972:109-12,153,191-96,204); Zavaleta(1972:65); Gutierrez(1972: 91-92,136); Grant(1979); Liddle(1977:99).

With respect to social recruitment and interaction, similar patterns reappear. Recruitment is primarily from privileged civilian upper middle and lower middle classes with some internal recruitment. Upper middle class officers are disproportionately represented in the higher ranks. Countries without significant middle classes such as Mali, Bolivia, or Cambodia had recruited a substantial number of peasant offspring into the lowest commissioned ranks, whereas internal recruitment was more significant in Brazil and Chile—nations with long military traditions. In general, officers appear to have "married up," and to have associated with civilian upper middle classes—especially at the senior ranks—when they were not socializing exclusively with each other. There seems to have been a ubiquitous aversion to either social interactions or "nation building" activities with peasants or workers among "professional" officers. Useful sources on these variables are: Stepan (1971:34-37,94-97,176-77,186); Goff(1972:79); Gutierrez(1972:101); Jacobs(1966:168); Evans(1973:228,233); North(1974:8,10-11); MacEoin(1974:150); Schneider(1959:42-43, 214,314-15); Adekson(1976:259); Bretton(1975:19).

15. In a number of cases (Iran, Bolivia, Cambodia, Mali, Guatemala, Indonesia, and perhaps Ghana), it is unclear why commanders who were believed to be loyal failed to act decisively during the height of the crisis. Subornation is one possibility. As noted in Chapter 1, Agee(1975:512) records that "although the Agency usually plays the anticommunist card in order to foster a coup, gold bars and sacks of currency are often equally effective." Other possibly relevant factors include institutional loyalty of the military class, simple opportunism, surprise, and the failure of Mossadegh, Sihanouk, Keita, Sukarno, and Arbenz to offer courageous leadership. Finally, in Bolivia and Brazil, NCOs who had been exposed to Marxist ideas organized within the command structure. There is little reason to doubt that this deterred some "loyalist" officers from actively opposing the coup (Goffs, 1969: Stepan, 1971).

16. In Cambodia, a rural guerrilla force had fought Lon Nol's units for several months during 1967 following antileftist repression. A shift in domestic policy after Sihanouk's return was reflected by a suspension of the insurgency. It resumed however in late 1969 when the Lon Nol-Siri Matak regime again resorted to repression and launched offensive operations in rural areas. There is little reason to believe that the existence of this small force played a significant role in motivating the March 1970 coup. Concern over foreign aid sources—major reliance upon Soviet Union and/or China rather than a resumption of U.S. loans and grants—appears to have been more significant. Such a change would have required shifts in top military personnel, an end to collaboration with U.S. Special Forces, and a settlement of some sort with the Khmer Rouge.

17. Thus Capt. Yoro Diakite, Director of the French-dominated Malian Military Academy, boasted that planning had begun 2-3 years earlier. CIA preparations to overthrow Arbenz were initiated in 1953. The Indonesian Council of Generals began meeting in January 1965, and three months later U.S. Ambassador Howard P. Jones—a good friend of Bung Sukarno—announced he would be replaced within eight weeks. Marshal Green arrived in June to oversee the CIA operation that apparently was scheduled for October 5th, Armed Forces Day. Only in July did Sukarno announce the impending creation of a popular militia—a project which apparently did not get off the ground until sometime in August. In Ghana, attempted conspiracies involving high military officers antedated the coup by approximately two years, and as of early 1966 the 7,000 man Workers' Brigade had

not been armed. Furthermore, it was only in 1965 that the POGR was fully dissociated from the army and a decision made to increase it from one to two battalions.

18. In virtually all of the cases, a handful of senior officers remained loyal to the deposed reformer. One or more of the following motives were probably operative: personal friendship; noblesse oblige; leftist ideological exposure; internalization of a professional noninterventionist role orientation; and opportunist miscalculation.

19. Horowitz(1969) cogently analyzes that coincidence of class and national interests within the framework of contemporary international relations.

20. Sources that provide detail on how these mechanisms operate include: Wolpin(1972); Agee(1975); Western Massachusetts ACAS(1979); and *NACLA's World Empire Report*. It is not clear that serious attempts were ever made to negotiate with Allende and several of the other deposed reformers considered here(Arbenz, Nkrumah, Torres).

21. S. Lens, "Perspectives," *The Progressive*, August 1976, p. 11.

22. Bebler(1972:91,129) discounts Moussa Troare's July 1968 invitation to France as well as the fact that ten out of fourteen members of the junta were French- and/or American-trained. According to *Africa Report*, November 1968, leaflets mysteriously appeared in Bamako a month prior to the November coup calling upon the armed forces to save the country from economic disaster. Within the weeks that followed, Moussa Troare visited Keita and demanded the militia be disbanded. Then an NCO came up with a list of 40 persons, including several officers, who were to be arrested following Keita's return from a trip to Niger. Needless to say the origins of the list are quite obscure.

23. Consistent with these acts referred to in Martin(1966) is Gutierrez's(1972:36-37) report that

> seven months after the PRD leader assumed the presidency, when the decision to overthrow him was being taken in Washington, Volman suspended his own activities in the Dominican Republic, dismantling FENHERCA, paralyzing CIDES, and leaving the country. A few weeks earlier, J. M. Kaplan had resigned as Bosch's lobbyist in the U.S. Congress.

CIA ties to these persons and institutions are examined by Gutierrez (24–39).

24. According to Agee, 1975, p. 52: '(i)n the past 25 years, the CIA has been involved in plots to overthrow governments in Iran, the Sudan, Syria, Guatemala, Ecuador, Guyana, Zaire, and Ghana. In Greece, the CIA participated in bringing in the repressive and stupid regime of the colonels. In Brazil, the CIA worked to install a regime that tortures children to make their parents confess their political activities. In Chile, The Company spent millions to 'destabilize'—that's the Company word—the Allende government and set up the military junta, which has since massacred tens of thousands of workers, students, liberals, and leftists. And there is a very strong probability that the CIA station in Chile helped supply the assassination lists. In Indonesia in 1965, The Company was behind an even bloodier coup, the one that got rid of Sukarno and led to the slaughter of at least 500,000 and possibly 1,000,000 people. In the Dominican Republic . . . the CIA arranged the assassination of the dictator Rafael Trujillo and later participated in the invasion that prevented the return to power of the liberal expresident Juan Bosch.' Wise & Ross (1964) reveal the CIA role in ousting Arbenz, Mossadegh, and its efforts to topple Sukarno in the late 1950s. On the CIA in Chile, see also Evans, 1973, Petras & Morley, 1975.

25. Possible exceptions are Indonesia, Ghana, and Mali. Nevertheless leading antireformist civilians were immediately brought into the military regime in one capacity or another.

26. Although some gaps exist, the following are instructive on military training and relationships with the United States, Britain, and France. Except for official U.S. sources, most are suggestive of personal involvement by the CIA or U.S. military officers in the conspiracy:

Iran: Hurewitz(1969:280-84); Nirumand(1969:85,227-28); Wise and Ross(1964); Agee(1975:52)

Guatemala: Melville(1971); Wise and Ross(1964)

Dominican Republic: Wolpin(1973:137); Martin(1966:480); Kurzman(1965:88,103,166-67); Gutierrez(1972:24-25)

Brazil: Wolpin(1973:136); Skidmore(1967:325-30); Stepan(1971:129,173-84); Agee(1975a:52)

Indonesia: Wolpin(1973:8); Agee(1975a:52)

Ghana: Price(1971); Adekson(1976:264); Nkrumah(1969:38-41); Agee(1975:52)

Mali: Bebler(1972:91-92); U.S. Department of Defense(1970:13-14)

Cambodia: U.S. Army(1968:306,311,321); Chomsky(1970:164,172-73); Chomsky(1973:197); Leifer(1970:183-84)

Bolivia: Goff(1972:79); Whitehead(1972:86)

Chile: North(1974:16); Wolpin(1972); MacEoin(1974:151-54,169-70); Blanco(1973:20); Petras and Morley(1975:126,131); Agee(1975a:52)

27. Assassination attempts, uprisings, conspiracies, or abortive coups directed against the reformer had occurred and been communicated to him in every single one of the cases, with arguable exceptions for Iran and Brazil. Both Mossadegh (who in his last months resided in the parliament to minimize his risk of assassination following a mob attack on his home and the murder of his police chief) and Goulart (after the March 13th rally and the March 20th military ultimatum) were, however, fully apprised of the nature and means being resorted to by their protagonists.

28. Thus, the Minister of Defense and Army Chief of Staff General Carlos Prats

understood the implications of the abortive coup of June 29th. According to one account, following the coup attempt, while the country was still under martial law, Prats advised Allende that the forcible retirement, exile or imprisonment of over a hundred officers of the growing military conspiracy was the only possible means of averting disaster. Rejecting Prats' advice, Allende instead entered into an alliance with the liberal wing of the Christian Democratic Party, a compromise under which the Popular Unity bargained away its organizational work within the military in return for the support of what had become an essentially powerless group. According to this account, Prats understood, perhaps not from political conviction but from military experience, that Allende's rejection of his plan in favor of a reformist alliance represented suicide for the left. NACLA(1974:37).

29. Chorley(1971) examined the relationship of military establishments to social revolution in Europe and came to similar conclusions.

30. These relationships are explored in the sources listed in note 5, and Chapter 8.

31. And when I asked an Embassy official in early 1967 why so much aid was being poured into Chile, he declaimed "we've got a lot of money here." Or more recently Nathaniel Davis—designated in 1971 as Ambassador to oversee the subversion of Allende—prior to departing from Guatemala told a meeting of the U.S. Chamber of Commerce in that nation's capital on April 20, 1971, that "money isn't everything. Love is the other 2 percent. I think this characterizes the United States' relationship with Latin America."

32. Drawing upon several case studies, Ellen Trimberger (1977) identifies four variables that have been associated with military "revolution from above": 1) exposure to nationalist ideology; 2) social isolation from a traditionally dominant upper class sector; 3) international room for maneuver; 4) economic stagnation or decline. These conditions hold today in much of the Third World.

5

The Communist Military Subordination Model

The principal contention of the preceding chapter was that the likelihood of "counterrevolutionary" or rightist success was measurably enhanced by sanguine reformist tactical assumptions. This chapter argues that successful social radicals have wisely eschewed such illusions. While the Marxists have disagreed for more than a half century about the feasibility of egalitarian reform and even structural change in industrialized parliamentary capitalist systems of the West, there has been little doubt that the right would attempt to use violence to deter similar changes in what we now call the Third World. If the Chilean Communists were an exception to this rule, their fate in 1973 constituted a clear lesson that European-style revisionism was unsuitable for export to "the English of South America." During the Popular Unity interregnum the Communists played a conservative role within the governing coalition, endeavoring to moderate the reformism of that regime. At bottom, their praxis was premised upon fear of conservative militarism and an inability to come effectively to grips with the problem of military "autonomy."[1]

One approach of demonstrated value for ensuring the subordination of the military to civilian governance during periods of egalitarian social change is that used by Marxist-Leninists in societies where state socialism has replaced monopoly capitalism. Thus, Hobsbawm(1973:179) stresses that "by and large communist-governed states have been passionately civilian-minded as even acknowledged heroes of the nation like Marshal Zhukov were to discover." The thesis elaborated here is not that the "Communist military subordination model" should be replicated, for (as I shall show) there are variations and nuances among the Communist regimes themselves. On the contrary, I wish to argue only that the institutional practices delineated in the following sections reflect policy patterns that are conducive to the goal of military subordination by leftist regimes. Whether they are imitated or supplanted by newly devised functional equivalents, some consciously adopted military policy to eliminate autonomy is necessary if radicals are to survive. Most or preferably all of the following aspects of the general "model" should be assigned high priority.

Social Recruitment

Since landlords and employers comprise the bourgeoisie whose property is nationalized by Communists, it is logical that persons from such background be excluded from command over military forces. Conversely, because Communist social policies bring new opportunities and welfare to laborers and poor peasants, it seems obvious that the offspring of these classes would not only be more predisposed to Party supremacy but also less captivated by corporative chauvinism and privileges within the armed forces. Hence, all Communist regimes have practiced class discrimination against men from privileged backgrounds in the competition for places at officer cadet training institutions. Within a decade of a new regime's establishment, a substantial majority of its officers hail from lower class backgrounds, while most of the remainder are sons of the salaried middle class and, to a lesser degree, artisans or shopkeeper-types. A few career officers from bourgeois and aristocratic backgrounds can also be found, particularly in staff assignments or as highly trained specialists.[2] In most cases, once the regime is consolidated — usually between 10 and 20 years after the initial conquest of state power — class background is deemphasized as a criterion for admission to officer candidate programs. While informal quotas or proscriptions may remain in some countries, in general a youth's excellence in school, his record in Communist Youth organizations, and/or performance during basic training become the principal criteria.[3]

Because lower class youths who have benefited from compensatory discrimination are more likely than others to regard a regime that introduces egalitarian policies as legitimate, social bias in officer selection and promotion is an excellent way of promoting maximum loyalty during the critical consolidation phase. In this context, Abrahamson (1972:53) is categorical: "obviously employment in the armed forces was one such form contributing also to the political control of the army by the party structure."[4] And the subsequent termination of class tests means that some of their own sons can aspire to become officers. Needless to say, officer offspring often enjoy a de facto competitive advantage.[5]

During the struggle for revolutionary power, discrimination against individuals with bourgeois origins tends to be more political than social. It is generally manifested by assiduous scrutiny of the officers' views and behavior. Clearly, the outcome of the struggle for power is seldom predictable and the dangers obvious. Upon occasion, bourgeois who agree to serve or volunteer – often former junior officers from the ancien regime's armed forces – do so at great personal risk in the event of defeat and bring valuable technical skills.[6] Except for the German Democratic Republic where an essentially new class-based army was created in the mid-1950s, former officers were used during the struggle for state power in most East European countries(1945–49). Then many of them, even those who did not oppose socialism, were gradually retired or reassigned to nonmilitary positions. In the words of the official Soviet manual, *Marxism-Leninism on War*(1972:265):

A crucial factor in the development of the socialist armies is the replacement of officers who formerly served in the bourgeois armies by well-trained officers from among workers, peasants, and the people's intelligentsia.

As we have seen, Marx certainly would have endorsed such a policy, and its value to the Soviet Union may have been demonstrated in 1956 and 1968 when Hungarian and Czechoslovak officers for the most part declined to engage actively in nationalistic and arguably anti-Communist movements.

In the long run, the only military personnel from bourgeois armed forces who remain seem to be former conscripts and NCOs who were given officer training by the Communist government. However, this may hold only for those countries where the struggle for state power did not at the outset involve a seemingly hopeless guerrilla war. Officers or others of bourgeois origin who joined Communist-led guerrilla struggles for national liberation in Yugoslavia, Albania, Mongolia, Korea, China, and Vietnam have been properly regarded as dé classé. In Russia, this would in all likelihood apply to a few thousand Imperial officers who volunteered to serve in the Red Army during 1918. The existence of such a survival pattern is of course speculative, and in the Soviet case it is complicated by the consequences of Stalin's paranoia.[7]

Less problematic is the fact that most Communist regimes were organized in essentially agrarian societies with traditional values, economic dependency problems, and conservative militarism similar to that which afflicts Third World nations today. While the officer recruitment policies favored urban workers, the very size of the new or reorganized armies made this an inadequate source of manpower.[8] Hence, in a majority of cases, many of the new officers were necessarily recruited from modest peasant backgrounds.[9]

Socialization

Certainly the relationship between Stalin's forced rural collectivization and the widespread military discontent that culminated in protests by Tukachevsky and other Soviet marshals suggests that, under certain circumstances, there can be more than a grain of truth in conclusions of Kolkowicz and Wolfe(Lang,1972:112) that "the requirement that military officers participate in political activity and provide in the army a 'school for communism' contradicts professional orientations. . . ." What is required for purely professional tasks (e.g., maintaining the morale of peasant conscripts) will inevitably limit the extent to which beliefs, values, and attitudes can be structured after one enters a Red Army.[10] While there is considerable emphasis upon formal socialization via lectures, films, discussion groups, and courses, and some indications (Griffith,1967:130; Lang,1972:81) that this actually enhances combat efficacy, an indeterminate number of officers in the Soviet Union and presumably elsewhere have often objected to the amount of time (roughly 20 percent in the USSR and possibly double that in China prior to the late 1970s) devoted to political education and activity.[11]

Although Kolkowicz(1967) can never bring himself to admit that there may be purely military benefits to be derived from such character building, his own discussion of officer motives reveals that "natural" elitist, if not neomilitaristic attitudes, may be at the root of the problem. Even here he unwittingly neglects two equally serious socialization obstacles. First, there is the heritage of nationalism and its special meaning for almost all armies attached to states. To even the most socialized Communist officer, I suspect that national symbols spark a greater affect than any associated with proletarian internationalism. It is hardly coincidental that after the Nazi "sneak attack" in June 1941, Stalin stressed traditional patriotic appeals. Considering the inexperience of Soviet officers at the time, this inspiration probably contributed to the heavy casualties which they inflicted upon the Germans during the first 18 months of the war. Hence, when a Communist regime is also sovereign, the nationalist legacy will reinforce the socialization process. The efficacy of the process is partially vitiated, however, when sovereignty is nominal.

While I do not doubt that Soviet intervention preserved state socialism in Hungary during the 1956 uprising, it seems equally clear that, insofar as the Hungarian People's Army was concerned, radically altered social origins, intensified indoctrination, and the presence of former Soviet officers did little more than avert full-scale resistance against what the Chinese call "social imperialism." Thus, an anti-Soviet author (Vali, 1961:318) notes that many officers who were not noted for pro-Soviet views "refused to take the ultimate step of opposing the army of the 'Socialist Fatherland.'"

When, at last, orders were issued to put up resistance [to the Russians], the widely scattered units of the regular army participated only sporadically in the renewing battle, because effective centralized leadership was lacking (orders had generally not reached the troops) and because pro-Soviet officers sabotaged the efforts and others hesitated. The police were also unfitted to take part in open or street battles. Only the National Guard, some workers' units, some cadets, and a few small military units stood at the disposal of the revolutionary command when the combat opened on November 4.[12]

If the nationalist heritage prevented the army from actively defending the discredited pro-Stalinist Party elite, the limited impact of prior Communist-directed socialization nevertheless probably did spare Europe another World War.[13]

Formal intramilitary socialization should be regarded as complementary to premilitary exposure to Marxist theory and interpretations of current events. The character and political consciousness of officer candidates must be recommended in most Communist countries by nonmilitary Communist Youth organizations in the candidate's home district or boarding school.[14] From there he is dispatched to the military academy which, according to Van Doorn(1969:19-20), is "a key institution . . . where much time is devoted to political studies." After being commissioned, the young officer is, along with his men, exposed to periodic special education and propaganda campaigns. The officer who has been selected for promotion to senior levels takes special courses. In Korea, for example, Chung(1963:118) reports "great attention is given to the advanced training of senior command personnel, and their political study is conducted in a special course under the military academy."

An equally, if not more important, supplement is the informal socialization derived from institutional experience. In most Communist armies and particularly in Asian ones, the deference and material privileges given to officers are modest when compared to Western and Third World military establishments. Officers are expected to treat their men with respect and to base their leadership upon personal example with minimal reliance upon command discipline.[15] Sessions in which officers engage in self-criticism and accept that of their subordinates are clearly egalitarian in tendency. Prior to the rise of Teng-hsiao Peng, the Chinese People's Liberation Army (PLA) had pushed such practices (Joffe, 1965:129-38; Griffith, 1967:180-81) to their probable limits: 1) officers spent a few months a year in the ranks; 2) the insignia of rank had been deemphasized or eliminated; 3) noncommissioned personnel and officers discuss military and political questions together. Such egalitarian and socially democratic behavior constitutes positive reinforcement for the directed inculcation of Communist norms. At the same time, there is little hard evidence that it interferes with combat readiness or expertise. During peacetime, armies are seldom fully occupied by purely military activities. Junior officers are thus indirectly prepared to assume the responsibilities of their seniors. And it must be remembered that under actual battlefield conditions, unity of command is unquestioningly honored. When engaged in combat, only suspected treason limits the officer's purely military authority over his men.

In sum, given past and contemporary Soviet hegemony in much of Eastern Europe and the circumstances of the Hungarian rebellion as a test case, it seems that Communists have done as well as one could expect in socializing their officer corps. In the aftermath of the Hungarian rebellion, one suspects that a "New Deal" for East Europe combined with intramilitary egalitarian reforms along Chinese lines would have been a better long-range antidote than simply cashiering most of these officers.[16] The Soviet-led Warsaw Pact intervention in Czechoslovakia undoubtedly reinforced nationalist sentiments and vitiated "socialist" indoctrination of militaries in the region. Although most obvious in Yugoslavia—which resumed importation of U.S. arms before Tito's death—latent antagonism toward the Soviet Union is probably widespread among East European officers. With the possible exception of Bulgaria, many are probably indifferent to or even alienated from the Soviet variant of socialism. While this may not hold for Bucharest, there is no doubt that Soviet foreign affairs leadership is widely disrespected among that nation's officers, as it has been for decades in Yugoslavia. It is problematic, however, whether this extends to Soviet-style socialism in the latter country and is unlikely in the former. A new Soviet leadership which both established a detente with China and respected national autonomy within Eastern Europe would strengthen rather than undermine the intramilitary socialization process.

A less salient military dilemma stems from the ambiguity of the "People's Army" concept that mandates armed forces socially representative of, as well as integrated with, the masses. But precisely how unequal should the life styles of officers and men be? More seriously, if the conferral of new privileges upon officers strengthens Party supremacy (Kolkowicz, 1967), at what point might such privileges undermine the egalitarian norm of Marxian socialization and military subordination itself? Since, for Marx, the armed forces are an interim "necessarily evil," the very existence of an ideologically foredoomed yet even modestly privileged body of professionals is dialectically pregnant with the seeds of future conflict. So for that matter is the exceptionally low social prestige of military officers as compared to their ideologically more legitimate counterparts in the bourgeois societies of the West and especially in the Third World.[17]

Political Officers and Party Organizations

While a relative paucity of material privileges and nominal sovereignty may contribute to the low popular esteem accorded the military profession in such lands as Poland, we should not ignore the fact that in the Marxian scale of values, military activities are nonproductive consumers of resources that would otherwise be invested or allocated to welfare.[18] Furthermore, to the extent that the powerful are esteemed in all societies, we can say without hesitation that Communist armies lack the aristocratic continuity or heritage as well as the de facto autonomy necessary for such prestige. These are Party-dominated armies whose primary function is to serve the Party leadership, rather than to safeguard a constitution or the national patrimony.[19]

While an egalitarian recruitment policy may predispose many officer beneficiaries to accept the principle of Party supremacy, special pains are taken to institutionalize this relationship by bringing Party organizations into the armed forces themselves. Political officers are directly accountable through an independent hierarchy to some kind of Military Affairs Committee within the Central Committee or Political Bureau of the country's Communist Party. These political officers generally receive some military training; and should the army enter combat, they are expected to set a courageous example whenever required by tactical exigencies.[20] They are schooled as a rule in special military academies. Occasionally regular officer candidates who fail on technical tests may be permitted to enter the military by becoming political officers.

The political officer is responsible for developing and guiding party bodies, committees, departments, and cells throughout the military establishment. Party bodies or committees usually exist down to the regimental level, though where membership is high they may be formed in the battalions. Their function is to involve officers and men in discussion of Party issues or policy and to instill an interest in Marxism. Political officers directly socialize cadets within the various military academies, and the brightest serve on war college faculties.[21]

Direct control over regular officers is exercised by the de facto requirement of membership in the Party, or in the case of younger ones, in the Party Youth. While all officers do not join, the proportion of members grows markedly as one ascends the rank hierarchy.[22] At the senior levels, only a small minority—largely staff specialists—may remain outside the Party during the revolutionary struggle for power. During the consolidation process, this category gradually disappears as some join and others retire or are transferred to responsible positions in non-military state agencies. In any case, young officers quickly recognize that to be promoted in a self-consciously political army, they must reject the "bourgeois myth" of apolitical professionalism.[23] In the Soviet Union and possibly elsewhere, many officers particularly in the technetronic weapons specialties seem to be pro forma or nominal Party members (Kolkowicz, 1967).[24]

The efficacy of Party membership as a control device depends upon the organizational vitality of branch units. In China, considerable emphasis has been placed upon using Party committees for discussion and activities with nearby community organizations. This diminishes military isolation from civilians. Within Party discussion groups, enlisted men can, upon their own initiative or as surrogates for political officers, confront and criticize officers.[25] And ultimately Party control commissions have the authority to sanction regular officer members with penalties that can in the extreme involve loss of rank.[26]

While friction occasionally surfaces between regulars and their counterpart political officers (who can be found down to the company level, generally holding lower rank), such conflict appears to be rare.[27] The political officer is expected to maximize combat potential by raising troop morale through cultural and political activities. Although in Maoist China and during periods of acute crisis everywhere, the political officer's authority has equaled or even exceeded that of his counterpart, in general he can only appeal against the regular officer's decisions to political departments associated with higher level commands. On the other hand, officer promotions commonly require (Brezinski, 1954:9) a recommendation from the political officer.[28]

Military subordination is also ensured through periodic removal of the more independently minded of the officers. At the highest levels, purges have in a regime's early years occasionally involved imprisonment or execution, though in most cases forced retirement tends to be the officer's fate. While this practice has much to recommend it during peacetime, it may conflict with the need for daring leadership if an actual war erupts. Hence, in 1939, 50 percent of the officers whom Stalin had purged (Brezinski, 1954:24) were restored to active duty. Since the military officers are deliberately politicized, it is natural that, when great national debates take place, some may end up on the losing side. The risks are greatest for those ranking military men who had been rewarded with a seat in the Central Committee or Political Bureau. Historical experience suggests that co-optation at the national level offers highly valued honors to regular officers who actively support Party supremacy, and the dominant faction within the Central Committee. But, it does not necessarily produce ironclad conformity of opinion.[29]

Political officers themselves will respond to and reflect intramilitary sentiment: in 1936 there was no apparent cleavage between the Tukachevsky faction and the majority of Soviet military commissars or Zampolits! According to Schapiro(1956:66), most political officers agreed with their military colleagues that Stalin's forced collectivization was professionally harmful because of its deleterious effects upon conscript morale. This episode suggests that political officers alone may not be sufficient to ensure military subordination in armies of consolidated Communist regimes. On this point, the situation appears to have come full circle since the Stalin purges of 1936–38. Thus, Warner(1977:270) notes that

the deputy commanders for political affairs, the Zampolits who are affiliated with the Main Political Administration, direct the massive political training efforts and supervise the various Party organizations in all of the major combat units and staffs throughout the military establishment. As outlined in Chapters 1 and 2, over the years the political officers have apparently come to view themselves as military professionals and thus seem to identify with their fellow officers of the Ministry of Defense rather than with the men of the Central Committee apparatus of which the Main Political Administration is nominally a part.

On the other hand, where unit Party committees are freely elected, they can forcefully represent rank-and-file egalitarian sentiment and optimally constrain elitist officer tendencies. Only thus can both prestige and organizational vitality infuse Party organizations within the armed forces. Ultimately, the subordination of regular officers requires that they be accountable to higher level Party organs and to their politicized subordinates, both officers and conscripts. While this cross-pressure model was most highly developed by the Chinese, a variant can be found within the Soviet Union where, for example, "all Party officials . . . are selected . . . by a higher political officer [e.g., the Regimental Party secretary is selected by the divisional Zampolit], and presented to the membership meeting by the unit as the nominee of the Party." Brezinski(1954:19–20) goes on to report that the membership does not necessarily acccept the nominee. Hence, the hierarchical designation of political officers is not merely independent of the military chain of command, but it also is in some genuine measure responsive to Party sentiment from below.

Since Party officials are generally one rank below political officers at the same level, this vote can strengthen their representative or oversight function. It can also neutralize elitist tendencies among political officers. To the extent that these Party organizations initiate the critical scrutiny of decisions of regular commanders, in that measure will Party supremacy be safeguarded from the natural "bureaucratic" tendency of many political officers to prefer harmony with regulars to possible conflict.[30] Where this process seems to have been carried out most fully, in People's China, the Party leadership has been able to use the PLA to purge elitist elements from the Party itself as well as in other institutions. As early as October 1951, a general purge of the Party was carried out to eliminate those guilty of corruption, waste, and bureaucratism. Griffith(1967:176) informs us that among those ousted were an indeterminate number of "high regional and provisional officers." Chinese egalitarianism has been reinforced by subsequent "rectification campaigns" in the mid-1950s and early 60s. During the Mao era, there were no longer rank insignias for officers nor special privileges for Party members. Although they have "better opportunities for promotion and education," Party members were expected to work hard and set high standards according to Griffith(1967:180). But, since the early 1970s, hierarchical tendencies have become more pronounced within the PLA.

Civilian Linkages

In approaching the problem of military subordination from another perspective, Chorley(1943:163) took pains to emphasize her belief "that contact with the civil population during the course of his military life is an important influence in undermining that conception of the impersonal instrument which has been set up for the soldier as his ideal mentality." Isolation of draftees is necessary to create a reliable command structure for the officer corps.[31] This is less important for nonconscripted enlistees and NCOs, for these groups have voluntarily opted to follow military careers. Yet, in both cases, the best method of preventing officer independence is to maximize civilian contacts or what is called fraternization between the rank and file and the masses.[32]

During the struggle to institutionalize state socialist regimes in East European countries, an early Soviet policy (*Marxism-Leninism on War*, 1972:264) required that local Communist Parties be permitted to recruit members and carry on propaganda among the rank and file soldiers. Initial proselytization was facilitated by demands that enlisted men be treated with greater respect and that NCOs be given expanded opportunities to enter special officer candidate schools. Similarly, in China and Imperial Russia, Communists had actively infiltrated ancien regime military units. This contributed to the breakdown of both command structures, though other factors created an extremely propitious environment for conscript demoralization.[33]

Once the Communist Party has established an organizational infrastructure at various levels within the armed forces, civilian linkages, while continued, apparently become somewhat less able to ensure officer subordination. In China, Vietnam, Albania, Mongolia, Cuba, and

North Korea, the armed forces have been used for clearing agricultural lands, building factories, constructing dams, and so forth. Although this is primarily for economic purposes, it impedes the development of a relatively idle and privileged officer elite, enhances Party legitimacy as a "nation building" institution, establishes relations between military men and local Party members, and probably increases military prestige. Provided that the time allocated to such projects is reasonable – in China it has been about eight to ten weeks – military capabilities will not be seriously affected.[34] A number of specialized Chinese military organizations have also played a major role (Szuprowicz, 1977:3-19) in the development and administration of industries that are essential to armed forces capabilities.

While, in the past, activities of this sort were undertaken in the Soviet Union and Yugoslavia, they appear to be less important today in those countries and were never emphasized for the unreliable East European People's Armies. In East Europe, the pattern seems to have been a voluntary one, possibly stimulated by wage incentives. According to *Marxism-Leninism on War* (1972:266):

Much attention is given to strengthening the links between the army and the people. Although these links take different forms, the most important among them are the participation of the soldiers in socialist construction and the participation of the working people in the country's defences. When off-duty, soldiers help the working people in the factories and in the agricultural produce cooperatives to develop the socialist economy.

Civilian sector linkages have also encompassed cultural and social activities between military units and localities or economic enterprises nearby. Generally, both responsibility and initiative rests with the Party committees within military units, the political officers, and especially the Party organizations of civilian institutions.[35] Efforts have been made to tie particular enterprises to specific military divisions under some type of sponsorship arrangement. It is unclear how extensive or effective this practice is, though it may ironically have contributed to the immobilization of the Hungarian People's Army in November 1956. When the Party is unpopular because of external imposition or policy failure, such linkages may deprive it of the armed forces as a reliable instrumentality for domestic suppression. Hence, we may hypothesize that the more popular the regime – especially in such sovereign and generally self-created regimes as China, Russia, Mongolia, Albania, Yugoslavia, Cuba, Korea, and Vietnam – the linkages can be intensified without "dysfunctional" consequences.[36] In the Chinese case, the Cultural Revolution has entailed the actual dispersion of some units into communes where army men could work and live with the people. To the extent that officers and soldiers are cultivated by Party organizations within the communes and their political interest aroused by local and intramilitary Party committees, they are immunized from becoming obedient followers of militaristic officers. Hence, when Lin Piao and his extremist clique rebelled and were purged in 1970, there was scarcely a ripple of support within the PLA. This despite the very important role (Godwin, 1976:1-20) army officers played as chairmen, deputy chairman, and members of provincial Party committees between 1967 and 1972. By 1973, when the major excesses of the Cultural Revolution had been effectively constrained, these officers were gradually replaced by civilian cadres.

Within revolutionary Cuba, the armed forces have not only enhanced their professional skills by assisting threatened revolutionary regimes in Angola, Ethiopia, South Yemen and Nicaragua, but they too have played a major role in creating a developmental infrastructure. Thus, Duncan(1978:78-80) maintains:

The central argument here is that forging a modal personality and common national identity oriented to attitudes and values that support the activities and outlooks required for the tasks of economic and political development, can be performed in part by the military of a developing country. . . . Cuba well demonstrates the central argument. The Cuban military, long the instrument of coercion and support for dictatorial rule before Fidel Castro's revolution of 1959, became a key modernizing agent once Castro and his followers assumed power. That is, it was a major instrument in building a new modal personality and common national identity geared to development. With the military's new role came legitimate authority for Fidel Castro and the Cuban government, increased institutionalized change as the mid-1970s approached, and certainly a development consciousness within the Cuban population. These developments in turn have conditioned the armed forces' willingness—as well as that of the civilian population—to cut sugar cane, to build roads, dams, and schools, and to engage in mass literacy campaigns. The military has remained loyal to the regime (indeed, it very much is *the regime*) throughout many years of Castro's rule, and it has actively performed much of the organizational and socialization work involved in the revolutionary economic and political changes pursued since 1959.

As these observations make clear, it is not only the tangible projects and physical structures that are important; more significant are the new values and norms into which youthful conscripts are socialized. "These values," Duncan stresses (1978:101), "included work, struggle, commitment to the revolution, revolutionary consciousness, discipline, duty, and self-sacrifice for the Cuban collectivity and for socialist brothers and sisters in other countries."

In concluding this section, it is necessary to emphasize that for new Third World state socialist mobilizational systems, military infrastructural and socialization "missions" seem to assume a secondary or residual character after about two decades. Initially they play a major role in these areas because of necessity. That is, domestic and external counter-revolutionary forces require temporary militarization as does the weakness (Leo Grande, 1978) of the Party and civilian institutions. During this transitional period, there is dire shortage of organizational and technical skills in the latter areas. At the same time, the absence of in-stitutionalization is generally manifested by diffuse leadership roles, i.e., the same group of socialist revolutionaries leads and moves between both military and civil hierarchies. It is only with the conscious elaboration of disciplined and effective Party and civilian organizations that a clear in-stitutional separation appears. During the interim, special security troops ensure against lower level military insubordination. Subsequently, party organizations are structured and given increased authority within the armed forces. This occurs at the same time as a new generation of truly professional officers begins to rise through junior ranks. Their political consciousness is distinctly inferior to the first generation of revolutionary leaders and their careerism or corporate interests conjointly require con-tinued oversight by both Party and security organizations.

Paramilitary Security Forces

While those being purged are invariably ejected from the Party and/or retired from the army, in serious cases dismissal from service is accom-panied by arrest and even summary trial. Working closely with—and largely recruited from—the most devoted members of the Party is the paramilitary security police in each state socialist system.[37] Because of the dangerous and unpleasant character of much of their work, these of-ficers may at times receive special material dispensations.

Like the political officers, security police elites hold military rank, but in addition they operate independently of the military chain of com-mand. Although exceptions can be found, the security police generally report directly to the Minister of Interior who, in turn, also supervises a number of paramilitary organizations such as the Frontier Guards, Railway Police, Industrial Police, and the Citizen's Militia. These units are somewhat more carefully screened than the regular army, both at of-ficer and enlistee levels. They are voluntary and probably contain a large number of highly motivated Communists, as well as a fair number of "toughs" or "lumpen" types—the latter essentially among the noncom-missioned ranks.[38]

Screening for elite troop detachments assigned to the security police is assiduous, and their indoctrination is very carefully administered. A combination of tight discipline, high motivation, careful training, and the superior educational level of its officers makes the security police and its troops so effective in ensuring military subordination. For in terms of numbers, these units seldom exceed 5 percent of the regular armed forces.[39] If one adds the less dependable frontier units, militia organizations, and other types of armed police, the percentage ranges from 15 to 30 with variations occasioned by war or other security problems. Van Doorn(1969:22) notes "this dualistic policy may be expected to be particularly in evidence in those countries where the party is not fully confident of the conforming effect of selective recruitment and indoctrination of the officer corps."

Prior to regime consolidation in a number of countries, many security police officers were recruited from Communists belonging to minority groups that had suffered acute discrimination under the deposed ancien regime (Brzezinski, 1954:74; Pool, 1955:110–11). This situation existed in the Soviet Union until the mid-1930s and in East Europe for more than a decade after World War II. Not coincidentally, the first ministries which the Communists held in most East European countries were Interior and Defense, with priority assigned to the former. During initial conflicts associated with the onset of the Cold War and domestic reform struggles, voluntary Workers' Militia units that had been organized by the Party and/or Interior Ministry and which were backed by nearby Soviet forces acted as a key deterrent to as yet unpurged bourgeois regular army officers. It is noteworthy that security troops were the only national armed units to oppose rebellious Poles and East Germans in 1953 or Hungarians in 1956.[42]

Within the regular army, the security police have departments at all levels of command down to divisional and at times even regimental levels. Referring to the Soviet military establishment, Brzezinski(1954: 57–62,76) notes that unlike political officers, they do not give "advice" or even "suggestions" to the counterpart regular commanders, who

are supervised by their own superiors and by the political, Party, and [security] organs. The political and Party organs are likewise subordinated to their superior levels but are also controlled by the [security police]. The [security] officers participate in certifying (e.g., for promotion purposes) the military commanders as well as the political personnel. . . . The [security police] officially has no right to meddle openly in the decisions of the military and political officers nor to criticize them openly. Its role is to watch and to report.

Although the security police is officially considered to be a counterintelligence agency, its essential role lies in ensuring state security and the political loyalty of the Army. Threats to security are watched for throughout the Armed Forces: among the soldiers, the officers, the generals, and the marshals, their Party membership notwithstanding. Rank and prestige mean nothing to the security police. Every soldier and officer is a potential enemy of the state in the eyes of the security police.

In performance of these duties, the security police are expected to monitor all military gatherings and activities. They have the right to inspect, even without prior authorization by unit commanders, the unit's military stores, financial accounts, arms, etc. Of supreme importance is their creation of a network of agents:

Special efforts are made to recruit informers from among the commanding staff, especially the aides-de-camp, the secretaries, the orderlies, etc. Since no informer is ever fully trusted, efforts are made to have mutually checking informers in all staff units.

Some of the information reported may have military utility because it is supposed to encompass "the military condition of the unit, the political morale of the troops, and their material and medical welfare."

Unsurprisingly, then, in their effort to achieve an autonomous status for the Red Army, Tukachevsky and his followers endeavored not only to reestablish genteel social practices and to reduce political officers to educational work, but also actually succeeded for a short time in expelling security sections from the military establishment. The newly titled "Home Guard" was reassigned to the armed forces when the 1937 military purges began. During the Civil War, they had worked very closely with the political officers, and it may be assumed that this again eventually came to be the case.[43]

One final point warrants brief mention. During actual combat, sentences administered by the security police tend to be more extreme and there is often only cursory regard for procedural norms. Yet at the same time, the scope of what is defined as a treasonous attitude or expression is narrowed considerably. Not only is more freedom to criticize the regime tolerated (Brzezinski, 1954:71), but we know that the authority of political officers was also sharply curtailed in 1942. At such times, the ultimate responsibility placed upon regular military officers literally requires that their authority be broadened for the duration of the military conflict.

In concluding this section, it is important to emphasize that as far as the Workers Militia is concerned, once the Communist regime is consolidated, these organizations generally function as auxiliary defense forces and maintain internal order rather than deter a possible coup d'etat or other form of military pressure. Thus Revolutionary Cuba abolished the militia by 1975 and shifted to (Duncan, 1978:100) "increased reliance on a system of reservists." In several countries, such as China, possibly Korea, and the Soviet Union, the militia have actually been placed under army or joint control. Elsewhere, there are units of volunteer auxiliary police which are de facto militia organizations when the latter do not formally exist.[44] Everywhere the elite organization dedicated to ensuring military subordination is the security police and its own armed detachments. The voluntary militia is nevertheless important because its existence may avoid the necessity of having to use unenthusiastic conscripts to preserve internal order in the event of local rebellion. Thus it neutralizes dysfunctional fraternization effects and diminishes the likelihood of military mutinies. These problems, however, have been minor for most Communist regimes — Poland, Hungary, and possibly Czechoslovakia excepted. Only during the actual process of seizing state power and undertaking initial purges of the army can it be said that the militia or Red Guards play a vital and direct role in securing Party supremacy.

Force and Military Subordination

The role of armed force has been everywhere vital to the initial seizure of state power. No Communist regime has been established let alone consolidated without the threat or actual use of armed coercion. Here the contribution of the Soviet Union cannot be exaggerated. The Bolsheviks initially seized power in Petrograd and elsewhere by relying upon armed volunteer workers who had been organized by the Party into decentralized Red Guard units. Because the Imperial army's command structure had been undermined by mass demoralization, the initial seizure was successful in most cities and towns. Within several months, a democratic and relatively undisciplined 100,000 man Red Army was constituted by volunteers largely from these very same Red Guards. Yet, with the onset of external intervention and Civil War, this Red Army had to be reorganized and rapidly expanded. Under Trotsky's forceful leadership, it was transformed into a disciplined professional and explicitly political army.[46]

Not only did it play a determinative role in establishing the first Communist government known to the world, but the Soviet Red Army played some part in the struggle for state power or consolidation of almost every other Communist regime. And whether these relied primarily upon the Soviet Union or upon indigenous forces, victory in all cases required a preponderance of force. In the interests of clarity, I shall break them down into three categories: 1) Soviet-assisted; 2) Soviet-imposed in premodern or traditional agrarian societies; and 3) Soviet-imposed in bourgeois institutional settings. Generally, because of an inability to assimilate the nationalist legacy, the maintenance of Communist institutions in the last group has required a continuing Soviet presence and/or occasional military intervention. And this, in turn, has partly vitiated the effort to consolidate the regimes.

Soviet-assisted governments have come to power in China, Vietnam, Laos, Yugoslavia, and arguably in Albania. In all of these states, the brunt of the struggle against some form of imperialist rule and often simultaneously against anti-Communist movements has been borne primarily by indigenous and nationally led Communist movements. Yet leaders and officers of these guerrilla national liberation struggles have all received varying amounts of training and advice from Soviet military experts both within Russia and (to a limited extent) in the field. This was supplemented by Soviet military equipment, though its quantity was seldom impressive until after a successful revolutionary struggle culminated in seizure of state power. The Russians also gave some diplomatic support to these regimes either before or after the initial victory in the revolutionary struggles. [47]

In two countries where the Soviet Red Army played a direct role in setting up Communist governments, there had been no institutionalized national party system with any mass support. During the early 1920s, Mongolian insurgents jointly invaded their country with the Red Army and ousted a White Russian regime that had previously occupied the country and deposed a short-lived monarchist government. When in the early 1930s a widespread anti-Communist rebellion almost ousted the pro-Soviet Mongolian People's Revolutionary Party, Russian forces re-entered the country and saved the day. [48] In Korea, under wartime agreements the Russians entered and disarmed Japanese troops who had supported a neocolonial administration for well over a decade. Again, small guerrilla units under indigenous leaders entered with the Soviets and organized the government. Initially, thinly veiled front governments functioned in both Korea and Mongolia, while Communist-led armies were organized from the outset under Soviet aegis. Nor were there any ancien regime armies to purge or incorporate. Officers who had served the Japanese in Korea fled to the south or were arrested, and a similar fate befell those who had fought for Baron Von Sternberg in Mongolia. [49] What distinguishes these regimes is that since the late 1950s, Korea has followed an independent or national foreign policy and both countries have developed a genuine mass base internally. This may be partially accounted for by two factors: 1) the masses were first incorporated into national politics by the Communists; and, especially, 2) the regimes defeated by Soviet-assisted insurgents were of alien origin—more so than the Soviet-backed Kim Il Sung- or Sukhe Bator-led movements. [50] The long-term improvement in mass living standards has also enhanced systemic legitimacy.

Throughout East Europe, the presence of Soviet troops either as occupation forces (Germany, Hungary, Bulgaria, Rumania) or to safeguard communication lines (Poland, Czechoslovakia) played a direct role in: 1) the resurgence of formerly outlawed Party organizations; 2) formation of Party-led armed militia forces; 3) weakening of bourgeois parties by widespread civilian and military purges of those who had sympathized with Nazi Germany against Russia; and 4) the imposition of early Communist control over Interior Ministries and to a lesser degree Defense Ministries.[51] In the Czech case, the Red Army having liberated two-thirds of the country ensured that local militia were armed. Even though Soviet forces had withdrawn by early 1948, their reentry was threatened (Hoffman and Neal, 1962:106) if Benes plunged the country into Civil War by refusing to accept the anti-Communist resignations that February. Only in Yugoslavia did no foreign Communist troops play an important role in the Communist seizure of state power. There Tito's brilliant and patriotic leadership of the anti-Nazi guerrilla movement and the Chiang Kai-shek-type of performance by his rivals gave Tito the nationalist mantle which subsequently enabled him to force out the small Soviet forces that had entered part of the country. Albanian liberation too was accounted for by indigenous guerrilla forces heavily aided by Yugoslav personnel and material.

With the exception of Rumania, which has had an independent foreign policy since the early 1960s, only Albania and Yugoslavia seem to have fully consolidated regimes. Ironically, in these two countries, foreign policies have at various times opposed Soviet goals and the Communist leadership had remained within the country during World War II to organize national liberation struggles. Except for Czechoslovakia, Communism had been outlawed in East Europe during the interwar period. Hence, internal organizations were weak and many leaders had lost contact with their societies due to years of exile in the Soviet Union. Upon their return, these exiles were to some extent "foreigners," while those Communists who had fought with the partisans were distrusted by Stalin. Add to this the fact that nationalistic Communist leaders were purged in the 1949–51 period as Titoists and one can begin to comprehend some of the reasons for the failure of these regimes to become fully legitimated. In the cases of the Soviet-imposed Mongolian and Korean regimes, the leaders who were installed had actually led guerrilla national liberation struggles within or in border regions of their own countries until shortly before the entry of Soviet troops.[52]

In passing, it should be noted that the new Communist armies were generally organized (or in the case of those being purged, reorganized) along Russian lines. Soviet equipment was introduced, and officers were sent to the USSR for advanced and specialty training. Soviet officers — some of local ethnic origin or recent exiles — served as advisers often down to company levels. In some countries they assumed command responsibilities for retraining (Wolfe, 1970:42) or for safeguarding the consolidation process (Pool, 1955). While the advisers in an indeterminate number of cases were undoubtedly Soviet political or intelligence agents, many also concentrated upon improving the technical and organizational capabilities of newly organized or restructured Red armies.

Conclusion

The relation of the military to Communist regimes is no more devoid of conflict than the Party's dealings with any self-conscious elite of professionals within a society whose norms are a synthesis of bourgeois tradition and socialist aspiration. Because the material abundance that Marx envisaged as a precondition for the internalization of unselfishness—religious types excepted—has nowhere been attained, at least some of those with superior political resources will invariably be attracted by the idea of converting them into scarce material amenities. Hence, tension and at least latent conflict will exist and should be regarded as normal. The more efficacious recruitment, socialization, and promotion mechanisms are, the less support there will be for an elitist professional orientation. In an ultimate sense, however, elitism cannot be totally eradicated so long as military expertise and even a relatively authoritarian command structure—both apparently necessary to the conduct of modern warfare—are maintained. Thus, in summarizing the contemporary situation in the USSR, Warner(1977:270) concludes that:

The Ministry of Defense appears to enjoy considerable autonomy and unrivaled expertise in these questions. The Defense Ministry is greatly assisted by the fact that, unlike most Soviet government ministries, it does not have to contend with a specialized department within the powerful central apparatus of the Party, which actively monitors the vast majority of its day-to-day activities. Although three of the departments of the Central Committee—Administrative Organs, Defense Industries, and the Main Political Administration—deal with military matters, none of these appears to play a significant role in such key areas as the drafting of the defense budgetary plans, the development of operational military plans and doctrine, or the myriad of activities connected with the routine administration, training, and exercise of the Soviet armed forces.

Notwithstanding such apparent de facto autonomy, Deane's(1977) analysis reveals that, at the highest Politburo and Defense Ministry levels, the Brezhnev civilian leadership has dominated budgetary and foreign policy conflicts as have predecessor Party leaders.

Even so, similar tensions do appear to constitute a problem elsewhere in the "socialist camp," especially in those systems where revolutionary consolidation and institutionalization have yet to be attained.[53] As Dominguez(1976) and LeoGrande(1978) demonstrate, this has been less true of the early stages of such revolutionary socialist regimes as China and particularly Cubá where the political and military leadership were initially unified so that overlapping roles rather than specialization was the dominant pattern. Soviet training assistance did contribute to the emergence of a "traditional" type professional (i.e., expertise and elitist) oriented sector within the Chinese military by the late 1950s and this also appears to be the case for Cuba by the late 1960s. Hence, with the passing of guerrilla-originated groups from leadership positions during the early 1980s in China and toward the end of the coming decade in Cuba, we can predict that the model will for these and similar regimes (Korea, Vietnam, Laos, etc.) begin to approximate the institutionalized one common to Soviet and East European state socialist systems.

Ultimately, it can be argued that corporate or class aspirations of officers in such systems will remain operative so long as the societal milieu is itself highly stratified in terms of social amenities and political roles. Until a peaceful classless society becomes established as a new world civilization, some ranking officers will continue to be attracted by the idea of "autonomy" and the class privileges which are consequential to power. In the interim, an effective if uneasy military subordination can be imposed only at the price of unceasing vigilance and timely purges. At the same time domestic military policies resembling, if not necessarily identical with those summarized in the sections above, must be effectively imposed if radical survival prospects are to be maximized.

The preceding chapter examined the fate of mildly egalitarian Third World regimes which were deposed by rightist military coups. A few had begun to introduce elements or functional equivalents of the military subordination model delineated above. Civil leadership deficiencies, a "porous" or "soft" state open to external destabilization, and an absence of leftist coercive resources were key obstacles to exercising control over the military. Before turning to an assessment of contemporary radical Third World regime prospects, consideration should be given to the potential responsiveness by at least some officers to "socialist" appeals, the performance of various regime types on a number of development indicators, and the relationship of both of the foregoing to arms transfers.

Notes

1. "Autonomy" is a de facto state of affairs which is commonly rationalized by reference to the nature of professionalism. The latter does require limited autonomy with respect to the inculcation, evaluation, and application of military science principles and skills. But no threat to professionalism inheres in its limitation to internal managerial practices that do not contravene highly regarded civilian norms. In the modern era, all traditional and new professions are governed in part by societal constraints. Military aspirations for domestic power, privileges, and prestige are probably more common as sources of peacetime conflict with civilian sectors than the desire to be irresponsible (i.e., unaccountable) in the application of expertise. To what extent the perfection of expertise occasions a corporate desire to

be irresponsible in its application is of course unknown. Nor have its alleged (Abrahams-son, 1972:15-17) linkages with other militaristic motives been firmly established.

2. In those countries (Yugoslavia, Albania, Mongolia, Korea, Vietnam, Germany) where no bourgeois army existed when Communist forces triumphed, the new armies were primarily officered by sons of peasants and/or workers. They were, of course, supple-mented by dé classé students or intellectuals who generally came through the Party or its mass organizations. With the exception of East Germany, peasants were the dominant class of origin. As far as the GDR is concerned, in 1965 approximately 82 percent of the army of-ficers were of proletarian origin while 3 percent were peasant (Van Doorn, 1969:17). A few years later (Marxism-Leninism on War, 1972:265), it was reported that "in the National People's Army of the GDR nine-tenths of the officers were in the past workers and peasants, one-tenth—members of the people's intelligentsia." This can be contrasted with the German Federal Republic where in 1960 less than 1 percent of the officers or cadets were proletarian while the upper middle class seemed to be even more represented among cadets than by existing officers (Cvrcek, 1969:98). The remaining armies were essentially guerrilla in origin. Mongolians and Koreans who had served in the Soviet Red Army were also assimilated by those two countries. General (as opposed to quantitative) social origin references appear in: Hoffman and Neal(1962:71-73); Hammer(1954:82-102); Sohn(1969: 271-75); and Giap(1968:46-47,53), who records that regular Vietminh troops were recruited from battle-tested local guerrillas and emphasizes rigorous political scrutiny for officers from nonproletarian origins: "our army has always been concerned with the train-ing of officers and warrant officers of worker and peasant origin or revolutionary intellec-tuals tested under fire." Referring to the outbreak of war in December 1946, Giap notes that "peasants, workers, and intellectuals crowded into the ranks of the armed forces of the Revolution. Leading cadres of the Party and State apparatus became officers from the first moment."

Elsewhere Communist success either involved the use of ancien regime officers in the course of Civil War (primarily through conscription in the USSR and defection in China) or the manipulation of army factions in such countries as Poland, Czechoslovakia, Hungary, and Bulgaria. While one analyst (Joffe, 1965:34) has referred to "the plebian nature of the officer corps" in China, the only countries for which published quantitative data are available are the Soviet Union, Poland, and Czechoslovakia. According to Garthoff's(1968:246-48) research on the USSR, between 50,000 and 100,000 former Im-perial officers entered the Red Army while more than double this number served the Whites. As soon as the Civil War was over, the Bolsheviks began to dismiss those uninterested in Party membership while simultaneously training lower class offspring for officer careers. Although the Imperial army had included officers from middle class and kulak backgrounds, the following figures are nevertheless instructive: in 1923, 13.6 percent of the officers were of worker origin, while 52.7 percent were peasant and 33.7 percent from "other" backgrounds; by 1927, these percentages were 22.4 percent, 56 percent, and 21.6 percent. At least until 1928 and possibly through 1937, these figures understate lower class representation at junior levels and overstate it for the senior grades. In the case of Poland, by the end of 1957 (Graczyk, 1969:88-89), 51 percent of the officers were from worker background, while 34.1 percent came from poor peasant homes. By the year 1964, these percentages were 47.7 percent and 33.4 percent. The slight decline is accounted for by a rise in officer recruitment from urban salaried employees of the state and by a small in-crease from artisan backgrounds. Close to 60 percent of the senior officers in 1964 were from worker or poor peasant backgrounds. This can be contrasted with Pool's(1955:57) description of the pre-World War II Polish Army where

> out of 58 interwar generals in our sample only six stopped their schooling at the secondary level and 26 had been to a civilian university. The large majority came from upper or middle class homes. Their fathers were often professional men or

landlords. Many belonged to the nobility or had wives of aristocratic birth.

According to Wiatr(1969:234), "the elitist character of the officer corps was strengthened by provisions regulating the selection of spouses: the officer was not supposed to marry a woman of a lower status and President's Order No. 20 (March 18th, 1937) stated that he might be dismissed from the service for disobeying this regulation." This is of course an unwritten norm for upwardly mobile officers in most bourgeois military establishments. If the Polish one represented the agrarian traditional past, that in industrialized Czechoslovakia symbolized the modern model.

Thus Cvrcek(1969:95) estimated that only 7 percent of the officers prior to 1948 were from large landowning or big business families, while 32 percent were the offspring of tradesmen and a high percentage came "from families of former civil servants." The changes were nevertheless sweeping. According to Pool(1955:46–47), by "1950 General Cepicka could claim that 50 percent of the entering students and 40 percent of the students in both years of [the] Czechoslovak Military Academy were of proletarian origin in contrast to 7 percent in 1945." And Cvrcek(1969:99–100) reports the occupational background of new officers in 1957 and 1966 to be: worker, 67 percent, 65.7 percent; farmer, 12.2 percent, 6.9 percent; clerks and intelligentsia, 15.1 percent, 18 percent; employees, 2.6 percent; tradesmen, 3.0 percent, 2.2 percent; other, 0.0 percent, 7.2 percent. In all of these countries, some of those from worker backgrounds and large numbers of peasants were in the early period drawn from conscript and NCO levels of the ancien regime military establishment. Some workers of course were nominated from Party-led trade unions and paramilitary units.

3. It may have been assumed, perhaps a bit prematurely in East Europe, that the regimes were consolidated. Hence, the educational system could be relied upon to inculcate socialist patriotism and hopefully "proletarian internationalism" along with the rudiments of historical materialism. The tightening up of educational requirements was also intended to improve the military efficiency and capabilities of the armed forces. Thus, in 1957, Cvrcek(1969:100) reports that 44 percent of the new Czech officers had completed secondary school while 55 percent had not. By 1966, almost 87 percent were secondary school graduates with an additional 3 percent who completed university. All Communist regimes have stressed mass expansion of educational opportunities both for economic development and socialization purposes. Recruitment for officer courses seems to be carried out among conscripts and enlisted men during basic training or subsequent service in the ranks.

4. Commenting on the Rumanian experience at the height of the cold War, Pool(1955:95) observes:

> the majority of officer candidates who are chosen from among soldiers in training though members of the Young Communist League may be admitted directly to officer candidates' school. The candidates are chosen above all for social origin, are screened carefully, and are given political as well as technical training. . . . To some extent this training scheme undoubtedly works to produce effective and reliable officers. A refugee source has admitted that "officers who have completed the Communist schools are well prepared from the professional point of view and the majority are devoted to the Communist regime." This is due to the fact that a majority are people of low social origins who now have a material situation and social position such as they could not have dreamed of before and who know that if this regime collapsed they would lose all their privileges.

5. In the Soviet Union, special officer cadet schools may exist (Brzezinski, 1967). Needless to say, internal recruitment such as has traditionally characterized France and in recent years the United States contributes to military isolation from external reference groups. In the absence of a relatively egalitarian military establishment, it has the long-run

effect of enhancing the potential for conservative militarism. Thus far, there is a "complete absence" (Van Doorn, 1969:18) of self-recruitment in Poland, the GDR, and Czechoslovakia.

6. At the same time, Party members with limited or no military experience were often directly commissioned as were large numbers NCOs and soldiers from the ancien regime's armed forces. The latter groups received very limited training. Hence in summarizing several recent studies, Van Doorn reports (1969:18): "the authors describing the situation in the DDR, Czechoslovakia and Poland agree that in the first period of army construction, the criterion of political loyalty weighed more heavily than that of professional ability." Because of the nearness or presence of Soviet forces, "the socialist countries of the second generation moved somewhat faster in recruiting new officers and discharging those they replaced." The process of replacement begins with the highest levels and top commands at once (Pool, 1955:3).

7. Where these officers actually participated in combat (Soviet Union, China, Vietnam, Yugoslavia, and a handful in Albania and Korea) against capitalist forces, or in Soviet-sponsored anti-Nazi East European divisions, it is probable that retirement was natural rather than deliberate. Pool's analysis (1955:84-92) of post-World War II data for East Europe is consistent with this view. Others who joined the party may also have been exempted even in the absence of pro-Communist combat experience. And for those commissioned from conscript and NCO ranks, it is almost certain that there was no purge. While the reports on replacement trends do not in general make such distinctions, Cvrcek's data(1969:97) seem to support this contention as does the assumption of minimal rationality. The latter can be seen in the fact that as new officers became available, even the partisan-type Communist officers were often retired in favor of better trained men (Pool, 1955:3). Some in East Europe of course were purged because of real or suspected nationalistic sentiments—even though they had impeccable Communist credentials. Less rational was Stalin's purge of more independent-minded and experienced Soviet officers between 1936 and 1938. While this reduced the professional competence of Red Army officers—particularly at senior levels—it opened promotion opportunities to junior officers who had been trained under Soviet auspices. In assessing its overall impact upon Soviet forces in 1941, few Western analysts mention that: 1) Hitler's invasion plan actually failed; 2) during the first 18 months of the war, Soviet units fought well enough to exact nearly a million German casualties; and 3) had Stalin not delayed mobilization during the critical weeks before the attack, the German salient might have been considerably more modest.

8. While Polish data (Graczyk, 1969:88) imply a preference for urban workers, virtually all published Communist statements emphasize class alignment rather than the character of one's locale. Thus Griffith(1967:41) records the following policy guidelines from the "Final Decision Concerning Red Army Problems" adopted at the first All China Congress of Soviets in December 1931:

> the Red Army is the most important defender of the Soviet power; it is a class army, and in mission or in spirit, it is fundamentally dissimilar from the Kuomintang army and the imperialist armies . . . the Red Army is the Army of the masses of workers and peasants themselves. . . . All toilers, workers, hired farmers, poor peasants, middle peasants, and urban poor have the right and privilege to take up arms to defend the Soviet political power; all who belong to the ruling classes and their flayers —warlords, landlords, bullying gentry, bureaucrats, capitalists, rich peasants, and those who belong to their families—are not permitted to join the Red Army.

Until about 1936, this policy was also followed by Russia. The end of discrimination in the Soviet Union was followed a decade later (Pool, 1955:125-26) by Chinese willingness to incorporate defecting Kuomintang officers for the duration of the Civil War. Yet their limited numbers and/or demobilization was reflected by the early 1950s in Pool's conclusion that "very few of the Communist officers have much education and they are poorly equipped for the intricacies of modern warfare." The Korean performance belied the accuracy of the latter claim. By 1954, persons of all social backgrounds were being conscripted into the Chinese PLA at 18 years (Joffe, 1965:39).

9. Landless peons or agricultural laborers are probably as amenable to socialist norms as urban workers. Peasants who owned land, however, are likely to be committed to private property as are their offspring. While we lack systematic data for the countries dealt with here, the response pattern of such groups to Marxist parties in Cuba, Chile, Russia, and in Eastern Europe is consistent with the hypothesis.

10. The purge of the Red Army elite eliminated most officers who did not owe their position to Stalin — ex-Imperial and Communist alike. According to Kolkowicz (1967:56),

> Leonard Schapiro lists the following as possible causes of Stalin's drastic measures:
> (a) Opposition from some military leaders to certain aspects of collectivization . . .
> (b) The military's growing self-assertiveness . . . (c) Substantial military support for Bukharin. Allegedly, all the senior officers on the Central Committee supported the majority against Stalin during the Central Committee meeting in the autumn of 1936, with the exception of Voroshilov and Budennyi.

The actual votes (Schapiro, 1956:67–68) on which Stalin found himself in the minority called for internal Party democracy and curtailment of the collectivization drive. Claiming that forced collectivization was lowering military capabilities due to its impact upon peasant conscript morale, most military leaders gave their backing to the rightist Bukharin (Mackintosh, 1956:63). They did this after having over more than a decade successfully struggled to reduce the authority of political officers to little more than troop education supervisors (Schapiro, 1956:68). The assertion of military independence during the 1930s was thus associated with support for the rightist Party faction and with the heightening of the privileged class status of officers. Garthoff(1968:247–49) reports that, under the leadership of the ex-lieutenant of the Guards, nobleman Mikhail Tukhachevsky, officer's clubs were established, dancing, and polo lessons begun, salary gaps increased and wife changing became common — in terms of "marrying up" presumably!

11. With respect to the USSR, Brzezenski(1954:47–48) contends that "professional officers, whose main concern is with the military and tactical preparation of their troops, consider the political education as an imposed duty and treat it without enthusiasm." Fifteen year later, Garthoff(1968:252) estimated that about 240 hours per year were assigned to troop indoctrination — a period that hardly seems excessive. What is unique here is that both political and regular officers participate in two hour activities for their men two or three times each week (Brzezinski: 1954:34–43). This generally involves a discussion of current events and Party policy. When officers are not doing this or attending a course at one of the 135 evening universities of Marxism-Leninism located in all garrison towns, they were supposed to attend study sessions on national history, Marxist classics, and leading topics in current periodicals. A cycle of some sort involving these obligations was repeated every two years. "The essential objective of the political education of the Soviet troops has always been to develop in the soldiers a firm conviction of the superiority of Soviet society, to strengthen their loyalty to the Party and its leader and to convince them of the inevitability of the collapse of the capitalist world." Soviet military authorities maintain (*Marxism-Leninism on War*, 1972) that this type of activity does not involve a reduction in or diversion from necessary combat training. The roles specified for Soviet officers encompass: 1) carrying out policies and directives of the Party; 2) defense of the state against internal or foreign threats; 3) cooperation with Party organizations within the armed forces; and 4) acceptance of egalitarian intramilitary practices (Kolkowicz, 1967:20). It goes

without saying that political education both at cadet or officer's training institutions and within the army was begun during the first year of the Red Army's existence (Chamberlain, 1935:34-37).

With some variations, intensive political education characterizes officer education in the armed forces of all Communist regimes. When fighting occurs, the courses of study tend to be short. Once security has been guaranteed they are gradually lengthened from the initial 2-6 months to about two years. Thus, the first Chinese Red Army Military Academy offered an eight month course in 1933. This was reduced to four months after the Long March, when "of the ten courses on record, only three could be considered purely military; the others were political." Between 1936 and 1950, periods of study were lengthened and the number of training institutions proliferated. In the mid-1950s, Lin Piao emphasized that "politics is unquestionably first and most important." However, from the viewpoint of the time required for political and military training, the latter is more important (Joffe, 1965:7-16). Griffith(1967:5-6) estimates that approximately 40 percent of training time is devoted to ideological work.

As far as Eastern Europe is concerned, during the initial years of restructuring new People's Armies, Pool(1955:17) reports that "indoctrination has been stepped up to fantastic proportions. The political departments undertake immense programs of indoctrination. All high officers are required to take courses at political military institutes, and many are sent to Russia for political as well as technical training." Later he notes with respect to Poland

> an important new theme is the role of the officer from the general down as the teacher and protector of the soldier. Much is said about incidents of camaraderie between enlisted men and officers both during the war and after. The humble background and the revolutionary record of the generals is emphasized; on the other hand their military record is not overplayed (80).

Once apparent consolidation of the new regime has been attained through the massive introduction of newly trained officers, the time devoted to formal socialization may be reduced. Referring to Czechoslovakia, an American officer (O'Ballance, 1964:29) informed his readers that "political training and constant indoctrination is carried out in the armed forces, although this is not overdone." Conceivably the time formerly allocated to political education has been used to introduce such subjects as "the theory of management and command, sociology, philosophical anthropology, psychology, and adult pedagogy" (Cvrcek, 1969:102). Whether or not these courses were taught from a Marxist revolutionary perspective is not indicated.

12. Yet "no Hungarian Army unit participated in the fight against the insurgents."

> If they were called out for concrete tasks, they either malingered or joined the revolutionaries. In some barracks, officers and soldiers deserted to avoid executing unpleasant orders. . . . We may add that although the Hungarian Army did not participate in the attempted suppression of the rebellion, neither did it fight openly in organized units against the Soviet forces. (Vali, 1961:314)

Clearly, had they been so motivated, the officers could have led their units against Soviet troops without fear of mass insubordination — hence it was the officers' role that was determinative. On the other hand, the command structure would have collapsed at the troop level had they ordered the men to fight the so-called National Guard and other "Freedom Fighters." As it was (Macartney, 1962:241), "army depots and munition factories opened their stores; the people armed themselves" in the initial phase of the rebellion.

13. Unlike the Czech situation in 1968, it was unclear whether the United States would have come to the aid of a beleaguered but fighting Hungarian Army. In the more recent Warsaw Pact intervention, it seems that the Soviets actually informed Washington prior to their invasion of that country. Latent anti-Soviet nationalism is probably most intense in

Poland despite a step-up of indoctrination in 1948 and repeated purges since 1950, when General Marian Spychalski and 300 officers were replaced by an alleged 5,000 Soviet officers—though many of them were probably of Polish origin. The Spychalski faction was restored to rank some years later (Gorlich, 1967:30–34).

14. When nominated from conscript ranks—a common practice—this task would be discharged by intramilitary Party organizations. Where as in Albania officer candidates are apparently recruited from "the third-year student population at the State University" on a voluntary basis (Gardiner, 1968:37–38), Party youth organizations probably furnish the recommendations. In most Communist countries, Marxism-Leninism and rudimentary military training have been gradually introduced in secondary and to some extent even in primary schools on an obligatory basis.

15. Hierarchical features and variants are nowhere treated in detail or compared. They are however referred to by Kolkowicz(1967), Joffe(1965), Griffith(1967), Basseches(1943), Pool(1955:80). A retired officer's (King, 1972:75–198) pungent rendition of caste and class in the contemporary U.S. Army provides a striking contrast to the Communist regime armies, as do the vignettes in Vagts(1959). This is not to deny that we need much more data or that there are considerable variations in elitism both within the Communist and the capitalist areas. In the Albanian case, Gardiner(1968:38) reports high officer morale despite the following monthly pay scale: conscripts, $37.00, lieutenants, $75.00; majors $83.00; generals, $92.00.

16. Although large numbers of Hungarian officers had trained in the Soviet Union before 1956, only 20 percent were willing to sign an oath approving the intervention after the rebellion was suppressed. The remainder were dismissed while units which had covertly or actively assisted the rebels were disbanded. The air force was deprived of bombers and a small number of officers were brought to trial. By 1959, the army's size had been reduced by more than 50 percent, and many Soviet advisers reintroduced. Officer selection was given greater care and indoctrination intensified. Elected Party committees replaced the former appointive ones within army units. (Vali, 1961:434–35); *Marxism-Leninism on War,* 1972:265).

17. Apparently the more inegalitarian the army, the greater the prestige of the officer corps. Thus Wiatr's (1969:77) cross-national survey ranked countries in terms of declining officer prestige: Pakistan, Indonesia, Denmark, Philippines, West Germany and the United States, and Poland. It is possible of course that imperialism may also contribute to such a rank ordering. Both German and American armies had been unsuccessful in recent imperialist campaigns. The Poles had in turn failed to oppose Soviet hegemony over their nation, Hungary, and Czechoslovakia.

18. Nor does military spending function positively as a source of high aggregate demand (i.e., prosperity) as it has in advanced capitalist countries. Quite apart from the labor theory of value, an ubiquitous commitment to rapid economic growth tends to focus mass attention upon investment rather than consumption in Communist societies.

19. While Mao recognized the value of the army in securing areas where the Party could be organized, he never deviated from the principle (Griffith, 1967:214) that "the Party commands the gun." Or in the categorical terminology of another renowned Communist military leader (Giap, 1968:100,103),

the Party's leadership is the decisive factor of all the successes of our army. . . . The Party's leadership . . . enable[s] the army to maintain its class nature and carry out its revolutionary task. The Party's leadership of the army is an absolute one. This leadership reveals itself politically to imbue the army with the Party's revolutionary line in order to make of it the faithful implement of the Party in the carrying out of the revolutionary task.

20. The textual discussion is based upon: Chamberlain(1935); Brzezinski(1954);

Pool(1955); Joffe(1965); Kolkowicz(1967); Griffith(1967); Gorlich(1967); Sohn(1969); and Keefe(1971).

21. There are generally three parallel though related political structures within Red armies. The first to be constituted is the administrative hierarchy with political departments attached to commands at regimental or higher levels. Below that, political officers accountable to these departments are attached to battalion and company commands. Once this chain of administration exists, Party units are structured from top down: committees at the military district, army, corps, and divisional levels, and basic membership cells within the companies, and where circumstances permit within platoons. For young personnel — generally under 27 years of age — there is a Party youth organization or in some cases a front mass organization. Everyone is encouraged to join such groups and the criteria for admission are far less demanding than for the Party itself.

22. During the Korean War era, Brezinski(1954:14) estimates that about 86 percent of the Soviet officer corps were in the Party or its Komsomol, while Griffith(1967:180) asserts that for China in the early 1950s "all senior officers belonged to the Party, as did most company commanders and a high proportion (about two-thirds) of the platoon leaders. Another 50 to 60 percent of all personnel were enrolled either as 'probationers' or as expectant candidates who hoped to 'establish merit and enter the Party'. . . ." He regards these cadres as the backbone of the PLA which fought so well in defending the North Korean regime. Within the Korean People's Republic (Sohn, 1969:282-83), about 45 percent of the officers were Party members in 1956 while the remainder belonged to the Democratic Youth League. For Poland, Gorlich(1967:33) states that "in 1963 nearly 100 percent of the generals and staff officers, 72 percent of the noncommissioned career officers, and 28.6 percent of the officer candidates were members of the Communist Party." More recently it was reported (*Marxism-Leninism on War,* 1972:265) that 75 percent of Polish officers were members of the Party, as were 85 percent of Bulgarian officers and "most" of those in the German Democratic Republic. And in the case of Albania,

> all or nearly all officers in the regular services were Party members in 1970. All cadets over eighteen years of age in candidate military schools were also Party members. Younger cadets were members of the Union of Albanian Working Youth. Probably only a very few of the conscripts were Party members, but nearly all were members of the youth organization (Keefe, 1971:175).

In Vietnam, 90 percent of the officers are Party members (Giap, 1968:49).

23. In some East European countries after World War II, "as soon as the Russians came in, they insisted upon identifying each officer with a political party . . . in the period of coalition the Communists even went so far as to compel career officers to associate themselves with non-Communist parties rather than to stay neutral (Pool, 1955:16)." In most of these countries, officer membership in the Party has risen more quickly than it did in the Soviet Union. There is also extensive participation in Party committees (Van Doorn, 1969:19,21).

24. Brzezinski(1954:20) notes that "party meetings usually begin late and Party members, according to some reports of former Soviet officers, bring to them all sorts of reading matter or simply take a nap during the proceedings." Under Stalin's rule this would be expected because of the constraints upon internal Party democracy. Similarly, to the extent that the Party's control function totally eclipses its representative potential, the participatory quality of membership will remain low.

25. This is militarily functional because it enhances morale. Although it is practiced in Russia and presumably in East Europe, there seems to be greater officer resentment in the Soviet Union (Kolkowicz, 1967) than in China or other Asian countries. Ho Chi Minh(1957:313) clearly attached immense value to these sessions:

> as a result of this, the proletarian class stand and the viewpoints of each of you have

been strengthened further, and the confidence in the Party's leadership raised higher, creating good conditions for the strengthening of the solidarity and single-mindedness between high and low ranks, which is the most important condition for all success of the army. This is the good result of the democratic life, of correct criticism, and self-criticism in the Party.

26. Brzezinski(1954:22) reports that Soviet "party disciplinary courts have jurisdiction over all matters involving the Party and during wartime Party commissions are known to have exercised a major role in imposing disciplinary penalties, not excluding even the penalty of a military demotion for a Party violation."

27. Kolkowicz(1967) and Brezinski(1954) seem to imply a generalized conflictual pattern, but nowhere offer substantiating evidence. The better view would be that independently minded personality types who are unusually devoted to the cultivation of professional expertise will resent Party controls, while others—the overwhelming majority—will adjust reasonably well to such supervision. Yet since the art of war does require great expertise and often considerable personal risk, these sentiments in latent form will be widely shared. Gratuitous interference by political officers especially if the latter have failed to study military subjects will naturally occasion overt resentment. Because leaders like Tukachevsky, Zhukov, and Peng Teh-Huai forcefully articulated professional grievances and sought to diminish permanently the authority of political cadres, they constituted a clear and present danger to Party supremacy.

28. While political officers sometimes receive additional military training and become regular officers, the latter have seldom if ever opted to become political officers. The one-way flow is also apparent in the direct commissioning of veteran Communists into regular commands during periods of acute struggle: USSR in 1918–19, East Europe between 1945–49. A few of the Party men later take formal military training courses, but most leave as quickly as possible since the military life style had never held any appeal for them. On the other hand, Party activists who at a young age joined the Red Army or guerrilla struggles are more likely to become military professionals. For this reason, once most of Russia's Imperial officers were demobilized in the 1920s, the role of political officers was for a decade (Schapiro, 1956:68) steadily diminished and some argued for complete abolition. Similarly, they are less important for control purposes in China, Korea, and Vietnam than in most East European countries.

29. According to one recent study of the Soviet military, the post-Khrushchev era of collective rule has been associated with considerable articulation of military views including interservice conflicts over military and defense-related policies. Thus Warner(1977:269) stresses that:

> The leaders of the Soviet military establishment do not appear to keep their beliefs and preferences to themselves. Their assertive public declarations and the available memoirs of Soviet political and military figures suggest that the leaders of the Ministry of Defense have often sought to have their points of view accepted and acted upon by the political leadership. Military spokesmen have also shown themselves willing openly to attack Soviet writers like Talensky and Bovin outside the military establishment who have voiced opinions on the catastrophic nature of nuclear weapons and the impossibility of attaining victory in a modern world war. These attacks were probably motivated by concern within the military that these views clearly threaten the budgetary fortunes of the Ministry of Defense and might serve to undermine the morale and motivation of Soviet servicemen as well. There is also ample evidence that the senior military commanders and their partners in the defense production field have utilized their direct access to the political leadership both to press their requests for the development and production of new weapons and to resist vigorously any attempts to cut back on the Soviet defense effort.

30. Giap(1968:105-11) views Party committee supremacy at all levels and internal democracy as functional to military ends by raising morale and increasing the likelihood that several persons in the course of a discussion will spot an error which would be overlooked by an individual.

31.

The fiction of the "impersonal instrument" paid the officers was in reality centered not on a civil government chosen by the nation they were enlisted to serve, but on their own professional esprit de corps. But this means the officers could hold the rank and file politically in the hollow of their hands. . . . The [non-Communist] examples quoted above show clearly enough that in a long-service army the theory of the "impersonal instrument" works only in so far as the rank and file is concerned. The officers are never apart from politics in any genuine sense, and the rank and file can be so conditioned that they will only be roused from their apathy in rare circumstances. (Chorley, 1943:180)

32. Chorley(1943:181) seems to feel that even when conscripts form the rank and file, the basic solution is simply to variegate the social composition of the officer corps.

33. By all accounts, the hardships associated with World War I along with internal grievances led to the virtual disintegration of the Russian command structure by November 1917. Inept and frequently corrupt leadership, again associated with military failure (Griffith, 1967:79-101), resulted in the gradual disintegration of Kuomintang armies. Here, perhaps also because the Communists had championed a nationalist struggle against the Japanese and the 100,000 Americans who came to aid Chiang, many officers defected along with their units, though one suspects that defeatist opportunism was ubiquitous by 1948.

34. Until 1960 or thereabouts (Joffe, 1965:85-87), the Soviet-oriented PLA faction argued that 100 percent of training time should be devoted to perfecting modern weaponry skills. Lin Piao and his ultimately triumphant "Maoist" colleagues defended allocating two months of the military year to development projects by citing three benefits: 1) such activities were essential to national economic construction; 2) this in turn is what supports the defense budget; and 3) "through productive labor, the officers and men will receive more political training, will increase their appreciation of labor and raise Communist consciousness to higher levels." For descriptions of the types of activities that are performed in Mongolia and Albania, see: Gardiner(1968:35,30); Dupuy(1970:436-37,444); and Keefe (1971:181).

35. A Yugoslav colonel (Krajacevic, 1968:24) emphasizes that while his army

has always been in close contact with the people and has associated itself with the efforts they have invested in the country's development. . . . The reorganization undertaken in the League of Communists of Yugoslavia has resulted in even closer organizational and action unity between the Communists in the Yugoslav Army and branches of the League of Communists outside of the Army.

36. It may be hypothesized too that where Communists seized State power as a consequence of victory in a civil or antiimperialist war (China, Russia, Vietnam, Yugoslavia) or where the ancien regime (Korea, Mongolia, Albania) was colonial or purely aristocratic, Communist rule will be more popular at the mass level than where (as in many East European countries) some form of parliamentary government had been institutionalized and an external power played an important role in bringing local Communists to a position of internal dominance. Rumania is probably an exception to the latter pattern thanks to the flexibility and national perspicacity of its Party elite.

37. The pattern has its minor variations. Thus while in Yugoslavia "all members of

OZNA were Communists (Hoffman and Neal, 1962:85)," the situation in neighboring Albania is that a higher percentage of officers and men in the security police are Party members than in the army. In 1945, 5,000 of the most reliable resistance fighters were selected to staff this force (Keefe, 1971:193). Many former NKVD (Soviet) security police officers were assigned to East European Interior Ministries after World War II, of which a goodly number were of local ethnic origin (Pool, 1955). Some were recruited from Communist-led partisan guerrilla movements—all of which became quite active after Stalingrad.

38. Thus, even before the Second World War had ended, the Bulgarian Interior Ministry organized a "people's militia"—backed by the Soviet army and the NKVD—and composed of Communist partisans, lower class ex-convicts, and Bulgarians who had served previously in the NKVD. Between October 1944 and April 1945, they arrested 11,667 suspected Nazi collaborators, of which 2,850 were executed. The same (U.S. Congress, 1954:8-9) and other sources (Pool, 1955) suggest that the category "collaborator" was upon occasion liberally construed to include anti-Soviet elements.

39. During the early years of the Soviet regime when there were several million men in the Red Army, maximum Cheka strength (Chamberlain, 1935:79) seems not to have been in excess of 31,000, while as late as 1936 there was a combined total of 250,000 NKVD troops and Frontier Guards as compared to (Mackintosh, 1956:61) 1.3 million in the Red Army. In Maoist China (Griffith, 1967:219-20), as against an estimated 2.3 million in the PLA, there were about 300,000 security troops and People's Armed Police. A security battalion was stationed at each Army headquarters.

40. In Eastern Europe, where national sentiment limits the popularity of some Communist regimes, the ratio of security forces to regular troops tends to be high. Thus, in the mid-1960s there were (O'Ballance, 1964:28-29) "approximately 45,000 men with the internal security forces and the frontier guards" in Czechoslovakia as compared to a modest 185,000 or so in the army. After the Hungarian People's Army was reorganized in 1957 and reduced to about 120,000 men, a new Worker's Militia was created (American, 1957:15) with 25,000-30,000 "former AVO men and loyal Communist Party people." Under the personalist Albanian regime, there are more than 12,500 security police and approximately 30,000 regular army troops (Keefe, 1971:181,193).

41. The Soviet military manual, *Marxism-Leninism on War* (1972:261) stresses their contribution to the February 1948 coup d'grace in Czechoslovakia when all anti-Communists had resigned their ministries in protest against Communist control of the Interior Ministry security police. Although no Soviet occupation troops were inside Czechoslovakia, mass marches of Red militia units which had been armed by the USSR before its forces withdrew were sufficient to induce Benes to acquiesce in the coup and thus avoid Civil War and certain Soviet military intervention. In terms of the actual sequence, the militia seem to have been initially organized by special Party contingents that were returning with Soviet forces:

> the Communist and Workers' Parties created special armed detachments which were manned according to the class principle by revolutionary workers and peasants fully devoted to the socialist cause. These were the national security forces and the state militia, as well as the workers militia, that is, the armed workers detachments set up at factories, mines, etc. (*Marxism-Leninism on War*, 1972:261)

42. In Poznan, regular troops—unlike militia units—reportedly (Gorlich, 1967:31) disobeyed officers and refused to fire on rioters. And in Hungary, "the only organized armed unit of Hungarians that sided with the Soviet forces" in 1956 was the AVO security police. The same source (American, 1957:14-15) records that the morale of the *Frontier Guards* was quite low: "it is characteristic of the attitude of the men that after the revolt they replaced the red star on their caps only under the strictest orders to do so. . . ."

Vali(1961:439) acknowledges that it not only was advised by Soviet specialists, but the Frontier Guards' "membership has been recruited from among enlisted soldiers and these were encouraged to serve several terms. The officers, many of them subsequently dismissed because of disloyalty to the regime, were selected from among the most reliable noncommissioned officers of the army or members of the Security Police."

43. The background is succinctly recounted by Basseches(1943:109,181–82):

> later, long after the controlling functions of the commissars had ceased, their relations to the officers' corps were disturbed by the close contact which had grown up between the commissars and the Cheka during the Civil War. . . . For years these political police officials enjoyed special privileges. They were better paid than the officers, enjoyed easier and more rapid promotion. As the political police had a special military department, to which the police post within the army division was subordinated, the police officers felt themselves to be superior to the army and its officers' corps. The political police behaved as if it were the highest and most important organ of the revolution. Although this was no longer true, the political police continued to act as though every professional soldier was suspect, as in the time of the Civil War.

44. Similarly the size of these and other paramilitary forces generally exceeds that of the regular armed forces—but again the fear here is not of a possible coup. In China, as more recently in Vietnam, the militia were initially organized by the political department of the army to serve as local self-defense forces and a source of tested regular army troops (Griffith, 1967:265–77): "the militia's loyalty was ensured by its class composition and the constant, close supervision which Party cadres and the reliable Red Army men exercised." By 1945, there were in excess of 2 million peasants in the militia against about 1 million or less in the PLA. After Chiang's defeat, the People's Militia remained under PLA supervision and performed rural police and coastal defense duties. During the 1958 Quemoy/Matsu crisis, the militia were rapidly expanded to about 30 million, although (Clemens, 1964:103) "only 4 million had practiced marksmanship with live ammunition. More recent information suggests that the militia's 'first line' numbers 10 to 15 million men, but even these are too lightly and poorly armed to be used as light infantry." Between 1962 and 1964, the militia had been purged and reorganized; only "workers and poor and middle peasants who are politically reliable" were retained. Even so only about one-quarter of the units were armed as "core" detachments staffed largely by Party cadres and those of untainted class origins—all under 30 years of age. The remainder were used as productive labor battalions. Both training and ideological indoctrination was carried out under the joint supervision of the PLA and the Public Security Forces. The size of the PLA was, of course, less than 3 million active duty personnel.

With respect to Korea, Koh(1969:24,18) reports that in 1962 a militia called the "Workers-Peasants' Red Guards" was created "to serve as an adjunct to the regular armed forces in case of need." By the late 1960s, there were 1.2 million men and women in the militia as compared to less than 400,000 in the armed services. A similar situation exists in the Soviet Union, though there was obviously less fear of an invasion. Clemens(1964: 84–105) notes that in the 1930s, "brigadmits" were constituted in the USSR to aid the police and NKVD in the forced collectivization campaign. By the late 1950s, they had atrophied, and a volunteer auxiliary People's Police of more than two million was organized for internal order. In addition, there is a paramilitary organization called DOSAAF with more than three million which operates as an auxiliary or civil defense-type force for the regular armed services. Between 1923 and 1939, there had also been a territorial militia which in the latter year actually exceeded the size of the Red Army. Military opposition to its reconsitution in the early 1960s was based as in China a few years earlier not on the premise that such forces are "antimilitary." Arguments generally stressed cost effectiveness and the need of the regular armed services for budgetary shares which were designated for the militia.

45. Chorley(1973:185) assigns paramount importance to the relationshp between a new revolutionary army and the regime's short run survival:

> since no deep revolution has come to power without leaving in its wake a trail of dispossessed and embittered classes, this implies that a revolutionary government on the morrow of its seizure of power will probably be met by a certain degree of violent opposition, whether spasmodic and spontaneous or organized into open rebellion. Moreover, a deep revolution has serious repercussions on foreign countries and it may well happen, as in the case of Russia in 1919 and of France in 1792, that the revolutionary government finds itself not only faced by internal rebellion, but also by armed foreign support for the rebels, or even by invasion from the troops of frightened foreign governments. It follows, therefore, that a first and basic problem is the creation of revolutionary armed forces, capable not only of liquidating disorder and insurrection at home, but also if necessary of fending off external foes.

46. Chorley's thesis(1973:223-37) is that ad hoc or guerrilla-type formations may be invaluable during the insurrection but must be replaced by a hierarchical and well-trained regular army if the regime is to defend itself against similarly well-trained counterrevolutionary armies. While the progress of weapons research and development alone supports her contention, as does Soviet and Chinese history, this does not answer such questions as how hierarchical a military establishment need be nor whether a major defensive role might nevertheless be well within the capabilities of a popular militia. The Chinese appear to have struck a reasonable balance which seems fully consonant with the parameters of developmental socialism. See also Wulf(1979).

47. With respect to China, Griffith(1967:251-55) observes the Leninist concept that no army could be politically neutral "was part of the intellectual baggage the Russians brought to Canton in 1924, when they arrived there at Dr. Sun Yatsen's invitation to help him organize a revolutionary army." The same author maintains that this approach was drawn upon by Mao after 1927, while Pool(1955:24) argues that both before and after 1928, Chinese Communism "learned much of its military lore from Russian advisers." And according to North(1952:72), much of the Red Chinese leadership "was Russian trained." Yet this was true only of top leaders and a very small minority of 1949 Red Chinese military commanders since "very few of the Communist officers have much formal education and they are poorly equipped for the intricacies of modern warfare (Pool, 1955:125)." In 1945 the Russians (*Marxism-Leninism on War,* 1972:255) had provided Red Chinese forces with some captured Japanese weapons and claim that they "prevented the transfer of any considerable contingents of US troops to China." After the Red victory, the PLA absorbed considerable quantities of Soviet equipment, an appreciable number of advisers at higher staff levels and reorganized along Soviet lines. Even in this period of Sino-Soviet harmony (1950 to 1956, and in lesser measure until 1958), the dominant (Joffe, 1965:101-11) though not exclusive train of Chinese military thought was that Soviet approaches should not be blindly imitated but selectively adapted. Thus, for years Chinese military commanders had been accustomed to a more collectivist approach to the exercise of authority, and political officers served more commonly as military commanders than in the Soviet Union. As in Korea, Mongolia, Albania, Yugoslavia, and Vietnam, many of the top Party leaders had become military commanders during the struggle for State power. These and other differences in the Chinese heritage were celebrated and possibly exaggerated after the final break in 1960 when Soviet advisers were withdrawn. They are being narrowed since Teng Hsiao-ping's emergence as China's dominant figure in the late 1970s.

China aided Vietnam after 1948, while Soviet forces joined Tito's units in the final liquidation of Nazi control over Yugoslavia. After World War II, Soviet advisers and equipment (Hoffman and Neal, 1962) helped Tito create a modern Soviet-style army until the 1948 break. Earlier Stalin and Churchill had agreed to aid Tito and to share influence equally in that country. Tito, in turn, had aided Hoxha's Partisans in Albania where the Yugoslavs and Soviets jointly helped that country establish an army from 1945 until the 1948 expulsion of Yugoslav units by Hoxha, who remained pro-Soviet until 1960. "General Petrit Dume, who was commander of the [Albanian] People's Army during its dependence on the Soviet Union and still was in 1970, had said in November of 1952 that his force was an integral part of the Soviet Army." Until 1961, when Chinese aid replaced Russian, Albanian "training was based on Soviet methods, and specialized schools were scaled down copies of those in the Soviet army. Training manuals were translated from the Russian (Keefe, 1971:182,192)."

In these four countries, once the indigenous Communist movement was victorious, large quantities of Soviet aid were offered for security and influence purposes. With the exception of Vietnam, pro-Soviet officers in the other three countries were purged at one time or another.

48. As for Mongolia, the Russians (*Marxism-Leninism on War*, 1972:254–55) acknowledge that

> in 1921 the Mongolian working people, relying on the fraternal assistance of the Soviet Red Army, won the armed struggle against foreign oppressors and local feudals . . . the Soviet Union helped to equip the Mongolian Army with the latest weapons, the Mongolian Army mastered advanced Soviet military science, and the two armies supported each other in combat actions. In 1939, the Soviet and Mongolian soldiers jointly inflicted a crushing defeat to the Japanese aggressors. In the summer of 1945 the Mongolian People's Revolutionary Army, in joint action with units of the Soviet Army and the People's Liberation Army of China, contributed to the rout of the Kwantung Army and the liberation of the Chinese people from the Japanese invaders.

For details on the Soviet role in setting up the government in Ulan Bator between 1921 and 1923, and its massive intervention during the early 1930s, see: Rupen(1966); Bowden(1968:264); Dupuy(1970).

49. The Korean case is rather more complex than that of Mongolia. In the late 1930s, Kim Il Sung and several dozen guerrillas began to fight the Japanese from Manchurian base areas. They were forced to flee into Russia in 1941 and returned with Soviet forces in 1945. Between late 1945 and early 1948, the USSR created a number of Korean internal security forces such as the Peace Preservation corps and the Railroad Guards (Sohn, 1969:270). During this period, "the basic Russian strategy was to place native Koreans . . . in positions of the highest formal authority, and to place Soviet-Koreans or Russian advisers in locations of de facto power (Paige, 1966:29)." Kim had returned with about 50 guerrillas as his personal following and approximately 250 Soviet Koreans with Red Army backgrounds (Sohn, 1969:274). In 1948, these two groups—many of whom had commanded the paramilitary organizations—reorganized the latter as the Korean People's Army, and Soviet forces left the country. Nevertheless, Chung(1963:110) refers to

> a one year programme under the supervision of the Soviet advisory group which was set up on the withdrawal of the Soviet Army. These Soviet advisers are said to have been specially instructed "to possess the knowledge of the Korean language and customs." It is also said that "several Soviet general officers and a number of field grade officers were attached to the National Defence Ministry" as well as to the military academies and the naval training schools where they were acting as instruc-

tors. The allocation of advisers was thought to have been as many as 150 per division, but the number was reduced to twenty per division and one per company after the fulfillment of the one year program.

Although a few thousand Korean guerrillas returned from Manchuria in 1945–46, the bulk of those who were fighting under Chinese auspices—the 40,000 man Korean Volunteer Corps—didn't return until 1949. These men were "retrained" and amalgamated into the Korean People's Army as were a small number of Koreans who had spent the war in Yenan. Between 1952 and 1968, there was recurrent factional conflict and apparently an abortive coup d'etat in 1957 or 1958. Both the Maoist and Soviet factions were subordinated or purged, while Kim's own guerrilla followers seem to have consolidated their leadership.

50. Mongolia seems (Dupuy, 1970:439–40) in the 1960s not to have endeavored to offset Soviet influence, although a Chinese mission was accepted for a limited number of projects. During the earlier periods, Soviet influence was not, in contradistinction to Eastern Europe, intensely resented by the masses because traditionally China had endeavored to subjugate or exact tribute from the Mongolians. The very process of playing balance of power politics by Korea, Mongolia, Yugoslavia, and Rumania seems to have contributed to mass internal support. Albania's shift from dependence upon Russia to alignment with China also suggests a sovereign national orientation.

51. Acting through National or Fatherland Fronts which initially were genuine coalitions, the Communists demanded and generally obtained an exclusive right to politicize the rank and file within the armed forces and to supervise the elimination of Nazi collaborators. Between 1946 and 1948, these Fronts were transformed into Communist-led coalitions (*Marxism-Leninism on War*, 1972:261–64).

52. Hoffman and Neal (1962:106–7) stress that the only Communist-led undergrounds which amounted to much in terms of fighting were the Yugoslav and the Polish partisans. Yet even the latter needed overt Soviet military aid to finally defeat the Home Army in 1948. Hence, had Stalin not ordered that "Titoists" be purged throughout East Europe, it is at least conceivable that after a brief period, bourgeois-led nationalism would have restored capitalism in those countries as it almost did a few years later in Hungary and came close to doing in Czechoslovakia in 1968. In most East European countries, local Communists did not have Tito's nationalist appeal and more crucially they lacked personally loyal armed forces which had been forged through a lengthy guerrilla struggle. There had been insufficient time to restructure ancien regime armies, and in the event of protests against regime policies, it is likely that "Titoist" leaders would have been ousted or forced to follow what would in all likelihood become a restorationist current. For, as Nagy and Dubcek demonstrated, such "Titoists" could never bring themselves to call for Soviet military intervention. Rumanian patience, finesse, and an unusual Machiavellian character trait probably explain why they were able to bring off what others couldn't. The same, of course, is true for the Finns on the bourgeois side. Elsewhere the failure of bourgeois elites to recognize that the status quo ante could not be restored also contributed to East European instability, as did their anti-Soviet interwar cordon sanitaire.

53. Kolkowicz(1967:323–28) concludes his study of the abortive Tukachevsky and Zhukov challenges to Party supremacy by citing Polish sociologist Jerzy Waitr's admission of continuing tension between regular officers in the Polish People's Army and the Party leadership. He reportedly attributes military discontent to such "professional" traits as discipline, specialization, risk of one's life, and their view of the military role as "honorable." The officers are said to dislike: Party political activities within the military; class bias in the recruitment of officers; the rejection of traditions associated with bourgeois armies; and officer recruitment from the ranks. Although it is unclear how widespread or intense such sentiments are or whether they are more prevalent within East Europe than elsewhere, or if they be on the rise or decline, Kolkowicz nevertheless con-

cludes: "in the communist nations the problem of how to integrate the military into the political system is far from solved. Although it would be alarmist to call it acute, it is festering within the power structure of many of these states and given the right conditions, could become very serious." His implicit solution is that of all exiles: the Party should take its hands off the officer corps and allow it to play an independent role. A corollary holds that Churchill's famous solution to the "problem" of Bolshevism would be at hand: "strangle the baby in the crib!" Perhaps the Party's continuing "distrust" for a military "whose members desire exclusiveness, cultivate elitism, and at the same time control powerful means of violence" is well placed!

6

Marx and Radical Militarism: Can Officers Be Surrogates for Proletarians?

The very question posed by this chapter's title would outrage many Marxists because of its inconsistency (as we have seen) with one of Marx's most important predictions and the pains Communists have taken to subordinate the military. Like the adherents of more traditional religions, some of Marx's followers have sanctified his every utterence, investing each with the quality of dogma. Perhaps for this reason most social scientists in North America have excluded Marxian paradigms from their analytical frames of reference. An exception occurs when off-handed comments are made on apparent discrepancies between what Marx anticipated and contemporary developments. One apparent anomaly referred to in preceding chapters has been the emergence of radical or "socialist" military factions and regimes. Earlier chapters were preoccupied with sources and implications of *rightist* militarism — admittedly the most prevalent form. Nevertheless, the question must be posed whether leftist militarism can be reconciled with the Marxian paradigm. In this chapter I shall argue that such radical propensities by a minority of officers necessitates revision of Marx's prognostication, and the belief of many Marxists, that military men are invariably counterrevolutionary. But to construe this qualification of a specific prediction on military conservatism as a rejection of usefulness of Marx's *general* paradigm of social change for understanding the relationship between the military and socio-economic underdevelopment is wholly unwarranted.

What such an opinion overlooks is that, in addition to the plethora of doctrinal platitudes which primarily serve the agitational needs of Marx-ist political movements, there is also a Marxian-inspired scholarly tradi-tion that has existed and of late flourished (Miliband, 1977:5) at the fr-inges of orthodox Marxism. Although inspired by Marx's socialist values and paradigmatic orientation, some of these analysts have nevertheless been willing to reject doctrinal citation in favor of empirical analysis of class relationships and institutional change. One of the most cogent statements of Marx's empirical method is provided by McQuarie (1978). While this nondogmatic approach has occasioned the rejection, revision, replacement, or neglect of some of Marx's interpretive or predictive statements, it has substantiated others and generated new theoretical in-sights.[1] And at a more fundamental level, there is a consensus that both Marx's methodological orientation and general paradigm of socio-historical development remain useful in elucidating the sources of some if not all major conflicts in the 20th century.[2]

Unfortunately, most Marxian scholarship on the developing areas refers to civil-military relations peripherally if at all. It has tended to focus upon neo-colonialism and structural dependency as constraints upon economic development and national self-determination.[3] Marxian analysis of advanced capitalist societies has, on the other hand, sought to come to grips with such questions as if, how, and under what conditions bureaucratic state institutions function autonomously vis-à-vis the bour-geoisie.[4] In his last years, Marx himself explicitly warned against any assumption that his theory of capitalist development in Western Europe was necessarily applicable to Russia or presumably other nonindustrial-ized areas.[5] Following his admonition, I shall eschew the approach which *relies* upon doctrinal citation in attempting to explain the seemingly anomalous occurrence of leftist-oriented military regimes — ones which expropriate property-owning upper classes. Much of this analysis also applies to military support for radical civilian regimes. My preoccupa-tion is less with reconciling such an explanation with specific predictions than with its conformity to Marx's overall paradigmatic orienta-tion — what he variously called "the materialist conception of history" or historical materialism.[6]

The Materialist Conception of History

Marx was preoccupied with understanding the process of historical change in order to improve the prospects for effective control over the future. He assumed that, so long as socialism had not been institu-tionalized, groups controlling the means of production within particular societies would resort to coercion to maximize their share of available surplus. Insofar as such groups self-consciously entered into conflict with other groups to increase or maintain existing shares of surplus, these groups were defined as classes.[7] Historical change occurred when the emergence of new underutilized forces of production made it rational for a particular class to alter existing relations of production, and when that group became conscious of the potential for bettering its position by struggling for a change in the mode or organization of production. The class or classes which anticipated a decline in the share of surplus appropriated by them under the old mode of production would naturally oppose the structural changes advocated by the rising class.

Although catalyzed by malutilization of existing forces of production or growth opportunities, revolutionary class consciousness projects institutional alternatives by creatively elaborating proposals influenced not only by socialist ideas but also by the cultural legacy and experience of one's own or conceivably other societies.[8] Hence Marx maintained that while successful efforts to engender basic socio-economic change involved class conflict, the precise form or details of economic reorganization could not be predicted in advance of struggles to replace it. On the other hand, the character and development of preexisting forces of production did of course set the general parameters of short-run aspirations and practicality. Thus Marx's famous dictum that "men make their own history, but not in any way they please." If the rising social classes change and shape new institutions when existing conditions make this feasible, they are nevertheless constrained by this same institutional legacy.

Of all man's social institutions where material scarcity prevailed, the mode of production was (in Marx's view) the most basic in that it profoundly constrained the functioning of judicial, religious, educational, political, and military institutions. Marx assumed that a society's economic output or livelihood, and how it was produced, was so fundamental an activity for any people that it tended to be reflected in their values, routines, and panoply of cultural artifacts. Prior to capitalism, there was no formal separation of economic, military, and other institutions. Only with the growth in the division of labor associated with capitalist industrialization and especially its more modern forms did separate (or functionally specialized) institutions appear to operate autonomously. Yet it is important to stress that such superstructural elements were not directly or entirely "determined" by the prevailing mode of production. As in the case of class consciousness and the emergence of conceptions of alternative modes of production, superstructural institutions were conditioned or limited though not wholly determined by a prevailing mode of production.[9] Put differently, a capitalist mode of production was associated with and accounted for the way insitutions customarily routinized values in their performance, and biased them against some (though not necessarily all) alternative operationalizations which Marx therefore classified as idealistic. Hence major egalitarian reform efforts (i.e., "utopian socialism") by the state would wither if its officials ignored the fact that control over investment, production, and marketing decisions resided elsewhere. Unless, that is, those administering the state were capable of radically altering capitalism by assuming control over the means of production.[10]

Bureaucracy and the State in the Marxian Paradigm

It follows from Marx's expositions that, once capitalism became established and so long as it was developing and maximizing its productive potential, the state would ordinarily be constrained in its policymaking by the general interests of the capitalist class. The repressive and capital accumulative promotional role of the state operated in four areas: 1) against general protests by workers; 2) to ensure that goal seeking activities by particular capitalists or sectors of that class did not jeopardize general class interests; 3) defense of national capitalists against possible threats by foreign capitalists; and 4) in the case of some countries, furtherance of capitalist development through colonialism and neocolonialism.

Marx's view (Avineri, 1969:41-64) of the modern state stressed the gap or contradiction between ideology and reality. It proclaimed universalistic ideals but in practice implemented policies whose content was biased in favor of the particularistic needs of the bourgeoisie and in some cases the state's bureaucracy. Yet he also recognized that under unusual circumstances the state might become temporarily autonomous in the sense of not being deferential to the dominant sentiments of the capitalist class. These conditions were: 1) when a Napoleonic strongman emerged as a result of a hegemonic stalemate among antagonistic social classes; 2) when, as in some Asian countries, the state itself exercised direct control over surplus generating property, i.e., land; 3) when one class administered the state upon behalf of another; 4) when the costs of suppressing politically radical mass movements increased markedly.[12]

Marx did not, of course, entertain the view that a completely autonomous state would promote capitalist development under its own aegis in a more efficacious manner than the bourgeoisie itself could.[13] Nor did he regard state officialdom as capable (Avineri, 1969:48-52) of administering society impartially, i.e., in accord with neutral or universalistic norms. Thus if, under appropriate conditions, those directing the state did assert their independence from the bourgeoisie, their own particularistic class interests would merely be substituted for, and/or complement, those of the bourgeoisie. In his 1843 *Critique of Hegel's Philos-*

ophy of Right, Marx implied bureaucratic autonomy but placed most of his emphasis upon the authoritarianism and materialistic careerism that constituted core interests of the bureaucratic class:

The bureaucracy has in its possession the affairs of the state, the spiritual being of society; it belongs to it as its private property. The general spirit of bureaucracy is the official secret, the mystery . . . conducting the affairs of state in public, even political consciousness, thus appear to the bureaucracy as high treason against its mystery. Authority is thus the principle of its knowledge and the deification of authoritarianism is its credo. But within itself this spiritualism turns into a coarse materialism, the materialism of dumb obedience. . . . As far as the individual bureaucrat is concerned, the goals of state become his private goals: a hunting for higher jobs and the making of a career. . . . Bureaucracy has therefore to make life as materialistic as possible. . . . The bureaucrat sees the world as a mere object to be managed by him.

No distinction was drawn by Marx between military and civilian bureaucrats. He was writing of course in 1843 and Prussia was foremost in his mind. In *The Communist Manifesto,* he had identified three sources of bureaucratic bias against a hypothetical socialist revolution as: 1) their predominantly privileged social backgrounds; 2) the emoluments and privileges of office; and 3) socialization into the norm of hierarchical accountability. Almost 30 years later, Marx returned to the question of bureaucracy in his appraisal of Louis Napoleon's "Second Empire." That his views had remained consistent is apparent from the draft for his *Address on the Civil War in France.*[14]

Despite this essentially negative assessment of civilian and military bureaucrats, the picture is not quite so dismal. First, it bears reiteration that Marx's change-oriented focus highlighted not only the institutional matrix at any point in time but also its developmental tendencies, or potential for becoming something else. Thus he saw the process of industrial growth as a source of a class with truly "radical chains"—the proletariat.[15] Classes were for him both social aggregates with distinct occupations or life styles and, most fundamentally, self-conscious groups opposed to other groups within society. His use of the word was a matter of convenience, though its latter meaning was his major concern from the standpoint of altering the institutional structure. Second, even bureaucratic state rule would be to a limited degree "progressive" for Marx provided it was a necessary and efficacious means of developing formerly malutilized productive forces. It is at least conceivable that if in less developed areas "national capitalists" were incapable of leading the process, and international dependency inhibited maximum industrialization, Marx—had he been cognizant of such circumstances a century later—was open and empirical enough to assimilate radical military changes in property relations to end such impediments to the growth of the forces of production. This would be especially true where the proletariat was miniscule.

The Parameters of Military Radicalism

Before elaborating upon the thesis that "leftist" military regimes can be reconciled with Marx's "materialist conception of history," I shall briefly distinguish two more common types of contemporary military interventions. The first are military seizures intended to prevent Marxists from implementing a socialist revolution. Often, of course, the "Marxists" are in fact a variegated collection of populist reformers, economic nationalists, and socialists. Examples of such conservative militarism include the coups discussed in Chapter 4 against Mossadegh, Arbenz, Lumumba, Bosch, Goulart, Sukarno, Nkrumah, Keita, Sihanouk, Torres, and Allende. To the extent that Marx elaborated a general theory of the state, he viewed it as repressive toward popular aspirations. In these cases, whether the military was acting as a self-conscious corporate class, or merely as dependent elite responsive to cues of the bourgeoisie, or both, its coercive function in suppressing any emergent mass movement against the prerogatives of property owners is consonant with his theory of the repressive state under capitalism. Thus, in his *Address on the Civil War in France,* Marx emphasizes (Feuer, 1959:365) that the 1871 Paris Commune "could resist only because, in consequence of the siege, it had got rid of the army and replaced it by a National Guard, the bulk of which consisted of workingmen. This fact was not to be transformed into an institution. The first decree of the Commune, therefore, was the suppression of the standing army and the substitution for it of the armed people." And McLellan (1974:184) notes that "in 1871 Marx reminded Kugelmann of the passage in *The Eighteenth Brumaire* where he talked of the destruction of the bureaucratic-military machinery and described it as 'the precondition' of any real popular revolution on the continent."[17]

A second type of intervention — one which may or may not culminate in seizure and retention of civil offices — is occasioned by nonideological grievances of an institutional, subinstitutional, ethnic, personal, and/or national character. These necessarily pit the armed forces against civilian politicians who are incompetent, meddlesome, or unresponsive to personal, budgetary, and other institutional concerns of the military. This kind of intervention by officer cliques or intraclass factions is of course the most common (Thompson, 1973) variant in the contemporary era.[18] It is distinguished from normal pluralistic interest group activity by the use of coercion. While Finer(1975:28–53,225–30) identifies a broad range of single or (what is more common) multiple institutional and subinstitutional motives which result in forcible interventions within "low" political cultures, i.e., those distinguished by an absence of high civilian procedural consensus and organization, his stress upon "corporate self-interest"—analogous to the term "class interest" which I have used—as a primary behavioral influence deserves emphasis because of its contribution to understanding ideological as well as nonideological interventions.

Citing Needler's work on the anti-Arosemana 1963 Ecuadorean *golpe,* Finer(234-35) argues with considerable acuity that

this skein of selective induction, professional training and social code, along with the organization and often the social self-sufficiency of the military establishment, give rise to the narrower corporate interest of the military: a continuing corporation which has acquired or aspires to a certain social status, political significance and material standard. Interestingly, it has been suggested that this, and not so-called "middle-class values" is what results from the increasingly middle-class composition of the officer corps. . . . In concrete terms this corporate self-interest reflects itself in demands for bigger budgets and better pay, etc.; in intense and lethal opposition to the constitution of any rival armed forces like workers' militias or presidential guards; and in a determination to have a say in public policymaking.

The budgetary data considered in Chapter 7 is consistent with this view as is Thompson's(1973) conclusion that "corporate" grievances were a major source of coups. But he found subcorporate interests such as personal or factional advancement were even more significant quantitatively.

Although Marx believed that, within certain cultural traditions, the development of modern industry under capitalism would be associated with the institutionalization of parliamentary government, he never excluded the possibility of military interventions in what have since been characterized as transitional or developing societies. Marx distinguished Great Britain, Holland, and the United States where even peaceful struggle for socialism was regarded as a serious option because of the relatively advanced level of material and cultural development, from such neo-agrarian societies as Prussia, Russia, and France. Thus in assessing the 20 year reign of Louis Napoleon—a personalist regime which approximates our second type of nonideological intervention because of the prior suppression of the left—Marx stressed: 1) that such a state can function autonomously for a period—even "humbling" the interests of the bourgeoisie; 2) while Bonaparte's following was petit bourgeois and peasant in character, the regime nevertheless acted independently of their aspirations too; and 3) that France was in fact governed by the bureaucratic classes.[19] The corruption, authoritarianism, and personalistic opportunism associated with such bureaucratic regimes were commented upon in Chapter 2. Hence, while Marx did not predict the occurrence of Bonapartism or simple militarism within the colonized areas, the analogous characteristics of such regimes are not wholly inconsistent with his view of the French state of the mid-19th century which ruled over a developing capitalistic society. Some recent data indicates that military regimes in Third World areas have slightly higher rates of industrial growth than civilian-administered systems.[20] This seems to "fit" well with the Bonapartist model which, according to Marx,

> was acclaimed throughout the world as the savior of society. Under its sway bourgeois society, freed from political cares, attained a development unexpected even by itself. Its industry and commerce expanded to colossal dimensions, financial swindling celebrated cosmopolitan orgies, the misery of the masses was set off by a shameless display of gorgeous, meretricious, and debased luxury. The state power, apparently soaring high above society, was at the same time itself the greatest scandal of that society and the very hotbed of all its corruptions. Its own rottenness and the rottenness of the society it had saved were laid bare by the bayonet of Prussia. . . .[21]

While there haven't been numerous wars in the Third World, the dozen or so international ones which have occurred in recent years (Arab/Israel, Ethiopia/Somalia, Algeria/Morocco, Indonesia/Timor, El Salvador/Honduras, North Yemen/South Yemen, Pakistan/India, China/India, Uganda/Tanzania) don't reflect favorably upon the performance of the military governments in question. The armies of these corrupt regimes tend to exhibit greatest success when their own unarmed civilians are the "enemy." Even in counterinsurgencies, as the Portuguese and Nicaraguan cases make clear, they generally require extensive foreign assistance or direct involvement to succeed. Yet to understand the appeal of radicalism to some officers in these areas, it is necessary to recognize that corruption and administrative inefficacy constitute but a small number of links in their "radical chains."

My purpose here then is less to fault Marx gratuitously for the absence of such a specific prognostication than to draw upon his general theory of historical materialism in order better to explain the occurrence and limits of radical militarism in the Third World. First, it should be noted that Marx's assessment of colonialism appears to have been rather evenhanded. While he viewed it as exploitative in the sense that surplus was withdrawn to the imperialist center where it accrued to the bourgeoisie and to the working classes, prior to the 1860s he considered it to be a positive phenomenon. This because it would begin the process of industrialization and concomitantly attenuate parochial outlooks and particularist loyalties. Thus, for Marx, imperialism was the highest stage of capitalism not because it engendered cataclysmic wars but rather because it extended the bourgeois mode of production and its modern universalistic norms to the traditional feudal or tribal societies.[22] As noted later in this chapter, Marx revised his assessment of colonialism where it stifled indigenous entrepreneurship (i.e., Ireland). Over the century and a quarter since Marx essayed the likely consequences of colonialism, his views have if anything been confirmed. While formal colonialism has been repudiated, the yoke has not been thrown off altogether. Our contemporary era has thus been denoted as one of "dependency" or neo-colonialism by an appreciable number of social scientists and political leaders.[23] On the other hand, these analysts and even less radical ones like Barnet and Muller (1974) have recognized that, enclaves or "export platforms" notwithstanding, most less developed societies are not only unable to control "their" industrialization but are failing to close the per capita GNP gap with advanced industrial societies.[24] Put differently, adherence to the "open door" for foreign investment has deformed and artificially limited the industrialization of these structurally dependent Third World systems. Since the 1930s, an ever-growing constituency, including some radical officers, have come to accept the view that existing neo-colonial relations of production are in conflict with maximizing the potential productivity of existing forces of production—labor, plants, technology, and, potential capital.[25]

The Appeal of Military Radicalism

For radical social change to occur, Marx maintained that, in addition to the existence of a contradiction between the mode (i.e., existing organization) and the emergent forces of production, there had to be a particular social group whose material interests would be served by a new and more productive system of ownership and control (i.e., property relations). These were necessary but not sufficient conditions for structural change. Otherwise service workers, the urban lumpenproletariat and marginal peasants would, along with insecure if less miserable factory workers, constitute an adequate social base for such radical transformation. The condition which they fail to meet is class consciousness backed by organization and sufficient coercive resources to succeed in a revolutionary undertaking.[26] This condition ironically may be in some circumstances most easily met by the military. Engendered by its distinctive life style, hierarchical organization, national defense mission, and heroic elan, the military has a unique corporate identity. Particularly when reinforced by physical isolation and limited social interaction with the dependent bourgeois and landowning sectors, such self-consciousness needs only an ideology which will provide a basis for active opposition to one or more of the classes which had heretofore controlled the means of production.

In the contemporary era, an amalgam of ideas incorporating economic nationalism, social welfarism, and what we might call state capitalism as a catalyst of development constitute such an "ideology." Some officers have been imperfectly exposed to these perspectives in a variety of ways, ranging from books to war college courses, university experiences, orientation tours to socialist societies, direct contacts with Marxist cadres, visits to radical nonaligned nations, and even through counterinsurgency campaigns. The socialization or resocialization of (usually junior) officers to radical beliefs and values is a process that has not been systematically studied. Woddis (1977:24–90) cites a number of factors associated with radical coups or the leftward movement of military regimes. These include the: 1) inability of existing regimes to "govern" in the face of rising and organized mass demands; 2) effects of leftist movements upon officers; 3) decline in the proportion of upper class officers; 4) desire to incorporate modern technology into their societies; 5) influence of leftist intellectuals informally and within staff colleges; and 6) hostility of imperialist Powers to "initial" domestic reform programs. The findings of a recent study by Rejai(1979:182–204) of prominent leaders in 12 revolutions are of immense heuristic value, even though most of his revolutionary elite were civilian and only about half of the revolutions could be loosely classified as Marxist or populist: Mexico 1910; Russia 1917, China 1949, Bolivia 1952, Vietnam 1954, Cuba 1959, Algeria 1962, and France 1968. The remainder (England 1640s, America 1776, France 1789, Hungary 1956) were bourgeois revolutions. Even so, the following characteristics were associated with the 32 revolutionary leaders:

1. youthfulness (20–45 years of age) especially in the 20th century
2. early exposure to revolutionary ideology and participation in revolutionary activities
3. early and consistent exposure to urban life
4. mainstream religious and ethnic backgrounds (though substantial proportion of non-Islamic opted for atheism)
5. large number from lower middle and lower class backgrounds especially for 20th century revolutions in the underdeveloped areas
6. an "overwhelming majority" are from large families and a majority tend to be oldest or youngest children
7. a minority had stormy childhoods or came from broken homes
8. though only "a fraction" were trained in the social sciences, humanities, or arts, they tended to be "a well-educated group" with "many in law and medicine." "A few have formal military training, some acquire military experience through conscripted service, and others in the course of their revolutions."
9. a large number publish writings often on revolutionary theory and practice

10. an impressive number are professional revolutionaries or combine this with another occupation; many were "arrested with regularity and imprisoned."
11. while virtually all are indigenous to their societies, most had traveled widely and many remained abroad for long periods of time, thus exposing themselves to foreign cultures, languages, and ideologies
12. optimistic views toward human nature and their own country, though the international community is divided into friends and foes—especially by those with nationalistic or Marxist ideologies
13. ideologies which were indigenous variants of "nationalism, Marxism or a mixture thereof"

Schools, interestingly, were most radicalizing for those from turbulent homes, and "the relatively small number of revolutionaries who are radicalized in school come from undeveloped or semideveloped countries, and they hold ideologies of Marxism/Leninism or nationalism/Marxism-Leninism." Finally, travel was "more likely to function as a radicalization agent if one has experienced a stormy childhood or school radicalization."

At the level of individual psychological traits, as with exposure to the radicalizing agents considered above, there was no single mix of background characteristics that was associated with the emergence of the revolutionary leader. In the case of (largely 20th century) "planned revolutions," leaders did tend to be defined by "marginality, an inferiority complex, and a compulsion to excel." Similarly a substantial majority were distinguished by "commitment to a rugged, spartan, puritanical style . . . in an effort to drive out all societal evil and to bring about a reign of virtue."

Vanity, asceticism, and marginality have greater explanatory power than estheticism, relative deprivation, and status inconsistency. Oepidal complex has least explanatory potential. While the particular "mix" of psychological dynamics varies from revolutionary to revolutionary, vanity, asceticism, estheticism, and marginality recur with greater frequency than any other mix.

Yet while "virtually all situational revolutionaries [were] vain," about "half of the leaders from planned revolutions [were] not."

As far as class and ideology were concerned, Rejai discovered that "most democrats come from upper and middle social strata, a majority of Marxist-Leninists and nationalists from the middle class, and a majority of nationalist/Marxist-Leninists from the lower class."

A surprisingly large number of Marxist-Leninists come from a Jewish background, while democrats, nationalists, and nationalist/Marxist-Leninists come from Protestant, Catholic, Muslim, Jewish and other origins. While all leaders with a Jewish heritage shifted to atheism, all Muslim revolutionaries retained their religious commitments.

Islam tended to be reinforced by revolutionary commitments in the Algerian case and it was found that "some revolutionary leaders deliberately dilute their ideologies in order to maximize popular support and, perhaps, to forestall foreign intervention." As one would expect, most exhibit oratorical skills and often organizational ones as well. As far as the military variable was concerned, it was found that although the

revolutionary leaders necessarily gather a great deal of military experience as a result of their prolonged activities, they are not necessarily drawn from the military ranks. A few have professional military training and some gather military experience as a result of conscripted military service. As a component of their organizational skill, however, many leaders acquire substantial military experience in the course of their revolutions.

Hence, while this group of civilians tends of necessity to become military-oriented, it would be fascinating to ascertain the degree to which the characteristics of radical military leaders converge with those of the civilian revolutionaries. My own research (Wolpin, 1981) on 20 prominent Latin American leftist officers suggest they: (1) were recruited from nonprosperous families; (2) had alien ethnic ties; (3) were exposed to urban national and foreign cultures, though originating in hinterland towns; (4) experienced personal crises that could be attributed to the economic system; (5) interacted with leftist relatives or political partisans; (6) were youthful, highly intelligent, and professionally accomplished; (7) exhibited both social extraversion and probity; and (8) frequently had intellectual interests. These patterns remain tentative until comparative research is undertaken of their radical officer counterparts in other Third World areas.

Here it is crucial to recognize that when the military opt to function as industrializing surrogates for a weak or nonexistent national capitalist class in this way, they also do so as a result of favorable circumstances—not historical inevitability. Such determination is, as I have argued, wholly alien to Marx's own approach to class roles in historical development.[27] The most Marx would say, I think, is that material conditions including the international environment are becoming increasingly propitious for the appearance of radical military regimes, and therefore we may predict a greater number of them in the decades ahead.[28] In the 1960–74 period alone, a United Nations(1974a) report on nationalizations and takeovers recorded 875 cases in 62 countries of the world—predominantly in the underdeveloped areas. Africa accounted for 340 of them and "led in all categories of industry except petroleum— that is, in instances of nationalization of mining, agriculture, manufacturing, trade, public utilities, banking and insurance." A serious student of this trend in Africa concludes his analysis (Rood, 1976:446–47) with the following prediction:

The pattern of takeovers during the last decade in black Africa, as well as that in the rest of the world, suggests very strongly that they will continue to nationalize and indigenize enterprises whenever they believe it will serve their own interests. The only limitations will be practical ones . . . the growing strength of the national resource blocs such as OPEC, the spread of socialism, and the increased acceptance of nationalization vastly improve the bargaining position of the nationalizing countries.

Even conservative military analysts such as Kennedy(1974:67) acknowledge economic nationalism as a major catalyst for radical militarism in an era of declining Western hegemony:

While considerable evidence has been accumulated of the alleged relationship between Third World economies and the industrialized economies, and much of it is critical of the relationship, the growing independence of the economic managers of these countries, their aggressive assertion of their own national interests and their general noncompliance with behavior that would be expected from dependent partners to a dual form of exploitation, which is what is implied by the theories of neo-colonialism, suggests that the relationships that were thought to be apparent in the 1960s are not as naked or as direct, and that new explanations are needed.

The three major forces working in favour of military intervention as a solution to the legitimacy crisis are therefore: the failings of the implanted political party system in the cultural milieu of the developing countries; the strategic position of the military—a small force with leverage; and the growing realization of the potentialities of independence among the elites, or, to put it another way, the realization that the European powers are less committed, and less able, to intervene against governments or policies they disapprove of.

Radical appeal is enhanced by a number of domestic variables which have complemented the slow but perceptible decline of the United States as a world power. These affect both the prestige and the material self-interest of the military class itself. Thus it seems clear now that economic dependency and underdevelopment is associated with chronic balance of payments deficits which have resulted in increasingly unsupportable external debt burdens for many, if not all, such countries.[29] The consequences are recurrent austerity budgets and limitations upon potential financial and human resources for military institutional needs.[30] Officers must then become ever more dependent upon external creditors or donors for equipment, training, etc. They are under pressure to reduce institutional needs, divert resources from other societal sectors, or solicit additional foreign assistance with its concomitant erosion of self-esteem. A sense of malaise is also engendered by their awareness that, in comparison with officers in military aid donor countries, they represent states whose dependent capitalist economies are incapable of closing the technological and welfare gaps. Hence, the self-esteem as well as the institutional interests of the military are promoted by adopting a new national development mission involving a sharp break with the past.[30]

In a slightly different historical context, Skocpol and Trimberger(1978:123-24,130) not only underline the limited yet real developmental role of state-based and authoritarian "revolutions from above," but they join Block(1978:35-36) in stressing the "autonomy" of the state and an elite revolutionary commitment that is essentially reactive to international pressures or threats.

Actual historical revolutions, though, have not conformed to Marx's theoretical expectations. From the French Revolution on, *they have occurred in predominantly agrarian* countries where capitalist relations of production were only barely or moderately developed. In every instance, political military pressures from more economically advanced countries abroad have been crucial in contributing to the outbreak of revolution. And, most important, the objective contradictions within the old regimes that explain the emergence of revolutionary situations have not been primarily economic. Rather they have been political contradictions centered in the structure and situation of states caught in cross-pressures between, on the one hand, military competitors on the international scene and, on the other hand, the constraints of the existing domestic economy and (in some cases) resistance by internal politically powerful class forces to efforts by the state to mobilize resources to meet international competition. . . . And if states are extractive organizations that can deploy resources to some extent independently of existing class interests, then it makes sense that revolutions create the potentials for breakthroughs in national economic development in large part by giving rise to more powerful, centralized, and autonomous state organizations. This was true for all of the revolutions from above and below that we studied, although the potential for stateguided or initiated national economic development was more thoroughly realized in Japan, Russia, and China than it was in France and Turkey.

Such an innovative mission brings radical officers prestige and the expectation that their role in the nation's history will be accorded honor by future generations. Thus, as with every rising class in Marx's schema, their particular interests would be legitimized as — and at least for a limited historical period actually promote — the general interests of society. And in the short run, both career mobility and immediate budgetary needs are satisfied by replacing civilian politicians and rightist officers who have been preoccupied with siphoning off surplus for themselves or associated speculators, promoters, etc. Hence, to the extent that military officers develop a "socialist" perspective and recognize that it requires political intervention, they can be viewed as a new ruling class with at least limited "radical chains" — a material and social interest in challenging bourgeois privilege and hegemony heretofore secured by the pre-existing mode of production.

The Constraints upon Military Radicalism

If the developmental prognosis in much of the Third World is as problematic as I have argued, why then have not more radical military regimes emerged? Or from the Marxian perspective, why have officers so often been content to remain as an elite dependent upon the willingness of those in control of capital to invest surplus in the economy? Insofar as they defer to capitalist incentive structures or "laws," capitalists become the ruling class and the military are at most — even when hegemonically administering the state — a "governing elite." The state apparatus in such circumstances has no control over the forces of production.

An attempt to explain the preference for a conservative or "moderate" political orientation would in itself require a monograph. Here I can at most simply mention a number of variables — several of which have been analyzed at greater length in Chapter 2 — that seem to have functioned as impediments to military radicalism. First, it is but two decades since many of the "new nations" have come into existence. Such issues as the ownership of capital, terms of trade, crippling external indebtedness, the need for price indexing, and a "new economic order" have only become salient at international meetings during the 1970s. The struggle in short has only begun and is far from played out. We should look instead to the next 20 to 40 years.

Second, many officers have never been exposed to state socialist systems, "radical" systems or the interpretations of underdevelopment which socialism offers.[31] Domestic and external socialization often has tended either to ignore such alternatives or to denigrate them systematically. This has been particularly true of the U.S. Military Assistance Program which attempts to socialize foreign officer trainees against the "radical" options of public ownership and non-alignment.[32] Thus questions of "threat perception" posed recently during interviews of Indonesian and Philippine senior officers (average age: 48) elicited response patterns which were summarized (Maynard, 1978:148-49) as follows:

Senior officers in neither country fear a conventional external attack; they are far more concerned with domestic stability. Both groups fear China as a *potential* threat due to its overwhelming size, proximity, and ideology; but officers cannot provide recent examples of Chinese interference in either Philippine or Indonesian domestic affairs. . . . And one gets the impression that officers in both countries would prefer incorporation of Sabah to allowing an independent and radical regime to set up house in northern Borneo. . . . Senior officers in both

Indonesia and the Philippines rank radical Muslims and communist remnants as the foremost threats to their countries. Essentially they view these threats as domestic problems receiving very limited external assistance. . . . Communism is opposed by both military elites, ostensibly because it appears foreign and antireligious and because in both countries it has preached the forceful overthrow of the national government. Senior officers in both militaries have had personal experience fighting communists and radical Muslims; they are not likely to easily forgive or forget these two threats. Senior officers in both militaries describe corruption as a threat to the government in general and to the military in particular. In Indonesia, corruption is usually portrayed either as financial mismanagement perpetrated by a few senior officers or as a corruption of time, using office hours for the conduct of private business. In the Philippines, officers perceive corruption among both civilian bureaucrats and military personnel, in the upper ranks as well as at lower levels. Although abuses at the lower levels tend to be related to physical misbehavior in public, those in the higher ranks tend toward clandestine financial dealings. Senior officers in both militaries seem chagrined that the actions of a few individuals have been allowed to discredit the entire armed forces.

What is especially noteworthy in this summary is the conservative socio-political bias manifested by the frequent deprecation of financial abuses — a common phenomenon in both regimes — coupled with a stereotyped devil image of "communism" and an equally rigid antipathy toward "radical" forces. Even more than in other bureaucratic occupations, officers tend to be task-oriented, i.e., they are "doers" as opposed to being contemplative intellectuals. Third, like most of us they tend to be more preoccupied with immediate or visible problems than with longer term structural dysfunctionalities. Thus today's budgetary conflict can usually be more easily dealt with by simply forcing a reallocation of funds from nonmilitary items or through additional foreign indebtedness.

Fourth, it is likely that, in many military establishments, senior grade officers more often than not do interact socially and perhaps economically with civilian businessmen, landowners, and/or their relatives. As suggested in Chapter 2, a larger proportion of officers at these ranks are probably *upper* middle class in origin and even those who aren't — especially in Africa — tend to "marry up" or assimilate some values associated with the life style of their social betters. Investments, corruption, double job arrangements, high salaries, and other perquisites of office also operate to introduce an element of conservative bias in many Third World countries.

Fifth, there is the bureaucratic aversion to risk-taking. Even regimes led or supported by military radicals have (in more than a few instances) been deposed or otherwise coerced into "moderating" their economic policies and toning down their nationalism. As occurred during the 1970s in Egypt, Peru, Portugal, and to a lesser extent recently in Algeria, radical officers have been supplanted by more conservative factions whose policies promised greater rapport with the interests of transnational corporations and their local representatives. Finally, the assumption of administrative responsibility for economic development implies the acceptance of new missions for which many officers have little training, experience, or attraction. Furthermore, these activities, because of their civilian and economically mundane aura, have often been the object of disdain by those socialized into the martial ethos and its heroic self-image. Such "traditional" attitudes are probably more prevalent among senior officers who are older and co-opted from combat specialties.[23]

The foregoing survey of antiradical influences is presented only for the purpose of explaining why the failure of dependent capitalism to spur development has not already led to a greater number of radical military regimes in the Third World. Thompson(1973:44), as we saw in Chapter 2, found only 8 percent of Third World coups from 1946–70 were "strikingly reformist" in terms of grievances. These factors predispose a substantial majority of politicized officers toward suppressing both radical counterparts and socialist or populist mass movements. This, of course, does not exhaust the range of antiradical influences. Others, such as the problematic economic performance of many shortlived state capitalist regimes, "subimperial" or U.S.-backed proxy interventions, unusual economic performance, and the efficacy of the CIA—heretofore unheralded in many cases—might be added.[34] Despite them, quite a few radical officers have emerged and at times won varying degrees of rank and file support.[35] And for the reasons delineated, we can expect more in the future.[36]

Marx would not have foreclosed the possibility of at least minority sectors of the military class developing entrepreneurial or management skills sufficient to initiate a capital accumulation process in lieu of a nonmodernizing or dependent and largely commercial "national" bourgeoisie. A state capitalist regime of this sort could be, as I have argued, reconciled with his "materialist conception of history." Roughly a century after Marx wrote, military leftists are attempting a distinct yet analogous developmental "function" which resembles yet differs in crucial respects from that performed by Louis Napoleon's autonomous "bureaucratic military" regime.[37] As will be made clear in Chapter 9, these radical military experiments are unstable because corporate loyalty, intramilitary weakness, and/or ideological ambivalence prevents radicals from purging "moderate" fellow-officers who seek to limit the state role, and in some cases (Adams, 1975:127–28) use their positions to acquire agricultural or other investments. This of course was the Turkish experience and one that Trimberger(1977) views as the most probable pattern of military-led state capitalist development elsewhere.[38] Certainly policy shifts away during the 1970s from state capitalism toward a mix with greater monopoly capitalist elements in such countries as Egypt, Sudan, Portugal, and Peru are indicative of this instability, as are the reactionary coups referred to earlier in this chapter.

On the other hand, just as Western intervention endeavors to strengthen such factions and tendencies, we must recognize that state socialist countries whose regimes differ markedly from the "pure" state capitalist model are also supporting and encouraging more "extreme" military factions.[39] Even though Marxist-oriented officers such as Siad Barre, Ngouabi, Mengistu, Kerekou and Ratsiraka—a handful within the radical minority—have upon occasion insisted that they were instituting a socio-economic order inspired by principles of "scientific socialism," such pretensions are properly classified as utopian. It is one thing for the military class to endeavor to direct an industrialization process, but quite another for it to introduce socialism which itself presupposed civilian supremacy and a democratization of the military bureaucracy. The wage earning industrial and agrarian workers were to promote further development themselves through civilian political parties or governmental processes that were under their day-to-day control. Socialism, in short, implied democratic mass control for Marx—and nothing less.[40] Its rhetoric notwithstanding then, a military-dominated state capitalist system is at best likely to accumulate industrial capital, promote national control over the economy, and of course create a modern proletariat. At worst, it will fail in this mission for one or more of the reasons already mentioned. In either case, it will at some point confront a contradiction between the new mode of production and an underutilized potential in the forces of production.[41] While a total—or what seems more common—partial reversion to monopoly capitalist dependency constitutes one "reactionary" outcome in the short run, a state-socialist alternative may be another. The latter implies a coalition between an armed Marxist-Leninist movement and a socialist officer faction that has responded favorably to Marxist ideology. No social revolution has succeeded (Chorley, 1971; Russell, 1974) in the absence of military defection or neutralization (i.e., disunity, command structure breakdown, defeat, etc.).

While state socialist systems share two key characteristics with military state capitalist regimes (state control of the means of production and bureaucratic class rule), they also differ in several key respects, all of which are important from a Marxian standpoint. Of especial importance is the utilization of economic surplus primarily if not exclusively for productive investment rather than ruling class consumption, civilian party supremacy, and Marxist ideology with its commitment to democratic values.[42] At the risk of appearing dogmatic, I contend it is very unlikely that a fully socialist—and therefore democratic—system can be created under the aegis of a radical military regime. One of the signal failures of such systems has been their inability to develop mass civilian participation or mobilizational party systems. On the other hand, Leninist state socialist systems provide the civilian organizational vehicles, the ideological legitimacy, mass social welfare improvements, and the economic development that gradually create the material conditions and propitious cultural environment for subsequent attempts to establish workers' control. Even these systems which have, for the most part, subordinated the military elite to a civilian political class may revert in some measure toward the state capitalist variant as seems to have occurred in the Yugoslav case.

Concluding Remarks

The foregoing exposition, which has perhaps unduly highlighted the ambiguities and empirically open character of Marx's "materialist conception of history," explains in part why dissensus as well as general paradigmatic agreement characterize the work of contemporary Marxian analysts. Insofar as underdevelopment is concerned, many theorists take the position: 1) that this situation is a consequence of exogenous intrusions, i.e., Western imperialism; and 2) that it can be negated only by introducing a (state) socialist mode of production.

In support of this view, it is commonly maintained (Johnson, 1968-69; Rhodes, 1970; Frank, 1972; Mittelman, 1975; Sklar, 1976) that potentially developmental national bourgeois classes are either nonexistent or in the final stages of subordination to transnational corporations, i.e., "the world capitalist system." Further, bureaucratic elites, including the military, are by definition incapable of functioning as an autonomous class vis á vis the capitalist and landowning classes. Bureaucratic authoritarianism, high compensation, fringe benefits and perquisites of office, socio-economic interaction at higher levels with property-owning classes, and concomitant propensities toward various corrupt practices are held to predispose such elites toward subordination.[44] Marxists inclined toward "structuralism" maintain that, short of socialist revolution, the state must function in a dependent manner because of the objective necessities or laws of capitalism within the societies or, more commonly, those operating on a world level. Thus, from an orthodox Marxist standpoint, as Kennedy(1974:59-60) points out:

This view of the army as an agency of modernisation is challenged by those who exclude the idea of independent social forces other than the bourgeoisie in the early period of industrial capitalism or the proletariat in the 20th century. What this view boils down to is this: that the only progressive social force is the political movement which "represents" the historical interests of the latter-day proletariat, that is, the Marxist revolutionaries. There is inevitably bitter disagreement among Marxists as to which of the "Marxist parties truly represents the proletariat's interests. If this question is indeterminate it reduces the concept of an "historical force" in the form of a Marxist party to the level of a myth agreed upon by its exponents.

Hence, performance rather than a priori deduction is the only empirical or scientific means of resolving this dilemma.

Despite a legacy of short-lived radical regimes, others within the Marxian tradition like Woddis(1977) adopt a more sanguine and longer historical perspective that does not necessarily counterpose armed socialist revolutionary struggle to the alternative of stagnation and dependency. Openness to other alternatives is quite consistent with Marx's increasingly empirical bent and his aversion to "supra-historical" orthodoxy. Further, I have argued that the radical or state capitalist developmental strategy can be reconciled with his general emphasis upon malutilization of existing productive resources given a prevailing organization of the economy at a particular time in history. The fact that such contradictions are increasingly perceived in the Third World and are slowly being reflected by movement in the state capitalist direction as well as in the appearance of new radical regimes — some led by prestige-oriented military officers — implies the need for theoretical circumspection and revision. Except for identifying the "main outlines" of an epoch, Marx held that middle range or particular theories had to be developed and revised in light of varying human responses to the historical challenges confronting each generation. McQuarie(1978), for example, stresses Marx's empirical method of "successive approximations" following initial identifications of a "central tendency" in relationships. This approach could and did lead him to reassess his own predictions. Especially relevant to the growing appeal of state capitalism was Marx's initially sanguine view of 19th century capitalist diffusion under the aegis of the British Empire. Considerations of its actual impact upon Ireland led him (Mohri, 1979:32–42) to regard imperialism as an an obstacle to Third World development rather than a process with both negative and equally significant positive by-products (see note 22).

From the standpoint of Marx's socialist goal, of course, it is quite clear that neither officers nor civilian radicals can act as surrogates for proletarians who are as nascent as a class as the national bourgeoisie is nonhegemonic. Yet the military may still have at least limited "radical chains" derived from their esteem and professional needs as well as from the standpoint of more material interests, especially those of a long-run nature. The relative paucity of military radicalism is accounted for by a broad range of constraining forces at the transnational, systemic, institutional, subinstitutional, and of course individual levels. These have been identified rather than analyzed at length here for two reasons. First, they were discussed in Chapter 2. Second, my focus has been upon general or structural (McFarland, 1969:125–42) tendencies that account for the emergence and slowly growing Third World appeal of state capitalism ("socialism"). Even though the performance of such regimes is uneven and unspectacular on most economic indices, I think it would be premature, even dogmatic, to define this alternative to bourgeois control over the means of production out of existence as a viable option in the contemporary world.[45] A few have survived destabilization attempts for almost two decades and, as the changing world balance of power continues to erode the traditional hegemony of the advanced capitalist states, one might predict the emergence of new radical military regimes and that more of these struggles to attain national dignity and development will endure for sufficient time to effect a significant expansion in heretofore underutilized forces of production.

Whether they do will be influenced not merely by leadership capacity, cohesion, and a favorable international environment. At bottom, both survival and extension of military state capitalism hinges upon the socioeconomic performance of such regimes. Magdoff(1978:1–7) and many other Marxist social scientists regard the "radical" or "non-capitalist road" to development as historically unviable. Thus Woddis(1977:90) cautions that:

All experience shows that, at best, radical military regimes can play an objectively progressive role at a certain stage of national development; but this can only be a temporary phase, short or long. If military leaders do not deliberately pave the way for democratic civilian rule, with deeper and more fundamental social and economic programmes, they will inevitably come into conflict with the rising social forces or become the victims of a preemptive coup by more right-wing military elements who seek to prevent the assumption of power by the more progressive forces of the nation, and to swing the regime back decisively into the camp of imperialism and domestic reaction.

Before assessing the validity of this pessimistic prognosis, it may be useful to compare the performance of state capitalism with that of other developmental approaches discussed in this book. The following chapter summarizes a number of empirical studies on the impact of military rule. Then I compare a range of empirical indicators which not only distinguish military from civilian performance, but also reveal varying political and socio-economic performance patterns for not only the state capitalist, but also the state socialist and monopoly capitalist systems in the Third World.

Notes

1. Exemplary of this Marxian empirical tradition—one which note 5 indicates Marx himself was strongly committed to—are such Anglo-American journals as: *Monthly Review; Socialist Revolution; Politics & Society; Kapitalstate; Insurgent Socialist; Critique; Socialist Register; New Left Review; Economy and Society; Marxist Perspectives; New Political Science.*

2. In the following section of this chapter, his general theory of societal change—sometimes referred to as historical materialism or more often in his own words as "the materialist conception of history"—is summarized. It may be distinguished from various "special" or intermediate range theories which he elaborated, such as those dealing with capitalist development within Western Europe, the role of the state, or the impact of colonial expansion. Similarly, it should not be confused with his empirical methodological approach which is incisively described by McQuarie(1978:218-33).

3. A number of the more outstanding dependency studies are referred to in note 23, and in Chapter 8.

4. Most such studies conclude however that autonomy exists only with respect to particular capitalist class sectors and not insofar as its general bourgeois class interests are concerned. Among the most incisive of these analyses are those of Miliband(1969); Offe(1972); Weinstein(1968); O'Connor(1973); and Poulantzas(1973).

5. Thus in his 1877 *Reply to Mikhailovsky* (McLellan, 1974:135-36), Marx cautions

> now what application to Russia could my critic make of this historical sketch? Only this: If Russia is tending to become a capitalist nation after the example of the Western European countries—and during the last few years she has been taking a lot of trouble in this direction—she will not succeed without having first transformed a good part of her peasants into proletarians; and after that, once taken to the bosom of the capitalist regime, she will experience its pitiless laws like other profane peoples. That is all. But that is too little for my critic. He feels he absolutely must metamorphose my historical sketch of the genesis of capitalism in Western Europe into a historico-philosophic theory of the general path every people is fated to tread, whatever the historical circumstances in which it finds itself. . . . Let us take an example. . . . Thus events strikingly analogous but taking place in different historical surroundings lead to totally different results. By studying each of these forms of evolution separately and then comparing them one can easily find the clue to this phenomenon, but one will never arrive there by using as one's master key a general historico-philosophical theory, the supreme virtue of which consists in being suprahistorical.

The consistency of this historical and comparative orientation with the so-called young Marx is apparent from this 1846 *German Ideology* (McLellan, 1974:191) excerpt:

> Empirical observation must in each separate instance bring out empirically, and without any mystification and speculation, the connection of the social and political structure with production. The social structure and the State are continually evolving out of the life process of definite individuals, but of individuals, not as they may appear in their own or other people's imagination, but as they really are; i.e., as they operate, produce materially, and hence as they work under definite material limits, presuppositions and conditions independent of their will.

6. My interpretations are based in part upon the work of McLellan(1974), and in lesser measure upon Avineri(1969).

7. While the textual passages reprinted by McLellan(1974:152-65) and Marx's overall approach support such a conceptualization based upon conflict and its necessary precondi-

tion, consciousness, it is equally true that sometimes Marx used the term simply as an empirical referent to groups which often were occupational in nature and/or exhibited distinct life styles. These included "peasants," "middle classes," "financial" as distinguished from "industrial capitalists," "national class," "ideological classes," "lower middle class" or "petite bourgeoisie," and of course "lumpen proletariat." Although in his theory of European capitalist development Marx predicted that gradually two major polarized classes would emerge, he never limited himself to a two class model in analyzing the evolution or conflicts of particular societies.

8. Avineri(1969:79-86,183-84,215-21).

9. His rejection of voluntaristic idealism as well as historical or economic determinism is elucidated in several early works. Thus in 1846 *German Ideology* (McLellan, 1974:129), Marx stresses

> that [in history] at each stage there is found a material result: a sum of productive forces, a historically created relation of individuals to nature and to one another, which is handed down to each generation from its predecessor; a mass of productive forces, capital funds and conditions, which, on the one hand is indeed modified by the new generation, but also on the other prescribes for it its conditions of life and gives it a definite development, a special character. It shows that circumstances make men just as men make circumstances.

A year earlier in *The Holy Family,* (McLellan, 1974:125), Marx had sharply impugned the reified historicism of his Young Hegelian protagonists by admonishing that

> history does nothing; it does not possess immense riches, it does not fight battles. It is men, real, living men, who do all this, who possess things and fight battles. It is not "history" which uses men as a means of achieving—as if it were an individual person—its own ends. History is nothing but the activity of men in pursuit of their ends.

During the same year, in his third *Thesis on Feuerbach* (McLellan, 1974:124), Marx dissociated himself from crudely determinist materialism by cautioning that "the materialist doctrine concerning the changing of circumstances and upbringing forgets that circumstances are changed by man and the educator must himself be educated." These views, it might be added, are quite consistent with Engels' observation (McLellan, 1974:124) decades later that

> Marx and I are ourselves partly to blame for the fact that the younger people sometimes lay more stress on the economic side than is due to it. We had to emphasize the main principle vis-á-vis our adversaries, who denied it, and we had not always time, the place, or the opportunity to give their due to the other elements involved in the interaction. But when it came to presenting a section of history, that is, to making a practical application, it was a different matter and there no error was permissible.

10. Thus, in one rather categorical statement which appears particularly relevant to the rise of left-wing military regimes, Marx noted that

> the state cannot abolish the contradiction which exists between the role and good intentions of the administration on the one hand and the means at its disposal on the other, without abolishing itself, for it rests on this contradiction. It rests on the contrast between public and private life, on the contrast between general and particular interests. The administration must therefore limit itself to a formal and negative activity, for its power ceases just where civil life and work begin. Indeed, in the face of the consequences that spring from the unsocial nature of this civil life, this private property, this commerce, this industry, this reciprocal plundering of different civil

groups, in the face of these consequences, impotence is the natural law of the administration. . . . If the modern state wished to do away with the impotence of its administration, it would have to do away with the contemporary private sphere. . . . *Critical Notes on "The King of Prussia and Social Reform"* (McLellan, 1974:189–90).

11. Such historically observed West European state roles are referred to in Marx's *Review of E. Girardin's Socialism and Taxes, The Communist Manifesto,* his other writings as cited by McLellan(1974:162–63,192) and Avineri(1969:170). Elsewhere in his *German Ideology* and *Address on the Civil War in France,* Marx acknowledged that the state performed allocative or distributive functions with respect to intracapitalist conflicts, and of course general police or order-maintaining activities which would not necessarily evaporate when bourgeois hegemony was ended. Again it is crucial to stress that he was open-minded about state roles in the future because methodologically Marx did not believe that theorizing in his era could do more than predict general trends. His rejection of utopian idealism explains the absence of detailed models of future social organization. Hence, the specific contours of future societies could only become an object of theory after subsequent historical developments were known. This clause, ongoing, and reciprocal relationship between theory and contemporaneous conflictual activity is often referred to as Praxis.

12. This range of possibilities is recognized on historical grounds in *The Class Struggles in France, The Eighteenth Brumaire of Louis Bonaparte,* his *Review of E. Girardin's Socialism and Taxes,* and in *The Civil War in France.* (McLellan, 1974:182–83; Avineri, 1969:50–1).

13. With the possible exception of several historical Asian cases where the state directly controlled the means of production (i.e., land, irrigation, etc.), Marx regarded the independence of the state as temporary, necessary to the maintenance of bourgeois control over the economy and the latter's growth, and ultimately then more nominal then real. Furthermore, there is no doubt that in his analysis of European capitalist development such cases were regarded as exceptional. Thus, the key to genuine independence for the state is direct control over the means of production. While in his own epoch Marx did not anticipate such an eventuality short of a socialist revolution, it is worth stressing that his conclusions were empirically derived from the history of Napoleon II's regime, its emergence, and the short-lived aftermath known as the Paris Commune. The last-mentioned case was treated by Marx as fully rather than spuriously independent even though it was not socialist (it retained private ownership of the means of production). Thus a city state ruled by a petit bourgeois-working class coalition represented at least one historically derived option. In Marx's view, its defeat became highly probable after the National Guard failed to take the offensive following Thiers' initial withdrawal from the city. Yet even if the Commune had avoided the siege and somehow neutralized the Prussians, there is no doubt that eventually continued state independence would have necessitated some form of social ownership. Thus in *The Eighteenth Brumaire* (Tucker, 1972:522), written some two decades before the destruction of the Commune, Marx predicted:

as the executive authority which has made itself an independent power, Bonaparte feels it to be his mission to safeguard "civil order." But the strength of this civil order lies in the middle class. He looks on himself, therefore, as the representative of the middle class and issues decrees in this sense. Nevertheless, he is somebody solely due to the fact that he has broken the political power of this middle class and daily breaks it anew. Consequently, he looks on himself as the adversary of the political and literary power of the middle class. But by protecting its material power, he generates its political power anew.

Fear of such a trend—evidenced by widespread "corruption of hardened Bolsheviks" — played a significant role (Ticktin, 1976:29) in the Soviet decision to terminate the NEP in 1928.

14.

> This parasitical excrescence upon civil society, pretending to be its ideal counterpart, grew to its full development under the sway of the first Bonaparte. . . . But the state parasite received only its last development during the Second Empire. The governmental power with its standing army, its all-directing bureaucracy, its stultifying clergy and its servile tribunal hierarchy had grown so independent of society itself, that a grotesque mediocre adventurer with a hungry band of desperadoes behind him sufficed to wield it. . . . Humbling under its sway even the interests of the ruling classes, whose parliamentary show work it supplanted by self-elected Corps Legislatifs and self-paid senates . . . the state power had received its last and supreme expression in the Second Empire. Apparently the final victory of this governmental power over society, it was in fact the orgy of all the corrupt elements of that society. To the eye of the uninitiated it appeared only as the victory of the Executive over the Legislative, of the final defeat of the form of class rule pretending to be autocracy of society by its form pretending to be a superior power to society. But in fact it was only the last degraded and the only possible form of that class ruling, as humiliating to those classes as to the working classes which they kept fettered by it. As quoted in Avineri(1969:50–1).

15. By "radical chains" Marx meant the class possessed a general material interest in economic restructuring. Thus socialism would reduce the economic insecurity of the workers, bring about a rise in their living standards, and of course their social status. This could only be accomplished when workers became conscious that economic restructuring required political action directed at overthrowing the state whose essential characteristic was repressiveness, i.e., it safe-guarded bourgeois control over the means of production. The only class allies that Marx envisaged were agricultural laborers, a sector of the declining petite bourgeoisie and some bourgeois intellectuals. While no mention was made of military officers, in the next section of this chapter, I shall argue that those who have opted for state capitalist developmentalism can nevertheless be regarded as having limited though genuine "radical chains" of their own.

16. This is consonant with his general theory of historical change that holds

> at a certain stage of their development the material forces of production in society come into conflict with the existing relations of production, or — what is but a legal expression for the same thing — with the property relations within which they had been at work before. From forms of development of the forces of production these relations turn into their fetters. Then comes the period of social revolution. (McLellan, 1974:196).

17. Such contemporary civil-military relations theorists as Chorley(1943), Kling(1956), Vagts(1959), Needler(1966), Huntington(1968), Nun(1969), and Nordlinger(1970) also tend to interpret military interests as generally hostile to mass socio-economic demands in the underdeveloped areas. While Nun stresses middle class reference groups as the key explanatory variable, neither Huntington nor Nordlinger limit themselves to this factor. The latter adds such professional values as order and hierarchy while the former stresses extra-military environments characterized by a decline in procedural legitimacy when at a certain stage of development political institutions lack the extractive capability to process increased demands occasioned by the entry of new aspirant groups into the system.

18. Of 73 coups which occurred between 1950 and 1970 in Africa, Asia, and the Middle East, only 29 could be classified (Wolpin, 1973:123–24) as ideological. The latter were

coups involving policy shifts toward either foreign investors and/or nonalignment. Thompson(1973) found only 40 percent of 226 coups from 1946–70 in the Third World involved ideology to a significant degree.

19. McLellan(1974:183–84). Immediately prior to the passage quoted in note 14, Marx observes that "every minor solitary interest engendered by the relations of social groups was separated from society itself, fixed and made independent of it and opposed to it in the form of state interest, administered by state priests with exactly determined hierarchical functions." Although Marx does not refer to bureaucratic "priests" or "parasites" with the term "class" as I have here, he does use that word flexibly to refer to other groups and upon those occasions when he is referring to autonomous state bureaucracies he does resort to the term "caste." This occurs when he refers to the Prussian state in his 1843 *Critique of Hegel's Philosophy of Right,* as it does nine years later in *The Eighteenth Brumaire of Louis Bonaparte* wherein he observes that

> an enormous bureaucracy, well-dressed and well-fed, is the "idee napoleonienne" which is most congenial of all to the second Bonaparte. How could it be otherwise, seeing that alongside the actual classes of society, he is forced to create an artificial caste, for which the maintenance of his regime becomes a bread-and-butter question? Accordingly, one of his first financial operations was the raising of officials' salaries to their old level again and the creation of new sinecures.

And again some twenty years later in his *Drafts for the Civil War in France,* the term "caste" is used with the same frame of reference. McLellan(1974:183,193); Tucker(1972:520).

20. Tanahill(1976:233–44). From 1948–67, the same author also found substantially greater use of government sanctions (i.e., repressive acts) by South American military regimes, a larger proportion of revenues generated by indirect taxes, lower percentages of budgets allocated to social welfare and little apparent difference in budgetary shares for the armed forces. Yet with respect to the last mentioned datum, he proffers the following plausible — if difficult to document — explanation:

> while military rulers might be relatively unconcerned with increasing the size of the armed forces, as we found above, would they not be interested in increasing its slice of the budgetary pie? Certainly so. The anomaly likely results from two factors. First, military appropriations can be hidden in several budgetary categories (Weaver, 1973:64) and thus the official figures may be misleading. Secondly, incumbent civilians may find it expedient to buy off the military. There is evidence for this in Table 2 in that the two countries with the least threat of military intervention during the period, Chile and Uruguay, also had two of the lower average defense budgets proportionally speaking.

21. *Address on the Civil War in France* (Tucker, 1972:553).

22. This benign perspective upon what Marxists today call the dependency or "diffusion model" is I think unduly emphasized by Avineri(1969:163–71). For, insofar as economic development was concerned, Marx envisaged the necessity of either revolution in the center or a successful anti-imperialist struggle in the periphery. Foreign investment within the relationships structured by colonial dependency could do no more than lay the basis for full industrialization. Thus, in his perspicacious 1853 tract on *The Future Results of British Rule in India* (Tucker, 1972:586–87), Marx is explicit in warning that

> all the English bourgeoisie may be forced to do will neither emancipate nor materially mend the social condition of the mass of the people, depending not only on the development of the productive powers, but on their appropriation by the people. But what they will not fail to do is to lay down the material premises for both. Has

the bourgeoisie ever done more? Has it ever affected a progress without dragging individuals and peoples through blood and dirt, through misery and degradation? The Indians will not reap the fruits of the new elements of society scattered among them by the British bourgeoisie, till in Great Britain itself the now ruling class shall have been supplanted by the industrial proletariat, or till the Hindoos themselves shall have grown strong enough to throw off the English yoke altogether. At all events, we may safely expect to see, at a more or less remote period, the regeneration of that great and interesting country. . . .

23. Because these issues have been given considerable publicity over the past ten years as a consequence of demands made by a majority of Third World nations at the U.N. and in various international conferences, I assume general familiarity with them. Some of the better Marxian treatments of the relationships include those by: Baran(1962); Frank(1967); Magdoff(1969); Horowitz(1969); Jalee(1969); Rhodes(1970); Amin(1974); Wallerstein (1976); Girvan(1978); Magdoff(1978).

The uses of the term "dependency" vary, but all imply the subordination of domestic economic and often other policies to the approval of external governments and transnational corporations due to their control over export markets, investment capital and the ability to import as a consequence of pre-existing import/export structures, associated terms of trade deterioration and the growing need for loans, credits and grants to compensate for this. See note 29.

24. See Jalee(1969) for data on the 1950s. According to the U.N.(1974), the annual average rate of per capita growth in Gross Domestic Product—which includes that contributed by foreign investment—for the 1960-72 period was: 3.8 percent for Developed Market Economies; 2.7 percent for Developing Market Economies; and 5.7 percent for Centrally Planned Economies.

25. Serious analyses of the "open door" and its sources are provided by Williams(1962), Gardner(1964), Kolko(1968), Hayter(1971). A November 10, 1976 dispatch from Cairo to the *New York Times* underlines the contemporary relevance of this perspective:

a new Cabinet involving major changes in Egypt's economic leadership but none in political figures was sworn in today by president Anwar el-Sadat. Dr. Abdel Moneim el-Kaissouny, Chairman of the Arab International Bank, was named a Deputy Prime Minister for financial and economic affairs. The post, which places Dr. Kaissouny above four Cabinet ministers dealing with economic matters, did not exist in the previous Cabinet. Dr. Kaissouny, who held the same Cabinet economic position in the 1960s under President Gamal Abdel Nasser, is known and respected in Western economic circles as an advocate of fiscal restraint. Western sources said that Dr. Kaissouny, as an informal advisor to President Sadat, was one of the founders of the "open door policy" announced by the President in 1973 to encourage foreign investment in Egypt. Cf. Fagen(1979).

26. The difficulties of developing such consciousness at the mass level—even in the absence of repression—appear to have been as underestimated by Marx as they have been exaggerated by some of his more brilliant contemporary followers. See, for example, the incisive if pessimistic analysis of legitimacy at the mass level in advanced capitalist societies by Mueller(1975).

27. Thus, the three dimensions of Marx's "materialist conception of history" help us analyze this phenomenon: 1) the contradiction between an existing organization of production and the potential which inheres in the forces or means of production; 2) a class whose socio-economic interests would be enhanced by changing the organization of production; and 3) the importance of assessing material conditions in any consideration of the viability or probability of altering the mode of production.

28. During the two decades from 1953 until 1973, quite a few radical regimes — some military-led and others with varying degrees of intramilitary support — have existed and been overthrown: Mossadegh; Arbenz; Peron; Bosch; Kassem; Goulart; Sukarno; Torres; Nkrumah; Keita; Allende; Velazco. To this one might add the shifts which occured in Egypt, Sudan and Syria during the 1970-72 period, those of Peru and Portugal in 1975, and Somalia in the late 1970s. Regardless of the vulnerability of such regimes to externally backed military subversion, it is important to recognize that such radicalism keeps reappearing because of an accentuating contradiction between the widening development gap associated with dependence upon foreign capital and the potential for closing that gap by exercising control over the means of production. Thus, despite the "destabilization" of the regimes listed above, a glance at the contemporary horizon indicates that at least ten and conceivably up to to twenty such "radical" states continue to lighten the horizon: Tanzania; Congo; Guinea; Afghanistan; Algeria; Iran; Guyana; South Yemen; Malagasy; Libya; Nicaragua; Ethiopia; Mali; Burma; Angola; Guinea-Bissau; Mozambique; Grenada; Zimbabwe.

While the radicalism of such regimes is controversial — many Marxists share a sense of skepticism with their pro-capitalist antagonists in the West — I justify the term on the following grounds: 1) they tend to be so depicted by their own elites and by those in the West both in mass communications media and in official pronouncements; 2) they have actively sought to dissociate themselves from alignment and its concomitant dependency upon Western nations; 3) they have rejected a pattern of deference to foreign investors in favor of attempting to impose conditions and controls extending in more than a few instances to expropriations — the timing or terms of which were objectionable to the corporations; 4) they have allowed Marxists liberty to organize a mass constituency and/or have attempted to deliver immediate welfare benefits to at least some mass sectors. While all of the regimes may not share the four characteristics, most of them conform to at least three of the four criteria. Hence, regardless of their deficiencies — some of which will be discussed in Chapter 9 — I believe it is useful to differentiate them from what are eumphemistically termed "moderate" regimes in the West. See also note 39 for system classifications.

29. These have been occasioned not only by changes in the level of economic activity in advanced capitalist states, but increasingly by foreign exchange deficits due to declining terms of trade and large net capital outflows. Consequently, external indebtedness has with the exception of the major OPEC producers risen to unprecedented levels, thus deepening the dependency and increasing the humiliation of the status quo. A look at the dimensions of this crisis is provided by Cheryl Payer(1976:5) when she notes

> the total debt owed by Third World countries to national governments, international agencies, commercial banks, and other private lenders is likewise a matter of guess-work, but all the guesses are very large. *Business Week* puts the total at $130 billion. Somewhat more precise are the figures for the annual payments deficits of non-oil-producing developing countries: these mounted from $9 billion in 1973 to $28 billion in 1974 and $38 billion in 1975. For this year the deficit is expected to fall to "only" $31 billion, but even so, no one seems to know exactly where the money is going to come from. The executive director of Chase Manhattan's London bank appraised the total debt of Third World countries at $145 billion in December 1975, and estimates that $150 billion more will be needed to cover deficits from 1976 through 1980.

With respect to capital outflows, see Barnet and Muller(1974:152-62), and Girvan(1978).

30. Such "defensive modernization" is intended to maximize the power of the state vis-á-vis other states. Officers who have studied or otherwise enjoyed lengthy or varied exposures over time to industrially advanced societies are likely to be professionally superior (Dishman, 1979) to their national counterparts and to experience such discontent.

31. See note 39.

32. Klare(1972); Wolpin(1973); Etchison(1975). Cf. Price(1971).

33. While many of these characteristics are less pronounced at middle and especially junior officer ranks, successful coups by the latter are far less probable than by senior headquarters' officers (Thompson, 1976:263).

34. Fortunately, the number of serious or authoritative accounts of such C.I.A. roles has increased substantially in recent years. Some of the better ones are provided by: Marchetti and Marks(1974); Agee(1975; 1975a); Borosage and Marks(1976); Lemarchand (1976). All of these treat military coups as one among several mechanisms of external intervention. Cf. Wolpin(1973), and Watson(1977).

35. A systematic investigation could probably double or even triple the following list of prominent military radicals who have appeared and sometimes headed regimes in the underdeveloped areas since the 1930s: Arbenz; Kassem; Boumedienne; Cardenas; Ngouabi; Camaano; Sabri; Prats; de Carvalho; Prestes; Alves; Siad Barre; Mercado Jarrin; Velazco; Torres; Sanchez; Bachelet; Barwah; Dhani; Untung; Lister; Nasser; Kedafi; Torrijos; Prestes; Yon Sosa; Turcios; Peron; Mengistu; Abdul Qadir; Torres; Ratsiraka.

36. Naturally, much remains to be learned about why such officers are predisposed to internalize radical outlooks and how this process occurs. Although some recent research (Needler, 1964:45; Abrahamsson, 1972:42,102–3; Kourvetaris and Dobratz, 1973) casts doubt upon the relevance of social origins, these and other variables associated with career experiences, internal socialization, interaction with nonmilitary elements, etc., require systematic investigation. See Wolpin(1981).

37. With however certain rather important historical differences. The regime in 19th century France did not have to play a national major directive economic role because that country: 1) possessed a dynamic entrepreneurial bourgeoisie in Paris and other northern urban areas; 2) was not technologically far behind other modern industrial nations; 3) benefited from a growing colonial empire abroad through access to cheap raw materials, outlets for surplus population and markets. The absence of these conditions and the diffusion of socialist or state developmentalist ideas accounts in large part for this new orientation manifested by internal efforts to extend state control over the means of production and external challenges to pre-existing economic dependency relations.

38. Trimberger's(1977) historical analysis of several developmental ("revolutions from above") military-led regimes – Japan, Turkey, Egypt, and Peru – lays heavy stress upon the existence of all of the following four conditions: a) social isolation of the officers from a declining landed upper class; b) a centralized state bureaucratic apparatus; c) an indigenous nationalist movement; and d) international room for maneuver. Although she was properly pessimistic with respect to ultimate goal fulfillment by the Velasco regime in Peru and presumably analogous contemporary state capitalist approaches, elsewhere Horowitz and Trimberger(1976:40–43) appear somewhat more optimistic concerning military developmental capabilities and believe that military autonomy and economic nationalism are the order of the day in Latin America. Philip(1976) argues that the Peruvian and presumably other examples of military radicalism are best explained by unique conjunctures of historical influences. Thus in addition to noting the absence of a threatening leftist mass movement, the failure of prior reform programs and not least the overbearing behavior of the U.S. and the I.P.C., Philip adds "French influence" at the CAEM (war college) and associated exposure to the U.N. Economic Commission for Latin America's sharp critique of the developmental prospects of the "open door" approach. Cf. Monteforte Toledo(1970).

39. Because of the plethora of works and publicity in the United States as well as other Western nations on Soviet or other Eastern "meddling" in Third World nations, I have not felt it necessary to dwell upon such intervention in this book. Some of the more useful sources analyzing both Eastern and Western activities are those by Cottam(1967), Leitenberg and Sheffer(1979), and Volman(1980).

40. Thus in his 1879 *Circular Letter* against reformism, Marx denounced (McLellan, 1974:178) at the same time the paternalism of many Social Democrats: "the emancipation of the working classes must be conquered by the working classes themselves. We cannot therefore co-operate with people who openly state that the workers are too uneducated to emancipate themselves and must be freed from above by philanthropic big bourgeois and petty bourgeois." Elsewhere both McLellan(1974:172–74,210) and particularly Avineri (1969:182–84) establish Marx's hostility to authoritarianism on the left. Thus Marx did anticipate the possibility—if not desirability—of authoritarian socialism where low pre-existing development of the forces of production and proletarian cultural levels constitute major impediments to democracy. In such circumstances material scarcity would catalyze class conflict as hegemonic factions endeavored to appropriate surplus from the producing classes.

41. The source of this contradiction will be the tendency for military and subordinate bureaucratic classes to appropriate for their own consumption increasing investible shares of economic surplus generated by the economy. Stratification initially based to a great extent upon superior power and function will be transformed into privilege due to the absence of a anticonsumerist ideology and mass accountability.

42. Even if routines in the contemporary era generally deviate from such values in varying degree, Marx's 1871 *Address on the Civil War in France,* his statement the following year on *The Alleged Splits in the International,* and the sources referred to in note 40 above leave little reason to doubt that socialism was synonomous with the socialist democracy.

43. Based upon a general reading of Marxist literature in this area, it seems that the points of disagreement center upon: 1) the effects of capitalist penetration into peripheral regions; 2) whether a truly national bourgeoisie exists in most of these countries; 3) the potential or viability of radical state capitalist developmentalism; 4) whether the change in the world balance of power and domestic environments imply a substantial probability that guerrilla warfare or other violent forms of struggle would be successful. Andre Gunder Frank(1976), for example, contends that state capitalist regimes are too vulnerable to subversion by monopoly capitalist elements to offer a viable developmental alternative to socialist revolution. Szymanski(1976), on the other hand, argues that data on foreign investment, dependency, and growth are not wholly consonant with Frank's(1967) theory of underdevelopment. In general, those who attribute essentially negative effects to foreign investment also deny the existence of a national bourgeoisie, the feasibility of state capitalist options—military or civilian—and maintain that the entire repressive apparatus of the state must be destroyed to unfetter the forces of production.

44. A MERIP(1976:8–9) report may be suggestive:

the little-publicized Syrian "opening" to the West has had similar consequences to Egypt's famous "opening!" "A new middle class has grown up in the shadow of the Baathists. Because it was able to adapt itself to the system we installed, it has become richer and larger than the old owning class," the minister in charge of the economy has been quoted as saying. Corruption within the government is also rampant, generally taking the form of real estate speculation, and the dolce vita has replaced the austerity of "Arab socialism." The bigger hotels, high-priced restaurants, cabarets and discotheques are always full.

45. It seems that, given the lead time necessary for a "learning curve" and to compensate for transitional costs associated with reorganizing traditional structures (e.g., capital flight, administrative disorganization, etc.), most of these state capitalist regimes have not existed for the twenty to thirty years that are probably required to assess the underlying viability of this development strategy. Thus, on the basis of U.N.(1975) compilations, the average an-

nual percent increase in per capita GNP between 1961 and 1970 was only 1.3 percent for the following thirteen countries which during that period tended to be state capitalist: Algeria; Burma; Cambodia; Congo; Egypt; Guinea; Iraq; Mali; Somalia; Sudan; Syria; Uganda; Tanzania. Average industrial growth rate percentages for this group (less Guinea, Mali and Somalia) from U.N.(1974) are 9.4 percent which was 1.6 percent above that for the Third World as a whole.

7

Developmental Strategies: Cost/Benefit Comparisons

One requires neither Marx's optimism nor his humanist vision to recognize that the masses of increasing numbers of Third World countries are finally benefiting from the right to a decent life as a consequence of the diffusion of socialism. Indeed who would have predicted in 1917 the virtual collapse of all European imperial systems within a mere three generations and the spread of Marxian socialism to encompass almost half of the world?

During this post-1917 era, Marxists have played a prominent role in assuring that both national economic development and the simultaneous diffusion of welfare benefits to the masses would become paramount issues in the underdeveloped areas. U.N. General Assembly resolutions, the "Alliance for Progress," proclamations of North/South conferences and, of course, the data regularly published by the Economic and Social Council attest to the universality of such aspirations, as do the public goals of aid programmes by major donors. Needless to say, Marxists have consistently maintained that unless socialist mobilizational systems were introduced, Third World peoples would never be able to close the economic and mass welfare gap with the advanced capitalist societies of the First World. Put differently, their fate was to be haunted by the twin spectres of exploitative economic stagnation and mass margination from the benefits of modern technology.

One of the central objectives of this chapter is to assess the validity of this Marxian thesis on development and welfare. Is socialism a viable option? And if it is, has the performance of such systems really outpaced that of the others? Clearly, some analysts in the underdeveloped areas and even more in the advanced capitalist countries reject such a dichotomized alternative as a tacitly ideological oversimplification. During the 1950s, early 1960s and again with the resurgence of Cold War in the late 1970s, numerous scholarly works in the West argued that the costs which communism imposed upon present generations were excessive. Thus present generations were being "sacrificed" for future generations—witness the flight of refugees from Eastern Europe, Kampuchea, Afghanistan, Cuba, etc., and the revelations of the Stalin era. Further, they maintained that with adequate foreign aid and investment, civilian-led systems could modernize and grow incrementally until they reached the point of "take-off" into self-sustaining growth.

Gradually as authoritarian non-Communist civilian regimes replaced competitive party systems, and both sorts became increasingly haunted by the spectre of domestic militarism, the political costs to present generations became a less pronounced theme in "Western" modernization literature. While interim socio-economic burdens and political restraints upon the masses were regarded as essential to the capitalist accumulation process, economic growth and stability assumed utmost importance as preconditions to overcoming underdevelopment. Not only were Marxist-led movements regarded as a threat to this developmental strategy, but so were all "rhetorical" populists and "irresponsible" or even "nonrational" economic nationalists. By the mid-1960s, Western governments and many analysts had discovered a third option for the Third World—modernizing praetorianism. The armed forces were necessarily sensitive to external modernizing trends, manifested patriotic dedication to the "national interest," and possessed the organizational capabilities to lead their nations to the promised land.[1] One need not put up with the demagogy of electoral politics, the corruption and incompetence of civilian regimes nor allow the situation to degenerate to the point where socialist revolutionaries were offered an opportunity to destroy "Western" values. The military professionals would "keep the lid on" and nurture growth to the point where civilian policy-making could again be restored and the masses might be gradually reincorporated into the political process.

Following from this implied and frequently explicit denigration of civilian capabilities per se, a second major objective of this chapter will be to contrast the performance of military and nonsocialist civilian regimes. Is the military an actual or potential political class that can bring about more socio-economic change at less cost than the civilians they usurp? Even if one excludes civilian-led socialist systems, a number of recent analyses—to be summarized shortly—cast considerable doubt upon the thesis that military capabilities in this area are superior to those of non-Marxist civilian governments. Although not cited by him, they tend to confirm the recent conclusion of Gerald A. Heeger(1977:247–48) that:

the military decade (1965-75) that has just ended in Africa and Asia has been highly disillusioning. Contrary to most scholars' earlier depiction of the military as a highly modern force, able to transfer its organizational and technological skills to the art of governing, most military regimes have hindered the development of their countries. Explanations for their incapacity abound. Military organization is now seen as incapable of dealing with the more elusive problems of development; the military is seen as preoccupied with its own class interests; military rulers are described as so antipolitical as to frustrate their efforts to gain popular support. Regardless of the cause, the important fact is that, in the current literature, the societal and political conditions that originally fostered military intervention are seen as persisting.

Even worse (if Heeger is close to the mark) then, the 1965–74 increase in Third World military expenditures (U.S.A.C.D.A., 1976:14,54–55) from less than 25 billion to more than 50 billion in constant dollars represents for the most part a potential loss of developmental resources of considerable magnitude. So does the rise in largely unproductive armed forces from 11.2 million men to 15.6 million during the same period. Per capita military expenditures have increased from $10.25 (constant) to $16.84, while arms imports soared from $2.1 billion to $6.6 billion with little more than a third of this being accounted for by OPEC members. Finally, the societies have become somewhat more militarized as armed forces to population ratios climbed 13 percent, from 4.7 to 5.3 per thousand. Because Hibbs(1973:113) has found a positive correlation of moderate strength between high military spending and armed forces coups, the implications of this trend may be portentous even for those regimes which remain as yet under civilian leadership. Since the early 1960s, the proportion of civilian governments has of course steadily declined, so that by the early 1970s more than 40 percent of the nonsocialist Third World nations listed on Table 7.6 were military-dominated, whereas only 15 percent belonged to that category a decade earlier. By 1980 it could be said that civilian dominance had been eclipsed in a majority of these polities.

After surveying the findings of empirically oriented analysts who, upon the basis of quantitative data from the 1950–70 period, addressed themselves to aspects of Heeger's thesis, I shall present more recent performance data for the decade to which Heeger explicitly refers — 1965 to 1975. But with several differences. First, I will avoid the tacit ideological bias which accounts for the absence of explicit treatment of state socialist systems as alternatives to both military and other civilian variants. Second, nonsocialist civilian and military regimes will be subclassified according to their developmental strategies. Like civilian counterparts, some officers (as we saw in the preceding chapter) have attempted to pursue radical nationalist and state capitalist goals, while their more "moderate" counterparts have opted for what might be called the "open door" pro-Western approach. Finally, I shall compare the performance of the few remaining competitive electoral civilian systems with all others to discern what if any differences emerge. In contrast to the studies essayed below, I have also added a number of both cost and performance indicators that more comprehensively explore the overall distribution of burdens and benefits to citizens.

Distinguishing Costs from Benefits

At first glance the meaning of these terms appears so self-evident that elaboration would obfuscate matters rather than elucidate regime failures and achievements. The jargon-laden typologies so common in modernization studies by scholars in advanced capitalist societies do more to impede communication and understanding than one imagines. As indicated in the preceding section of this chapter, Third World political elites and intellectuals who have addressed themselves to the goals of promoting socio-economic change and "development" provide us with a general if not uniform consensus of what types of changes are regarded as beneficial. We can also discover substantial agreement on governmental policies viewed as intrinsically harmful or at best as a necessary expedient for promoting beneficial changes. By defining my terms in accordance with meanings ascribed to them by the colloquial or contemporary Third World political culture, I am merely following the methodological dictum that endorses conventional or customary meanings in the absence of a strong case for specially created terminological definitions.

The sources to which I have referred, as well as the publications of U.N. development agencies generally, treat beneficial changes as those which better the physical and socio-cultural welfare of the general population. Thus, I will focus upon benefits to the civilian masses. While most of the benefits to be compared will be both direct and immediate, several are either indirect and/or long-run in nature. In the latter category fall such widely desired economic changes as higher rates of per capita growth, increased capital formation, and, of course, an expansion of manufacturing output. Direct mass benefits will be measured by changes in such areas as health, education, housing, and employment.

With respect to costs, I shall follow a similar procedure. In the economic area, both inflation and a growth in external debt burdens are commonly depicted as undesirable by development agencies, political elites, and intellectuals concerned with development. High consumer price increases limit or reduce the real income of workers and often redistribute wealth from the masses to entrepreneurial or other highly organized groups in a position to keep ahead. The fragmentation and weakness of blue collar and peasant unions in the underdeveloped areas suggests that, aside from business elements, those other groups tend to be bureaucratic in nature, i.e., "white collar" state employees. Similarly, unless the tax structure is progressive—which in de facto operational terms it seldom is—rising external debt burdens imply an eventual day of reckoning when sacrifices must be imposed upon the masses. The subsequent austerity measures that are customarily introduced to combat foreign exchange crises and high rates of inflation usually mean (Hayter, 1971) unemployment for workers and lower level "white collar" employees, a cutback in social programs for the popular sectors and restrictions upon wages and the availability of basic necessities.

Other costs that are often characterized as negative include increases in the regressiveness of the tax structure and a growth in resources allocated to the military. Thus, although he joins but does not cite Benoit(1973) in arguing the contrary, Gavin Kennedy(1975:179) nevertheless acknowledges: "that defence is a burden is an almost unanimous view among economists and decision-makers, and as it is generally believed to be standing in the way of the competing claims of alternative uses, it is in consequence under budgetary pressure in all countries."

Finally, it can be stated even more categorically that political repression is universally regarded to be a cost. This phenomenon embraces not only the destruction of political parties but also political disappearances, executions by official or quasi-official agencies (e.g., "death squads"), detention, and of course torture. Because of the nearly universal opprobrium attached to them, I shall also classify riots and deaths from domestic violence as negative parameters.

Any conceptualization of benefits and costs assumes a normative frame of reference. Mine is egalitarian and therefore necessarily mass welfare-oriented. Such an anti-oligarchic bias implies that this assessment will be devoid of sympathy for those who view society from the top down or from the reasonable standpoint of preserving their class privileges. While I am cognizant that political elites in quite a number of underdeveloped countries may not take their own rhetoric seriously—even when formalized in multilateral declarations or U.N. resolutions—I *do* because of partiality to mass aspirations for a better life, dignified treatment, and meaningful citizenship.[2] The prevalence of such desires may explain the ubiquity of such rhetoric and (even more) the popularity of the word "socialism" in much of the underdeveloped world. It may even have a little to do with the appeal and diffusion of Marxism, though observers who attribute this primarily to Machiavellian conspiracies will probably disagree. Even these cynics would tend to share my view that governments should exist in order to serve their citizens. Hence I shall now turn to empirical studies of civilian and military regime performance to ascertain what differences emerge. If they all perform badly on balance, perhaps we should reconsider anarchism as a serious normative option.

The Performance of Latin America's Military

Well before domestic militarism emerged as an important phenomenon in the "new nations" of Asia, Africa, and the Middle East, so-called "gorilaismo" had joined "caudilloismo" as recognized sources of governmental instability in the Western Hemisphere.[3] Separate treatment of Latin America is warranted not only by this heritage, but more importantly because of the availability of a number of pertinent quantitative studies.

One of the earliest and least pretentious was published by Needler a decade and a half ago. While his preoccupation was less with the performance of military governments than the conditions associated with their onset, Needler's findings are nevertheless quite suggestive. Insofar as reformism is construed as bringing benefits to the "popular" (worker, peasant and lower middle) classes, Table 7.1 indicates that this tendency has become less pronounced during the Cold War era. The remaining characteristics indicate that militarism has become an ever more significant obstacle to the growth of citizen political participation and has heightened violent repression. The cross-sectional analysis by Robert Putnam(1967:83–110) for the 1956–65 decade is also consistent with the view that the growth of citizen participation is impeded by militarism.

Table 7.1 *Characteristics of Successful Latin American* Golpes: *1935-64*

	1935-44		1945-54		1955-64	
	Number	Percentage	Number	Percentage	Number	Percentage
Reformist	8	50	5	23	3	17
Low in violence	13	81	15	68	6	33
Overthrew constitutional government	2	12	7	32	9	50
Occurred around election time	2	12	7	32	10	56

Source: Martin C. Needler, "Political Development and Military Intervention in Latin America; *American Political Science Review,* 60 (September 1966): 616-26.

Both the stability and aggregative function of political parties were inversely correlated with military intervention. These trends have continued since the mid-1960s. Thus, in the fifteen years between 1964 and 1979, there have been only four reformist coups in Latin America, and three of them—Velazco in Peru, Torres in Bolivia, and Lopez in Honduras—were terminated by rightist military coups. Only Panama's Torrijos survived and his active reformism was moderated in 1973.

Although Thompson's(1975) conclusions after replicating Needler's analysis imply caution in accepting the latter, his criteria were markedly different. Hence, publicly announced goals rather than policies of the conspirators were used to identify the military government's ideological character, inclusion of the regime required that it maintain itself in power for only one week, and no "strikingly reformist" military seizures were recorded for the 1966–70 period. Yet there had been 5 percent in 1961–65, and 7 percent in 1956–60 for the "strikingly reformist" category. While Ecuador's Rodriquez and Bolivia's Ovando might have been excluded on that basis, the utility of his conclusion is vitiated by the absence of Velazco(1968), Torrijos(1968) and Torres(1970). Whether a regime is reformist is determined by its policies, not its rhetoric. And even if subsequent developments constrain the imposition of new reforms, the reaction to such events would have differed had not the predisposition existed beforehand.

An analysis of intercorrelations among more than 125 variables which focused upon the relationship between military rule and certain policy patterns was undertaken by Philippe Schmitter(1971:425–506). Using both longitudinal and cross-sectional approaches, he found that indirect taxes—particularly on imports and exports—tend to be proportionately higher for military governments. When such governments had been entrenched for a long period, they tended to be characterized by lower per capita military expenditures and a smaller share of the GNP was allocated to the armed forces. On the other hand, military regimes of long duration devoted a larger share of their budget to the armed forces and exhibited the highest rates of increase in their military expenditures. Furthermore, Schmitter found that civilian governments which were not plagued by threats of *golpes* not only spent markedly less on the armed forces but also devoted a larger share of their budgets to welfare spending. And regardless of the level of economic development, party competitiveness and civilianism were positively associated with a greater ability to extract resources for the pursuit of public policies.

Several years later Schmitter(1973:117–87) again used both cross-sectional and longitudinal correlations to identify what (if any) associations existed between military aid, armed forces expenditures, and military rule in both the 1945–61 period and the Alliance for Progress years,

1962-70. This time he used Edwin Lieuwen's assessment of military dominance—one that appears to have exaggerated civilian power for the middle category of "transitional" or "Constitutional Guardian" systems. His cross-sectional tabulations revealed a much stronger association between military aid and especially GNP levels and per capita military spending than the type of regime (especially in the 1962-70 years). Nevertheless, if one looks at the two most civilian-dominant regimes for this same period, both per capita military spending and expenditures per soldier were far below those of the remaining countries. Hence Schmitter concedes (1973:146) that "Mexico and Costa Rica do, however, stand out as both low spenders and low aid recipients. So does Bolivia for the earlier [1945-61] period." And in his assessment of the time series data, the author concludes (1973:177) that "the probabilistic evidence suggests that incumbent generals will raise total DMS above levels predicted by GNP for that country and incumbent civilians will do the opposite." This assessment would probably be strengthened and the cross-sectional curvilinear military budget share pattern for increasingly military-dominated regimes might be rendered more comprehensible by recognizing that expenditures for the armed forces are often hidden by military-controlled governments.

Although it seems unlikely that appreciable concealment would be necessary or applicable to such countries as Costa Rica, Weaver(1973:64-65) cautions:

Military budgets and the overall costs of maintaining a military establishment are extremely difficult to measure since without exception Latin American governments hide military appropriations in several budget categories (the Ministry of the Interior or Justice expenditure, for example, may conceal funds ostensibly programmed for military controlled "public safety"); moreover, debt repayment and service charges on loans made to military and counterinsurgent programs, or for equipment, are usually not included in the formal accounts of the armed forces.

As for military aid, Schmitter's cross-sectional analysis revealed a strong .53 correlation coefficient between total military assistance (credits, surplus deliveries as well as grants) and increased military budget shares for the 1945-61 period, and a more pronounced one (at .74) for the *Alianza* years. The effect of such "aid" was to improve the proportion of governmental spending devoted to military purposes rather than to permit the reallocation of other funds to welfare or economic development programs. While Schmitter found a weaker longitudinal relationship between such aid and military spending, and "no impact" of aid upon the incidence of military rule, there are good reasons to believe that external training is directly associated with the likelihood that when ideologically motivated coups occur, they will be anti-leftist in nature.[4] Furthermore, after the massive influx of military aid to Latin America during the decade of the 1960s, given a few years lead time, it now seems that direct or indirect military hegemony over governmental policy is well-nigh universal in the region. Today actual or threatened coups are inconceivable only in miniscule Costa Rica which prudently abolished the army several decades ago, and revolutionary Nicaragua, whose newly organized armed forces and militia place that country's civil-military relations in a special category—one closer to Cuba than other Latin American states.

Before turning to several nonregional studies of differential regime performance, brief reference should be made to R. Neal Tannahill's(1976:233–44) analysis of government policies in 10 South American countries between 1948 and 1967. Although he treats all regimes not headed by an officer as "civilian," and thus fails to take account of indirect military coercion in his sharply bifurcated regime classification, Tannahill's findings are nevertheless quite consistent with most of those previously discussed.

With respect to beneficial change, several new variables are highlighted. First, military governments perform slightly better on three economic indices. Their average annual increase in per capita GDP is 2.4 percent as compared to 1.3 percent for governments with civilian presidents. The average annual increase in manufacturing production is 6.3 percent vs. 4.5 percent, while the average annual export surplus as a percentage of total trade is 7.3 percent as against 3.7 percent for civilians. Insofar as the percentage of the budget allocated to social welfare is concerned, the gap is not only favorable to civilian governments but is also substantially higher: 23.2 percent on the average as compared to 17.4 percent. This last difference incidentally is the only one that is statistically significant (T-Test .01).

Two cost indicators in which we can be equally confident statistically are the proportion of taxes that are indirect and the rise in the cost of living. With respect to regressive taxation, the civilian average was 61.7 percent as against 70.8 percent for the military. As for inflation, the average annual increase in prices was 11.4 percent for the latter and 23.6 percent for the former.

Other cost patterns for which however the T-test was in excess of .10 were military spending and repression. Although civilian governments allocated an average of only 0.7 percent less to the formal military budget categories, Tannahill argues that one must interpret this by taking account of Weaver's(1973:64) previously quoted caveat and stresses (1976:242) "that the two countries with the least threat of military intervention during the period, Chile and Uruguay, also had two of the lower average defense budgets proportionately speaking." Hence, while the civilian mean was 17.2 percent, for these two nations it was little more than 12 percent. As for repression, the average number of government sanctions for the military regimes was 18.2 compared to 12.1 for the civilians. The author(1976:240) adds that even though

the T-test falls short of significance, this is a case where the statistical test does not tell the whole story. In the first place, the difference between the two pooled means is relatively large. Secondly, within the table a clear trend emerges. For the two countries with no military involvement in government during the time frame (Chile and Uruguay), the annual mean score is relatively low. Of the eight countries experiencing both military and civilian rule, six register higher government sanction scores during years of military tenure. Finally, of the other two, the difference between mean scores in Peru is slight and, for the case of Venezuela, one could make a strong argument that the military regime of Perez Jimenez was far more repressive than the figures indicate.

Given the widespread fear of opposition that many military regimes evoke after the initial imposition of sanctions, it may be that this particular indicator systematically underplays the repressiveness of some such regimes. A similar pattern of bias would also apply to civilian governments which were characterized by an absence of genuine party competition. This assumes of course that the severity and probability of being victimized by such sanctions were sufficient to terrorize many potential opponents into acquiescence, exile, or less commonly participation in guerrilla-based national liberation struggles, i.e., internal war.

Tannahill's(1976:242) overall assessment of militarism's impact upon the peoples of Latin America is more comprehensive but not inconsistent with the findings of Needler, Putnam, and Schmitter:

the major difference in the performance of military and civilian governments, however, is a political one. On every indicator of political responsiveness to demands for reform—government sanctions, social welfare spending, and direct taxes—the military as rulers opt for more conservative or more repressive policies than do their civilian counterparts. We must concur with Nordlinger(1970:1134), then, that military rulers are commonly unconcerned with the realization of reform, and where there are civilian organizations pressing for such changes, the military purposefully oppose them.

Notwithstanding a few exceptions like Peru (1968–75) and perhaps Panama (1970–74), his statement does not appear overdrawn. It is certainly consonant with the policy orientations of most contemporary Latin American military-dominated regimes.

Third World Patterns of Military Performance

Two cross-national studies of civilian vs. military performance suggest global patterns which are similar to those previously discussed. Both investigations emphasize the absence of striking differences in the socio-economic performance of the two types of regime. A key thesis in Nord-linger's(1970:1131–48) analysis is the antipopulist (reformist) orientation of the military because of their reference group identification with the middle classes.[5] As Table 7.2 makes clear, the only region where the degree of military influence is moderately correlated with any change indicators — and these refer to economic growth rather than egalitarian or populist reforms — is Africa south of the Sahara. This positive association is attributed to the nascent character of "the middle class" on one hand, and to the weakness of politically oriented mass organizations.[6] It is undoubtedly true that more business was in the hands of "middle class" foreigners within Africa and it is also evident that a larger proportion of officers were recruited from "popular" or peasant backgrounds than elsewhere. But other factors may also be germane to explaining the apparent "radicalism" or marked change brought about by African military regimes on the first four indicators.

That their deviation is probably meaningless from the standpoint of

Table 7.2   *Correlation of Political Strength of the Military and Economic Change*

	Latin America	Middle East and North Africa	Asia	Tropical Africa	All
Per capita GNP rate of growth: 1950-63	.01	-.28	.03	.45	.13
Industrialization: 1950-63	.16	.03	-.02	.42	.29
Agricultural productivity: 1950-63	-.06	-.03	-.39	.60	.07
Growth of educational enrollments: 1957-61	-.43	-.12	-.31	.34	.08
Gross investment rate: 1957-62	-.38	-.32	-.26	.06	-.11
Change in effectiveness of tax system: 1950-63	-.14	-.11	-.07	.07	.04
Leaders' commitment to economic development	-.43	-.16	-.17	.08	-.22
Mean correlation	-.18	-.14	-.17	.29	.04
	(N = 21)	(N = 15)	(N = 15)	(N = 23)	(N = 74)

Source: Eric A. Nordlinger, "Soldiers in Mufti: The Impact of Military Rule Upon Economic and Social Change in the Non-Western States." *American Political Science Review*, 64 (December 1970):1131-48.

relative military capabilities is suggested by the following considerations. First, militarism in that area was not associated with even a moderately strong officer commitment to economic development. This is also apparent from Olorunsola's(1977:119–28) case study of the 1970–74 performance of the Gowon regime in Nigeria, as it is with Chikwendu's(1977:531–41) analysis of a decade of military rule in Nigeria. Nor for that matter were there an appreciable number of "strikingly reformist" coups in Africa according to Thompson's(1973:44) study of coup grievances between 1946–70. For this region there were none prior to 1956. In subsequent years, there were one out of two (1956–60), none of 10 (1961–65), and two out of 22 (1966–70). Sub-Saharan Africa's overall percentage of 9 was almost doubled by the Arab world! Second, while the first three indicators are based upon the 1950–63 period, military dominance is calculated as an independent regime variable only for the 1957–62 years. Since a much larger proportion of African states became independent during this period and especially from 1960–62, these indicators may be more reflective of performance by colonial administrations than that of the regimes in question. This interpretation concurs with the lack of correlation between militarism and the gross investment rate for 1957–62. And it can be squared with the only fairly strong correlation$-.60$ for agricultural productivity—since colonial policy in Africa tended to assign priority to expanding the production of such export crops as groundnuts, cocoa, cotton and coffee. Furthermore, the increase in educational enrollments is only weakly correlated with militarism and may reflect in part colonial and post-colonial foreign aid priorities.

Even if these objections are viewed as not well taken, it can be argued that during the initial years of independence the external military socialization and neo-colonial reference groups of the military (Price, 1971) were sufficient to ensure interim confidence by largely nonindigenous commercial property-owning elites and aid donors to account for the moderately positive "performance." Nordlinger himself contends that it is not really the superior performance capabilities of the African military, but the smaller size of the middle class and the lower level of mass economic demands during the period that account for the positive indicators. Needless to say, if one combines these three last-mentioned factors—limited egalitarian organizational demands, a small indigenous and largely bureaucratic middle class, and a neo-colonial military—he has a recipe for confidence by largely foreign export-oriented owners of plantations, mines, finance and commercial firms, along with external aid donors. The foregoing fits well with Nordlinger's(1970:1144) attempt to reconcile the fact that in the 29 countries with miniscule middle classes (less than 10 percent white collar and entrepreneurial), the highest correlation (.34) with the rate of GNP growth occurred despite a negative (−.04) correlation with the governmental leaders' commitment to economic development.

This would suggest that economic change is due to the officer-politicians' permissive orientation toward change rather than any sustained efforts on their part to bring it about. And this makes good sense according to the class interpretation: economic change is in accord with the interests and prestige-seeking identities of the middle class officers, but since they themselves have already achieved many of the prerequisites of middle class life there is not sufficient motivation for them to undertake strenuous programs of economic modernization.

In the final analysis, as the overall .04 correlation suggests, what the African data imply are unique and temporary situational conditions rather than socio-economic performance capabilities of hegemonic military classes. Otherwise, one would have to explain why markedly less well-educated and experienced African military officers were superior in economic management to their counterparts in Asia, the Middle East, and Latin America.[7]

That they are not is suggested by the more recent analysis of McKinlay and Cohan(1976:850–64) who failed to discern any significant performance variations between African and Asian military regimes.[8] They did find that the differences between civilian- and military-led governments were most pronounced in both of these regions and that in most cases these indicate somewhat better economic performance by civilian regimes and much higher costs to the citizens under military government — especially those of long duration. Their cross-sectional analysis of 25 dependent variables for 101 non-Communist nations was methodologically superior to Nordlinger's because they corresponded in all cases to the period in which the governmental types were in existence rather than drawing upon a longer time span for a number of crucial variables.

McKinlay and Cohan emphasize that populations under the military governments experienced higher cost of living increases and political repression (i.e., restrictions upon political activity). As Table 7.3 indicates, this pattern was most clearly associated with and hence largely explained by the duration of the regime. Hence, the longer a military government is in power, the more repressive and inflationary will be its performance.[9] The importance of this pattern is underlined by the fact that long-term military regimes do have an opportunity to demonstrate their capabilities in both the cost and benefit areas. Furthermore, while less stable — as measured by the number of constitution and executive changes — than civilian governments, long duration military regimes are more stable on both of these indicators than 2–5 year military governments. Furthermore, such repressiveness is unaffected by economic development levels nor is it transferable (1976:855).

Table 7.3   *Political and Economic Costs of Third World Military Regimes*

Type of regime	Mean percent years constitution not fulfilled[b]	Mean percent years legislature banned	Mean percent years parties banned	Mean percent military in cabinet[b]	Rate of growth cost of living index
Civilian[a]	11.5	4.5	14.2	4.2	5.74
Military	34.7	36.0	22.1	22.3	11.28
Military (0-2 yrs)	8.5	9.0	19.1	11.4	3.92
Military (2-5 yrs)	31.1	40.2	24.4	20.2	6.04
Military (5+ yrs)	56.5	45.3	20.4	32.2	21.66

a Excludes civilian-ruled nations with per capita GNP in excess of $900.
b Statistically significant at .01 level.
Source: R.D. McKinlay and A.S. Cohan, "Performance and Instability in Military and Nonmilitary Regime Systems," *American Political Science Review*, 70 (September 1976): 850-64.

Table 7.4   *Military Regime Duration, Characteristics, and Resource Diversion*

Type of regime	Military size (in thousands)	Military expenditure (as percent of GNP)	Mean percent of military in cabinet[b]	Number of main executives[c]	Number of constitution changes[b]
Civilian[a]	44.9	2.7	4.2	2.1	0.4
Military	47.9	3.2	22.3	4.1	1.7
Military (0-2 yrs.)	45.8	2.7	11.4	4.1	1.1
Military (2-5 yrs.)	41.5	2.4	20.2	4.5	2.0
Military (5+ yrs.)	61.9	4.6	32.2	3.4	1.8

a Excludes civilian-ruled nations with per capita GNP in excess of $900.
b Statistically significant at the .01 level.
c Statistically significant at the .10 level.
Source: See Table 7.3

While restrictions on political activity in low-income nonmilitary regime systems increase slightly from low to middle GNP levels and then decrease substantially, the restrictions in military regime systems are fairly constant. Thus, while there is an expected downward trend in restrictions on political activity in low-income nonmilitary regime systems as GNP increases, this does not hold true for military regime systems where restrictions are generally uniform regardless of the particular level of GNP. The restrictions on political activity would seem to be a function of the military regime in the military regime system, and no transference of restrictions to the civilian regimes in the military regime system occurs once the military regime is terminated.

In addition to their greater regressiveness and disposition to allow substantially higher prices to be imposed upon the consuming masses, Table 7.4 reveals that long duration military regimes devote markedly more national economic resources to the armed forces whose size is 38 percent larger than for the civilian regime category.[10] The latter, on the other hand, exhibited a markedly higher rate of growth in military expenditures—one on the order of 33 percent. The implications of this civilian pattern are manifested in Figure 7.1 where Hibbs identifies a positive correlation between high governmental budgetary shares for the armed forces and coups.[11] Coups in turn are associated with the imposition of government sanctions, as are the presence (which he interprets as "availability") of large "internal security forces" per square kilometer. The costs of such sanctions—which predictably are negatively correlated with civilian electorally accountable governments—are underlined by the consequential pattern of public protest and armed resistance. While organized struggles are often defeated and difficult to mount in the post-coup decade, the sufferings of the people from such regimes are cast in relief by the inability of repression to inhibit subsequent expressions of mass protest which continue notwithstanding guerrilla failures. Despite Hibbs' contention that the inverse relation between Communist regimes and collective protest or internal war is attributable to superior repressive techniques, it may well be that regime performance in socio-economic and cultural areas plays a complementary role in accounting for this (−.378) negative correlation. Before turning to my data, which are consistent with this interpretation, a brief summary of McKinlay and Cohan's economic performance patterns may be of some value.

While they failed to introduce controls for civilian development ideologies or electoral regimes, McKinlay and Cohan(1976:857,861) did find that "the military regime systems do score consistently lower than the nonmilitary regime systems" in economic performance. And while noting that the variations were not of sufficient magnitude to warrant statistical confidence, they reiterate that "what differences do exist place the military regimes in the weaker position." As Table 7.5 indicates, with

Figure 7.1 Source and Consequences of Repression in The World: 1960-1970

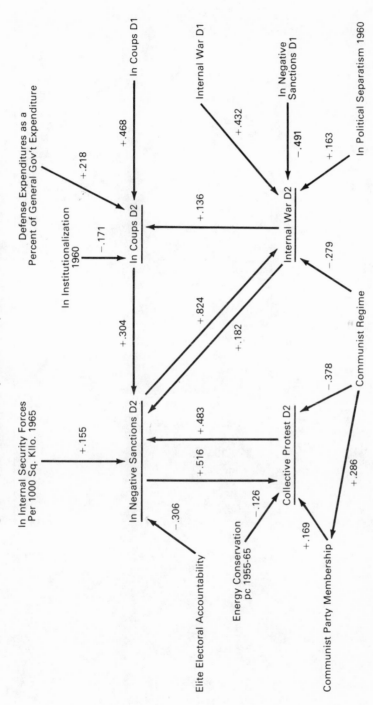

Source: Douglas A. Hibbs, Jr. *Mass Political Violence: A Cross-National Causal Analysis.* New York: John Wiley, 1973.

Table 7.5   *Socio-Economic Performance of Third World Military Regimes*

Type of regime	Rate of growth of constant per capita GNP	Rate of growth of exports	Direct investment balance as percent of GNP	Exports as percent of GNP	Imports as percent of GNP	Number of doctors
Civilian[a]	2.71	9.20[c]	2.00	27.2	25.6	29.8
Military	3.33	8.85	1.24	18.2	20.7	27.8
Military (0-2 yrs)	5.30	13.50[c]	1.68	24.2	24.5	17.4
Military (2-5 yrs)	2.49	11.33[c]	1.67	16.2	21.2	33.2
Military (5+ yrs)	3.29	2.73[c]	0.47	17.8	17.8	24.7
Per Capita						
$0 - $150 GNP[b]						
Civilian			0.98	22.0[d]	19.7	
Military			0.97	15.1	19.7	
$151 - $400 GNP						
Civilian			1.66	30.4[c]	27.4[c]	
Military			1.53	19.6	20.4	
$401 - $900 GNP						
Civilian			3.35[c]	28.0	29.7	
Military			1.28	26.0	26.2	

[a] Excludes civilian-ruled nations with per capita GNP in excess of $900.
[b] Data omitted by authors (McKinlay and Cohan, 1976-861). See note 12 for their textual comments.
[c] Statistically significant at the .05 level.
[d] Statistically significant at the .01 level.
Source: See Table 7.3

the exception of the number of doctors, all of the measures of performance are economic in nature. Even so, it is only on per capita GNP growth rates that the military manage to evidence any superiority. Yet the difference is not only less than 2/3 of 1 percent, but for the more stable long-term military regimes which have had ample opportunity to implement policies, the difference is but 0.58 percent. The interim 2–5 year military governments are actually inferior to civilians on the per capita GNP growth rate indicator. Interestingly, the long-term military are decidedly inferior when it comes to promoting direct investment, while in the equally crucial area of export promotion (which Tannahill found to be benefited by militarism), they also come off rather badly. If controls are introduced for economic development levels, civilians are superior whenever differences manifest themselves.[12]

The poor record of long-term officer regimes may not only demonstrate their low political bargaining and economic management capabilities, but also reflect their previously mentioned higher allocation of national resources to the class interests (i.e., equipment, salaries, and amenities) of the military itself. At the same time, the better performance of short-term military governments may be explained by the fact that as "gate-keeper" interregnum regimes receiving high initial aid injections, they function to restore confidence to capitalist sectors that had been threatened by collective protests and more organized articulation of mass interests.[13] From a conceptual standpoint, it may be useful to regard such "gate-keeper" interventions as acts by a dependent elite that remains psychologically deferential to the "ruling" property-owning investor class. The long-term military government may well reflect the rejection of such reference groups along with the emergence of the officer corps as both a ruling class and a governing elite. As Table 7.6 indicates, this assessment is supported by not only the greater stability of executive tenure in such semipermanent regimes but even more by the significantly enlarged military participation in the cabinets and the associated variations with respect to national resource allocations and military size. While the rate of growth in military expenditures is 11.7 percent for civilian governments as compared to 8.3 percent for these entrenched praetorian regimes, it seems reasonable to interpret this as a desperate attempt by civilians to "buy off" the armed forces and thus deter a coup.[14] S. F. Finer's(1975:234–38) recent addendum to his earlier incisive analysis of civil-military relations, *The Man on Horseback,* places considerable stress upon perceived threats to military class interests (life style amenities and political hegemony) as catalysts of intervention.[15] He closes the topic aptly by recounting both Schmitter's(1971) and Nordlinger's data indicating substantial military diversions of both budgetary and societal resources.

Table 7.6 Regime Classification by Development Strategy: 1960-67 and 1965-74

Civilian "Open Door"

1960-67	1965-74
Afghanistan	Cameroon
Argentina	Chad
Burundi (1963-66)	Chile (1965-70)
C. Af. Rep. (1961-65)	Colombia
Cameroon (1962-67)	Costa Rica
Chad (1961-67)	Ethiopia
Chile	Guyana (1967-74)
Colombia	Haiti
Costa Rica	India
Ethiopia	Iran
Gabon (1961-67)	Ivory Coast
Haiti	Jamaica (1965-71)
India	Jordan
Iran	Kenya
Ivory Coast (1961-67)	Kuwait
Jordan	Lebanon
Kuwait	Liberia
Lebanon	Malawi
Liberia	Malagasy (1965-71)
Libya	Mauretania
Malaysia	Mexico
Mexico	Morocco
Morocco	Nepal
Nicaragua	Nicaragua
Niger (1961-67)	Niger
Nigeria (1961-66)	Philippines
Panama	Portugal
Philippines	Rwanda (1965-73)
Peru	Saudi Arabia
Portugal	Senegal
Rwanda (1963-67)	Sierre Leone (1966-74)
Saudi Arabia	Singapore (1966-74)
Senegal (1961-67)	Somalia (1965-69)
Sierre Leone (1961-67)	Taiwan
Somalia	Trinidad
Taiwan	Tunisia
Tanzania (1962-67)	Turkey
Trinidad (1963-67)	Uganda (1965-71)
Tunisia	Venezuela
Uganda (1963-67)	Zambia
Upper Volta (1961-66)	
Uruguay	
Venezuela	
Zaire (1961-65)	

Civilian state capitalist

1960-67	1965-74
Cambodia (1961-67)	Guinea
Ghana (1961-65)	Jamaica (1972-74)
Guinea	Tanzania (1968-74)
Indonesia (1960-64)	
Mali (1963-67)	
Turkey (1960-65)	

Civilian Electoral Competitive

1960-67	1965-74
Ceylon	Chile (1965-70)
Chile	Costa Rica
Costa Rica	Guyana
India	India
Jamaica	Jamaica
Lebanon	Lebanon
Malaysia	Philippines
Mexico	Turkey
Pakistan	Uruguay
Panama	Venezuela
Peru	
Philippines	
Trinidad	
Uganda	
Uruguay	

Military "open door"

1960-67	1965-74
Ecuador	Argentina
Salvador (1963-67)	Benin (1965-73)
Guatemala	Bolivia
Korea, S. (1962-67)	Brazil
Pakistan	Burundi (1967-74)
Paraguay	C. Af. Rep.
Sudan (1960-64)	Chile (1974)
	Dominican Rep.
	Ecuador
	Guatemala
	Honduras
	Indonesia (1966-74)
	Korea, S.
	Nigeria
	Pakistan (1965-71)
	Paraguay
	Salvador
	Thailand (1965-73)
	Togo
	Upper Volta (1967-74)
	Zaire (1966-74)

Civilian state socialist

1960-67	1965-74
Albania	Korea, N.
Bulgaria	Mongolia
China	Poland
Cuba (1963-present)	Romania
Hungary	Yugoslavia

Military state capitalist

1960-67	1965-74
Burma (1963-67)	Algeria (1966-74)
Egypt (1960-66)	Burma
	Egypt (1968-72)
	Iraq
	Libya (1972-74)
	Malagasy (1973-74)
	Peru (1969-74)
	Somalia (1970-74)
	Sudan (1970-74)
	Syria (1968-72)

In those Latin American states (1950–67) whose military were not politically involved, the average proportion of defense expenditure to the central government's expenditure was 9.3 percent; for those with intermittent military involvement, it was 14.1 percent; for those ruled by the military circa 1960, it was 18.5 percent. In between 1960–65, the first group of states increased their military expenditure by 2.8 percent annually, the second group by 3.3 percent—but the third group increased it by 14 percent. What applied to Latin America applied, in a broad sense, to a sample of seventy-four states (including Latin American ones). The proportion of GNP devoted to defense was almost twice as large in countries ruled by the military 1957–62, as in countries whose military were not politically involved.

The adverse implications of such resource diversion are underscored by McKinlay and Cohan's(1976:858–59) finding that, while not statistically significant, military governments nevertheless tended to extract less resources from the economy to begin with than civilian systems. And even if we discounted this datum, had military regimes performed markedly better than civilians on socio-economic benefit indicators, such high costs could well be factored in as instrumentally functional. Yet as previously discussed analysts have demonstrated—notwithstanding inconsistencies here and there—no basis exists for concluding that the military is generally superior and a preponderance of evidence is consonant with the view that they impose far heavier burdens upon the people in political and to a lesser degree in economic cost areas.

I have not thus far considered Kennedy's(1974:162–64) comparative analysis of budgetary shares. In addition to finding that actual or imminent belligerency resulted in higher allocations to the armed forces regardless of the regime's character, he also identified a pattern of significantly higher military budget shares for noncivilian governments save in the Middle East where Israel and anachronistic monarchies accounted for an exception to the rule.

Of the 15 countries that have devoted to defence an average of over a fifth of their state budgets throughout the 1960s, 10 of them had military regimes for all or part of the years in question (Syria, Nigeria, Egypt, Burma, Indonesia, Iraq, Korea, Pakistan, Turkey, Colombia), and a further three, Jordan, Iran, and Ethiopia, were militant monarchies. Only 3, India, Lebanon, and Israel, were party states. At the other end of the scale, of the 10 countries that allocated an average of under 10 percent of their budgets to defence, 8 were party states (Chile, Ivory Coast, Uganda, Costa Rica, Liberia, Kenya, Sri Lanka, and Malawi). The two exceptions, Ghana and Honduras, were at the upper end of this bottom ranking (9 and 9.1 percent respectively). . . . Military governments in Asia, sub-Saharan Africa, and Latin America allocated about double the percentage allocated by nonmilitary governments on defense out of state budgets. The relative allocations in the Middle East group, after the adjustment of the nonmilitary regimes (21.9 percent), is still much closer to the military regimes than for those in other regions. This is explained by the intense pressure of Middle East insecurity, which is partly related to the Arab-Israeli War and partly also to the ever-present threats felt by the monarchical regimes who are under pressure from their republican neighbours.

The relationship between militarism and increased budget shares is also identified by Thompson(1973:20–23) who found for the 1946–66 period "that years in which military coups occurred were more likely to coincide with years in which relative defense expenditures increased, not decreased." Although this probably signified an attempt to buy off intramilitary support for the conspirators, Thompson warns against causal assumptions. Nevertheless, he adds, "more generally, it would appear that there is a tendency for relative defense expenditures to rise in the years after a coup, especially after successful coups." The same holds for post-coup increases in "arms trade" and "weapons stocks."

Higher budgetary shares for the military are burdens because they restrict consumption through taxes; they foment inflationary tendencies because little is added to the flow of goods and services upon which military salaries are ultimately spent; and, in the final analysis, military budgetary shares are competitive in some measure—at least under military-dominated regimes—with civilian budgetary allocations. Thus Kennedy's(1974:171,173) data indicates that, during the decade of the 1960s, military governments devoted about 18 percent of their average annual budgets to welfare (health and education) while civilians exceeded 20 percent. On a regional basis the differences for his selection of countries are as follows:

Area	Civilian	Military
Asia	26 percent	15 percent
Latin America	21	17
Africa	21	21
Middle East	13	19
Average	20	18

Sarkesian(1978:9) reports similar patterns from a statistical cross-sectional analysis:

Park and Abolfathi analyze military involvement in domestic politics and its consequences for foreign and defense policies. Five indicators of military influence (M.I.) were operationalized and correlated with approximately sixty variables across 150 countries (ca. 1970). Among other things, Park and Abolfathi found that "countries with a strong political rating of the military tend to spend a higher proportion of their governmental revenues for defense." They also found that health and education expenditures tend to decrease as military influence increases.

These probably understate the threat to mass opportunities and welfare represented by "moderate" (i.e., the vast majority of) military regimes. First, such budgetary reallocations usually are incremental over time. Second, the 1960s was a period of unusually high levels of U.S. and Western aid inputs for health and education. Hence, militarism in the 60s should be reflected by less pronounced disparities between allocations to the armed forces and civilian welfare than in the 1970s and 80s.

Class Parameters and Development Strategies

It may be argued that the foregoing analyses have not exhausted the entire range of independent variables, particularly those associated with military heterogeneity. While a number of controls for regime duration, economic development levels, coup incidence, and geographical region were introduced, fairness requires sensitivity to McKinlay and Cohan's caveat at the outset of their article that in terms of performance, military regimes were anything but homogeneous.

As emphasized in Chapter 6, during the post-World War II Cold War era, a growing minority of patriotic officers have sought to improve the condition of the masses and to spur industrialization under national control. Sometimes called populists, economic nationalists, radicals, leftists, Peronists, Nasserists, or military "socialists," they differ markedly from the majority of military rulers who are "moderate" or right-wing in ideological disposition. The latter typically persecute both populist social reformers and Marxists, while simultaneously endeavoring to create a propitious investment climate for the indigenous property-owning upper classes and often associated (Girvan, 1978) transnational corporate interests. As Christopher Jencks(1977:9) makes clear in the following passage, the Chilean junta has been the archtype of what we shall call the "open door" or monopoly capitalist approach. While more "extreme" than other rightist regimes such as Egypt's, Brazil's, or Thailand's, the patterns are analogous:

The Chicago-trained economists . . . persuaded the junta to curtail government expenditures sharply in an attempt to reduce aggregate demand and dampen inflation. But the junta made no parallel effort to reduce private spending. Instead it allowed private entrepreneurs to create "financieras" outside the conventional banking system, which provided new sources of credit to the propertied classes. The funds made available in this way were used largely for consumption and speculation, not investment, and thus fed the inflationary fires that the reduction in government spending was supposed to dampen. . . . The junta has followed orthodox laissez-faire principles. For example, it provides virtually no assistance to the unemployed. As a result, food consumption has fallen, malnutrition and infant mortality are on the rise, and starvation is a real threat to large numbers of Chileans for the first time in living memory. At the same time, the new opportunities for speculation opened up by the junta have softened the impact of economic contraction on the propertied classes. Letelier reports that property holders' share of national income rose from 37 percent in 1972 under Allende to 62 percent in 1974. No figures for 1975 or 1976 appear to be available, but the 1974 figures suggest that, despite the overall decline in living standards, the minority who own property are better off than under Allende. Indeed, they are probably better off than they were before Allende. So far as I know, no country in recent history has redistributed so much income from the poor to the rich in such a short period of time.

As I suggested in the preceding section, one can view the military who follow such a course as a governing elite which, because of its reference group orientations, is dependent upon what for want of a better term we shall call the investing or capitalist classes. At the higher levels, it is probable that recruitment origins, socialization, and interaction patterns condition such reference group identification.

The military leftists, on the other hand, are characterized by expropriations of the investing classes and by an attempt to assign developmental primacy to the state. Thus I call them state capitalists or radicals who in a Marxian sense function as a rising class because they enter into conflict with important sectors of those who formerly controlled the means of production. Their struggle then is to seize effective control over those productive forces rather than to defer to the property-owning bourgeoisie and often interlocked landowning classes. In such circumstances, the military may be regarded as a hegemonic ruling class as well as a governing elite.[16]

The performance of leftist and right-wing military regimes has been compared with those dominated by civilians. But now, the last category will also be subclassified by political affinity: "open door" civilian governments will be compared with their radical or state capitalist-oriented counterparts.[17] All of the foregoing will be compared to state socialist systems ruled by a civilian Marxist-Leninist political class, whose developmental strategy is distinguished by a mobilizational cadre party system, a democratic and egalitarian ideology, intolerance of a residual bourgeois property-owning and labor-employing class, and of course an emphasis upon ensuring that the professional military are an "objectively" or institutionally subordinate elite.

While I have both aggregated and subclassified these five civilian and military regime types in the following section, data on one additional civilian subtype were extracted largely from the open door category — the electorally competitive system. Although parliamentary or "bourgeois" democracy is and has been obviously on the decline in the developing countries for two decades, the ideal still exerts considerable appeal in not only these countries but also within the state socialist systems. Furthermore, balance and objectivity require that this variant be given its due, as does Marx's own conviction that popular struggles and accountability were fortified by civil liberties.

Applying these classifications was quite difficult, particularly because in a sense they are ideal types, whereas most regimes can be found on a continuum subject to movement in one direction or another. For example, while Chile may be regarded as an extreme, many open door regimes—civilian and military alike—are in the process of moving (Rood, 1976:427–47; Horowitz and Trimberger, 1976:223–43) incrementally toward the adoption of at least some economically nationalist measures. Similarly, as highlighted in Chapter 6, a number of state capitalist regimes like Peru and Egypt have reverted in the direction of the open door, while state socialist systems, such as Yugoslavia and more recently China, have reverted toward state capitalism.

This problem has been dealt with by requiring that a regime be characterized in large part by a specific orientation for at least seven of the ten years under study (1965–74). Because of the availability of a small number of political cost indicators for the 1960–67 period, in classifying regimes for those years, I have required a minimum of five for a particular orientation.[18] A number of countries were excluded because of abrupt shifts toward the middle of a period, and in other instances no data were available. Although any such classification required an element of judgement for "difficult cases" at the borderline, no systematic bias was introduced and in all likelihood the few "errors" will cancel each other out. With respect to the state socialist systems, I have excluded those three which are commonly viewed as industrialized and thus in a rough sense "developed" even though socio-economic performance data for the USSR, GDR, and CSR would probably have strengthened the showing.[19] I have also perhaps inappropriately included revolutionary Cuba which during much of the period was the target of an injurious economic blockade and destabilization activities that involved not only armed attacks but also the destruction of substantial numbers of livestock.

With respect to the electorally competitive civilian systems, I have sought to exclude those of a nominal character by requiring either that the government change hands as a consequence of the electoral defeat of the incumbent party or that the opposition receive in excess of 40 percent of the vote at least once during the seven years of the 1965–74 period. The importance of such criteria is pointed up by Kennedy's(1974:63) cogent summary of "common aspects of the electoral system" in the Third World countries as encompassing "the hiring of thugs to terrorize opposition candidates, the intimidation of electors, the partisan intervention of the state, the illegal disqualification of the candidates, and the large-scale personation of electors. . . ." His list omits only vote-buying which is probably even far more common as a means of undermining elections.

Because of limits on time, a different, less satisfactory approach was used for the 1960–67 period relying upon the incidence of electoral irregularities. Thus, only those "countries for which elections were scored as competitive and reasonably free" by Taylor and Hudson(1972:57) were so classified. Since Putnam(1967) concluded that the party structures were the primary victims of military intervention, their presence as viable "aggregating" organizations in a genuinely competitive environment might be expected to make a difference in regime performance. In sharply dichotemizing governments as civilian vs. military, I have rejected the approach utilized by Tannahill, McKinlay and Cohan, and adopted that of Sarkesian(1978), since what is at issue is not whether civilians can be found (as they usually are) at the higher levels of all governments, but rather if they or military men are imposing policy goals and co-opting compliant administrators. Hence regimes with nominal leadership by civilian executives whose tenure or eligibility was subject to military veto as well as those that were formally led by officers who did not win office via genuinely competitive elections were classified as military. Kennedy(1974:44) for example notes that:

In many Latin American countries the same type of formula is followed whereby the (not always) leading member of the military junta is endorsed as "Presidential" candidate by the other members to seek democratic endorsement of the takeover in an army-organised election. But as the military in these countries remains in a leading position within the governing elite, often providing cabinet ministers for key posts, and as a ghost "second chamber" for the regime, it is more accurate to class these regimes as military in composition.

On the other hand, where the civilian executive utilizes the armed forces for purposes of internal suppression but, as in Iran until 1979, nevertheless controls and otherwise determines appointments to general staff posts of the army, I have classified the regime as civilian. What is crucial then is whether the central headquarters is subject to civilian executive manipulation or is an autonomous "state within a state." Thompson(1976) has highlighted the cruciality of the central headquarters since it is from there that most successful coups are launched. Needless to say, even under civilian dominance, the general staff will function in some measure as a pressure group upon behalf of military professional and/or other class interests.

Political and Socio-Economic Cost Patterns

The distribution of political costs to citizens by regime type for the

1960-67 period appears in Table 7.7. Repression as measured by the average number of government sanctions is vastly higher — almost 100 percent — for military regimes and particularly those of the open door variety. While there are few differences with respect to the incidence of sanctions among the civilian regimes, this does not apply to the occurrence of riots where, in general, nonmilitary governments again impose much lower costs upon their citizens. Here interestingly the socialist and radical civilian-led systems may be distinguished from all others including the electoral ones for their exceptionally low costs.[19] And within the military category, left-wing officers obviously outperform conservative praetorians on both riot and sanction indicators.

Table 7.7   *Political Costs to Citizens by Regime Type: 1960-67*

Type of Regime	Government sanctions per 100,000[a]		Deaths from domestic violence per 100,000[a]		Riots per 100,000[a]		Internal security forces per 1000 working pop.	
Civilian (all)	8.9	(61)[b]	223.6	(61)[b]	2.7	(61)	3.3	(56)
Military (all)	16.8	(10)[b]	53.9	(10)[b]	4.5	(10)	3.0	(9)
Nonsocialist (civilian)	8.6	(51)	261.6	'(51)[b]	3.2	(51)	3.0	(47)
State socialist (civilian)	10.6	(10)	29.6	(10)[b]	.48	(10)[b]	4.7	(9)
Electoral (civilian)	9.6	(15)	83.4	(14)[b]	5.5	(14)	2.9	(12)
Open door (civilian)	8.43	(45)[b]	274.0	(45)[b]	3.5	(45)	3.1	(41)
Open door (military)	18.0	(7)	64.1	(7)[b]	5.1	(7)	2.8	(7)
Radical (civilian)	8.2	(6)[b]	168.7	(6)[b]	1.1	(6)	2.3	(6)
Radical (military)	14.8	(3)	30.0	(3)	3.3	(3)	3.8	(2)
	(N = 71)		(N = 71)		(N = 71)		(N = 65)	

[a] Base year for the population in first three categories of costs is 1965.
[b] Significant p < .05 for immediately following regime classification. The figure in parentheses indicates the number of regimes in this category.
Source: Charles L. Taylor and Michael C. Hudson, *World Handbook of Political and Social Indicators.* New Haven: Yale University Press, 1972; pp. 94-101, 110-123, 295-97.

When one turns to deaths from domestic violence, however, the military governments hold a clear advantage. A single exception applies to the state socialist systems whose costs are, as in the area of riots, the lowest of all types of regimes. Aside from that, radical or populist civilian governments do have a markedly lower — if still high — cost average on the death indicator than their open door nonmilitary counterparts.

Within the generally superior military category, left-wing officers again evidence far lower citizen costs — on the order of 100 percent — than do the open door military governments. In fact, the former's superiority in this regard is virtually identical with that of the civilian state socialist regimes.

When the cost phenomenon is approached more indirectly in terms of the relative size of the uniformed apparatus which dominates and/or must be supported by the workers, radical civilian governments appear to be the least costly of all, while the left-wing military regime is clearly the most burdensome within the nonsocialist categories. This fits well with my earlier contention that it is useful to treat the emergence of such regimes as the rise of a new ruling class which is likely to need all of the coercive or potentially productive units at its disposal. However, on the basis of other policies associated with leftist military regimes, "the burden" signified by their relatively larger armed forces may be moderately exaggerated by the 3.8 ratio to working populations for two reasons. First, the active labor force is relatively low for the simple reason that the average per capita GNP of Burma and Egypt during that period was less than $200. Second, the burden is lessened for such peoples because units are assigned to nonmilitary functions such as industrial construction, agricultural development, railroad or road building, and to other infrastructural undertakings. This of course is far more true of developing state socialist systems, and thus accounts for what I believe is a largely spurious high cost ratio here.

The foregoing clearly delineates: 1) the relatively lost cost character of socialism; 2) less marked but general superiority (except in the area of deaths attributable to domestic violence) of populist or radical civilian regimes; 3) an analogous pattern of lower costs (except in the one area of relative military size) for radical officers vis-à-vis their "moderate" praetorian counterparts; and 4) a decided edge for civilians on two of the three measures for which substantial differences appear. Yet how confident can we be in these findings? Put differently, if we analyze the cost patterns for similar regime classifications during the succeeding decade, do we find substantial parallels?

Furthermore, because of the contemporary interest in torture and other very immediate inflictions (disappearances, executions, political detentions), systematic data is currently available which more directly measure the costs to citizens for the various types of regimes. With some variations favorable in all cases to civilians, Table 7.8 appears quite consonant with the patterns of the 1960–67 period. This time however civilian governments are grossly superior on each and every indicator. The predictably very low costs associated with state socialism are once more starkly revealed. Only in the area of political detentions does one nonsocialist type evidence even lower costs. And these same civilian-led populist governments in turn rival the state socialist type by exhibiting extremely low costs in all areas except what may well be an ominous and substantial rise in armed forces size relative to population. Many of these governments retain Western training links and are subsequently forced to "moderate" their socio-economic policies or be deposed by externally supported coups.[20] The rightist military regimes which often replace them are also the type which Table 7.8 indicates to be the highest in repressiveness. On all measures they are more costly than other systems whether within civilian categories or for that matter even when compared to the consistently greater benignity of left-wing officers.

Table 7.8   *Political Costs to Citizens by Regime Type: 1965-74*[a]

Type of regime	Torture allegations[c]		Disappearance or executions allegations[c]		Political detentions allegations[c]		Percent increase in armed forces per thousand people	
Civilian (all)	25	(53)[b]	02	(53)[b]	36	(53)[b]	25	(53)[b]
Military (all)	48	(31)	32	(31)[b]	55	(31)	54	(30)[b]
Nonsocialist (civilian)	30	(43)[b]	02	(43)	40	(43)[b]	32	(43)[b]
State socialist (civilian)	00	(10)[b]	00	(10)	20	(10)[b]	-6	(10)[b]
Electoral (civilian)	40	(10)	00	(10)[b]	50	(10)	36	(10)
Open door (civilian)	32	(41)[b]	02	(41)[b]	42	(41)[b]	31	(41)[b]
Open door (military)	52	(21)[b]	43	(21)[b]	62	(21)[b]	66	(20)
Radical (civilian)	00	(02)[b]	00	(02)[b]	00	(02)[b]	57	(02)[b]
Radical (military)	40	(10)	10	(10)	40	(10)	31	(10)
	(N = 84)		(N = 84)		(N = 84)		(N = 83)	

[a] Averages for the first three columns are calculated on the basis of the 1970 population projections that appear in the second source. "Many" was defined as involving more than 10 persons if the country's population was less than a million, more than a hundred if the population was between one and 10 million, more than a thousand if between ten and 100 million, and in excess of a 100 thousand for the few countries with larger populations. Torture was operationalized as requiring allegations of brutality which involve more than the customary mistreatment that prisoners frequently receive such as being slapped around, threats, isolation, etc.

[b] Significant p ≤ .05 for immediately following regime classification. The number in parentheses indicates the number of regimes in this category.

[c] The percentages listed refer to the percentage of regimes in a particular category for which "many" allegations of torture and abuse were reported.

Source: Amnesty International, *Report on Torture.* New York: Farrar, Straus and Giroux, 1975. U.S. Arms Control and Disarmament Agency, *World Military Expenditures and Arms Transfers: 1965-1974.* Washington, D.C.: U.S. Government Printing Office, 1976.

A stark example of these costs, which may surpass the Chilean tragedy, is Suharto's Indonesia. Once nationalist officers were purged following the 1966 consolidation of Suharto's 1965 de facto coup against Sukarno, intense repression was continued while high-ranking officers joined foreign investing groups in materially benefiting from socio-economic sacrifices (Palmer, 1978) imposed upon the masses. The conclusion of a pro-Western scholar, Crouch(1978:350–51), portrays these consequences so well that it is worth quoting at some length:

While the policies of the new government favored part of the urban middle class, the free rein given to military-backed commercial activities gave rise to resentment in other civilian quarters. In the cities, students and sections of the press protested against high-level corruption and the apparent willingness of senior generals to sacrifice "national interests" to do business with foreigners, while indigenous businessmen complained about competition from military-backed firms, foreign enterprises, and increased imports of consumer goods. The irregular purchasing policies of the army-dominated rice-trading agency, Bulog, contributed to urban hardship when prices rose and rural hardship when prices fell, while the corruption-ridden endeavor to expand the Green Revolution through the Bimas Gotong Royong program provoked so much opposition among peasants that it had to be abandoned. Symbolizing the army's grip on the economy, the state oil corporation, Pertamina, became a major target of civilian resentment as it channeled much of the nation's rising oil revenues into the army's coffers and to other military-sponsored purposes. The feeling became widespread that "economic development" served primarily the interests of the military and their Chinese and foreign business partners, while the mass of the people in the urban slums and rural areas were neglected. . . . The decline of the political parties and the absence of other civilian organizations able to countervail the army's power meant that the system grew less capable of responding to popular discontent. When the emasculated political parties ceased to serve as channels to carry nonelite aspirations upward, popular resentments were deprived of institutional means of expression and army officers felt free to pursue their commercial interests with little concern for civilians harmed by their policies. Because they controlled the means of coercion and the distribution of patronage, the military leaders of the government were rarely under pressure to take account of civilian interests. But the failure of the government's program of economic development to bring about improvements for the mass of the people meant that popular frustration and discontent continued to spread, while the government showed no signs of being capable of tackling the basic long-term problems of growing unemployment, overpopulation, and poverty. Despite the government's achievement of political "stability," it had no program to cope with the inevitable growth of popular discontent which it faced except to rely on the instruments of repression.

It is worth noting that while there are many more radical-led military regimes in this later period, very few of the left-wing nonsocialist civilian governments survived the destabilization efforts. The fact that barely two can be found in that low cost category is consonant with my findings in Chapter 4.

Such a danger is also pointed up by the first column in Table 7.9 where populist governments evidence by far the greatest percentage rise in military expenditures per capita. On this indicator, with the marked exception of very low cost competitive electoral systems, the military regimes have a decided edge over the civilians — one that is substantially lessened in the second column and is completely reversed on the remaining three indicators. With respect to the rise in military expenditures as a percentage of the GNP (more important from the standpoint of economic burdens than per capita expenditure patterns), the civilian electoral governments and especially those in the state socialist category evidence substantially lower costs than other civilian types and also both military categories. Again the two populist-led or radical civilian governments appear as high cost regimes, though even moderate civilian systems are substantially more costly than the open door military variant. As with changes in military expenditures per capita, leftist officers appear to be diverting significantly greater resources to the armed forces than their more moderate counterparts, but again it is worth reiterating that such regimes customarily assign a segment of the military to nonmilitary economic development projects, as do state socialist systems to much greater extent.

The foregoing military expenditure costs are in a sense indirect ones to the population. To the extent that they occasion diversions from social welfare or economic development budgetary allocations, they result in lessened benefits for the citizenry. Such probable consequences for military and particularly civilian radical regimes will be delineated in the following section. Here we can, however, also identify a number of direct costs that military governments — especially the open door variety — excel at imposing upon the masses with the corporate-owning national and transnational sectors as the redistributive beneficiaries. Thus approximating Christopher Jenks' previously quoted observation on Chile, in the area of consumer price rises, the anti-trade union and pro-corporate orientation of the open door militarists is reflected by exceptionally high costs for the masses. On the other hand, the left-wing officers do deliver well on their populist commitments by holding down inflation. In fact, their record on this indicator is slightly better than similarly low cost radical civilian governments and both of these are outperformed only by the remarkable showing of the state socialist systems. In general, even without this last category, civilian governments are substantially less burdensome to the citizens on this very crucial indicator. The electoral systems, however, do not manifest quite as good a

Table 7.9   Socio-Economic Costs to Citizens by Regime Type: 1965-74

Type of Regime	Change in military expenditures per capita	Change in military expenditures as percent of GNP	Change in consumer price index[a]	Change in indirect taxes[a]	Change in foreign liabilities as percent of exports[a]
Civilian (all)	21 percent (44)[b]	78 percent (52)	69 percent (42)[b]	—	—
Military (all)	04 (24)[b]	73 (30)[b]	184 (26)[b]	213 percent (16)[b]	293 percent (24)[b]
Nonsocialist (civilian)	21 (38)	91 (42)[b]	71 (37)[b]	127 (28)	101 (37)
State socialist (civilian)	22 (06)	24 (10)	09 (04)[b]	—	—
Electoral (civilian)	05 (09)	38 (09)[b]	95 (09)[b]	160 (09)	028 (07)[b]
Open door (civilian)	18 (36)	84 (40)[b]	72 (36)[b]	126 (27)[b]	102 (36)[b]
Open door (military)	04 (17)[b]	60 (20)[b]	247 (18)[b]	267 (12)[b]	274 (16)[b]
Radical (civilian)	86 (02)	234 (02)[b]	55 (01)[b]	168 (01)[b]	073 (01)[b]
Radical (military)	12 (08)	99 (10)	43 (08)	051 (04)	331 (08)
	N = 68	N = 82	N = 68	N = 44	N = 61

[a] Because their values were a large multiple of any other in a category, several countries were omitted from each. For the consumer price index column, these were Yugoslavia and Uruguay. With respect to the rise in indirect taxation, they were Indonesia and Uruguay. In the last column, Indonesia and Yugoslavia. In all cases, one of the excluded was a military regime. The number in parentheses indicates the number of regimes in this category.

[b] Significant p ⩽ .05 for immediately following regime classification.

Source: U.S. Arms Control and Disarmament Agency, *World Military Expenditures and Arms Transfers: 1965-1974.* Washington, D.C.: U.S. Government Printing Office, 1976. *U.N. Statistical Yearbook, 1975.* New York: U.N., 1976; pp. 641-47. *U.N. Yearbook of National Accounts Statistics, 1975,* Vol. 3. New York: U.N., 1976; pp. 446-508. *I.M.F. International Financial Statistics.*

showing as even the open door civilian governments, perhaps because they are not as heavy-handed from the standpoint of repression against militant trade union leaders and other democratic sectors.

The pattern of civilian superiority with respect to inflation is replicated on the indicator of the rise in indirect taxes. These are commonly viewed as disproportionately burdening low income groups because of their regressive character. Here again the pro-corporate bias of the open door military regimes is manifested by extremely heavy increases of this burden upon the popular sectors. Predictably, the left-wing officers distinguish themselves again by "delivering" to the people, though the absence of data does not permit us to assess the state socialist record. While the electoral and radical civilian governments are markedly less burdensome than the right-wing military regimes, they are somewhat more costly than equally open door-oriented civilian governments. This anomaly may be explained by their inability to increase sufficiently direct tax burdens upon the property-owning sectors to finance reforms and their expansion of welfare programs. The threat and fear of right-wing military intervention may account for this inability since, as I have noted, many such governments have been deposed during the 1960s and early 70s by open door-oriented praetorians. They, in turn, have not only the will but fewer qualms or scruples than open door civilians when it comes to imposing extreme sacrifices upon the popular sectors.[21]

As in the realms of inflation and to a slightly lesser degree with respect to increases in regressive taxation, civilian superiority is again vividly illustrated on the measure of long term external debt burdens. Here, interestingly, both types of military regimes are associated with exceptionally high costs which may well be due to inefficiency in international bargaining skills, a lack of financial sophistication, and/or limited managerial capabilities when it comes to dealing with monetary matters. Equally noteworthy is the marked superiority of electorally competitive civilian systems and their radical civilian counterpart, both of which are clearly less burdensome than the open door civilian variant which, in turn, is far removed from the disastrous showing of the military regimes.

While the inferiority of so-called moderate military governments is not uniform in the socio-economic cost area, it does appear especially pronounced with respect to the most important direct short- and long-run costs associated with inflation, indirect taxes, and approaching external bankruptcy. These variables are themselves interrelated since policies imposed by Western financial institutions and "aid" agencies to ameliorate exchange of payment problems in the short run for example tend, according to Hayter(1971) and Payer(1974), to force devaluations, inflation of basic consumer necessities, and of course higher indirect taxes. While left-wing officers have performed quite well in resisting such inflation and indirect tax rises, it is worth emphasizing that like their civilian radical counterparts—albeit in lesser measure—they are frequently deposed by open door-oriented officers as Chapter 4 and the recent history of Syria, Bolivia, Peru, and Egypt illustrate. On the other hand, the state socialist systems which were exceptionally low cost on two of the three indicators for which I have data are yet to be victimized by externally supported destabilization conspiracies.

Economic and Socio-Cultural Benefit Patterns

If it is in the nature of politics that all systems impose varying burdens upon their citizens in the name of some "public," "national" or "proletarian" interest, the brighter side of the picture is that most deliver at least a quantum of benefits to the masses. As Tables 7.10-7.14 suggest, however, the welfare performance of various regime types is even less uniform than in the cost areas.

With respect to economic benefits, the most significant and widely cited indicator is per capita growth. Almost as universally emphasized in recent years has been the expansion of industrial manufacturing. On both of these, as Table 7.10 indicates, the civilians leave militarists far behind.[22] With respect to per capita growth, the spectacular superiority of the socialists is noteworthy because they are the only ones who are even slowly closing the developmental gap with the advanced capitalist societies of the so-called North.[23] As for industrial performance, COMECON statistics offer a reasonable basis for inferring a similar pattern.[24] Although the electorally competitive systems didn't perform well on the per capita GDP indicator, they (along with all other civilian regimes) did markedly better than the militarists in increasing manufacturing output. Interestingly, the military leftists did quite poorly on both measures. Their performance was somewhat better on gross capital formation where, as also appears in the case of stimulating manufacturing employment, the open door military governments evidenced superiority. Even so, the differences which favor the military on both of these indicators are substantially smaller than on the two more crucial ones first discussed. Yet it must be conceded that the civilian electoral systems and the military radicals failed to deliver as much as other regime types. Even the socialist systems did only moderately well in the area of manufacturing jobs, though this may be discounted by the availability of alternative employment in these countries which—with the exception of semi-state capitalist Yugoslavia—are distinguished from all other developing areas by labor shortages rather than 20-30 percent unemployment levels.

If my comments on socialist achievements in the economic area elicit surprise, this should be less true of their health benefits to the masses.

For as Table 7.11 demonstrates, the world reputation of these systems is well deserved. Only in the decline in number of hospital establishments do such regimes seem to fare badly, though this may be more than offset by the remarkable fact that only in socialist systems has the availability of hospital beds actually increased! The most crucial indicator of health here is the decline in infant mortality. Not only do the civilians again outperform the military, as they do on all save the least important hospital construction category, but the radical civilian governments are nothing short of spectacular. They are also strongest with respect to both increasing the availability of physicians and hospital construction. Electoral systems did well on reducing infant mortality and physician ratios, did less impressively with respect to hospital beds and evidenced the poorest nonsocialist performance in hospital construction. The inefficiency of right-wing military regimes is pointed up by the fact that while their hospital building record is outstanding, they also manifest the highest increase in population per hospital bed! As with open door civilian regimes, with which they share the lowest declines in infant mortality, it is reasonable to hypothesize that many of the "benefits" accrued to the construction contractors and upper class neighborhoods. This finding is quite congruent with the dependent elite role of such militaries, as it is with the notorious lack of probity that tarnishes rightist regimes in the underdeveloped areas.

When we turn to the socio-cultural benefits identified in Table 7.12, civilian superiority is again shown on three of the four indicators. And on the fourth — change in daily newspaper circulation — data was provided by only a small number of military regimes. Furthermore, while the civilian electoral and, to a lesser degree, the state socialist systems do rather poorly, the right-wing military are outperformed by both their radical officer counterparts, as well as by the open door civilians, who account for the largest civilian category. From the standpoint of educational benefits, teacher ratio changes are the most important measure. Here the performance of civilian electoral systems and especially the socialist regimes leaves all others, excepting Sekou Toure's Guinea, far behind. Both open door capitalist systems are low benefit regimes, whereas surprisingly the situation actually deteriorated under the radical military governments as it did under some of their radical civilian counterparts. Table 7.9 may suggest the reason: a marked diversion of resources to the armed forces. Hence while this applies to Tanzania and accounts for the datum for that regime in the first column of Table 7.12, it does not apply to Guinea, which is the only other government of that genre for which I have available data. While the state socialist systems also decreased relative resources assigned to education, their superiority and efficiency is underlined by the previously discussed teacher ratio in-

Table 7.10   *Economic Benefits to Citizens by Regime Type: 1965-74*

Type of regime	Rise in per capita GDP (constant prices)		Rise in gross fixed capital formation		Rise in manufacturing output		Rise in manufacturing employment	
Civilian (all)	37%	(34)	–		–		43%	(24)
Military (all)	27	(19)	54%	(15)	37%[a]	(15)	48	(11)
Nonsocialist (civilian)	31	(26)[a]	–		66	(21)	45	(18)
State socialist (civilian)	55	(08)[a]	–		–		38[a]	(06)
Electoral (civilian)	17	(07)[a]	44	(07)	60	(07)	28[a]	(05)
Open door (civilian)	32	(25)	52	(17)	67	(20)	44	(17)
Open door (military)	30	(15)[a]	62	(11)	42	(12)[a]	52	(09)
Radical (civilian)	07	(01)	–		56	(01)[a]	61[a]	(01)
Radical (military)	11	(04)	32	(04)	17	(03)	27·	(02)
	N = 53		N = 32		N = 36		N = 35	

[a] Significant p ⩽ .05 for immediately following regime classification. The number in parentheses indicates the number of regimes in this category.
Source: *U.N. Yearbook of National Accounts Statistics, 1975.* Vol. 3. New York: U.N., 1976; pp. 253-70, 303-34, 363-90. *U.N. Statistical Yearbook, 1975.* New York: U.N., 1976; pp. 100-104.

Table 7.11   *Health Benefits to Citizens by Regime Type: 1965-74*

Type of Regime	Decline in infant mortality		Change in population per physician		Change in population per bed in hospitals		Change in number of hospital establishment	
Civilian (all)	12%	(31)	-13%	(45)	+02%	(45)	+10%	(41)[a]
Military (all)	09	(14)	-11	(26)	+05	(26)	+29	(24)[a]
Nonsocialist (civilian)	11	(25)	-09	(37)[a]	+03	(37)[a]	+12	(35)[a]
State socialist (civilian)	13	(06)	-30	(08)	-04	(08)[a]	-02	(06)[a]
Electoral (civilian)	11	(07)	+01	(10)[a]	+02	(10)	+29	(10)[a]
Open door (civilian)	05	(22)	-08	(36)	+02	(36)[a]	+11	(34)[a]
Open door (military)	07	(11)[a]	-08	(19)[a]	+06	(19)[a]	+39	(18)[a]
Radical (civilian)	61	(03)	-47	(01)	+13	(01)[a]	+43	(01)[a]
Radical (military)	15	(03)	-21	(07)	+04	(07)	+01	(06)
	N = 45		N = 71		N = 71		N = 65	

[a] Significant p ⩽ .05 for immediately following regime classification. The number in parentheses indicates the number of regimes in this category.
Source: *U.N. Demographic Yearbooks, 1966-74.* New York: U.N. Charles L. Taylor and Michael C. Hudson, *World Handbook of Political and Social Indicators.* New Haven: Yale University Press, 1972. *U.N. Statistical Yearbooks, 1968-1975.* New York: U.N.

Table 7.12 Socio-Cultural Benefits to Citizens by Regime Type: 1965-74

Type of regime	Change in educational as percent of GNP	Change in ratio of teachers (primary schools)	Change in daily newspaper circulation per 1000 population	Average[a] annual number residential dwellings constructed per 1000 population
Civilian (all)	11% (28)	08% (41)	40% (34)	4 (20)
Military (all)	09 (19)	05 (24)	46 (08)	2 (13)
Nonsocialist (civilian)	14 (24)c	05 (34)c	46 (27)c	4 (19)
State socialist (civilian)	-5 (04)c	23 (07)	17 (07)	2 (01)
Electoral (civilian)	16 (08)	20 (07)c	13 (06)c	3 (05)
Open door (civilian)	15 (23)	05 (33)	50 (26)	4 (18)
Open door (military)	13 (12)c	07 (16)c	46 (06)c	2 (06)
Radical (civilian)	-16 (01)c	17 (01)c	-75 (01)c	1 (01)
Radical (military)	03 (07)	-1 (08)	48 (02)b	2 (04)
	N = 47	N = 65	N = 42	N = 32

a Includes only the 1971-73 period.
b Burma is excluded because the multiple is several thousand percent.
c Significant p ≤ .05 for immediately following regime classification. The figure in parentheses indicates the number of regimes in this category.

Source: *U.N. Compendium of Social Statistics, 1967.* New York: U.N.; pp. 380-92. *U.N. Statistical Yearbook, 1967.* New York: U.N.: U.N., 1968; pp. 734-55, 763-64. *U.N. Statistical Yearbook, 1975.* New York: U.N., 1976; pp. 854-72, 890-94. *U.N. World Economic Survey,* Pt. 1. New York: U.N., 1974; pp. 85-86.

dicator, as it is by their success in eradicating most illiteracy.

My last measures deal with extremely important mass consumption items — housing and food. With respect to the former, Table 7.12 reveals that civilian performance is almost double that of the military regimes. While the open door and electoral civilians did better than Tanzania and Cuba from a purely quantitative standpoint, the latter countries probably delivered more new units to the masses as opposed to the middle and upper classes. As for the military governments, there is little to distinguish them except the strong but unsubstantiated belief that the leftist officers are likely to construct more houses for the "little people" than are the Pinochets and Sadats of the world.

Internal distributive patterns again tend to be masked by the food availability indicators which are the basis of Table 7.13. Even though the differences are small, I think it is again significant that civilian governments outperform their military rivals on both of them. Whereas the latter have actually fallen behind in their per capita food production over what was (for the masses) a state of malnourishment in the mid-1960s, they have also raised the price of food to a greater extent than the civilians.[26] Ironically, while the output failure can be attributed in part at least to priorities upon military spending and manufacturing for regimes led by radical officers, they at least have miraculously held the line on prices. So for that matter have the Tanzanians whose expansion of food output was only 6 percent higher. Guinea and the electoral civilian governments did the best in per capita food production growth, while the relatively "good" performance of the latter as well as both open door regime types was undercut by their markedly higher food price increases. This is explained by the subordination of such elites to the bourgeois sectors, and additionally, in the case of the electoral variant, by the tendency of businessmen to pass on trade union wage increases to the masses in the form of yet higher prices. It squares well with my conclusion from Table 7.9 that these three monopoly capitalist-dominant regimes were by far the most costly in terms of general price increases visited upon the consuming masses. While we lack such food production data for the state socialist systems, there is no doubt that they are characterized by more equitable distribution and a virtual absence of both starvation and malnutrition — even when victimized by economic blockades and extensive war damage as in the case of Indochina. A comparison of nutrition in China and India is as revealing as are the per capita GDP data in Table 7.10 or the infant mortality patterns in Table 7.11. For it is an unquestioned dictum of the public health professions that without good nutrition and, in lesser measure, housing and sanitation, medical progress comes slowly, notwithstanding all the contracts that may be parceled out for new suburban hospital buildings by open door governments. This dictum would hold even if many of the hospitals had been erected in popular barrios and hinterland communities.

Table 7.13   *Food Availability to Citizens by Regime Type: 1965-74*

Type of regime	1971-74 Per capita food production (1961-65 = 100)		1973 Consumer food price index (1970 = 100)	
Military (all)	99	(26)[a]	146	(15)
Nonsocialist (civilian)	102	(32)	142	(21)[a]
Electoral (civilian)	104	(08)	199	(05)[a]
Open door (civilian)	102	(30)	143	(20)[a]
Open door (military)	103	(19)	158	(10)[a]
Radical (civilian)	100	(02)[a]	130	(01)
Radical (military)	89	(07)	122	(05)
	N = 58		N = 36	

[a] Significant p ≤ .05 for immediately following regime classification. The figure in parentheses indicates the number of regimes in this category.
Source: U.N. *World Economic Survey, 1974*. Pts. 1 and 2. New York: U.N., 1974; pp. 85-86, 49-51.

Conclusions

My previous consideration of the studies by Needler, Nordlinger, Putnam, Schmitter, Tannahill, Hibbs, McKinlay and Cohan who in one way or another elucidated the consequences of military interventions or rule stressed the differences in performance attributable to militarism. Before briefly commenting upon some similarities, I want to relate my findings, as condensed in Table 7.14, to the three major patterns which emerge from the previous analyses. First, the most stark contrast is political. Needler, Hibbs, Tannahill, McKinlay and Cohan all tend to emphasize increased repression. Tannahill treats inflation and indirect taxes as costs, while data on these indicators are also presented by the last two authors. As the civilian military dichotomy in Table 7.14 illustrates, my own data—notwithstanding the incorporation of such additional indicators as the growth of external debt burdens, rises in military expenditures, relative size of internal security forces, political detentions, riots, deaths from domestic violence, disappearances, executions, and torture—yields a similar general pattern of much higher costs for military regimes to their citizens. Only in four areas did they manifest lower costs: relative size of internal security forces; deaths from domestic violence; and the two measures of military expenditure increases. On all of the other previously mentioned cost indicators, as well as the incidence of government sanctions and increases in the relative size of the armed forces, the civilians were associated with lower burdens to the people. This pattern of civilian superiority is heightened slightly when the state socialist systems are excluded. Thus with the removal of one indicator (size of internal security forces), the military regime systems exhibit the highest costs on 75 percent rather than 69 percent of the measures.

Table 7.14   *Differential Regime Performance on Cost/Benefit Indicators[a]: 1965-74*

Type of regime	Costs lowest		Benefits highest		Costs highest		Benefits lowest	
Civilian	69%	(9)[b]	71%	(10)[b]	31%	(4)[b]	29%	(04)[b]
Military	31	(4)[b]	29	(04)	69	(9)[b]	71	(10)[b]
Socialist (civilian)	64	(7)[b]	30	(03)[b]	09	(1)	10	(01)
Electoral (civilian)	15	(2)[b]	14	(02)[b]	08	(1)	14	(02)
Open door (civilian)	00	(0)[b]	21	(03)[b]	08	(1)[b]	07	(01)[b]
Open door (military)	08	(1)[b]	07	(01)[b]	54	(7)[b]	00	(00)[b]
Radical (civilian)	39	(5)[b]	23	(03)[b]	15	(2)	39	(05)
Radical (military)	08	(1)[b]	07	(01)	08	(1)	36	(05)

[a] The number of cost indicators is 11 for the state socialist regimes and 13 for all others. For benefits, the respective totals are 10 for socialist systems, 13 for radical civilian governments, and 14 for the remaining regimes. Figures in parentheses refer to the number of indicators upon which a regime type scored lowest or highest.

[b] Significant p ≤ .05 for immediately following regime classification. The figure in parentheses indicates the number of regimes in this category.

Source: Tables 7.8-14.

While Schmitter and Tannahill discerned a tendency by civilian governments to spend more on social welfare, neither these scholars nor others have found uniform patterns of performance in the economic area. If anything, there was some evidence that South American and (more problematically) African militarism of an earlier era were characterized by slightly higher rates of economic and industrial growth, though not with investment. A similar finding on investment is reported by McKinlay and Cohan. They also note a tendency by civilians to outperform military regimes—especially those of long duration—on most socio-economic measurers.

From the standpoint of my own analysis, while Table 7.14 does establish military superiority in the areas of gross fixed capital formation, manufacturing, employment, hospital construction, and daily newspaper circulation increases, the basic pattern that emerges is one of great civilian superiority in both the welfare and socio-economic areas. This includes the following ten indicators: 1) rise in per capita GDP; 2) rise in manufacturing output; 3) rise in educational expenditures as a percent of GDP; 4) rise in the ratio of teachers to primary school students; 5) decline in infant mortality; 6) decline in population per physician; 7) change in population per hospital bed; 8) increase in per capita food production; 9) rise in the consumer food price index; 10) construction of residential dwellings. When the state socialist systems are excluded, the civilian performance on benefits is only moderately diminished. Thus, on the twelve indicators in which differences appear, eight (67 percent) of them demonstrate civilian superiority. The two upon which no differences appear are the ratio of teachers and newspaper circulation. But in the crucial areas of per capita GDP, manufacturing output, housing, food availability, infant mortality, and access to hospital beds, the civilian lead is maintained.

When we turn to specific regime types, the state socialist systems alone show not only a pattern of lowest costs and highest benefits on a large number of indicators, but also a paucity of highest costs and lowest benefits. These outstanding systems score lowest on the following: deaths from domestic violence; disappearances and executions; torture; increases in military spending as a percent of GNP; increase in military population ratios; rises in the consumer price index. As for benefits, such regimes were highest in the following areas: rise in per capita GDP; increase in student/teacher ratios; and decline in population per hospital bed.

The second strongest showing with respect to lowest costs and highest benefits was provided by civilian radical or state capitalist regimes. Because such systems were very few in number, simultaneously accounted for the lowest benefit performance on five indicators, and seem particularly vulnerable to externally supported right-wing destabilization, a positive assessment must be severely hedged. While their costs were lowest with respect to government sanctions, torture, disappearances and executions, political detentions, and the size of internal security forces, their associated benefits were highest only on population/physician ratios, hospital construction, and the very significant decline in infant mortality. On the other hand, their performance trailed all others in the following areas: per capita GDP increase; rise in educational expenditures; residential housing construction; population/hospital bed ratios; and daily newspaper circulation.

Both civilian radical governments and electoral systems tend to be subverted by right-wing military coups. These two governmental types also tend to be characterized by middling cost/benefit performances. While the populist or radical civilian regimes are subject to extreme variations on the benefit side, the electorally competitive systems evidence a greater tendency to occupy a mean position with respect to both costs and benefits. Thus, they score lowest on costs only for external debt burdens, and political executions and disappearances. Similarly, with respect to highest benefits, electorally competitive systems were the most outstanding on per capita food production increases and educational expenditure as percent of GNP rises. With respect to riots, they were the highest cost regime type and provided the lowest benefits in controlling inflation and decreasing population/physician ratios.

While the open door civilian regimes did distinguish themselves by failing to rank lowest on any cost indicators, they accounted for the strongest performance with respect to the growth of manufacturing output, daily newspaper circulation, and the construction of residential dwellings. Deaths from domestic violence was the only cost indicator on which they scored highest and the only benefit upon which they offered the worst performance was the crucial one of infant mortality. This is consonant with the exploitative industrializing role which Marx believed the bourgeoisie would perform in India and presumably other "open door" developing countries.[27]

The open door military regime distinguished itself in a more ominous way on the cost indicators. It ranked highest by far on more costs than any other regime type on: government sanctions; political detentions; disappearances and executions; torture; increase in size of the armed forces; consumer price inflation; and the rise in indirect taxes. As for benefits, it ranked highest on but one indicator — gross fixed capital formation. Military "moderates" did manage to rank lowest on one cost indicator — change in per capita military expenditures — though, as pointed out previously, such items may have been concealed under other budgetary classifications. Admittedly, they did not rank lowest upon any benefit measures.

Left-wing officers similarly distinguished themselves by ranking lowest on but one cost indicator — rise in indirect taxes. The importance of this to the masses and the fact that the only benefit for which they scored highest was the restriction of food price increases suggest that their populist commitments have a real substantive rather than rhetorical (Decalo, 1976) basis. While increasing the external debt burden was the only cost upon which they ranked highest, the fact that radical officers turned in the worst performance on five benefit indicators implies that despite the greater stability of their regimes, they may be if anything less capable of overcoming the development challenge than are civilian radicals. These five benefit areas were: rise in manufacturing output; rise in manufacturing employment; gross fixed capital formation; teacher/student ratios; and per capita food production. In sum, while right-wing officers do stimulate somewhat higher production than their radical counterparts, it is at a cost which is incomparably higher to the "little people" or citizens.[28]

Ultimately, we are confronted with the fact that, while most of the regime types are in varying degree authoritarian (some considerably less benign or civilized than others), all with the exception of the state socialist systems appear to be incapable of governing society in a manner that enables the masses to close even slowly the economic, social, cultural, and health gaps with the advanced capitalist societies. The state socialist systems are neither paragons of virtue nor really spectacular performers, but in terms of both costs and tangible benefits, they at least are inching their way out of the malaise engendered by dependency and underdevelopment. And for those to whom state socialism is unattractive, there is no doubt that noncommunist civilians are more capable of bringing about somewhat more socio-economic change at substantially lower costs than the military. Although it is obvious that left-wing officers are well intentioned and doubtlessly more humane than right-wing ones, short of a coalition with socialists who are accorded a leading role, they appear incapable of meeting the interrelated challenges of radical structural change and self-reliant development.[29] This military "failure" is of course consonant with a central concept of modernization theory. If functional specialization is integral to the modernization process, then the place for the military is obviously improving their professional skills within the barracks—in a subordinated institutional relationship to civilian policy makers. Ironically, such pattern maintenance can only be found within the developing state socialist systems. In the remainder of our Third World, both civilian dignity and developmental prospects are in a process of slow but steady erosion before the tide of domestic militarism.

Notes

1. Among scholars who in varying degree shared such an optimistic perspective were Pye(1962), Halpern(1963), Gutteridge(1964), Johnson(1964), Janowitz(1964), and Bienen(1971).

2.

Twelve thousand people in the world die of starvation every day. Ten million children are underfed and close to death. Four hundred million are inert from hunger and almost a billion, a quarter of the world's population, suffer from the effects of malnutrition. These are the figures of Jean Mayer, Chairman of the National Council on Hunger and Malnutrition and President of Tufts University. If something isn't done quickly, he warns, the future may bring a "global death wave." As reported in *Seven Days,* April 25, 1977, p. 26.

3. It may be objected of course that both party involvement and direct citizen participation in the political system are inherent characteristics of civilian government and therefore their suppression ought not to be regarded as "costs" associated with other regime types. Despite the reasonableness of such a position, there are at least two good reasons for its rejection. First, military is distinguished from civilian here and in most of the studies cited by reference to the single criterion of Executive dominance. One can of course identify civilian-controlled governments which suppress mass participation directly or via the party system. Similarly, some military governments have actively sought to organize mass parties and to encourage certain forms of citizen participation. Hence, neither the existence of one or more parties nor participation itself is necessarily intrinsic to either type of regime. In varying degree, they may be tolerated or encouraged by military or civilian elites as a consequence of ideological commitments over which acute contemporary intracivilian and intramilitary differences can be discerned. Second, given the normative referents specified earlier in this chapter, maximizing citizen involvement in the process of arriving at community decisions which affect their lives in vital ways is an intrinsically desirable value from the dual perspectives of respect for individual dignity and any notion of "political development" other than one (Huntington, 1965:386–430) which is little more than a euphemism for institutional stability and order. If that were indeed the case, however, then the empires of the Aztecs and Pharaohs would be examples of political development. Since the concept of development implies a goal, it is imperative to acknowledge that in the 20th century mass aspirations in this area are for the realization of greater not less democracy.

4. Among those who have seriously examined such relationships are Price(1971), Klare(1972), Wolpin(1973), Marchetti and Marks(1974), Etchison(1975), Agee(1975, 1975a), Lemarchand(1976), Borosage and Marks(1976), and Watson(1977).

5. He also attributes military conservatism to such institutional or professional values as hierarchy, order, and discipline.

6. Nordlinger's findings and the disproportionate contemporary incidence of left-wing militarism in Africa and the Middle East appear to be consistent with Huntington's(1968) theory of radical praetorianism. It may also be added that imperialism had totally discredited the legitimacy of traditional ruling classes where they had existed in these areas. For an equally stimulating neo-Bonapartist approach to "revolutions from above," see Trimberger(1977) who after comparing the Japanese, Turkish, Egyptian, and Peruvian experiences emphasized the cruciality of the following four conditions: 1) exposure to nationalist ideology; 2) bureaucratic centralization which socially isolates officers from traditionally dominant land-owning upper classes; 3) international room for maneuver vis-à-vis imperialistic Great Powers; and 4) agrarian economic stagnation or decline.

7. In his perceptive case studies of four African military elites, Anton Bebler provides little basis for assuming such superior capabilities. And he acknowledges(1972:153) that "in a certain sense, however, the class stratification of the colonial societies spills over into the new independent polity through the military hierarchy as privileges, access to secondary and high schools, capital accumulation in the form of savings invested into real estate and business ventures, and so forth are passed on to the next generation." Another student of the African military, J. M. Lee(1969:125,145) echoed this view several years earlier by noting that a "sense of privilege . . . extends throughout all ranks, and is not simply a characteristic of the officer cadre." Adding later that "the army looks like a lobby which can secure for itself a large proportion of the state's resources," he goes on to observe that "in conditions where wage employment is rare" there is a strong aversion by conscripts, and presumably officers, to return to rural areas to "apply what they had learnt" in the modern sector.

8. Thus, they (1976:858) note

the within-area differences correspond to the within-area political differences where Africa and Asia demonstrated the most pronounced differences between military regime systems and nonmilitary regime systems. In Africa, military regime systems have lower GNP, lower GDFCF, and fewer doctors. Each difference is significant at the .10 level. In Asia, military regime systems have lower GNP, smaller budgets, and fewer doctors. The differences are significant at the .05 level.

9. Their data on inflation (Table 7.3) and exports (Table 7.5) suggest civilian superiority; like mine (Table 7.9), they are at variance with Tannahill's findings on these two indicators for ten South American nations.

10. This is in conflict with Schmitter's(1971) previously cited Latin American findings on the relationship of regime duration to the percent of GNP allocated for military purposes and to rates of increase in such spending. Furthermore, it seems at variance with his(1973) Latin America data indicating that per capita GNP levels best predict the percent of GNP allocated to the military.

11. Coups in the preceding decade were even more strongly correlated with military seizures. Putnam(1967) thus identified a high correlation between historical and contemporary coup activity in Latin America. Social mobilization, on the other hand, was strongly and negatively correlated with military interventions.

12. I have only referred to those indicators upon which there are differences between civilian and military governments. Thus the frequency of coups has been omitted as have such dependent variables as Budget as a percent of GNP (though small differences did appear here), Primary Production as a percent of GNP, and Gross Domestic Capital Formation as a percent of GNP. The economic differences which do appear, the authors take pains to stress, are not of sufficient magnitude to warrant statistical confidence.

A similar conclusion is reached by Robert Jackman(1976:1078-97) after a statistical reanalysis of Nordlinger's data as well as analogous indicators for the 1960s. In sum, "military intervention in the politics of the Third World has no unique effects on social change, regardless either of the level of economic development or geographic region."

13. This is not to imply that all interventions are exclusively or even partially catalyzed by such motives. Nonideological motives include a desire for higher rank and perquisites, civilian incompetence or corruption, budgetary conflicts, excessive civilian interference in the command structure, fear of sanctions for military corruption, personal pique, etc. Decalo(1976) after four case studies goes to the other extreme by asserting that ideological influences mask such personal/factional interests.

14. Rates of military expenditure increase for military governments of short duration were also somewhat lower than those for civilians. Thus for military regimes of two or less years, it was 7.4 percent, while it reached only 9.6 percent for those lasting from two to five years. Yet again I emphasize that they made no effort to distinguish those civilian governments which were unthreatened by military coercion from those that were—an important demarcation which Schmitter made in his 1971 analysis.

15. The nature and sources of these class interests are analyzed in Chapters 2 and 6.

16. When right-wing officers intervene at the behest of dominant capitalist sectors and subsequently enter into conflict with them by declining to retire to the barracks once the Marxist and populist forces have been repressed, the military is faced with two choices. Either it must move in a state capitalist direction by asserting direct control over major means of production (i.e., act as a class for itself), or it will be forced to withdraw as investing sectors institute what has been termed a "capital strike." The mechanisms are demands and in some cases coups by pro-capitalist elite officer factions. Even when the class role is opted for, it is sometimes the case that hegemonic officers use their positions to enrich and transform themselves into a "civilianized" national bourgeoisie of sorts—albeit

usually parasitical rather than entrepreneurial. Indeed, this is an omnipresent danger to all radical or state capitalist regimes that survive initial externally supported destabilization attempts.

17. Aside from rejecting a posture of deference toward large property-owning and investing upper class sectors, radical regimes typically pursue a cluster of policies which distinguish them from antithetical policy clusters associated with open door elites: 1) some redistributive agrarian and other social reforms; 2) price controls or subsidies for basic necessities; 3) encouragement of trade unions, cooperatives, and other mass organizations; 4) organization of mass parties with mobilizational goals that usually prove abortive; 5) limited tolerance and co-optation of Marxists; 6) broadening of relationships with state socialist systems and adoption of a nonaligned or pro-Eastern foreign policy; 7) imposition of foreign exchange controls.

18. When possible, data were limited to the post-independence period and tabulated for only those years during which a particular class/developmental strategy prevailed. Nations with less than 1 million citizens were excluded. The choice of indicators was based upon their perceived appropriateness as measures of costs and benefits to the people, as well as their availability. Because, for quite a number of exceptionally useful indicators, data were not reported, the number of cases is at times quite low. Had I then attempted to control, for economic development levels, the numbers would have been reduced in many instances to the already unsatisfactory situation with respect to the civilian state capitalist category in the 1965-74 period. Even so, I am uncertain that differences on the order of several hundred dollars of per capita income have any real causal or explanatory significance when one assesses the yawning gap which distinguishes the mass poverty of most of these societies from the standards of living in the industrialized north. Furthermore, Jackman's conclusion — quoted above in note 12 — indicates that performance levels are not significantly affected by economic development levels. Table 7.13 is consistent with his findings. None of the 1965-74 regime types which I compare had a per capita income average for the category which reached $900.

19. There are of course other less behavioral or physical approaches to estimating political costs. Raymond D. Gastil's(1977) comparative survey of "freedom" ranks countries on a scale of 1-7 from "most free" to "least free." His criteria are governmental respect for political and civil formal rights. Among the 33 which were "least free" (excluding those not incorporated into my classifications because of size or industrialization), 30 percent were state socialist, 24 percent were open door military regimes, 18 percent were state capitalist military systems, 15 pecent were open door civilian regimes, and 3 percent were radical civilian governments. Taylor and Hudson's(1972) governmental sanctions indicator covers most of these however and it is more readily comparable with other studies such as Tannahill's. Furthermore, it is less judgmental and subject to formalist or ethnocentric bias.

20. See the sources listed in note 4. A colloquy on MAP (U.S. Congress, 1977:802) before a House of Representative's foreign affairs committee is suggestive in its own way:

> *Mr. Conte.* Did you find that having some MAP programs in some of these countries has really helped, for instance, Indonesia, one of the largest countries in the world? We didn't have a lot of military assistance in there but we did have a MAP program, did we not?
>
> *General Fish.* Yes, sir.
>
> *Mr. Conte.* We also trained some of their officers here at our War College; right?
>
> *General Fish.* Yes, sir; we have training programs with Indonesia.
>
> *Mr. Conte.* And it was a program that really helped throw out Sukarno at that time without costing any American lives or military equipment; is that right?
>
> *General Fish.* The Indonesians did turn away from the Soviets and to the West, to the United States.

21. This may be explained not only by their ferocious anti-Marxism but also by their traditional martial values which tend to be force-oriented, aggressive, and disdainful toward civilians and the latter's presumed lack of discipline, disorderliness, procrastination, and hedonism. Vagts(1959), Janowitz(1960), Price(1971) and Abrahamsson(1972) comment on this oft-noted chauvinism — one aptly paraphrased in the African setting by DuBois(1969:5):

> many military men feel they are better equipped than civilians to rule their countries, because, unlike civilians, they are politically untainted. This supposed political purity emanates mainly from the fact that as military men they are usually not a part of any political party, indeed, in their professional capacity as soldiers they have remained almost totally aloof from the internecine struggle that characterizes politics. To many military men political parties are at worst a cancer which must be excised if the nation is to survive; at best they are a nuisance which must be tolerated but only so long as they abide by the strictures of good behavior as set down by the military themselves.

22. These patterns as well as the previously mentioned civilian superiority with respect to inflation are consonant with Tannahill's general conclusion — though my economic growth, manufacturing output, and inflation indicators favoring civilians differ from his findings for the ten South American regimes.

23. According to one U.N.(1972:13) report, there is an "increasing economic 'gap' between" the advanced capitalist societies and most of those in the Third World. Between 1960 and 1973, the average annual rate of per capita GNP increased by 4 percent in developed countries, and 3.3 percent in underdeveloped areas. Even "at a rate of growth of 3.5 percent, average income per person in the developing world would rise from the 1970 level of $200 to the level of only around $280 (in 1970 prices) by 1980." Average industrial growth rates (U.N.:1974) for the state socialist systems of 8.6 percent compare favorably to 6.3 percent for advanced capitalist systems during the decade of the 1960s when the average growth rate in per capita GNP for this group (less the GDR, USSR, and CSR) was 5.3 percent.

24. According to an August 30, 1976 report in *Granma,* the industrial output of all COMECON member countries had risen by 45 percent between 1971–75, while that in the capitalist countries of the First World had increased by about 10 percent.

25. Sources on military peculation in the Third World are listed in Chapter 4, notes 14 and 15.

26. I am dealing with regime performance relevant to the availability of food rather than nominal adequacy of the total food supply. As for the latter, the 1969–71 average calorie supply as a percent of requirements — which may have reflected prior regime performance and casts no light upon distribution — is as follows: military: 102(18); nonsocialist civilian: 100(27); Cuba: 117; civilian electoral: 103(5); civilian open door: 100(26); military open door: 103(12); Tanzania: 98; military state capitalist: 98(6). Source: U.N.(1974, Pt.1:85–6).

27. Thus, in his perspicacious 1853 tract on *The Future Results of British Rule in India* (Tucker, 1972:586–87), Marx is explicit in warning:

> all the English bourgeoisie may be forced to do will neither emancipate nor materially mend the social condition of the mass of the people, depending not only on the development of the productive powers, but on their appropriation by the people. But what they will not fail to do is to lay down the material premises for both. Has the bourgeoisie ever done more? Has it ever effected a progress without dragging individuals and peoples through blood and dirt, through misery and degradation? The Indians will not reap the fruits of the new elements of society scattered among

them by the British bourgeoisie, till in Great Britain itself the now ruling classes shall have been supplanted by the industrial proletariat, or till the Hindoos themselves shall have grown strong enough to throw off the English yoke altogether. At all events, we may safely expect to see, at a more or less remote period, the regeneration of that great and interesting country. . . .

28. I am referring not merely to the costs delineated in Tables 7.7, 7.8, and 7.9, but also to certain intangible or qualitative dimensions. Thus, the mere fact that the people are governed by armed praetorians in uniform may be regarded as an overwhelming affront to the self-esteem of civilians, effectively denying them all semblance of citizenship. Similarly, national self-esteem is difficult to maintain when open door policies result in foreign control of the strategic sectors of the economy. If Europeans, Japanese, and OPEC potentates owned the major industries of the United States and 1/3 of the most productive agricultural land, would Americans feel it was *their* nation? Their self-respect would certainly be tarnished, if not transformed, into latent economic nationalism.

29. The research of Chorley(1971) and Russell(1974) is fully in accord with the thesis that social revolutionary success requires either a breakdown of the army command structure or one of the following: 1) division among the armed forces; 2) a general collapse of morale; 3) defeat in war; or 4) external assistance to revolutionary forces as occurred in the American Revolution.

8

Arms Transfers and Developmental Prospects

The global rise in arms transfers among nations during the past decade or so has been particularly pronounced for the Third World nations of Africa, Latin America, the Middle East and Asia. Between 1968 and 1977 alone (in constant dollars), Third World arms imports increased from 5.9 billion to almost 13 billion dollars, while their arms exports barely doubled, rising from an insignificant .3 billion to little more than .6 billion dollars. For developed countries, the U.S.A.C.D.A.(1979:113) reports a far less pronounced rise from 2.8 billion to 3.7 billion dollars for the same period. At the same time the latter's exports ascended from 8.4 billion to 16 billion dollars—most of which was destined for Third World nations. Equally apparent has been the association of such transfers with a process of militarization in the recipient states. Although not true in every case, on the average governmental resources allocated to military-related purposes rose over the period, including concomitant external debt service and repayment obligations. Furthermore, there has been marked growth in both the size of armed forces as well as military/population ratios.

If the foregoing relationships are fairly well established, others evoke considerable disagreement among both academics and attentive publics. This chapter will explore linkages between such arms transfers and "dependency"—a term which over the past 15 years has come into wide use in depicting North/South relationships that are commonly viewed as inimical to national sovereignty and socio-economic development. First, I shall distinguish the structural characteristics of economic dependency from its historico-political sources. Then, a number of socio-economic and cultural consequences will be examined. Finally, I shall elaborate a series of propositions relating distinct arms transfer patterns to the efforts by Third World elites to diminish or reinforce such dependency relationships.

Dependency as a Structural Relationship of World Capitalism

Although development and international relations theorists who have addressed themselves to the concept of dependency are by no means unanimous as to the range of relationships to which it refers, nor, for that matter, to the most appropriate means for transcending them, this is one of the few areas where a measure of agreement can be found between some Marxists and non-Marxists. One of the more cogently stated Marxian conceptualizations of dependency has been provided by Theotonio dos Santos:

Dependence is a situation in which a certain group of countries have their economy conditioned by the development and expansion of another economy, to which the former is subject. The relation of interdependence between two or more economies, and between these and world trade, assumes the form of dependence when some countries (the dominant) can expand and give impulse to their own development, while other countries (the dependent) can only develop as a reflection of this expansion. This can have positive and/or negative effects on their immediate development. In all cases, the basic situation of dependence leads to a global situation in dependent countries that situates them in backwardness and under the exploitation of the dominant countries. The dominant countries have a technological, commercial, capital resource, and social-political predominance over the dependent countries (with predominance of some of these aspects in various historical moments). This permits them to impose conditions of exploitation and to extract part of the domestically produced surplus.[1]

While dos Santos and other Marxists, such as Andre Gunder Frank and Dale Johnson, identify politico-military hegemony as the source of such dependency, they are not nearly as explicit in highlighting the military dimension as are Albrecht et al.(1974:173-74), who, from an historical perspective, focus explicitly upon substantive as opposed to formal continuity:

In spite of considerable changes in economic relations between capitalist metropoles and dependent peripheries, one fact remains: armaments and the military (whatever the institutional setting might be) are indispensable for the preservation of the metropole periphery structure. The appearance and pattern of arms and violence may have changed; basically, however, until today it is the same process: their application is an important determinant for the development of the world-wide capitalist system. Neither the replacement of private armies by big colonial armies during the 19th and beginning of the 20th century . . . nor the breakup of colonial armies and the reshaping into and set-up of "national" military apparatuses in peripheral countries could change the fundamental function of armaments and the military as far as they are used in the periphery. . . .

The penetration of the present underdeveloped countries characterised by production sectors totally dependent on and determined by outside powers was only
made possible by the use of arms, sometimes for many decades. This applies
especially to regions with complex social structures and highly developed productive forces. The process of increasing underdevelopment and dependence was carried out by means of robbery, trade, extraction of resources, partial industri-
alisation to create markets for cheap consumer goods, outdated and already
depreciated technologies, etc. The accumulation of these mechanisms resulted in
a structure characterised by unequal transfer relations. The enormous expansion
and unfolding of productive forces in Europe and the United States resulted in a
corresponding decrease of the potential for autonomous accumulation and the
retrogression or stagnation of productive forces in the capitalist periphery.

Dependency, therefore, is as much a source of underdevelopment as it
is a consequence of external politico-military hegemony.[2] The latter is
institutionalized through the creation and co-optation of indigenous
oligarchic allies.[3] Internal effects, however, are not limited to such
mutually reinforcing hierarchical power linkages, but as Gunder
Frank(1972:19–20) underscores in the following passage, the psychological reactions are both multifaceted and dialectical —
culminating in resistance:

dependence is the result of the historical development and contemporary structure of world capitalism, to which Latin America is subordinated, and the
economic, political, social, and cultural policies generated by the resulting class
structure, especially by the class interests of the dominant bourgeoisie. It is important to understand, therefore, that throughout the historical process, dependence is not simply an "external" relation between Latin America and its world
capitalist metropolis but equally an "internal" indeed *integral* condition of . . .
society itself, which is reflected not only in international and domestic economics
and politics but also has the most profound and far-reaching ideological and psychological manifestations of inferiority complexes and assimilation of metropolitan ideology and "development" theory. At the same time, this dependence
generates reactions which are visible through nationalism, the growing class struggle against the capitalist system. . . .

Thus we can summarize the elements of dependency in the modern era as
historically conditioned structural or institutional relationships that are
hierarchical in terms of both resources and benefits. Further, these extend beyond the economic realm into political, social, and cultural areas
within the dependent societies. And finally the exploitative character of
such economic relationships generate its own antithesis in nationalist and
socialist struggles for liberation.

Notwithstanding the tendency of non-Marxists to deemphasize the unequal character of such relationships, which at times are depicted as a
natural evolutionary division of labor, some theorists such as K. J.
Holsti(1977:89,91) have gone so far as to posit not only dependency's

asymmetrical dimension but also acknowledge its mutually reinforcing attributes.

Dependence characterizes the relations between the developing countries and the industrial West, where dependence is defined as unequal degrees of reliance on markets and sources of supply, and unequal ability of the members of a pair of states to influence, reward, or harm each other. Although there are some notable exceptions, such as the oil-producing countries, the actions or policies developing states undertake have little impact on the political or economic fortunes of industrialized states, even small ones. The policies of an industrialized state, on the other hand, often have significant consequences on a developing country; and any attempt to alter drastically or terminate the relationship is extremely costly to the latter, and less so to the former. . . . Dependence and interdependence are obviously relative concepts, or different ends of a continuum. State A can be dependent on B, but interdependent with C, and virtually irrelevant to D. Likewise, A can be economically dependent upon B, but militarily dependent upon C. Singer argues, however, that the various dimensions of dependence correlate highly with each other: If A is dependent in one dimension, it is likely to be dependent in all dimensions.

Hence, it may be hypothesized that once political hegemony is established and used to structure a subordinate economic relationship, other societal areas become similarly dependent. This however does not affect the entire institutional panoply but only certain aspects of the economic, socio-cultural, and even the political subsystems. Thus, as Sunkel and Fuenzalida(1976:3–8) have noted, "a process of disintegration" occurs in dependent societies.

Parts of the bourgeoisie, of the petty bourgeoisie, of the industrial working class, etc., are integrated into the transnational system while other parts are not. . . . This is most obvious in its effect on the economy—the setting off of a process of internal polarization, involving the expropriation of local entrepreneurial groups, the disruption of indigenous economic activities, and the concentration of property and income. But disintegration is also discernible in other organized social activities, such as scientific research, architecture, and urban/regional planning, medicine, education, the arts, and at a cultural/personal level. . . . The result of these contradictory trends has been an aggravation of internal polarization—increasing poverty and unemployment of the majority and growing affluence of a minority—and foreign dependence—the structural interlocking of the minority into transnational capitalism. The political tensions arising out of these phenomena may well be among the most important causes of the growing number of repressive and authoritarian regimes that nowadays characterize the Third World, and one of the strong nationalist reactions towards the industrialized countries.

Such nationalist reactions are evoked despite "unprecedented process of economic growth, industrialization, and modernization" caused by external economic penetration and investment. The Iranian uprising against the Shah is a case in point.

In sum, then, dependency is not limited to external relationships but involves concomitant domestic restructuring and antagonistic patterns of reactive nationalism. The appeal of such nationalism is enhanced by downturns of economic growth in a context of rising external debt burdens. And if contemporary national liberation struggles signify one important response to neo-colonialism, then, as Joseph Kahl(1976:187) has argued, dependency theory itself can be viewed as "the weak man's answer to imperialism; it was imperialism as seen from the bottom looking up and suggested that if the process could be better understood it might be mastered."

Politico-Military Sources of Dependency

Notwithstanding the mutually reinforcing character of dependency, analytical clarity may be sharpened distinguishing its historical politico-military sources from the consequential web of interlocking relationships. The causal significance of such hegemony has been pointed up by Marxists dos Santos, Johnson, and Gunder Frank as it has in a more indirect manner by the non-Marxist, Fernando Henrique Cardoso (Kahl, 1976:156–57), who stresses the primacy of the political in both its causal and reactive dimensions.

to explain economic processes in terms of social processes requires us to find a theoretical point of intersection where economic power is expressed as social domination, that is in politics. Through the political process, one class or economic group tries to establish a system of social relations that will permit it to impose its view on the whole society, or at least it tries to establish alliances to ensure economic policies compatible with its own interests and objectives. Thus we will emphasize the following: the economic conditions of the world market, including the international equilibrium of power; the structure of the national productive system and its links with the external market; the forms of distribution and maintenance of national power; and above all the socio-political movements and processes pushing toward change, with their various orientations and objectives.

Hence, in the remainder of this chapter, I shall discuss separately military or neo-colonial sources of dependency, the effects of arms transfer patterns, and the relevance of these patterns to national struggles for self-determination and development.

The historical origins of socio-economic dependency are directly traceable to imperial conquest by Britain, France, Spain, and several other powers that carved out smaller empires between the 15th and 20th centuries. Although the forms of empire varied, as did the circumstances and initial goals of conquest, the socio-economic outcomes were quite similar, with the exception of a handful of settler colonies. Dual patterns of raw materials production and export dependence were imposed, while indigenous manufacturing was stifled so that narrow markets for such products could be monopolized by the colonial power. In the process, indigenous para-military forces were organized to stabilize such a social order, while miniscule local elites were tied to it by being accorded positions and limited socio-economic privileges. Although the administrative center and a small number of economic enclaves were modernized, the remainder of the colonial territories were only marginally and occasionally affected. Consequently, social stagnation characterized a large domain within these societies, as did what Pablo Gonzalez Casanova(1970) has depicted in the Mexican setting as "internal colonialism," wherein politically hegemonic elements in the modernized "center" extracted surplus and labor from hinterland areas.

Such patterns persisted in Latin America when Spain's weakness during the Napoleonic era enabled independence movements backed by indigenous land-owning and comprador classes to establish formally sovereign states. Benefits flowing to these classes from the prevailing free trade system integrated them to such a degree that external military reinforcement was readily solicited or acquiesced to when domestic nationalist or lower class movements threatened the social order's stability. Such "free trade imperialism" or neo-colonialism involved the use of force, loans, military training missions, informal cultural exchange, and of course crass bribery at one time or another. While Britain played the dominant role during most of the 19th century, France, Germany and the United States (especially in the Caribbean region) were also quite active in furthering investor interests.

Analogous patterns appeared in the 20th century as "new nations" emerged in Asia, Africa, and the Middle East. Traditional colonial powers were defeated or weakened by war, while emergent socialist and trade union movements infused unheralded dynamism into the politics of many new states. The United States and other neo-colonial powers responded to the challenge directed against what was now euphemistically called the "open door" by institutionalizing a broad range of influences to either destabilize or strengthen Third World regimes. Initially, the primary focus of these programs was Latin America, but gradually increasing emphasis was placed upon other underdeveloped regions. The "nation-building" programs embrace not only military and economic aid but systematized cultural exchange, propaganda diffusion, and covert activities as well.

These inputs are anything but neutral with respect to recipient developmental strategies. The United States and, less uniformly, other Western programs mobilize bias in favor of regimes willing to follow an "open door" approach at the minimum, and optimally a corporate subsidization or privilege conferral role by the state. While some specific projects may not appear to carry ideological baggage, the context and associated programs customarily reveal such a framework of assumptions, beliefs, and attitudes.

This also holds for various sorts of aid and cultural exchange programs from Communist or state socialist systems. Their minimum objectives are an end to pro-Western foreign policy alignment and pursuit of an economic development strategy which may be characterized as at least a "partly closed door." The latter may be depicted as a state capitalist developmental strategy in which the state directs the economy and exercises control or dominates the major means of production. While at this historical juncture it is problematic whether such an approach can fully vitiate structural dependency upon advanced capitalist powers, the mere existence of major Eastern aid donors and trade possibilities tends to broaden options and thereby diminish the degree of dependency.

State socialist systems appear to be the only regime type that has been able to eradicate such dependency and grow rapidly enough to begin to close the per capita GDP gap vis-à-vis the advanced capitalist societies. With the possible exceptions of revolutionary Cuba and Afghanistan however, no state capitalist regime has, as a consequence of intraelite conflict, been transformed into a state socialist system. While the latter have usually followed from communist-led revolutionary struggles involving guerrilla and/or internal war, the most common fate of the state capitalist system is to experience a rightist "open door" coup. Although the new elite usually retains some of the socially owned sector, it nevertheless curtails or reverses many of the leftist policies that characterized the deposed regime. Cuba is the exception which may or may not prove the rule. Less than two decades of experience lie behind us and it is quite conceivable that, if others such as Afghanistan emulate the Cuban strategy, additional state socialist "revolutions from above" may be effectuated. This is not to minimize the difficulties — rather to stress that alternative futures do in fact exist. As the aid programs of existing state socialist systems grow along with their cultural and other infusions, a reinforcing external environment for such transformations will gradually develop in the 1980s and 90s. Hence the maximal objectives of state socialist donors may be attained in some cases. U.S.-backed destabilization strategies against Cuba, Angola, Ethiopia, and more recently Afghanistan imply that the costs will be extraordinarily high.

One of the newer developments associated with neo-colonial strategy is what has been called the "low profile" or "subimperialism." This refers among other things to arms transfers by proxy countries. While in some instances the arms or components may be of indigenous manufacture, the exports customarily are assembled or previously imported weapons systems. Iran, India, Israel, and Brazil are four Western countries that have upon occasion engaged in such activities, while Czechoslovakia and the German Democratic Republic have done so for the USSR. The latter however are fully industrialized.

Commercial arms transfers, particularly of weapons in use for some time, involve little political significance aside from their reinforcement of a particular regime's coercive resources.[4] However, those which include training and advisory support have obvious ideological and intelligence effects. It is not simply the training in how to handle specific weapons, but the hospitality programs, guided tours, and less subtle ideological exposure that accompanies U.S. and other Western training of foreign officers. In the former case at least, follow-up is handled by military intelligence who in turn cooperate with the CIA. As suggested in Chapter 3, the efficacy of such indoctrination is greatest among those who have done repeated training tours, and for armed forces with the highest proportion of officers exposed to such external socialization.

Patterns of Arms Transfers

Before elaborating a series of propositions that conclude this chapter, it might be useful to distinguish several patterns of arms transfers. The following list indicates the range of options available to Third World elites:

A. One dominant Western supplier
B. Multiple Western suppliers
C. Ideologically diversified suppliers
D. One dominant Eastern supplier
E. Multiple Eastern suppliers
F. Marginal/occasional suppliers

One factor of considerable importance is of course the technological and organizational capabilities of Third World nations. Politico-military hegemony is accentuated by low recipient capability levels because they tend to increase reliance upon external training and advisory programs. Hence, it is essential to reject both the importation of sophisticated weapons systems as well as attempts to produce them locally until the level of civilian technological capability has reached the general standard prevailing in advanced industrialized systems. Thus Wulf(1979:248–49) takes pains to point out that

the underdeveloped countries are likely to suffer from a double disadvantage if arms-production programs are initiated locally or modern equipment is procured by the armed forces; the scarcity of skilled personnel raises the cost of technology transfer and, subsequently, production and maintenance costs. Arms production, therefore, is not suitable to alleviate unemployment problems, as is often claimed. . . . On the contrary, the allocation of . . . financial resources to purchase or produce weapons reduces the potential for the promotion of development through labor-intensive technologies in civilian sectors of the economy. The argument of creating employment opportunities by producing arms is a rather paltry one and obfuscates the development issue. This is particularly true since the qualifications acquired in arms production or in the military services are only of limited value and only occasionally applicable in civil production.

Dramatically increased imports and greater production of modern military equipment in the periphery were necessarily based upon a multiplication of the number of technicians, engineers, and scientists from industrial countries working there. Without their services, it is impossible to keep the equipment operational according to the pattern of industrialized countries. The independent decision-making in the military sector which is hoped for, and expected through indigenous arms production, cannot be attained since local production is crucially reliant on the delivery of technology and personnel from abroad.

Besides the fact that modern equipment often lies rusting in ports or stores, since it cannot be maintained in actual fighting between peripheral countries, sophisticated carrier systems like fighter-bombers and main battle tanks have often proved a handicap. Because of poor logistics (like shortage of munition supplies), lack of special military infrastructures (like airfields and fortified bridges) and inferior training of soldiers, the modern equipment can be used only marginally or even not at all.

As will be made explicit in my final proposition below, such apparent rejection of military "modernization" need not necessarily deprive a Third World country of a viable interim national security strategy. On the contrary, in conjunction with a labor intensive economic development approach, it is fully consonant with both short and long-run maximization of defense capabilities.

Propositions on Arms Transfers and Dependency

The following propositions are offered primarily for heuristic purposes. While precise measurement may be quite difficult in some instances, in others the associational patterns can more readily be tested.

1. The descending progression of arms transfer patterns (A–F) listed in the preceding section is positively associated with the minimization of dependency. As noted in an earlier section, the intervening variables are the ancillary training and advisory programs. These in turn are related to the second proposition.

2. The extent of dependency is a function of the degree of politico-military domination. If, as I and others have argued, the source of socio-economic and cultural dependency is politico-military hegemony, then it follows that political independence is the key to transforming such struc-

tural relationships. In the West, this implies struggles by radical nationalist and socialist liberation movements—both objects of destabilization programs by U.S. military training and covert action agencies.

3. The sources of dependency vary in different historical epochs. Direct military conquest played a central role in the establishment of colonial empires, while intermittent force in conjunction with economic "aid," bribery, and "cultural exchange" programs have assumed primary importance in the contemporary neo-colonial era. During the past decade or so, similar resources have been employed through third party proxies and what has been called the "low profile." Direct interventions continue to be utilized occasionally, and the newly created U.S. rapid deployment force implies greater activity of this sort in the future.

4. The rapidly growing sophistication of modern weapons is an obstacle to the minimization of dependency. The inability of many Third World countries to master modern technological and organizational skills has induced weapons recipients to solicit external training and advisory groups. Even the "transitional," less underdeveloped Third World societies fail to escape this situation because of their desire for the most complex weapons systems.

5. Militarization in the Third World over recent decades has made it more difficult for monopoly capitalist and state capitalist systems to decrease their dependency upon Western neo-colonial powers. The sharp rise in military expenditures has led not only to increased imports and concomitant training programs, but also to skyrocketing external debt burdens and to the destabilization of many state capitalist-oriented radical regimes. The latter have included: Brazil, Indonesia, Ghana, Mali, Bolivia, Cambodia, Uganda, Egypt, Chile, and Peru.

6. State socialism has enabled countries to reduce their dependency by furthering the diffusion of state capitalism as well as socialism. The mobilization capabilities of most new state socialist systems and their Eastern orientation enable them to alter and redirect economic relationships with traditional Western powers and associated economic institutions. This is not to say that all existing links are severed, though U.S. embargoes have in some cases reduced the range of choice. Cuba, because of the state capitalist top-down origins of her socialism, has encountered considerable difficulties in efficiently utilizing volunteer labor. Nevertheless, she is following other new Communist-governed countries in developing in spirit of self-reliance, planned economic development, and a broad diversification (Levesque, 1978) of trading partners. The existence, performance, and diffusion of socialist systems in the present century has not only radicalized the consciousness of elite sectors elsewhere in the Third World, but has given them sufficient international room for maneuver to allow a real chance for survival during the initial

period of radical regime establishment.[5] If most such systems are socialist in name only, they nevertheless represent a marked departure from the monopoly capitalist variant.[6]

7. Although the propositions elaborated above offer a range of alternatives for Third World regimes intent upon reducing the degree of historical dependency, only the final option listed in the preceding section is consonant with eliminating all forms of dependency. This however signifies a qualitative change in a state's national security strategy to one premised upon and integral to a self-reliant mobilizational approach which implies explicit acknowledgment of the need to maximize the short-run allocation of economic resources to industrialization, full employment, and socio-cultural development. These processes, in the long-run, will ensure both far higher quality military manpower and a concomitant mastery of modern military technology. Since capital is scarce and manpower is abundant, labor intensive production of relatively unsophisticated "defensive" armaments should be promoted with a simultaneous reduction and diversification of external imports to the lowest possible level. Wulf(1979:255–56) suggests that:

Besides . . . infantry units equipped with simple wire guided anti-aircraft equipment, occasionally a small navy for coastal protection is required, whereas the protection against possible air attacks lies in the hands of decentralized infantry units.

To promote target dispersal and diminution, fewer logistical problems, and continued civilian production, mass involvement of citizen volunteers in militia or reserve units would make easy conquest more difficult while vitiating the economic costs of a relatively large standing force. Thus, the same author continues:

Since the defenders are not dependent upon external assistance the aggressor cannot hope to blackmail the defenders into surrender by cutting off . . . the supply of weapons and parts. On the contrary, the invaders are permanently harassed and attacked by a large number of lightly armed combatants with the intention not necessarily of defending the territory or the border of the country but of ultimately forcing the aggressors to surrender.

Because our range of historical vision is often circumscribed by the exigencies of the present it can be difficult to see the movement toward the left that has been occurring during this century. Such an "unconventional strategy" would not only drastically curtail the diversion of economic resources from vitally needed mass welfare programs that themselves contribute to taller, healthier, and better-motivated conscripts, but it would equally foment a spirit of self-reliance and mesh with a labor intensive developmental approach which would absorb the unemployed and avoid increased external indebtedness. Only in this way will mastery as well as transfer of new technology occur — a sine qua non for attenuating scientific and cultural dependency. At the same time, because this "unconventional" security strategy implies a non-repressive military, it is consonant with a socially radical regime committed to mass welfare. In such a setting military professionals will not only be maximizing the short and long-run strength of the nation, but they will be accorded the honor and prestige that those seriously devoted to this calling merit. Despite the reversals, and obvious shortcoming of both state capitalist and socialist systems, the global expansion of these regime variants contribute to the slow weakening of world capitalism and its exploitative structural relationships. OPEC is one manifestation of this trend, as are deepening North/South antagonism, renewed Western (i.e., U.S., Japanese, NATO) diversion of civilian resources to militarization, and the financial crisis that has weakened world capitalism since the early 1970s. On the other hand, a growing number of states have rejected the "open door" approach to development within the past five years — Vietnam, Kampuchea, Tanzania, Afghanistan, Ethiopia, Angola, Nicaragua, Jamaica, Guyana, Zimbabwe, et al.[7] Capitalism as a world system may be far from dead, but there is little basis for doubting that, with the consolidation of the Bolshevik Revolution, it began a long period of secular decline.

Notes

1. "La crisis de la teoria del desarrollo y las relaciones de dependencia en America Latina" (Santiago: 'Boletin del Centro de Estudios Socio-Economicos,' No. 3, 1968, University de Chile), pp. 26-27, as quoted by Johnson(1972:71-2).

With respect to dos Santos' references to "exploitation" and surplus extraction, the following is instructive:

> between 1950 and 1966 . . . corporations and private citizens brought into the country $59.0 billion in excess of all private dollar outflows; . . . direct investments have returned substantial income to their companies in the United States, far greater than the direct investment outflows; . . . from 1950 to 1966 these investments returned in dividends and royalties and fees alone $20 billion in excess of all outflows. . . . Recently Professor Behrman argued before the Joint Economic Committee that the payback period for outflows of the U.S. dollars for manufacturing investment abroad is about 2½ years on the average. If this is right — and I must say, this estimate comes close to my own experience — this is a very short term indeed.

From a speech by John J. Powers, Jr., President Charles Pfizer and Co., delivered at an American Management Association special briefing on "New Foreign Investment Controls," in New York City on April 10, 1968, reprinted in the *NACLA Newsletter* 2 (November 1968):8-10. Cf. Gordon(1968) and Magdoff(1969,1978).

2. Chase-Dunn(1978) elaborates a number of interesting hypotheses concerning not only core-periphery linkages but also on cyclical shifts of dominance among core powers. Recent data provided by McLaughlin(1979) is consistent with the thesis of deepening dependency or the "development of underdevelopment."

3. Thus Johnson(1972:73) acknowledges that "the combined economic and military power of the imperial countries became instrumental in keeping Latin American nations as de facto colonies." And he goes on to argue that "dependence relations also shape the social structure of underdevelopment. A principal factor in the development and perpetuation of underdevelopment was (and is) the coincidence of interest between national oligarchies and the economic structure of underdevelopment. National businessmen grew up with and benefited from their nations' position as de facto colonies."

4. Since the U.S. and other major Western Powers also encourage commercial sales and even training, it is impossible empirically to dissociate them from other external penetration activities that directly promote control and dependency. In the U.S. for example, the Defense Department's functions included active encouragement of commercial sales and training in some cases such as Saudi Arabia. Furthermore, as Vayrynen(1977:145–66) stresses, commercial sales, concomitant bribery and local production through licensing reinforce other structural aspects of economic dependency.

5. This and other factors that influence radical survival prospects are discussed in the next chapter.

6. Not only in the extension of public ownership or control over the means of production, but also in the area of egalitarian social reforms. For a summation of such measures by the "radical" regimes of Mossadegh, Arbenz, Bosch, Goulart, Sukarno, Nkrumah, Keita, Sihanouk, Torres, and Allende, see Chapter 4.

7. In the 1960–74 period alone, a U.N. report on nationalizations and takeovers recorded 875 cases in 62 countries of the world—predominantly in the underdeveloped areas. Africa accounted for 340 of them and "led in all categories of industry except petroleum—that is, in instances of nationalization of mining, agriculture, manufacturing, trade, public utilities, banking and insurance." Thus a contemporary analyst (Rood, 1976:447) of this trend in Africa concludes with the following prediction:

> The pattern of takeovers during the last decade in black Africa, as well as that in the rest of the world, suggests very strongly that they will continue to nationalize and indigenise enterprises whenever they believe it will serve their own interests. The only limitations will be practical ones . . . [as] the growing strength of the natural resource blocs such as OPEC, the spread of socialism, and the increased acceptance of nationalization vastly improve the bargaining position of the nationalizing countries.

Data on nationalizations are quoted from U.N. Secretary General, Permanent Sovereignty over Natural Resources, A/9716, Supplement to E/5425, Annex (New York: U.N., 1974), p.1. The global dimensions of this trend are more fully discussed in Chapters 6, 9, and 10.

9

Contemporary Radical
Third World Regimes

Two tendencies which first appeared in Latin America during the decade preceding the Second World War have now become forces for structural transformations throughout the entire Third World. The first was the emergence of communist-led parties, trade unions, and mass organizations. Even broader appeal, in the short-run at least, has been evoked by less far-reaching goals associated with populism and economic nationalism — what I shall term "radicalism," though in the contemporary era "socialist" is often utilized by Third World political elites.

A third related development — explored in Chapter 6 — is the growing attraction of radical socio-economic policies to professional military officers. Even in the 1930s, left-wing ideas inspired Latin American officers who led governments for periods ranging from several months to a few years in Chile, Bolivia, and Mexico. While Alfred Vagts(1959) may have been justified in discounting such deviations as exceptions to the general rule that officers have historically functioned as a conservatively inclined social group, the incidence of left-wing militarism since the 1940s requires revision if not rejection of this characterization. Thus, a mid-1975 classification of noncommunist Third World countries with populations of half a million or more reveals that of the 46 which were military-dominant, 16 were led by military radicals. Among the civilian-dominated regimes however, only five out of 36 were so led. This can be compared with the situation little more than a decade earlier when a far smaller proportion of military-dominated systems were led by radical officers while a substantial majority of Third World countries still boasted civilian supremacy.[1]

These shifts then imply not merely the subversion of civilian rule by militarists, but also a pattern of acute political instability with respect to both policy orientations and of course civil-military relations.[2] In the sections which follow, I shall: 1) set forth a number of propositions on the survival prospects of radical regimes; 2) identify the internal contradictions which account for their exceptional instability; 3) examine factors which at least temporarily ameliorate the intensity of such contradictions; and 4) assess the radical or state capitalist approach as a viable development strategy.[3]

Theses on Radical Survival Prospects

1. Although the average life of radical regimes may not be nasty or brutish, there is no doubt that it is short. As Table 9.1 indicates, radical elites who were either deposed or induced to moderate their commitments to structural change in 18 nations during the three decades following World War II lasted for an average of less than four years. Interestingly, the seven military-dominant regimes managed to impose radical structural change for more than two and a half years longer on the average than their civilian counterparts. This difference does not characterize radical regimes which existed in mid-1975, as the average duration of both civilian and military governments was slightly above six years.

2. The increase in the proportion of radical military regimes in the more recent period may help to account for the enhanced survival prospects for Third World radicalism. Table 9.2 reveals that military regimes constituted more than two-thirds of this category—a significant reversal of the earlier situation. Since structural change generally provokes violence by groups whose privileges are being reduced, it may well be that professional managers of violence are more capable than civilians of successfully confronting conservative opponents—at least in the short run. Decisiveness, combativeness, bravery, initiative, and abhorrence of disorder are qualities of the so-called military mind. These and the widespread military disdain for politicians, especially those regarded as hostile to the armed forces, may put the military at an advantage in adopting the coercive measures necessary to promote structural change.[4]

3. The survival of a small number of civilian regimes in the contemporary era for approximately the same length of time as the radical military ones is accounted for by civilian leaders who appear to have assimilated at least some of the forementioned qualities which characterize the "military mind." Leaders of Guinea and Tanzania, the two cases which are responsible for the comparable civilian average have exhibited decisiveness, initiative, flexibility, and some measure of ruthlessness in denying political resources to anti-"socialist" forces—civilian as well as military—within their polities.

4. Greater longevity for recent civilian and military radical elites

Table 9.1   *Duration of Deposed or Moderated Radical Regimes: 1945-74 (in years)*

Nation	Civilian-dominant[a]	Military-dominant[a]	Radical period
Algeria	Ben Bella[b] 3		1962-65
Argentina		Peron 10	1945-55
Bolivia	Paz Estenssoro 3		1953-56
— — —		Torres 1	1970-71
Brazil	Goulart 1		1963-64
Cambodia	Sihanouk 4		1963-67
Chile	Allende 3		1970-73
Dominican Republic	Bosch 1		1962-63
Egypt		Nasser 10	1960-70
Ghana	Nkrumah 5		1961-66
Guatemala		Arbenz 3	1951-54
Indonesia	Sukarno 4		1961-65
Iran	Mossadegh 2		1951-53
Mali	Keita[b] 5		1963-68
Sri Lanka	Bandaranaike 5		1960-65
Sudan		Numeiry 2	1969-71
Syria		Salah Jedid 7	1963-70
Uganda	Obote 1		1970-71
Venezuela	Betancourt 3		1945-48
Yemen		al-Sallal 6	1962-68
Average duration	3	5.6	

Combined average = 3.9

[a] Leader at the time of overthrow, removal, or policy reorientation.
[b] Exclusion reduces civilian average by .1. These coups may be interpeted as involving a change in civil-military relations rather than development strategy.

hinges upon superior leadership capabilities and also the adoption of policy approximations of "the Communist military subordination" model and/or the presence of reinforcing environmental conditions. With respect to imposing such controls upon the military, Nordlinger(1977:18–19) warns:

The penetration model is exceptionally effective once implemented. But the attempt to do so is inordinately risky, except under the unusual circumstances of a weak army, and even then the model can only be applied within a certain type of regime.

Sekou Toure took advantage of the break with France as well as abortive

Table 9.2 *Duration of 1975 Third World Radical Regimes (in years)*

Nation	Military-dominant	Civilian-dominant	Radical period begins
Afghanistan	Daoud 2		1973
Algeria	Boumedienne 10		1965
Benin	Kerekou 3		1972
Burma	Ne Win 13		1962
Congo	Ngouabi 7		1968
Ethiopia	Haile Mariam 1		1974
Guinea		Toure 15	1960
Guyana		Burnham 1	1974
Iraq	Hassan Badr 17		1958
Jamaica		Manley 3	1972
Libya	Qaddafi 6		1969
Malagasy	Ratsiraka 2		1973
Mali	Traore 7a		1968
Panama	Torrijos 7		1968
Peru	Velasco 7		1968
Portugal	Col. Vasco des Santos Goncalves 1		1974
Sri Lanka		Bandaranaike 5	1970
Somalia	Siad Barre 6		1969
South Yemen		Rubai Ali 6	1969
Syria	Hafiz al Asaad 5a		1970
Tanzania		Nyerere 8	1967
Average duration	6.2	6.3	

Combined average = 6.3

a Radicalism problematic.

conspiracies to structure what Kaba(1977:43) depicts as "a sophisticated repressive system" whose efficacy approaches Leninist "totalitarianism." As for Tanzania, Bailey(1975:40–45) underscores Nyerere's sagacity in taking advantage of an abortive mutiny not only to disband the existing two-battalion British-trained force but to utilize Chinese assistance in structuring a new highly politicized and party penetrated army.[5]

From the standpoint of reinforcing environmental conditions, both of these nonaligned regimes absorbed a substantial influx of Eastern military aid. Algeria and Iraq, two of the three radical military systems which had survived for at least a decade, benefited from similar assistance patterns in addition to large petroleum foreign exchange earnings for arms purchases. In the Burmese case, despite some Chinese aid, tight import controls, and rapid growth of industrial assistance, a severe foreign exchange crisis began to develop in the late 1960s because of poor rice harvests and the regime's inability to prevent large-scale smuggling of that key export commodity. Nevertheless, the dominant Revolutionary Command Council benefited from two exceptional circumstances that enabled it to maintain a high level of internal cohesion. First, several disunified but persistent minority ethnic and foreign-backed left-wing insurgent movements created a military threat of sorts through continued low-level attacks upon the armed forces.[6] Second, General Ne Win's hegemonic officer clique had developed considerable cameraderie as a result of common World War II combat experiences. As for the military regimes that had survived seven years, three of the four appear to have benefited from some unique reinforcing environmental condition and significantly the fourth, Peru, succumbed to an intramilitary conservative coup in its seventh year.[7] This brings us to my final thesis.

5. The destiny of radical Third World regimes is to be forced back toward an "open door" or monopoly capitalist system rather than to evolve into a full-fledged neo-Leninist state socialist society. With the exception of Cuba and more problematically Afghanistan, none of these regimes have evolved, experienced coups, or succumbed to revolutionary mass movements that resulted in the inauguration of a Marxist-Leninist system of the Soviet, Chinese, or Vietnamese type. In the past, some radical leaders were coerced into opening the door because of acute foreign exchange crises or, as in the Sudan, where Marxist sectors abortively attempted a coup. More commonly, they did so after a reactionary coup. This seems to be the fate of nearly all military-led regimes and most of those under civilian leadership. In a few cases, of course, radical civilians are ousted by radical officer cliques. Hence the Algerian and Malian episodes probably represent no more than an interim extension of state capitalism within the society in question, for the radical officer coalitions just as probably will eventually be supplanted by a "moderate" intramilitary clique. While it is undoubtedly true that most rightist shifts never fully restore the monopoly capitalist or ideological/political status quo ante, they create more propitious conditions for socialist revolutionary struggle. This is not only because of predecessor regime reforms but also due to the patent illegitimacy of their rule at the mass level, as well as their tendency to increase oppression of workers, peasants, and often lower middle class sectors. Thus almost all Marxist-led socialist revolutions have been victorious within systems characterized by right-wing rather than radical regimes.

The Contradictions of Radical Regimes

The altered East-West balance of power and the concomitant rise of new state socialist systems have obviously played an important part in both the emergence and increased regime duration for Third World radicals. At the same time, it is equally obvious that, despite their own internal contradictions, the stability of state socialist and in lesser measure monopoly capitalist systems is immeasurably greater than that enjoyed by military or civilian radicals. Notwithstanding one or two close calls, no state socialist system has even been supplanted by another social order. Furthermore, both the brevity of radical interregna and the much greater duration of the deposed capitalist or open door regimes are clearly delineated in Tables 9.1 and 9.3. A similar pattern indicating relatively greater stability—again on the order of two and one-half times—for 1975 open door systems appears in Tables 9.2 and 9.4. Thus, the average duration of the 1975 monopoly capitalist systems listed on Table 9.4 is almost 16 years and they represent about three-quarters of noncommunist Third World systems. Similarly, although Tables 9.1 and 9.3 reveal that while more than twice the number of rightist as leftist regimes have been deposed between 1945 and 1974, the proportion of the former, constituting about 80 percent of all regimes, was substantially lower.

At a superficial level, one can discern that the precondition for radical survival simultaneously functions as the source of its exceptional instability. The new East-West balance of power and radical "success" in playing off major bloc rivals have provided what Trimberger(1977) calls "international room for manoeuvre."[9] On the other hand, this has also allowed unprecedented opportunities for competitive intervention to create and reinforce externally oriented factions.[10] But what at bottom facilitates the success of such destabilizing intervention are the unintegrated values and incentive structures of the radical systems themselves. And these in turn contribute to the uneven and often poor performance of such weakly legitimized regimes in social, economic, and political areas.

The primary source of radical regime instability is not simply a pronounced gap between their official goal values and the routines that are supposed to implement them—a phenomenon found even in more stable systems—but an eclectic endeavor to graft incompatible values by fiat. In concrete terms, although the move toward socialist mobilization is conditioned by both idealistic appeal and pragmatic or opportunistic calculations of particular leader sets, the radical structural changes are limited in degree, of restricted scope and more often than not rationalized in national rather than class terms.[11] Hence while some upper classes are *par-*

Table 9.3   *Duration of Deposed or Radicalized "Open Door" Regimes: 1945-74 (in years)*

Nation	Civilian-dominant[a]	Military-dominant[a]	"Open door" period
Afghanistan	King Zahir Shah 28		1945-73
Bolivia	Paz Estenssoro 8[b]		1956-64
		Gen. Rene Barrientos 6	1964-70
Brazil		Goulart 18	1945-63
Burma		U Nu 3	1959-62
Burundi	Ntare V 4[b]		1962-66
Cambodia	Sihanouk 9		1954-63
Chile	Frei 25		1945-70
Colombia		Gen. Rojas Pinilla 12	1945-57
Congo	Massemba Debat 8		1960-68
Dahomey	Maga 3[b]		1960-63
		Ahomadegbe 9	1963-72
Dominican Republic		Trujillo 16	1945-61
Egypt	Farouk 7		1945-52
		Nasser 10	1952-62
Ethiopia	Haile Selassi 29		1945-74
Ghana	Nkrumah 3		1958-61
Guyana	Burnham 8		1966-74
Haiti		Magliore 12[b]	1945-57
Indonesia	Sukarno 12		1949-61
Iran	Reza Pahlavi 6		1945-51
Iraq	Faisal 13		1945-58
Jamaica	Shearer 10		1962-72
Korea, S.	S. Rhee 13		1948-61
Libya	King Idris 18		1951-69
Malagasy	P. Tsiranana 13		1960-73
Mali	M. Keita 3		1960-63
Niger	Diori 14[b]		1960-74
Nigeria	Tafawa Balewa 6[b]		1960-66
Panama		Arias 23	1945-68
Pakistan	Suhrawardy 11[b]		1947-58
Peru		Belaunde 23	1945-68
Portugal	Caetano 29		1945-74
Rhanda	Kayibanda 11[b]		1962-73
Sierra Leone	Stevens 6[b]		1961-67
		1[b]	1967-68
Somalia	Ali Shermarke 9		1960-69
South Yemen	Al Shaabi 2		1967-69
Sri Lanka	12		1948-60
	Senanayake 5		1965-70
Sudan	Khalil 2[b]		1956-58
		Mahgoub 10	1959-69
Syria		Karim Zahreddin 18	1945-63
Tanzania	Nyerere 7		1960-67
Uganda	Obote 8		1962-70
Uruguay	Bordaberry 28[b]		1945-73
Yemen	al Badr 17		1945-62
Average duration	11.3	11.7	
Combined average = 11.5			

[a] Leader at time of overthrow or policy reorientation.

[b] Exclusion increases civilian average by .2 and military average by 1.2. Combined average becomes 12. These coups may be interpreted as involving a change in civil-military relations rather than development policy.

Table 9.4   *Duration of 1975 Third World "Open Door" Regimes (in years)*

Nation	Military-dominant[a]	Civilian-dominant[a]	"Open door" period begins
Argentina	Videla 20		1955
Bangladesh		Mujib	1972
Bolivia	Banzer 4		1971
Brazil	Geisel 11		1964
Burundi		Micombero 9	1966
Central African Republic	Bokassa 9		1966
Cameroon		Ahidjo 15	1960
Chad		Tombalbaye 15[b]	1960
Chile	Pinochet 2		1973
China, Rep. of	Chiang 25		1950
Colombia		Lopez 18	1957
Congo	Ngouabi 7		1968
Costa Rica		Oduber 30	1945
Dominican Republic	Balaguer 10		1965
Ecuador	Rodriguez 30		1945
Egypt	Sadat 3		1972
El Salvador	Armando Molina 30		1945
Gabon		Bongo 15	1960
Ghana	Acheampong 9		1966
Guatemala	Langeraud 21		1954
Haiti		Duvalier 18	1957
Honduras	Lopez Arellano 30[b]		1945
India		Gandhi 28	1947
Indonesia	Suharto 9		1966
Iran		Reza Pahlavi 22	1953
Ivory Coast		Houphonet-Boigny 15	1960
Jordan		Hussein 29	1946
Kenya		Kenyatta 12	1963
Korea, S.	Park 14		1961
Kuwait		al-Salim al-Sabak	1963
Lebanon		Franjieh 30	1945
Liberia		Tolbert 30	1945
Malawi		Banda 11	1964
Malaysia		Abdul Razak 12	1963
Mauritania		Daddah 15	1960
Mexico		Echeverria 30	1945
Morocco		Hassan 19	1956
Nepal		Birendra 30	1945
Nicaragua	Somoza 30		1945
Niger	Kountche 1		1974
Nigeria	Mohammed 9		1966
Pakistan	Bhutto 18		1958
Paraguay	Stroessner 30		1945
Philippines		Marcos 29	1946
Rwanda	Habyalimana 2		1973
Saudi Arabia		Abdul-Aziz 30	1945
Senegal		Senghor 15	1960
Sierra Leone		Stevens 7	1968
Singapore		Lee 10	1965
Sudan	Numeiry 4		1971
Thailand		Pramoj 2	1973
Togo	Eyadema 8		1967
Trinidad		Williams 13	1962
Tunisia		Bourguiba 19	1956
Turkey	Demirel 10		1965
Upper Volta	Lamizana 9		1966
Uruguay	Bordaberry 2		1973
Venezuela	Perez 27		1948
Yemen	al-Hamdi 7		1968
Zaire	Mobutu 15		1960
Zambia		Kaunda 11	1964
Average duration	13.5	17.9	

Combined average = 15.7

[a] Executive or leader in mid-1975.
[b] Major violence.

tially expropriated and therefore antagonized, their remaining socio-economic resources provide a basis for corrupting and otherwise "subverting" inexperienced and often ideologically confused bureaucratic elites. The simultaneous attraction at the civil-military elite level of bourgeois amenities ("possessive individualism") and life styles (disdain for manual labor) makes it difficult for the new "socialists" to serve as an inspiratory model for mass sacrifice.[12]

Bourgeois consumerist and petty investment opportunities facilitate the use of residual or imported economic resources to corrupt regime strata at all levels.[13] At the same time the upper classes neutralize regime programs by curtailing economic investments, smuggling, capital flight, or negotiating for policy moderation as the price of new investments. Thus, while Block(1978:31–32) acknowledges the distinct interests and autonomy of such states, he stresses the structural constraints imposed upon "radical" regimes by the need to elicit investment from the financial-industrial bourgeoisie:

Regardless of their ideology, state managers are dependent upon maintaining adequate levels of business confidence for a series of different reasons. For one thing, the level of business confidence will determine the rate of investment and that will determine the rate of employment. The more unemployment there is, the less political support the regime is likely to have, in general. So in order to protect themselves from political dissatisfaction, state managers want to keep business confidence up. Business confidence is also important because the rate of investment determines the flow of revenues to the state itself. The amount of freedom that state managers have in a competitive nation state system to spend money on armaments is also then a function of the rate of business investment and the level of business confidence. Finally, the level of business confidence has other international ramifications. In a capitalist world economy where trade can move capital across national boundaries in response to market forces, a domestic decline of business confidence will usually generate a decline in international business confidence. International bankers are then reluctant to lend to that nation, and other businesspeople act to disinvest, so the consequence is an international payments crisis. Such a crisis presents state managers with a whole set of difficult problems that they would sooner avoid by acting in the first place to halt the decline in business confidence.

Ironically, even when state managers act to halt this decline, as in the cases of Bolivia, Mali, Peru, Cambodia, Nicaragua, Egypt, Ghana, and now Burma, the anticipated capital influx is seldom forthcoming. Despite growing shortages and the emergence of a general social crisis in the urban sectors, most radical leaders and key supporters recoil from expropriating and thus eliminating the residual bourgeois institutional apparatus for the simple reason that, in a partial yet important sense, the petty bourgeoisie constitutes a partial reference for all but the most "doctrinaire" elite sectors. The socialism of the latter is deepened not only by bourgeois intransigence, externally supported destabilization efforts, and an ability to assimilate the experience of others, but also by domestic and foreign Marxist political activists or representatives who stress the cruciality of new participatory mass roles and the universal adoption of a new ascetic work ethic at elite levels. In the absence of exceptional and usually short-term trade/aid infusions, the common result is an unstable stalemate yielding conflicting and abrupt policy changes. Conspiracies, attempted coups, purges, disorders, and eventually a regime displacement by moderate to extreme rightists is the usual denoument.[14]

Such regimes commonly experience what Welch(1978) has termed "breakdown" — violent displacement often by another military or civilian/military faction. Welch hypothesizes that the following factors, many of which are present in the case of radical regimes, increase the probability of "breakdown:" 1) economic crisis; 2) politicization and intensification of social or ethnic conflict; 3) broad objectives of the regime rather than limited ones; 4) low military cohesion; 5) efforts to suppress intramilitary dissent; 6) large size of the officer corps as compared to the upper ranks of the civil service; 7) high commitment to professionalism; 8) long duration in power without civilianization or a conscious attempt to civilianize.

If Welch's conditions are most typical of radical regimes, there is another "breakdown" paradigm that is even more explicitly focused upon the "state capitalist" system. Although they devote most attention to explaining the class dynamics and rightward shift of Syria (1970) and Egypt (1971), stressing military defeat/burdens as a major source of these regimes' economic crises, Farsoun and Carroll's(1978:152–54) conclusions are applicable to the state capitalist failures examined in Chapter 4 and to similar systems elsewhere in the Third World.

The rise of the "intermediary strata" leads to elimination of the landlord class and the big bourgeoisie. But their transformation of the productive forces through state capital evolves according to the laws of motion of capitalist institutions and the capitalist market both domestically and in the world system. Even the land reform leads to the development in the rural areas of a *Kulak* class which continues to exploit the peasantry, perhaps more efficiently than the old semi-feudal landlords. Around the state sector a *new* bourgeois — contractors, consultants, import and export specialists, distributors, as well as the expanded military-bureaucratic establishment — develops. These new bourgeois and parasitic classes are literally the *creation* of state capitalism. Their interests and their consciousness are fundamentally capitalist and contrary to the further development of socialism. As they become economically and politically influential, they disrupt the socialists' path. As they accumulate capital surplus they put pressure on the state-capitalist strata for opening the door to private, including foreign capital. Their voices and ideology become relevant for state-capitalists especially as the fiscal crises deepen and as the workers-peasants exhibit restiveness and become a threat. In alliance with the right-wing factions of the ruling intermediary state-capitalist strata, they impel revisions in policy leading to a bloodless coup against the left-wing faction (i.e., Ali Sabri in Egypt and Syria, respectively). . . . [Citing Petras(1976:22), Farsoun and Carrolls maintain that] state capitalism, while exhibiting many of the common external features of socialist development, is in reality the imposition of new forms on old "structures" leading to a socio-economic impasse in which the old "structures" increasingly inform the newer forms.

The dominance of Western neo-colonial cultural legacies stressing individualistic opportunism reinforces the "regressive" process which culminates in rampant corruption, the door being opened internationally "to Western imperialism, drawing away economically and politically from the strong links to the Eastern and Soviet bloc," and to restrictions upon "democratic freedoms and worker movements."

Ascendent state-capitalism and its leading strata rally the masses, divert them from a revolutionary path, and mediate between them and the discredited bourgeoisie. However, the state-capitalist project triggers its own internal contradictions and is unable to resolve either the national or class questions. (Again, in the Arab periphery, the threat of Israel sharpens the failure and crisis of Egyptian and Syrian state capitalism.) The state-capitalist ruling strata, in alliance with a new parasitical bourgeoisie and the resurgent old bourgeoisie fears displacement or destruction at the hands of mass-based revolutionary movements. They thus seek salvation via counterrevolution and integration into imperialism.

This pessimistic and perhaps oversimplified assessment is shared by many Marxian analysts including those like Hobsbawn(1973:190) whose approach is empirical rather than structurally deterministic. He concedes that:

Though the net results of their efforts may be substantial—it is virtually impossible to think of Egypt, Peru, and Turkey as returning to their respective old regimes—they are unlikely to be as radical as the results of the genuine social revolutions. Army radicalism remains a second-best choice; acceptable only because it is better to fill a political vacuum than to leave it. There is, moreover, at present no evidence to show that it can establish a permanent political solution.

There remains however another dimension that has been underplayed to some degree by the preceding analysis—one introduced in Chapter 6, hinted at by Hobsbawn, and particularly germane in view of the performance patterns delineated in Chapter 7.

The Radicalism of the Radicals

Because of the enormous difficulties which confront all proponents of structural change, even radicals who for a few years are buoyed up by an unusually favorable economic situation, it is relatively easy to dismiss the state capitalist approach to development as ill-conceived at best (Girvan, 1978) and crass hypocrisy or opportunism (Decalo, 1976) at worst.[15] The fact that radical elites seek power or advancement and value public office really tells us only that they are "political" actors. It does not explain why some have (and more will opt for) radical structural and egalitarian changes.[16] Nor does it help us understand the motives of their supporters. Clearly power can be used by those who aspire for historical prestige (Lenski, 1966) as well as by those seeking to preserve or improve material privileges.

To risk one's position as such Caribbean leaders as Manley and Gairy recently have by challenging Western imperialism and the socioeconomic status quo surely is more hazardous—as the instability data and common sense suggest—than accepting the parameters of one's dependent capitalist social order. Woddis(1977:79–89), for example, while not depreciating the "vacillations" and autocratic norms of "radical" officers, nevertheless acknowledges from a Marxist perspective that as far as such regimes are concerned:

Measures of land reform have been introduced, foreign enterprises nationalised, state industry built up, educational and other social reforms begun, closer relations established with socialist countries, and an anti-imperialist position taken up in external relations. . . . The anti-imperialist direction of their policies, in many cases, is not necessarily an initial motivation of their actions, but any serious attempt to slough off the inherited backwardness and outworn institutions and practices which predated the assumption of power by such officers can result in pushing them into anti-imperialist positions.

The adoption of such a posture toward vested Western interests of course invites "destabilization" as described in Chapters 3 and 4. And this process is facilitated by the contradictory economic and class forces described in the preceding part of this chapter.

More must be taken account of in appraising the significance of these regimes than their instability. The historical process in which we are living is·one of the rise of socialist values and an erosion of monopoly capitalism. Not only have substantial portions of the Third World opted for state socialism, the only development strategy that is viable from the standpoint of closing the income and welfare gap with the advanced capitalist societies, but even the state capitalist regimes in a less marked way have also reduced mass exploitation, provided greater welfare benefits and begun the process of transfering major economic resources to social ownership.[17] As mentioned earlier, even when radical elites are deposed, some of these new innovations are customarily retained and monopoly capitalism as a social system is therefore weakened.[18] The exceptions such as the Pinochet regime, which attempted to completely dismantle the state capitalist institutional panoply, generally end by alienating much of their own constituency, bringing on economic collapse, and being deposed. Even in those Third World countries ruled by "moderates," monopoly capitalism is being eroded by the selective adoption of state capitalist measures that, at least indirectly, reduce the sovereignty of the "market," i.e. deference to transnational corporate decisional processes. Thus Mauritania nationalized her largest mining company in 1974, Iran has played a vigorous role on OPEC, and Venezuela under the Acción Democrática (AD) has nationalized both iron ore and petroleum while El Salvador and pre-revolutionary Nicaragua backed Panama's demand for control over that country's major foreign controlled resource.[19]

Hence, from the standpoint of expanding public ownership of resources and the rejection of monopoly capitalist ideological hegemony, radicals do contribute in a limited but nevertheless significant way to the long-run struggle for socialism. And their concomitant aspiration for national self-determination has ofttimes been reinforced by Marxist analyses of dependency and imperialism. Thus the dual forces of socialism and "nationalism" — both integral to radical regimes — have contributed to the slow decline of monopoly capitalism as a hegemonic world system.[20] Despite the high probability that most will not evolve into state socialist systems, reactionary and conservative coups are not therefore inevitable. As the monopoly capitalist world system is weakened by its protagonists and own internal contradictions, manifested for example in the spectacular rise in public indebtedness (Payer, 1974) during the 1970s, the probability of avoiding reactionary destabilization will slowly improve. Nicaragua and Angola are cases in point.

The Cuban Model

Changes in the world balance of forces and superior communist system performance are but two factors enhancing socialist prospects. Closely related to this historical ascent is the development of an increasingly sophisticated consciousness by the more left-wing-oriented sectors within radical movements and elites. As J. P. Morray(1962) details in his incisive analysis of the Cuban revolutionary process, Fidel Castro, Che Guevara, and Raul Castro early on recognized the unviability and contradictory character of pursuing egalitarian and national developmental goals while simultaneously denouncing communists and limiting the radicalism of the "first" revolution. In recent years, unprecedented emphasis (Valdes, 1976:1–39; LeoGrande, 1978) has been placed upon institutionalizing a once personalist "second" or socialist revolution. While Cuba's road to socialist development through elite conversion was once regarded as "exceptional," in the 1970s it has been replicated in varying degree by radicals in such countries as Angola, Guinea-Bissau, Mozambique, Ethiopia, Grenada, Zimbabwe, South Yemen, and now perhaps Nicaragua. Some of these endeavors nevertheless will undoubtedly be subverted, but others will become state socialist through a combination of Soviet and/or Cuban aid and exceptional leadership capability that manages to institutionally subordinate a heretofore or potentially autonomous corporate military class.[21] Thus, in the coming decades, the "model" represented by Castro's revolutionary success will assume a less exceptional place in the world historical process. The developmental failures of Third World monopoly capitalism (i.e., moderate, "open door" approaches) will, along with the uneven performance and partial failures of radical regimes, also contribute in a modest way to the improvement of such socialist prospects, though in most cases violent insurrection or even civil war as in Afghanistan and possibly Nicaragua will be the necessary price for pursuing a Marxist option.

Radical Survival Prospects

Given the range of policy, environmental, and sociological factors discussed in preceding sections, it follows that prognostication for particular regimes is extremely hazardous. Nevertheless, in Table 9.5 we have attempted such an estimate—one that takes account of ethnic and other unique threats for certain elites (e.g., Ethiopia) and also places considerable weight upon the balance of external military training. Those in the medium survival category are distinguished by a shift in military training toward the East and at least three of the following factors:

1. a reinforcing economic and especially foreign trade environment;
2. relatively high elite cohesion and leadership initiative;
3. avoidance of conciliatory approach toward "moderates" and particularly reactionaries;
4. initiation of institutional military subordination policies;
5. increasing reliance upon state socialist aid;
6. absence of major Western-backed ethnic, religious, and/or ideological insurgencies;

Where most or all of these conditions exist in addition to demilitarization of the regime (when military in origin), reduction of elite socio-economic privileges, structuring of Marxist-Leninist cadre parties, and associated mobilizational organizations, radical prospects are estimated to be high.[22] Within such societies, the previously essayed contradictions of state capitalist regimes are being transcended slowly and at the cost of intense domestic conflict. Although any process of egalitarian structural change will engender interim dislocations and consumer goods shortages,

Table 9.5 *Survival Prospects for Contemporary Radical Regimes*

	U.S. Map trainees as percent of 1974 armed forces	State socialist trainees as percent of 1974 armed forces	State socialist trainees as of 12/74	State socialist military advisors advisors 1974	Armed forces 1974
Low Survival					
Benin	? France	—	—	—	3,000
Burma	.4	—	—	—	202,000
Ethiopia	7.3	—	—	—	45,000
Guyana	? U.K./Canada	—	—	—	4,000
Jamaica	? U.K./Canada	—	—	—	4,000
Malagasy	? France	—	—	—	11,000
Mali	? France .9	—	—	—	8,000
Panama	44.8	2.5	50	20	8,000
Average	6.7	.3	—	—	.0[b]

Medium
Survival

Afghanistan	.3	2.5	400	500	130,000
Algeria	—	2.8	50	650	80,000
Congo	? France	10.7	250	60	7,000
Guinea	? France	6.9	250	125	17,000
Iraq	.4	2.7	375	1,100	4,000
Libya	1.9	1.2	300	100 (50)[a]	25,000
Somalia	—	6.7	225	1,000	14,000
South Yemen	—	4.1	175	250	130,000
Syria	.01	2.7	550	2,200	130,000
Tanzania	Canada; W. Ger.	7.0	350	750	20,000
Average	.3	4.7	—		1.2[b]

High
Survival

Angola	—	—	—	((11,570)[a]	30,000
Guinea-Bissau	—	—	—	—	5,000
Mozambique	—	—	—	25)[a]	20,000
Average	—	—	—		2.1[b]

[a] 1976 Cuban
[b] As percentage of 1974 armed forces.
Source: U.S. Dept. of Defense, 1974. U.S. Arms Control and Disarmament Agency, 1976. U.S. C.I.A., 1975: Tables 69 and 70. Stevens, 1976: 145.

these will not seriously threaten the stability of a regime simultaneously engaged in a process of rewarding initiative and participation with dignity and status. Thus, as upper class material and institutional privilege is being eliminated, its resources and those of sectors identifying with the oligarchy are being negated through both mobilizational as well as repressive measures.

On the other hand, as Downton(1973), Hagopian(1974), and Petras(1978) make clear in a distinct but analogous context, when leadership is unwilling or incapable of mastering organizational skills and providing examples to inspire mass commitments, the inevitable interim market disruptions will grow into a general economic crisis gradually isolating the more radical officers and/or civilian leaders from both less committed elite sectors and mass constituencies as well. Intensification of cleavages and concomitant polarization then create propitious domestic circumstances for externally supported destabilization programs. And, as emphasized above, because of both the legacy of Western training as well as the socio-political characteristics (Nordlinger, 1977) of most officers, these subversive strategems frequently culminate in reactionary short-run outcomes.[23] Whether such denouements will be more likely under the belligerently antiradical and mildly militaristic Reagan administration remains to be seen.

Notes

1. Thus, using a minimum of five years for a specific policy orientation during the 1960–67 period, only two (Burma, Egypt) of 19 military-dominant regimes could be classified as radical while 42 regimes were civilian-dominant. The remaining 17 military-dominant systems were: Argentina; Colombia; Ecuador; El Salvador; Guatemala; Honduras; S. Korea; Nicaragua; Pakistan; Panama; Paraguay; Peru; Sudan; Taiwan; Turkey; Venezuela; and Zaire. The large civilian majority was accounted for by: Afghanistan; Burundi; Cambodia; Cameroon; Central African Republic; Ceylon; Chad; Chile; Costa Rica; Ethiopia; Gabon; Ghana; Haiti; India; Indonesia; Iran; Ivory Coast; Jamaica; Jordan; Kuwait; Lebanon; Liberia; Libya; Malaysia; Mali; Mexico; Morocco; Niger; Nigeria; Philippines; Portugal; Rwanda; Saudi Arabia; Senegal; Sierra Leone; Somalia; Tanzania; Trinidad; Tunisia; Uganda; Upper Volta; and Zaire. Military dominance implies control of armed forces commanders over the process of selecting the civil executive.

2. Similarly, Nordlinger(1977:6) after citing a number of studies for different Third World regions concludes that "it turns out that the military have intervened in approximately two-thirds of the more than 100 non-Western states since 1945."

3. As used here the term "development" refers to: 1) the goal of national political control over societal resources; 2) industrialization and rapid economic growth; 3) increased mass social welfare and equality. For a lucid discussion of these three components as the basis for Egyptian state capitalism ("socialism") under Nasser's leadership, see: Haddad(1973:54–68).

4. The relatively greater longevity of radical military regimes may also be a function of socialization into rigid hierarchical norms of obedience, the fact that state capitalist

developmentalism constitutes a new "mission" where external security threats are often minimal, and the corporate class consciousness occasioned by directed socialization and a distinctive martial life style. In such circumstances, it may be decidedly more difficult for reactionary plotters to develop a cohesive faction than when radical changes are imposed by civilian politicians who are not only the object of martial disdain but also commonly endeavor to subordinate the armed forces by creating paramilitary forces, introducing party organization, retiring opponents, promoting supporters, etc.

5. Western military aid was diversified (Israel, Canada, Federal Republic of Germany) and gradually reduced during the 1960s as were Soviet and GDR programs on Zanzibar. Although the Chinese became the preeminent donor between 1965 and 1970, new Canadian offers were accepted in 1973.

6. Burma illustrates the importance of coming to terms with major indigenous mass-based Marxist organizations. The anti-communism of the regime elite doomed efforts to extend social ownership into rural areas and ultimately led to its erosion in the urban sector by denying essential mobilizational resources to the "radical" elite. Thus, according to recent assessments (Silverstein, 1977: Tun, 1978:28), the meager economic performance has been accompanied by repeated exposures of regime corruption, administrative inefficiency and even an overt attempt by rightist junior officers to topple the regime. Major industries have thus far escaped denationalization and to its credit the government has contained insurgent elements.

7. Both the Congo and Mali were offered and accepted primarily Eastern economic and military assistance during this period, while Panama's Torrijos easily mobilized mass support through skillful development of a cluster of issues related to the Canal Zone. Few if any of the latter's military officers in the National Guard were recruited from Panama's upper class.

8. With respect to the exceptional costs imposed by such regimes upon the masses and the paucity of socio-economic benefits, see Chapter 7. Yet as Chorley(1943) and Russell(1974) emphasize, in the absence of demoralization or substantial intramilitary disunity, revolutionaries are unlikely to carry the day. More ominously, Hibbs(1973) found that heightened repression is strongly associated with a decline in internal war — though not collective protest — in subsequent years. The problem, it seems, is the inability of revolutionary organizations to remain viable while broadening mass constituencies under such conditions.

9. One of the most carefully balanced and perspicacious analyses of this global phenomenon is provided by Horowitz(1969). Thus, for example, Soviet military aid to Third World countries has risen markedly over the past two decades: $1.3 billion in 1955–60; $2.8 in 1961–1965; $2.8 in 1966–1970; and $5.2 in 1971–1974 (U.S. Congress, 1977:69).

10. Cottam(1967).

11. The apparent appropriateness and relevance of state capitalist innovations to opportunist short-run calculations (Girvan, 1976) explains the widespread and growing appeal of this developmental strategy. My critique centers on the reactive frame of reference of decision-makers who consequently limit the scope of radical change. Hence what appears extreme or "doctrinaire" within that framework may be considerably more pragmatic from the standpoint of avoiding a collapse or destabilization of the experiment. Leaders whose socialization inhibits the adoption of extreme socio-economic and political measures will lack the anticipatory initiative and ruthlessness essential for regime stabilization. Quite a few civilians who appear in Table 9.1 fit this description.

12. Hence the contradictory incentive structure at elite levels inhibits the internalization of new norms at the mass level thus accounting for the ubiquitous failure of "mass" parties to evoke enthusiasm, commitment, sacrifice, etc. The qualitative dimensions of mass participation, then, leave much to be desired, and mass parties often function as little more than parallel administrative apparatuses or paper organizations.

13. While state socialist systems are devoid of neither corruption nor elite consumerism, the qualitative emphasis (Aurthur, 1977:18-28) is upon rewards for production achievements, and there are virtually no potentially accumulative investment opportunities or significant property-owning sectors to bribe officials on a large scale. Thus many of the sources on contemporary radical regimes listed at the end of this work contain references to allegations or disclosures of corrupt activities by civilian and military radical elites. Some like the Siad Barre regime in Somalia appear decidedly less afflicted than others. The consequences of corruption depend not only upon its prevalence but also may be influenced by alterations in the external environment, e.g., a sharp rise in petroleum prices for exporters. In general, however, corruption would appear dysfunctional for the promotion of developmental collectivist goals by radicals because it: 1) engenders pressures to restrict the growth of social ownership of the means of production; 2) contributes to the failure of planning objectives; 3) diverts both investible surplus domestically and foreign exchange for the importation of industrial equipment or basic mass necessities; 4) makes it far more difficult to break down the barriers between mental and physical labor in order to create an example likely to evoke mass sacrifice and initiative; 5) diminishes systemic legitimacy.

14. Put differently, the "primary contradiction" of antagonistic incentives is occasioned by what might be called a transitional or mixed model of production—one which combines rather than harmonizes the class accumulative dimension of monopoly capitalism with the developmentally oriented collectivistic accumulation of state socialist systems. This contributes to understanding a broad range of "secondary contradictions" such as: 1) mildly sanctioned yet vehemently denounced official peculation; 2) an inability to fully employ both highly trained and unskilled labor despite a commitment to maximize economic growth; 3) paternalistic authoritarianism and elitism vs. commitments to promoting mass initiative and participation; 4) aspirations for national self-reliance accompanied by increased dependence upon external aid and project engineering; 5) dedication to promoting national sovereignty while maintaining systemic openness to competing Eastern and Western destabilization efforts; 6) regime self-designations as socialist or "popular" with continued middle class bias in recruiting party and bureaucratic elites. As used here the term "contradictions" refers to antithetical tendencies or policy incoherence reflecting conflicting leadership goals.

15. The "personal power" thesis was elaborated a decade and a half ago with respect to Castro by Draper(1965). More recently, Decalo(1976:24) cogently argued that its overriding importance to understanding political conflict in Benin and the Congo, as well as in non-"radical" states as Togo and Uganda. The primary motives are personal, factional or corporate aggrandizement, or defense in a setting of material scarcity while consequential fragmentation of army discipline is "only indirectly and secondarily along ethnic, class or ideological lines." In the final analysis, however, class and ideology seem deprived of even their secondary importance, for the author denies (1976:26-27) "there is much evidence beyond rhetoric and pious declarations of any sincere desire by most of the military regimes in tropical Africa to bring about fundamental social change or a rearray in the structure of power within African states. This is true of the so-called 'radical' military juntas. . . ." Of some note is a nearly identical conclusion by the African Marxist Issa Shivji(1976) with respect to Tanzania.

16. An attempt to explain this attraction by employing Marx's "materialist conception of history" appears in Chapter 6. Nordlinger(1977:66), for example, takes pains to stress that

personal interests are more or less significant in explaining any kind of elite behavior; there is no reason to suppose that they are especially salient in accounting for the interventionalist behavior of military officers. And in developing explanatory generalizations about elite behavior what is most important is not the various personal interests themselves, but the extent to which they coincide with, and their behavioral expression is facilitated by, other, more general factors. With regard to military coups, there is usually a close parallel between individual concerns and corporate interests. . . .

17. In the following paragraphs, some of the relevant socio-economic measures by several contemporary state capitalist systems are listed. Implementation of course leaves much to be desired in certain countries which are in the early stages of improving administrative and organizing techniques.

Tanzania. Emphasis during the past decade has been upon investments promoting rural collectivization and modernization. Nationalization has encompassed major industries, banks, insurance companies, wholesale trade, some retailing activities, and large rental buildings. Limited resources available for urban renewal have been used for slum eradication and construction of homes primarily for low income persons. Since the early 1970s, rents for public employees have been mildly progressive with respect to different income levels. "In Tanzania the bulk of governmental activity and development funds for the urban areas are intended to benefit 'workers' or 'lower-income groups'; at the same time, care is taken that cooperative, socialist activities are promoted, and that the gap between urban workers and rural peasants does not widen." (Stern, 1975).

Mali. Notwithstanding the denationalization of retail trade in 1968, elements within the military leadership who sought to sell or shut down 27 state enterprises were defeated—although they did manage to force the dismissal of 1/3 of the employees. Their leader, Yoro Diakite, was ousted from the government even though he had played a major role in overthrowing Keita in 1968. After conspiring against Moussa Traore, he was prosecuted and imprisoned. (Bennett, 1975).

Guinea. The early success of the PDG has been attributed to "both . . . the boldness of its social programme—its appeal to workers, women, castes, and poor people, notably . . . its opposition to the traditional oligarchy—and also . . . [to] Sekou Toure's organisational capacities." Nationalization embraced most major economic, financial, and commercial enterprises. Several state/foreign partnership agreements were entered into for extractive and industrial investments. People's stores were established in rural areas. (Kaba, 1977).

Libya. "Cradle-to-grave welfare state." "Assembly-line schools were ordered by the score" as free universal education at all levels was introduced. "New parks were being opened, new sports areas built for boys and girls alike" as "the position of women had changed greatly, largely for the better." "In and around the chief cities and towns rose block after block of new housing, much of it not quite finished with its future occupants camped nearby in shanty-towns." "A vast boom in middle and lower income housing." Free medical care and clinics were extended to many villages. Agricultural productivity was a weak spot as peasants migrated to urban areas. Yet Libyans "were eating better than ever and farm wages were high. Individual farms were being built and farm communes organized; state-owned factories dotted the landscape. Tractors and farm machinery were plentiful." Considerable "progress was being made in finding underground water, bringing paved roads and electricity to the countryside, planting miles of windbreaks, and setting out thousands of fruit trees." And to avoid early depletion of petroleum resources, production was limited in this vital nationalized industry. (Sanger, 1975).

Congo. Following an abortive coup attempt in early 1972, the Congolese Worker's Party was completely purged, a new constitution was introduced and ratified in 1973, and utilizing revenues from nationalized oil companies a broad range of measures were enacted in 1974 and 1975. Minimum wages were increased by 80 percent while price freezes were imposed upon many staples. Scholarships for education were limited to the needy. Rising oil revenues were

> channeled into the ailing and quasi-bankrupt state enterprises, and an ambitious three-year development plan. The oil bonanza also allowed the regime to reduce the national debt and to capitulate to unionist strikes for across-the-board salary increases that had previously been opposed (due to an official austerity policy). Other measures were announced in March nationalizing all private insurance companies and giving the state a majority holding in all foreign banks. At the same time the regime declared that it would not allow any new private investment projects unless state funds were also involved in the form of joint companies. (Decalo, 1976:171–2).

Benin. A series of nationalizations were carried out in 1974 and 1975 while newly constituted revolutionary committees "to spearhead . . . societal transformation" in a Marxist-Leninist direction began to function. (Decalo, 1976:81–2).

Panama. The implications of Panama's Canal Zone demands are highlighted by Torrijos' activities after he consolidated his position at the end of 1969. A Labor Code was introduced in 1972 which

> defines the rights of employees, protects employees from being discharged without just cause established by law, provides for a minimum wage and . . . requires employers to pay the equivalent of one month's salary . . . to all employees as a yearly bonus, recognizes the right of union organization as well as the right to strike, and provides for mandatory social security coverage of all occupational risks, including illness, accident, maternity, and old age pension for all workers of the state and private enterprise. . . .

"The Education Security Tax enacted in 1972 was a special 2 percent tax on all wages that was earmarked to augment operating budgets of rural farm schools, to provide loans and scholarships for needy students, and to finance the costs of nonformal literacy and adult training programs in the rural areas." The Housing Decree of 1973

> established rent ceilings in urban areas, provided incentives for low cost housing construction, required all wage earners to deposit one-third of (their extra month's bonus) in a special Ministry of Housing account . . . to be used to finance low cost housing construction projects, established safety standards for urban dwellings, and prohibited landlords from transferring the costs of garbage disposal to their tenants.

After personal and corporate income taxes had been consolidated and increased in 1970, loopholes were closed in 1974 while penalties and interest charges were to be added to tax arrears. Further, "the method of urban property valuation was changed so that the highest value among market price, property registry price, and cadastral value would be applied." Also in 1974 banana export taxes were raised as Panama joined the Union of Banana Exporting Countries which subsequently constituted the Multinational Banana Marketing Enterprise. Reacting to an investment strike during this period, the Labor Code was slightly weakened in early 1977. Yet at the same time prices of some basic foods (sugar, oil, beans, lentils) were reduced as were salaries of civil servants grossing more than $750 per month. (Bassford, 1975); (Burns, 1977); (Latin America, 1977:15,32), (Nicasio, 1977:16).

Somalia. Siad Barre sharply reduced the incidence of several forms of bureaucratic corruption and leveled down the highest salaries including his own which was limited to $250 per month. Clan favoritism in appointments to official positions was curtailed through the introduction of Somali as the national language. This was also viewed as the most expeditious means of tackling the 90 percent illiteracy rate. Hence in 1972, secondary schools were closed and the president called upon "all students [to] go out to the nomads to teach them to read and write. This programme met with some success and only minimal grumbling; indeed, when the drought became unmanageable by 1975, many students stayed out in the bush helping the Government to administer relief." The previously ignored nomads, constituting 86 percent of the population, were benefited in other ways. Thus primary school educational enrollments rose 300 percent in the early 1970s, no price controls were placed upon animal products during the draught, wells were driven along new highways, and thousands of destitute nomads accepted the opportunity to join new agricultural settlements. "All in all . . . it looks as if the Government has succeeded in reducing the rural-urban differential." This reflects a "major change in investment strategy" after 1970 so that in "the 1971–3 period . . . the rural sector received two and a half times as much development money as the urban sector." These funds included Soviet aid for a nationally owned meat factory and fishing industry and major efforts in the area of forestry, agriculture, animal husbandry, and irrigation. In urban areas, rents and prices on consumer necessities have been controlled while credit has been regulated by the nationalization of banking. Street beggars and the like have been removed to work on infrastructural projects while by the mid-1970s women were first accorded equal rights under the law. (Laitin, 1976).

Iraq. Even before the Baath came to power in 1963, the Kassem regime had confiscated and redistributed large rural estates, contracted in 1959 with the Soviet Union for the construction of 11 nationally owned factories, and denied the Iraq Petroleum Company much of its concession land. "Since 1958 the company has had to gradually surrender more and more of its revenue to the government. . . . During the 1960's, oil companies were progressively nationalized by increasing the government's share steadily until, by June 1, 1969, the process was complete." As early as 1964 "the government of Abdul Salem Aref (who with the Baath had overthrown Kassem in 1963 and toppled the Baath nine months later) nationalized all firms in which it owned 25 percent or more of the stock and formed a General Industrial Organization to manage them." A year earlier, however, the Baath had "conducted a series of unplanned nationalizations and reforms." These augmented the measures adopted by Gamal Abdul-Nasser in Syria and Abdul-Karim Kassem in Iraq. Since 1963 considerable emphasis has been placed upon establishing cooperatives and increasingly collectives or state farms. Although the strategy was to concentrate amenities upon collectives which would serve as models for area peasants, progress has been slow. On the other hand, since

> 1968 an intensive program has been [effectuated] to increase the quantity and quality of social services. According to government statistics, expenditures on medical services has increased 40 percent since 1968. The ratio of doctors to population has improved from 1/4,200 to (1972) 1/3,200. Seventy percent of the population is now covered by free health care services. The number of beds in hospitals also increased from 12,300 beds in 1968 to 20,322 in 1973, an increase of 8,000 beds. The number of medical assistants increased by 57.8 percent by 1972.

In addition, trade union organizing has been encouraged. (Ismael, 1975).

18. Most commonly, a much enlarged state economic enterprise sector is retained. Often newly created cooperatives and even welfare benefits for modern sector employees are also retained. This seems to be the case in such countries as Ghana, Mali, Argentina, Brazil, Indonesia, Sudan, Egypt, Uganda, and Portugal.

19. As noted previously, in the 1960–74 period alone, a U.N.(1974) report on nationalizations and takeovers "recorded 875 cases in 62 countries of the world—pre-

dominantly in the underdeveloped areas." Africa accounted for 340 of them and "led in all categories of industry except petroleum—that is, in instances of nationalization of mining, agriculture, manufacturing, trade, public utilities, banking and insurance." Anticipating the future, a serious student of this trend (Rood, 1976:446–47) concludes his analysis with the following prediction:

> the pattern of takeovers during the last decade in black Africa, as well as that in the rest of the world, suggests very strongly that they believe it will serve their own interests. The only limitations will be practical ones . . . the growing strength of the natural resource blocs such as OPEC, the spread of socialism, and the increased acceptance of nationalization vastly improve the bargaining position of the nationalizing countries.

Cf. Girvan(1978).

20. This is reflected not only by the wider appeal of state capitalism and nonalignment in the Third World during the past two decades, but also in the growing ability of state socialist systems to compete with aid offers, and the rising share of world territory and economic output accounted for by centrally planned economies. As Barnet and Muller(1974) take pains to stress, however, the technological, information, and other resources of the transnational corporation continue to confer substantial advantages over opponents.

21. The crucial import of institutional subordination arises from history of deposed radical regimes. Virtually all were ousted by the armed forces or more often sectors thereof. While civilian groups participated in a number of these subversive efforts, none succeeded without active military participation. In most instances, civilian roles were secondary or even nonexistent.

22. Objective or institutional military subordination can be distinguished from subjective "subordination." The latter implies reciprocity between civilians who respect military autonomy in return for military willingness to recognize the authority of civilians in nonmilitary policy areas. This model has been vitiated for a steadily rising number of Third World countries—especially those governed by reformist and radical elites. Hence, depsite admittedly hazardous implementation obstacles, dedicated radicals have no choice but to attempt to employ at least some approximation of a model which has proved viable for regimes characterized by successful egalitarian social change, i.e., the state socialist systems. This approach deprives military professionals of the resources and autonomy necessary to coerce civilians. The following, or functional equivalents thereof, must govern civil-military relations: 1) intramilitary political education and party organization; 2) a specially trained executive guard force and/or people's militia; 3) increased external training from state socialist systems; 4) highly trained security police detachments and informant networks within the armed forces; 5) use of less politically conscious army units in conjunction with civilian organizations for infrastructural and other projects; 6) promotion of line officers who exhibit both professional expertise and socialist dedication. What this does is to reduce the officer corps to a dependent elite status rendering it difficult if not impossible for its ruling class potential to be realized. The term "class" as here used is meant to refer to an identifiable group with a distinctive life style and substantially higher levels of interaction internally than with outgroups.

23. Their success in the 1970s and 1980s also has been enhanced by a considerable reservoir and interchange of coup experience. Thus by the beginning of the period a detailed (Luttwak:1969) tactical handbook for plotters was in wide circulation. Careful analysis by leftists might enable them to anticipate and even tactically neutralize some conspiracies in the "low" and especially "medium" survival categories. This would be equally useful for

more structural assessments such as that by Welch(1977:82–98) who concludes that the impact of coup conspiracies depends upon: 1) the extent of popular disenchantment with the government; 2) the salience of social values condoning violence; 3) the ability to organize resistance to the incumbent government; and 4) the conspirators' access to the means of training, equipping, and directing combatants. And Thompson(1976:263) has found that coups launched by senior headquarters' officers were far more likely to be successful than those launched by junior officers.

10

Conclusions

It is now approximately two centuries since the process of democratization began in what we call the modern Western world. Efforts to institutionalize genuine elite accountability to the mass citizenry continue and remain far from fulfilled. During this period of conflict, hegemonic groups have used ideologies or designed belief systems in the attempt to legitimize and thus stabilize their rule over others. In some basic respect, all "elitist" ideologies attempted to meet the challenge posed by the emergent ideology of egalitarian political democracy—one that has exhibited marked appeal in the last hundred years. Rival "elitist" ideologies usually attempted to do this by alleging that in substantive terms they were promoting the fulfillment of mass needs, i.e., democratic ends. Frequently it has been claimed that some form of elite domination was necessary in the short run because conditions simply weren't ripe for democratic institutions to flourish at the time in question. That this often was merely a rationale for administrative plunder was revealed by the absence of sustained efforts to create such conditions. And even when some genuine attempts were paternalistically introduced, they proved abortive for the simple reason that almost all permanent democratic advances have been achieved through the primary if not exclusive mechanism of struggle from below that directly involved and socialized the mass sectors concerned.

A second aspect of this democratic struggle that must be underscored pertains to the socio-economic dimension. Prior to the industrial revolution, democratic reform or "limited government" was viewed as a practical means to safeguard citizens from despotic arbitrariness, whether manifested in the area of civil liberties or as simple economic plunder. While these meanings have remained, in the 19th and particularly in the 20th century, democracy at the mass level has come to mean a mechanism for avoiding negative consequences (i.e., tyranny) and also a route to obtaining equality and the modern material amenities held necessary for a good life. The promise or at least hope for finally eliminating mass poverty was implicit in the industrial and cybernetic revolutions.

Military and other hegemonic groups that violate civil liberties and impose arbitrary administration upon citizens have generally endeavored to acquire legitimacy—which is a reliable source of stability—by stressing that they alone can deliver the substantive socio-economic benefits. Sometimes they go so far as to provide for controlled mass consultation while maintaining that over time the conditions for political democracy will be created. The credibility of such pretensions depends in the final analysis upon the performance of particular governments with respect to the needs of their populations.

Militarism and Imperialism

In the 19th and 20th centuries, external militarism was rationalized by the proto-ideologies of imperialism. The conquest by the United States of its "continental empire" was justified in the terms "Manifest Destiny." For Britain, it was the so-called White Man's Burden; for France a "civilizing mission," and so on. The natives were to be uplifted in some manner. Needless to say, those who accepted such rationales tended to be citizens of the home country and a miniscule number of natives who in one way or another received material benefits or bettered status from the hegemonic relationship. Even within what are now called the "core" areas or metropoles, there were many who did not gain materially from such external militarism and some who failed to regard it as legitimate. Thus during the late 19th century anti-imperialist movements developed in Britain, France, and the United States. These in turn were in varying degree coextensive with emergent socialist parties. Not coincidentally, the term "militarism" was first given prominence by French socialists who denounced overseas military expeditions by the regime of Louis Napoleon.

Since the First and especially the Second World War, neo-colonialism or "informal empire" has been legitimized by such proto-ideologies as anti-communism, modernization, developmentalism, etc. Despite the perpetuation of "dependency," relationships between center and peripheries have changed in some important ways. The effects of World War II upon Britain and France seriously weakened their traditional hegemony, while the emergence of a number of Communist-ruled societies stimulated the growth of both economically nationalist and socialistic forces in the underdeveloped areas. In short, the anti-colonial struggles were fueled by leftist ideas and organizations. At the same time, formal independence has come to mean increasingly that Western imperialist powers could not only rely in the first instance upon their own military forces to maintain the existing "open door" to foreign investment and profit-taking within dependent areas. Economic and military aid, cultural penetration, indebtedness, proxy interventions, and above all external elite socialization have become the primary mechanisms for maintaining informal control—with overt military occupation usually a last resort.[1] As should be obvious, this approach to ensuring domination is less reliable. Thus, indigenous leaders and elites—even when initially helped to power by external powers—prove difficult to control fully. The emergence of an actively competitive Eastern "bloc" has of course increased their international "room for maneouver" as have some continuing divisions among Western neo-colonial rivals.

The Rise of Authoritarianism

What seems clear is that the socio-economic systems which these new nations inherited have been incapable of meeting the substantive mass welfare aspirations associated with political democracy. Hence popular discontent and the growth of socialist appeal have been endemic "problems" for the West and allied indigenous elements in the underdeveloped countries. Gradually in "modernization" literature of the 1960s and 70s there has appeared the theme that authoritarian regimes are the most appropriate type for such peoples.[2] William R. Thompson, for example, concludes a sophisticated methodological analysis(1975:451–52) of Latin American militarism by rejecting "the once dominant traditionalist perspective."

Traditional analysts tended to view the military as an alien and demonic force which thwarted the future of Latin American democracy by turning inward against its respective society. Less subjectively, revisionist analysts view military intervention as a manifestation of political violence in systems lacking an accepted political formula. Within this new perspective, the politicized military are no longer regarded as causes of political instability but rather as symptoms of societal conditions.

A similar rationale is offered by Kennedy(1974:54,154) who maintains "the prevalence of military rule after 10 or 20 years of wrestling with this crisis can be seen to be a consequence of the violence rather than a cause of it." Or in the form of equally categorical propositions:

Where viable civilian government is present, its military form is not, and where military intervention is attempted and fails, this only serves to confirm the viability of civilian government. Where civilian governments fall and the military succeeds this expresses the crisis of civilian government and not the inherent pathology of the soldier.

Although with less fanfare, this trend is also manifested by the behavior of Western governments. Thus, in referring to the destabilization of Thailand's parliamentary democracy in 1976, the late Malcolm Caldwell stressed (Elliot, 1978:18) that "the alacrity and relieved welcome with which the October coup was greeted in ASEAN capitals and by the American Embassy in Bangkok spoke for themselves."[3]

The most prevalent forms of authoritarianism have been military-dependent civilian governments as existed in the late 1970s in Iran, Mexico, Saudi Arabia, Morocco, Philippines, and Jordan, or more commonly military-dominant systems. Gradually the latter have been replacing the politically democratic civilian systems directly, or sequentially after a civilian "strong man" (e.g., Pacheco in Uruguay, Tubman in Liberia) has become increasingly dependent upon the armed forces. Thus in the few remaining political democracies, when leftists demonstrate surprising strength both organizationally and in terms of rising appeal, destabilization by Western imperialism and its local allies can be predicted. While these anti-leftist coups are common, occasionally similar externally encouraged efforts by Communist military aid donors will cause a radical military coup. Infrequently, though more in the case of radical than rightist coups, the external involvement may be marginal or even nonexistent since the former have often occurred in countries with little or no history of Eastern or even nonaligned military aid. Egypt, Peru, Ethiopia, Iraq, and Libya are examples.

Radical and Conservative Militarism

Like their right-wing counterparts, the radical militarist factions seek to legitimize internal hegemony by espousing some ideological rationale promising mass betterment along with economic nationalism. The term "ideology" does not necessarily imply integrated or coherent belief systems for, as Hobsbawm(1973:195), has cogently stressed:

Separated from the rest of society by a life consisting (in peacetime) of fancy dress, instruction and practice, games and boredom, organized on the assumption that their members at all levels are generally rather stupid and always expendable, held together by the increasingly anomalous values of bravery, honour, contempt for and suspicion of civilians, professional armies tend almost by definition to ideological eccentricity.

In fact, as Thompson(1973) found, ideology was virtually insignificant as a motivating factor in almost two-thirds of Third World coups between 1946-70. Yet over the decades there has been Peronism, Nasserism, Arab Socialism, African Socialism, Ethiopian Socialism, the Peruvian Revolution, etc. Because they endeavor to mobilize the masses rather than to exclude them from the political system, military leftists assign greater importance to the elaboration and diffusion of ideology. Ironically however they have less need for it from the standpoint of mass threats to regime stability. Unlike rightist military strongmen (Perez Jimenez, Batista, Lon Nol), none of these leftists have been overthrown or even threatened by popular uprisings (except where—as in Ethiopia and most recently in Afghanistan—there was major foreign intervention). Their demise has typically been through coups by anti-Communist officer factions with rightist civilian and foreign support. In some cases, the radical "strongman" will react to internal organizations further to the left (usually Communists) by repression and orienting his regime toward the West as occurred in the Sudan with Nimeiry and Egypt with Sadat. In both instances of course their radicalism was superficial and opportunistic rather than a matter of firmly held beliefs. This is not to suggest that other radicalized officers may not be sincere and deeply committed.

The instability afflicting radical regimes flows from an absence of cohesion within the officer corps and the destruction of investor confidence without its replacement by a comprehensive socialist incentive structure. State capitalism is a mixed system at a midpoint upon a continuum between two internally coherent rival systems: state socialism and monopoly capitalism. It is not, however, itself an internally coherent synthetic system but rather an unintegrated "mix" of institutions and norms derived from both the Leninist and "open door" variants. This in turn is reflected in the role orientations of increasingly politicized officer corps. The radical sector—invariably a minority—has the consciousness of a ruling class, whereas those with an "open door" orientation regard themselves as a governing elite with the investing class as a reference group, at least insofar as basic socio-economic policies and institutions are concerned.

Ultimately, however, both military regime variants have in most cases failed to acquire legitimacy because of their incapacity to fulfill either the previously mentioned democratic procedural or substantive goals. Gavin Kennedy(1974:28-29) like Hopkins(1966:175) almost a decade earlier found a markedly higher incidence of coups among the least economically developed Third World states. But he also cogently demonstrates (1974:22-26) the overriding importance of legitimacy related not only to economic performance but also to mass expectations and the political character of the regime. Thus between 1945 and 1972, in 36 "party states" there were 63 (1.75) coups and coup attempts, while the ratio increased to 2.0 in 12 monarchies which experienced 24 coups and to 4.04 in military states whose low legitimacy was reflected by the fact that 27 were afflicted by 109 interventions. These were the types of regime in effect at the time of the interventions. Thus his conclusion that "the legitimacy of the regime can be diluted as the people develop new ideas as to political rights and obligations and, if this coincides with gradual or dramatic evidence of a regime's ineffectiveness, it is likely to create the conditions for revolutionary disorder." After exploring why it is that most military regimes are incapable of acquiring legitimacy, I shall consider why two alternative civilian-led systems do manage to acquire mass legitimacy, though in one case this does not ensure the loyalty of the officer corps. Hence only one of these systems offers the prospect of relative stability and development. The obstacles to introducing that system will then be considered.

From a procedural or "political" standpoint, it is self-evident that a military regime by definition cannot be democratic. For, whether the military rules in its own right as a class independent and in a sense above other classes in the radical variant, or as an elite, with land-owning and corporate investing classes as its reference groups, the officers do not submit or even make a pretense to mass accountability and electoral replacement by the citizens. And military authoritarianism itself, as Krishnamurthy(1977:391–400) has shown in the Burmese and Indonesian cases, does not necessarily even guarantee stability. True, radicals do encourage mass organization, but the domestic political liberty is quite limited, constituting little more than institutionalized consultation. While repressiveness is less pronounced and brutal than under rightist military regimes, it cannot be obviated short of jeopardizing the hegemonic position of the military class itself. Hierarchical and command or dictatorial norms are inherent in military institutions and socialization. Hence it would be illogical to assume commitments to a democratic political process with its inevitable disorderliness, irresolution of issues, and opportunistic politicians. The last mentioned are of course almost universally disdained by professional officers. Admittedly, in a small number of instances democratically oriented officers do seize control of the state with the objective of restoring political democracy. But these are temporary or transitional military regimes which acquire their legitimacy because of their self-liquidating policy commitments. When such officers attempt to postpone or manipulate electoral arrangements, their legitimacy erodes at the popular level. Reflecting in part the paucity of internalized democratic norms among officers, transitional democratic military regimes are rare and the exception that reaffirms the rule of military propensities for authoritarianism.

The Military as Modernizers

While in the substantive or socio-economic area most military regimes fail to acquire legitimacy because of their inability to satisfy mass aspirations for improved health care, education, and living conditions, radical regimes clearly outperform the "open door" variant in the social welfare area. Inflation for basic necessities is held down as are indirect taxes while there is substantial improvement in health standards. Yet only unusually well-endowed radical military regimes such as Libya deliver enough at the mass level to acquire some broadly based legitimacy. Similarly, agrarian and other structural reforms also make for somewhat greater legitimacy at least in the short run. This remains partial and limited to certain population sectors. Delivery in terms of both socio-economic performance and procedural accountability are essential for institutional legitimacy.

Although the high instability of radical military regimes can be traced to such factors as their special vulnerability to external pressure due to factional strife within officer ranks and to erosion of the traditional economic incentive structure, the developmental potential of these along with "open door" military regimes would be highly problematic regardless of such special problems. Right-wing militaries may do somewhat better on strictly economic indicators in the short run, but it is because they suppress policies and classes which threaten capitalist incentives and not because of any special modernizing capabilities of the military elite. Further, the attraction to amenities felt by most rightist and many radical officers—professional rhetoric concerning asceticism and spartanism notwithstanding—prevents them from inspiring the kind of mass commitment necessary to meet the challenge of industrialization and sustained high economic growth rates. Hopkins(1966:171) for example underscores the problematic dimension of the new "modernizing" role in declaring that:

The political intervention of the military seems to me to proceed not so much from its prior attitudes to social change but from its strategic position within the arena of social dissensus, from its relatively large size, and hierarchic organisation that facilitates a cohesion which no other elite group can match. . . . Nor does it seem very profitable to talk of a desire to modernise in the abstract. Such a desire may be widespread, like the desire to consume Western goods. What matters more is the order of priorities and of sacrifices. Who is going to be deprived of what in order that others should consume what goods?

The issue has been posed more starkly by Woddis(1977:87) who, while acknowledging the sincerity and reforms implemented by some "patriotic" officers, nevertheless pinpoints a key vulnerability of such progressive military regimes—one directly affecting "the order of priorities and of sacrifices":

In both their military and civilian spheres, the new States established in the Third World countries provide enormous scope for individuals in the upper echelons of the State apparatus, irrespective of their class origin, to utilise their State positions to become part of the new bourgeoisie. They can accumulate wealth through commissions on contracts given to foreign firms, and through other forms of corruption; they are often offered large bribes by imperialist agencies, including the ubiquitous CIA; they are able to acquire farms, to speculate in urban landed property, to enter trade.

Finally, J. Bayo Adekson(1978:33), one of the sharpest critics of the military-as-modernizers thesis, argues that even when military-dominated governments opt to impose some "modernizing" socio-economic policies, not only is the overriding objective frequently to enlarge military power per se, but a usual concomitant is

military-institutional "role expansion" measured, for our purpose, by increased diversion of scarce resources from what we choose to call gari (food) production to gun procurement, as well as by quantitative increase in the armed forces. Sometimes, this military-institutional role-expansion, or military extractive tendency, may grow at such a rate as to throttle real "modernisation."

Another way of putting what we have been arguing in the preceding few paragraphs is that the extent of military "modernisation" that takes place under given circumstances is inversely proportional to the ratio of military extraction from society. By military extractive ratio (MER) is meant that proportion of national wealth more or less forcibly appropriated to and unproductively utilised by military members of a society in any given period. The greater the MER, the less the military "modernising" function (MMF); and, vice versa, the smaller the MER, the greater the MMF—all things being equal.[4]

In light of the budgetary and performance patterns examined in Chapter 7, Hopkins and Adekson's scepticism is well placed, while Middle Eastern analyst Hurewitz's(1970:430) admonition almost a decade earlier appears to be vindicated, particularly insofar as "moderate" military regimes are concerned:

Modernising armies, whether they intervene in politics or not, are often said to be modernising agents at large in their societies, because military investment in men and machines invariably produces positive nonmilitary side effects. . . . Such a claim may be good sales talk but it is poor social science. It might have been ignored but for endorsement by reputable social scientists. . . . The double-duty enthusiasts trip over hard facts. They resort to deductive reasoning and tend to overlook the empirical evidence.

Predictably, because of high MERs, corruption, repression, and managerial deficiencies among other things, these regimes are not closing the gap with advanced capitalist systems. Hence, despite short-run socio-welfare benefits and limited structural change from the radicals, neither military approach is viable from a longer-run developmental perspective.[5] The most probable route then to state socialism in the Third World will be insurrection against military rightists. But this will be infrequently successful and, as the Nicaraguan case makes clear, exceedingly difficult—even with petit bourgeois and external support—in the absence of military disunity. In the interim, rightist militarism will continue to subvert not only radical military regimes, but also civilian governments of a similar policy orientation, those of a "moderate" nature, and even preexisting rightist military dictatorships. Although we have seen that military regimes "score" lowest in terms of the partially interrelated characteristics of legitimacy and socio-economic performance, Kennedy's(1974:53) data indicate they are not much more war or insurrection prone than "party systems," which have been increasingly replaced by military regimes due to the former's insufficiently better socio-economic performance, corruption, and institutional weaknesses vis-à-vis better organized and increasingly ambitious or avaricious military elites.[6]

Ignoring the role of dependency and frequent external intelligence manipulation, Kennedy(1974:56,57) nevertheless captures a number of structural characteristics that are often present when officers move against civilians whose electoral systems are often a facade and where short-run calculations of advantages in political conflicts are

prismatically reflected in the whole social structure by the acceptance of corruption. Corruption is a tax on getting things done, it raises the cost of activity. It ensures that a minority redistributes income towards themselves, by virtue of their position in the state bureaucracy, and this transforms the state into a semi-private "taxation" system. The struggle for power in the state is also a struggle for access to this "taxation franchise." Illegal taxes have always been a source for sedition, and for cynicism. These are two sufficient conditions for a crisis in legitimacy, and a challenge to civil order. . . . The army in many African countries is equipped, trained, and motivated for intervention. The civilian government deploys the military essentially for an internal security role, but the military is able to transform its subordinate role into a dominant one. By kinship and peer-group affiliation it is aware of the prizes flowing from command of the state. By observation of the behaviour and living standards of the European it has acquired, like everybody else with ambition, an envy for living standards commensurate with its conceptions of its special role. It can only look with paternalistic disapproval on the struggle between political factions for power, which in no way resembles party politics in a traditional Western state in the intensity and ferocity of competition and the struggles between competing social groups for a share in the resources of the country. . . .

These and other previously mentioned cleavages within radical regimes undermine performance, and in conjunction with an absence of any spirit of fair play, vitiate aspirations for legitimacy. Thus, Farsoun and Carroll(1978:154) after analyzing Syrian and Egyptian developments, conclude that "the future of state capitalism is tenuous. For its demise will come either at the hands of another group of 'intermediate strata,' which sets the anti-imperialist/pro-imperialist cycle in motion again, or at the hands of a revolutionary party representing the interests of the proletariat and peasantry. . . ."

Over the next several decades, it is likely that a substantial number of these radical regimes will be supplanted by "open door" military-dominant ones, while a growing proportion of military progressives will survive, provided that the lessons of regime experiences during the 1960s and 70s are well learned. Such an outcome will be facilitated by the world capitalist crisis and the altered East/West balance of power, though the dangers occasioned by the attenuation of detente must surely increase. A few may be driven by the intensification of the "new" Cold War to opt for the Cuban and perhaps Ethiopian or Afghanistani route to a Leninist state socialist system. These three countries have of course survived rightist externally supported destabilization efforts only because of massive Soviet intervention and commitments.

Socialism and Civilian Supremacy

The significance of the foregoing is underscored by Chapter 7's finding that state socialist regimes are the only variant that is slowly closing the socio-economic gap with the advanced capitalist systems. The political class tends to be far more homogeneous and cohesive than in the state capitalist systems—civilian or military. Further, it is specialized functionally to promote maximum mobilization of human and natural resources for domestic accumulation. Even more than other civilians, Marxists tend to be optimal performers of the "modernization" role. They, in turn, confine the military to an appropriate specialized role: development of professional expertise in the "management of violence."

Military failures to perform effectively civilian socio-economic and political functions then are inconsistent with the modernization paradigm and demonstrate the value of its emphasis upon role specialization. As Hobsbawm(1973:188) notes with respect to military roles

one reason for this rather negative character of military [development] politics is, that army officers rarely wish to govern themselves, or are competent at any activity except soldiering, and sometimes not even that. The increasing professionalization and technification of modern armed forces has not substantially changed this.

This in turn can be reconciled with the special role assigned to the party in the Marxian paradigm. It is also, interestingly, possible to reconcile the limited structural change which military radicals bring about with the same theoretical paradigms. Thus the inability of "open door" derived policies to employ existing and potential productive resources fully is so obvious that some junior officers become more receptive to socialist ideas. Despite their usually good intentions, their efforts to alter the property system so that it will be more equitable and productive generally meet with only limited success. This for the previously cited reason that their specialized expertise lies elsewhere.

While military radicals do succeed in weakening the position of traditional large property-owning sectors and expanding the sphere of social ownership, they fail to activate the productive forces fully in part because they cannot mobilize mass initiatives. Hence in these respects and their lack of ruling class cohesion and of coherent ideology, military radicals compare unfavorably with the hegemonic Leninist political class which not only creates the organizational network to employ potential fully and completely restructures the forces of production, but also provides both immediate socio-economic benefits to the masses and simultaneously accords them meaningful if not determinative participatory roles in the policy process. These features – carefully analyzed in the revolutionary process of Cuba by Fagen(1969) and Duncan(1978) – of internally imposed Leninist systems, along with a strong commitment to national self-determination, account for the ability of most such regimes to build a broadly based sense of legitimacy. Thus in the context of measuring revolutionary Cuba's domestic achievements, Duncan(1978:79) stresses:

Passive acceptance and compliance are not enough for dynamic change. Active involvement in economic and political processes is mandatory if public policy goals are to be met, rather than either checked by countervailing power or by public apathy. Institutionalizing change has been variously defined by scholars, but it is defined here as the creation of statewide political institutions and values that stress active participation within shared organizations. These institutions and values become the mechanisms for positive acceptance and support of the regime's development goals, on the one hand, or on the other, for resolving conflict in ways that do not undermine those goals. Without institutionalized change, political instability and violence are potentially high, and systematic problem solving and conflict resolution are potentially low.

While the military and militarized programs can be used temporarily (LeoGrande, 1978) when civilian institutions are in their infancy, both institutionalization and socio-economic breakthroughs require exemplary leadership, the strengthening of Party and other civilian organizations, limitation of the military to residual infrastructural missions, and above all creation of a new ethos reinforced by meaningful consultative/participatory roles.[5] This, more than "terror," accounts for Communist stability and mobilizational success. None have been overthrown by the armed forces which – notwithstanding occasional professional and/or corporate inspired tensions – are institutionally subordinated as a dependent elite. Leninist practice in tandem with socio-economic performance account for consonance with Huntington's(1968) preconditions for "objective" control of the military: 1) relatively stronger civilian institutions; 2) the political systems' institutionalization; and 3) Party respect for the perfection of military expertise. Where there is a delay in implementing the first two conditions, direct administration of the armed forces by socialist revolutionaries and widespread use of the former in socio-economic mobilization will insure interim subordination. This is the implicit lesson (LeoGrande, 1978; Duncan, 1978) of the Cuban case. Although the diffusion of state socialism in the Third World will be inhibited by counterrevolutionary Western intervention, the performance deficiencies of alternative developmental approaches will assure its steady if irregular extension as the emergent "world system" of the 21st century.

This may sound simplistic but so did Marx a century ago to his bourgeois critics. Which of them predicted that within a mere five generations 50 percent of the earth's surface would be civilian-ruled by Marxist-oriented governments? Or that in another third of the world—advanced capitalist and underdeveloped—that the struggle for socialism would constitute one of the principle sources of political conflict? Marxism as an ideology has been "disproved," and socialist movements have been discounted ad nauseam. Yet vitality and growth characterize this tradition while decay, avarice, and crisis afflict capitalism. Even one of the foremost pro-Western African intellectuals, Ali Mazrui(1978:170–83), acknowledges a future characterized by rising Marxist appeal on a continent where Marxism is alleged to be most alien and least theoretically relevant insofar as its orthodox versions are concerned. Yet according to Rejai(1979:199) who systematically examined the backgrounds of 32 revolutionary leaders, "the most typical pattern is the eclectic adaptation of foreign ideologies to conditions of one's own society." Given this qualification, he found that "the most prevalent revolutionary ideologies have been democratic, nationalist, Marxist-Leninist, and nationalist/Marxist-Leninist, with the last two gaining prominence in the 20th Century." If the trends of this century continue then, we can anticipate that socialist civilian rule will bring social revolution to the Third World and perhaps to our own as well. Hence while the etiology of intervention is admittedly multifarious, the contemporary rise of militarism and militarization in the underdeveloped areas are best viewed as transitory anti-socialist yet unviable developmental alternatives.[7] Civil-military analysts such as Perlmutter(1977) are looking so intently at the new saplings that they are unable to sense that as the decades progress the forest itself of "praetorian" militarism is shriveling at its perimeters.

The process will be slow and arduous as recent socialist successes demonstrate. This is not merely a matter of Western determination and intervention – the 1978 coordinated reaction to CNLF advances in Shaba and the civil war fomented since then in Afghanistan being a case in point. But more fundamentally it is necessary to take account of historical patterns of social revolution. As Chorley(1943) found, with respect to Europe, and Russell(1974), with a statistical sample drawn from a broader geographical base, unless the preexisting armed forces are divided and defeated, it is exceedingly unlikely that social revolutionaries will triumph. It is from this standpoint that Western military assistance discussed in Chapters 3 and 8 is so crucial. Depending upon the absorptive capacity of recipient military establishments, this aid strengthens their organizational capabilities vis-à-vis social revolutionaries and weakens radical military tendencies. Such aid programs will undoubtedly be strengthened due to the breakdown of detente during the 1978–80 period.

Hence from the standpoint of praxis, a dual mission confronts those committed to development. In donor nations, their activity should be directed at ending military aid to developing areas on one hand while simultaneously opposing economic assistance that indirectly contributes to militarization. Within the Third World, those holding similar commitments are confronted by a greater challenge. Despite repression, they must prepare organizationally for insurrection and whenever possible endeavor to expose members of the armed forces to socialist ideas. Thus Woddis(1977:23) properly stresses how

hazardous [it is] to allow one's political thinking about the State and questions of political power to be influenced or dominated by conceptions arising from a strict verbal meaning of these terms. Armed forces are an instrument only in a very particular sense. They certainly include instruments, weapons, machines, such as guns and ammunition and so on, with which they are equipped. But whether or not the ruling class is able to rely unconditionally on this institution depends in the last resort not on the equipment or firing power of the armed forces, important as this may be, but on whether the armed forces are prepared to use their weapons against the rulers' opponents. In other words, it depends on social and political factors. This is why it is misleading to try and reduce everything to the slogan "political power grows out of the barrel of a gun." Political power grows out of the total political alignment of forces including the strength and organization of the people. It is this which, in the last resort, determines if, when and *in what direction* the guns are going to be used.

Progressive movements, he argues, can win over or at least neutralize sectors of the armed forces by seeking democratic reforms, improved conditions, and military education through electoral and other campaigns which seek to isolate only monopoly sectors and the right.[8] Despite the counterrevolutionary role of most armed forces, a sufficient number of left-led factions have appeared during recent decades to warrant a revised conception of the state in Third World areas plagued by "the development of underdevelopment." To define simply such an institutional apparatus as a bourgeois instrumentality even in a structural (Block, 1978) sense is reductionism which cannot be reconciled with Marx's empirical acknowledgment that class conflict may occur within the state itself and that the bureaucratic "caste" may—when cohesive—place its own interests above those of other classes. It is altogether likely that, in the 1980s, we shall see increasing evidence of officers (albeit a minority) pursuing their interests in a manner incompatible with existing dependency relationships, even if they do not do so in a manner consonant with either "Marxist" socialism or one that is effective in mobilizing their societies in a manner that meets fully the challenge of developmental modernization. In a fundamental sense, this process underscores the salience of nationalism as perhaps the most potent force in the Third World today—one which increasingly catalyzes radical and socialist policy goals.

Notes

1. Aside from Korean and Indochinese-type wars, between 1945 and 1975 military force has been employed more than 215 times—largely in Third World areas—by the United States alone according to a recent systematic analysis by Blechman and Kaplan(1978). Cf. Luttwak(1974).

2. The unsuitability of liberal democracy is argued or implied by Heilbroner(1963), Sinai(1964:217-23), Moore(1966:414-508), Black(1966:66-80,98-99,140-47,151-52,165-67), Tullis(1973:52), Huntington and Nelson(1976:18-29).

3. While the rationale whenever possible is articulated in political (i.e., anti-Communist or radical) terms, when no immediate threat of such a character is manifest, economic reasons tend to be stressed. Thus in a recent paper (Dernberger, 1979:27) Thomas E. Weisskopf argues

as did Myrdal in his study of the countries of South Asia, that any differences in the results of their development efforts can be traced to differences in their social, economic, and political institutions and policies. . . . Recognizing the relatively small size of his sample and the possibility of alternative explanations, Weisskopf draws the following conclusions:

1. Higher growth rates in the nonrevolutionary societies are directly related to "authoritarian" governments which assign a high priority to growth among the various objectives of development.

2. Compared with the more "democratic" regimes, these "authoritarian" governments have a greater preference for liberal, i.e., free-market and internationalist, as against interventionist, economic policies.

3. These policies lead to higher growth rates because higher growth rates in the nonrevolutionary societies are directly related to capital inflows. . . .

4. Adekson(1978:35) cogently adds that

the idea that the army possesses technical superiority as against the remaining society, of a "competence gap" as Fred Green calls it, is fallacious. To begin with, the question may be asked: Can the technical qualities, resources, and capabilities of any army possibly exceed those of the society within which it operates; and this, whether the society concerned is a "closed" or "open" one? As regards a "closed" society (one untouched by external influences, in short an autarky), the answer, which is a definite no, is too evident to require further comment.

With reference to an "open" society (defined as one subject to what in contemporary terminology is called the transnational influence of technology and ideology), however, this answer may not be that obvious. In fact, it is tempting to answer in the affirmative, if one concentrates on the formal and superficially distinctive characteristics of the military (such as organisational charts, drill-regulations, weapons, in short the material) which are known, of course, to be mostly foreign-derived. But these are artifacts which in themselves are of no use to society until operated by *men*. . . . Nor measured in terms of *skills* (learned methods of performing increasingly specialist and complex jobs competently) is the assumption of technical superiority on the part of the army vis-à-vis society empirically supported at least in Sub-Saharan Africa. For one thing, a greater number of skilled people available in the average state here (whether administrators, engineers, doctors, economists, agronomists, geologists, architects, chemists, statisticians, accountants, or machinists) tends to be found practising their skills in the civilian rather than in the military sector. Few, if any Sub-Saharan African armies have established corps of engineers; few, if any corps of doctors and nurses; and few, if any research scientists. On the contrary, rather than being a repository of scarce skills, the average army, since independence, has depended for its technical and managerial expertise largely upon the civil society. Thus, it seems most inappropriate to speak à la Professor Janowitz of "transferability of skills" from the military to society.

5. The necessity of a radical or syncretic futurist orientation as a rupture with the past has been underlined by both Sinai(1965) and Goulet(1968). Because what must be at issue is a struggle for unconditional victory over underdevelopment, military rhetoric has sometimes — especially where the leadership has guerrilla origins — been employed. Thus, Duncan(1978:103) recalls that in the Cuban case

> to "work" and "battle for the homeland" — both in defending its sovereign territory against outside enemies and in domestic development projects — have been common features of the modal personality stressed over the years. Development projects, work brigades, technological and industrial achievements, planning activities, and even sporting events have been frequently characterized as "battles" and "struggles." This emphasis led Fidel to depict the 1970 goal of a 10 million-ton sugar harvest (which was not achieved) as a "historic battle decisive for the future," for which the entire nation was mobilized, including the armed forces, who were "mobilized" for the 10 million-ton sugar harvest as they would for war. At times during recent years in Cuba, planting grass, removing weeds, picking guavas, learning artificial insemination, water conservation projects, winning baseball games, training military reservists, improving bureaucratic efficiency, being a good communist, and graduating more agronomists and technicians — all were moral imperatives to do battle.

Close functional equivalents have been used in other Third World state socialist mobilizational systems. Military rhetoric has been less pronounced, I suspect because Party socialization preceded the leadership's guerrilla and/or governmental roles while in Cuba the guerrilla leaders created the party after defeating the counterrevolutionary forces. None of this should obscure the fact that whatever the precise style of the terminology, the spartan and dedicated example of the leadership is, along with a perception of national purpose, essential to engendering morale and motivation at the mass level. This is as true for armies as it is for developmental struggles.

6. A broad range of structural and situational factors also contribute to domestic militarism in underdeveloped countries. Taylor(1977:103–8) for example, using a multiplicative rather than an additive equation, found a substantially higher incidence of government change through the threat or actual use of force in systemic environments characterized by the following cluster of variables: 1) low per capita GNP; 2) small size; and 3) low legitimacy as measured by a high incidence of government sanctions. Others attribute growing militarism in the Third World to personal (Decalo, 1966), institutional (Huntington, 1968), and global (Horowitz, 1977) forces. With respect to the last, Laemmle(1977:327–33) concludes that while some evidence of international contagion appeared within various regional subsystems, its significance as a pure macrosystemic phenomenon was found to be severely constrained. Thompson's(1973) analysis stresses the conjunction of low alternative (civilian) support for regimes and high salience of corporate or more commonly subcorporate grievances akin to those essayed by Decalo(1966).

7. The "anti-socialist" dimension is not meant to imply specific motives of this character for all interventions. While many have been neither ideological nor explicitly anti-leftist, it is equally apparent that the military have functioned as the major obstacle to socialist movements in the Third World. Further, that the United States and other Western powers have created, trained, and strengthened these institutions and finally as Adekson(1978:34) warns:

> No evaluation of the "theory of modernizing soldier" can be complete which does not take due account of the fact that it was originally formulated by Western social scientists as a conscious alternative to Marxism-Leninism-Maoism, under the ideological influence of the "Cold War" beginning from the late fifties. Furthermore, it was strongly conditioned by "containment" (meaning counterrevolutionary) objectives of American foreign policy. Guy Pauker, one of the school's founding fathers, admits in his seminal article on "Southeast Asia As a Problem Area in the Next Decade" that its aim was to work out a preventive alternative to "Communist takeovers." When approached by the U.S. State Department and other government agencies for advice, scholars such as Pauker recommended that, among the elites of new states, "members of the national officer corps as individuals and the national armies as organizational structures" be considered the "best equipped to become an effective counterbalance to the spread of Communism." To the extent that all the contributors to the Johnson volume on *The Role of the Military in Underdeveloped Countries* more or less shared similar "cold war" concerns and the values of capitalist liberalism, its alternative title could well have been "A Non-Communist Manifesto."
>
> It is important to stress these dogmatic origins of the theory, not because they are directly relevant to its empirical validity, but because they lead many Western scholars, researchers, and statesmen, especially the Americans, to support soldiers' rule first and justify it later in terms of "modernisation," even where such a rule is known to retard the very process through widespread corruption and repressive control as was the case in pre-1975 Vietnam.

8. While he is ambivalent about unions in the military, Woddis continually stresses the importance of forging a leftist majority—including petit bourgeois and new middle class sectors—both of which are increasingly drawn upon to officer armies. The latter he maintains have a legitimate external defence role for socialist systems. This strategy is viewed as appropriate for both Third World and West European societies. With respect to the latter, Woddis stresses the importance of conscription as it opens the armed forces to external political currents. Wright(1978:251–52) proffers a similar caveat:

it is because of this threat of military intervention that Western European Communist parties ascribe such importance to the current international equilibrium of forces. Their hope is that the general balance of power between the United States and the USSR will make it unlikely that direct military intervention would occur if a Left government came to office. This does not mean, however, that the threat of internal military counterrevolution can be treated lightly. Even in Chile, where American involvement was quite important in the fall of the Allende government, it was unnecessary for the United States to invade the country directly. Any socialist strategy in advanced capitalism must therefore involve serious organization within the military itself, efforts at changing life within the military in order to break down the social and ideological isolation of the army from the working class and so on.

Bibliography

Abrahamsson, Bengt. 1972. *Military Professionalization and Political Power.* Beverly Hills, Cal.: Sage.

Adams, Richard. 1968-69. "The Guatemalan Military." *Studies in Comparative International Development* IV (5): 99-109.

Adekson, J. Bayo. 1976. "Army in Multi-Ethnic Society: The Case of Nkrumah's Ghana, 1957-1966." *Armed Forces and Society* 2 (February): 251-72.

_____. 1978. "On the Theory of the Modernising Soldier: A Critique." *Current Research on Peace and Violence* 1: 28-31.

Agee, Philip. 1975. *Inside the Company: CIA Diary.* London: Penguin Books.

_____. 1975a. "Playboy Interview." *Playboy* (August): 49-70.

Albrecht, Ulrich; Dieter Ernst; Peter Lock; and Herbert Wulf. 1974. "Armaments and Underdevelopment." *Bulletin of Peace Proposals* (V): 173-85.

Alexander, Robert J. 1958. *The Bolivian National Revolution.* New Brunswick, N.J.: Rutgers University Press.

Allan, J. A. and K. S. McLachlan. 1976. "Agricultural Development in Libya after Oil." *African Affairs* 75 (July): 331-48.

Allman, T. D. 1970. "Anatomy of a Coup." *Far Eastern Economic Review* 67 (April): 17-22.

Aluko, Olajide, ed. 1977. *The Foreign Policies of African States.* London: Hodder and Stoughton.

American Friends of the Captive Nations. 1957. *Hungary under Soviet Rule: A Survey of Developments since the Report of the U.N. Special Committee.* New York: American Friends of the Captive Nations.

Amin, Samir. 1974. *Accumulation on a World Scale: A Critique of the Theory of Underdevelopment.* New York: Monthly Review Press.

_____. 1976. *Imperialism and Unequal Development: An Essay on the Social Formations of Peripheral Capitalism.* New York: Monthly Review Press.

Amnesty International. 1975. *Report on Torture.* New York: Farrar, Straus and Giroux.

Apter, David, ed. 1970. *Philosophers and Kings: Studies in Leadership.* New York: George Braziller.

_____. 1970. "Nkrumah, Charisma, and the Coup." In *Philosophers and Kings: Studies in Leadership.* New York: George Braziller; 112-47.

Arraes, Miguel. 1969. *Brazil: The People and the Power.* Baltimore: Penguin Books.

Arrighi, Giovanni. 1978. *The Geometry of Imperialism.* New York: Schocken Books.

Arthur, Jonathan. 1977. *Socialism in the Soviet Union.* Chicago: Workers Press.

Avery, Peter. 1965. *Modern Iran.* New York: Praeger Publishers.

Avineri, Schlomo. 1969. *The Social and Political Thought of Karl Marx.* Cambridge: Cambridge University Press.

Bailey, Martin F. 1975. "Tanzania and China." *African Affairs* 74 (January): 39-50.

BalaKrishnan, N. 1976. "Sri Lanka in 1975: Political Crisis and Split in the Coalition." *Asian Survey* 16 (February): 130-39.

Baran, Paul A. 1957. *The Political Economy of Growth*. New York: Monthly Review Press.

Baran, Paul and Paul M. Sweezy. 1966. *Monopoly Capital*. New York: Monthly Review Press.

Barnet, Richard. 1967. *Intervention and Revolution*. Boston: Little, Brown.

Barnet, Richard F. and Ronald A. Muller. 1974. *Global Reach: The Power of the Multinational Corporations*. New York: Simon and Schuster.

Basseches, Nikolaus. 1943. *The Unknown Army*. New York: Viking Press.

Bassford, Henry H. 1975. "Panama's Political Economy of Development." Thesis for Norman Uphoff. Ithaca, N.Y.: Cornell University.

Bebler, Anton. 1972. *Military Rule in Africa: Dahomey, Ghana, Sierra Leone, and Mali*. New York: Praeger Publishers.

Bechtold, Peter K. 1975. "Military Rule in the Sudan: The First Five Years of Ja'far Numayri." *Middle East Journal* 29 (Winter): 16–32.

Be'eri, Eliezer. 1970. *Army Officers: Arab Politics and Society*. New York: Praeger Publishers.

Bendix, Reinhard. 1967. "Tradition and Modernity Reconsidered." *Comparative Studies in Society and History* 9: 292–346.

Bennett, Valeri Plave. 1975. "Military Government in Mali." *Journal of Modern African Studies* 13 (June): 249–66.

Berger, Martin. 1977. *Engels, Armies and Revolution*. Hamden, Conn.: Shoe String Press.

Bienen, Henry, ed. 1971. *The Military and Modernization*. Chicago: Aldine.

Binder, Leonard. 1962. *Iran: Political Development in a Changing Society*. Berkeley, Cal.: University of California Press.

Black, C. E. 1966. *The Dynamics of Modernization*. New York: Harper and Row.

Blanco, Hugo et al. 1973. *The Coup in Chile: Firsthand Report and Assessment*. New York: Pathfinder Press.

Blechman, Barry M. and Stephen S. Kaplan. 1978. *Force without Wars: U.S. Armed Forces as a Political Instrument*. Washington, D.C.: Brookings Institution.

Bliss, Shepherd. 1977. "Setting Its Own Course." *Cuba Review* VIII (April): 22.

Block, Fred. 1978. "Marxist Theories of the State in World System Analysis." In *Social Changes in the Capitalist World Economy*. Ed. by Barbara Hockey Kaplan. Beverly Hills, Cal.: Sage.

Bobrow, D. B. 1971. "Adaptive Politics, Social Learning, and Military Institutions." In *The Perceived Role of Military*. Ed. by M. R. Van Gils. Rotterdam: Rotterdam University Press; 295–307.

Borosage, Robert L. and John Marks, eds. 1976. *The CIA File*. New York: Grossman.

Bosch, Juan. 1965. *The Unfinished Experiment: Democracy in the Dominican Republic*. New York: Praeger Publishers.

Boyd, David. 1973. *Elites and Their Education*. United Kingdom: National Foundation for Educational Research. As cited in Salaman and Thompson(1978:303).

Bretton, Henry L. 1966. *The Rise and Fall of Kwame Nkrumah*. New York: Praeger Publishers.

Brzezinski, Zbigniew, ed. 1954. *Political Controls in the Soviet Army*. New York: Research Program on the USSR, East European Fund.

Burns, E. Bradford. 1977. "Panama: A Search for Independence." *Current History* (February): 65–7, 82.

Carranza, Mario Esteban. 1978. Fuerzas armadas y estado de excepcion en America Latina. Mexico: Siglo Veintiuno Editores.

Chamberlain, William H. 1935. *The Russian Revolution: 1917–1921*. Vol. 2. New York: Macmillan Co.

Chase-Dunn, Christopher. 1978. "Core-Periphery Relations: The Effects of Core Competition." In *Social Change in the Capitalist World Economy*. Ed. by Barbara Hockey Kaplan. Beverly Hills, Cal.: Sage.

Chikwendu, Ebitimi. 1977. "Considerations of the Freedom Value in a Military Regime: A Decade of Military Rule in Nigeria." *Verfassing und Recht in Ubersee* (Hamburg) 10(4): 531–41.

Chomsky, Noam. 1970. *At War with Asia*. New York: Random House.

_____. 1973. *For Reasons of State*. New York: Pantheon Books.

Chorley, Katherine. 1943. *Armies and the Art of Revolution*. Boston: Beacon Press. Reissued 1971.

Chung, Kiwon. 1963. "The North Korean People's Army and the Party." *China Quarterly* (April-June 1963): 105–24.

Clemens, Walter C., Jr. 1964. "The Soviet Militia in the Missile Age." *Orbis* 8 (Spring): 84–105.

Clinton, Richard Lee. 1971. "The Modernizing Military: The Case of Peru." *Inter-American Economic Affairs* 24 (Spring): 45–64.

Clotfelter, James. 1968. "The African Military Forces." *Military Review* 48 (May): 23–31.

Corbett, Charles D. 1972. *The Latin American Military as a Socio-Political Force: Bolivia and Argentina*. Gainesville, Fla.: University of Miami Press.

Cottam, Richard. 1964. *Nationalism in Iran*. Pittsburgh, Pa.: University of Pittsburgh Press.

_____. 1967. *Competitive Interference and 20th Century Diplomacy*. Pittsburgh, Pa.: University of Pittsburgh Press.

Crouch, Harold. 1978. *The Army and Politics in Indonesia*. Ithaca, N.Y.: Cornell University Press.

Current World Leaders. Journal of Bibliography and News. Santa Barbara, Cal.: International Academy of Santa Barbara.

Cvrcek, Jaromir. 1969. "Social Changes in the Officer Corps of the Czechoslovak People's Army." In *The Military Profession and Military Regimes: Commitments and Conflicts*. Ed. by Jacques Van Doorn. The Hague: Mouton; 94–106.

Davidson, Alastair. 1968. *Antonio Gramsci: The Man, His Ideas*. Melbourne: Australian Left Review Publications, 1968.

Davis, Nathaniel. 1971. Statement to a U.S. Chamber of Commerce Meeting in Guatemala City (April 20).

Decalo, Samuel. 1976. *Coups and Army Rule in Africa: Studies in Military Style*. New Haven: Yale University Press.

Dernberger, Robert F. 1979. "Aspects of Contemporary China: Economic Development." *Social Science Research Council: ITEMS* 33 (June): 27–30.

Dishman, Benton G. 1979. Interview on 31 May. A Lt. Col. in the USAF, he has considerable experience giving flight training to Third World officers.

Downton, James V., Jr. 1973. *Rebel Leadership: Commitment and Charisma in the Revolutionary Process*. New York: Free Press.

Draper, Theodore. 1965. *Castroism: Theory and Practice*. New York: Praeger Publishers.

DuBois, Victor. 1969. "Military Rule: Repercussions in West Africa." *American University Field Staff Reports: West Africa Series* 13 (September): 1–13.

Duncan, Cam. 1977. "Manley Unveils His Economic Reform Plan." *Guardian* (February): 16.

Duncan, W. Raymond. 1978. "Development Roles of the Military in Cuba: Modal Personality and Nation Building." In *The Military and Security in the Third World: Domestic and International Impacts*. Ed. by Sheldon Simon. Boulder, Colo.: Westview Press.

Dunn, John M. 1961. *Military Aid and Military Elites: The Political Potential of Ameri-*

can Training and Technical Assistance Programs. Princeton University, Ph.D. Dissertation.

Dupuy, Richard E. and Trevor N. 1970. *The Encyclopedia of Military History.* New York: Harper and Row.

Dupuy, Col. T. N. USA Ret. and Col. W. Blanchard, USA Ret. 1972. *The Almanac of World Military Power.* 2nd ed. New York: Bowker.

Dye, Thomas R. 1976. *Who's Running America.* Englewood Cliffs, N.J.: Prentice-Hall.

Eckhardt, W. and A. G. Newcombe. 1969. "Militarism, Personality and Other Social Attitudes." *Journal of Conflict Resolution* 13 (June): 210–19.

Elliot, David. 1978. *Thailand: Origins of Military Rule.* London: Zed Press.

Ellis, John. 1974. *Armies in Revolution.* New York: Oxford University Press.

Emmanuel, Arghiri. 1972. *Unequal Exchange: A Study in the Imperialism of Trade.* New York: Monthly Review Press.

Etchinson, Don L. 1975. *The United States and Militarism in Central America.* New York: Praeger Publishers.

Evans, Les, ed. 1974. *Disaster in Chile: Allende's Strategy and Why It Failed.* New York: Pathfinder Press.

Fagen, Richard. 1969. *The Transformation of Cuban Political Culture.* Stanford, Cal.: Stanford University Press.

_____. 1979. *Capitalism and the State in U.S.-Latin American Relations.* Stanford, Cal.: Stanford University Press.

Farley, Philip; Stephen S. Kaplan; and William H. Lewis. 1978. *Arms Across the Sea.* Washington, D.C.: Brookings Institution.

Farsoun, Samih K. and Walter F. Carroll. 1978. "State Capitalism and Counterrevolution in the Middle East: A Thesis." In *Social Change in the Capitalist World Economy.* Ed. by Barbara Hockey Kaplan. Beverly Hills, Cal.: Sage.

Feld, M. D. 1971. "Professionalism and Politicalization: Notes on the Military and Civilian Control." In *The Perceived Role of the Military.* Ed. by M. R. Van Gils. Rotterdam: Rotterdam University Press; 267–76.

Feuer, Lewis S. 1959. *Marx and Engels: Basic Writings on Politics and Philosophy.* Garden City, N.Y.: Doubleday-Anchor.

Fields, Rona M. 1976. *The Portuguese Revolution and the Armed Forces Movement.* New York: Praeger Publishers.

Finer, S. E. 1975. *The Man on Horseback.* 2nd ed. Hammondsworth, U.K.: Penguin Books.

Frank, Andre Gunder. 1967. *Capitalism and Underdevelopment in Latin America.* Revised ed. 1969. New York: Monthly Review Press.

_____. 1970. *Latin America: Underdevelopment or Revolution.* New York: Monthly Review Press.

_____. 1972. "Economic Dependence, Class Structure and Underdevelopment Policy." In *Dependence and Underdevelopment.* Ed. by James D. Cockcroft, Andre Gunder Frank and Dale L. Johnson. Garden City, N.Y.: Doubleday-Anchor.

_____. 1972. *Lumpen Bourgeoisie – Lumpen Development.* New York: Monthly Review Press.

_____. 1976. Personal communication with the author.

Furniss, Edgar S., Jr. 1957. *Some Perspectives on American Military Assistance.* Princeton, N.J.: Princeton University Press.

Gardiner, Lt. Commander Leslie. 1968. "Albania: The People's Army." *Military Review* 48 (May): 32–40.

Gardner, Lloyd C. 1964. *Economic Aspects of New Deal Diplomacy.* Madison: University of Wisconsin Press.

Garthoff, Raymond L. 1968. "The Military in Russia 1861-1965." *Armed Forces and Society.* Ed. by Jacques Van Doorn. The Hague and Paris: Mouton; 240-56.

Gastil, Raymond D. 1977. "The Comparative Survey of Freedom — VII." *Freedom at Issue* 39 (January-February): 5-18.

Gerassi, John. 1963. *The Great Fear.* New York: Macmillan Co.

Giap, Vo Nguyen. 1968. *People's War, People's Army.* New York: Bantam Books.

Gilbert, Stephen P. 1970. "Soviet-American Military Aid Competition in the Third World." *Orbis* 13 (Winter): 1117-31.

Gimbel, Jon. 1968. *The American Occupation of Germany: Politics and the Military, 1945-1949.* Stanford, Cal.: Stanford University Press.

Girvan, Norman. 1978. *Corporate Imperialism: Conflict and Expropriation.* New York: Monthly Review Press.

Godwin, P. H. B. 1976. "The PLA and Political Control of China's Provinces: A Structural Analysis." *Comparative Politics* 9 (October): 1-20.

Goff, Fred and Michael Locker. 1969. "The Violence of Domination: U.S. Power and the Dominican Republic." In *Latin American Radicalism.* Ed. by Irving Louis Horowitz, Josue de Castro, and John Gerassi. New York: Random House.

Goff, James and Margaret Goff. 1972. "Setback in Bolivia." *Christianity and Crisis* 32 (April 3): 78-84.

Gonzalez Casanova, Pablo. 1970. *Democracy in Mexico.* New York: Oxford University Press.

Gordon, Wendell C. 1968. "Has Foreign Aid Been Overstated? International Aid and Development." *Inter-American Economic Affairs* 21 (Spring): 3-18.

Gorlich, Joachim George. 1967. "The Development of the Polish People's Army." *Military Review* 47 (January): 29-34.

Goulet, Denis. 1975. *The Cruel Choice.* New York: Atheneum. Reissue of 1971 ed.

Graczyk, Josef. 1969. "Social Promotion in the Polish People's Army." *Military Profession and Military Regimes: Commitments and Conflicts.* Ed. by Jacques Van Doorn. The Hague: Mouton; 82-93.

Gramsci, Antonio. 1957. *The Open Marxism of Antonio Gramsci.* New York: Cameron Associates, Inc.

_____. 1971. *Selections from the Prison Notebooks of Antonio Gramsci.* New York: International Publishers.

Grand Pre, Don R. 1970. "A Window on America — The Department of Defense Information Program." *International Education and Cultural Exchange* 6 (Fall): 86-93.

Grant, Ronald M. 1979. "Indonesia 1978: A Third Term For President Suharto." *Asian Survey* XIX (February): 141-46.

Griffith, Samuel B., II. 1967. *The Chinese People's Liberation Army.* New York: McGraw-Hill.

Gutierrez, Carlos. 1972. *The Dominican Republic: Rebellion and Repression.* New York: Monthly Review Press.

Gutteridge, William. 1964. *Military Institutions and Power in the New States.* New York: Praeger Publishers.

Haddad, George M. 1973. *Revolutions and Military Rule in Middle East.* Vol. 3. New York: Robert Speller and Sons.

Hagopian, Mark N. 1974. *The Phenomenon of Revolution.* New York: Dodd, Mead.

Halpern, Manfred. 1963. *The Politics of Social Change in the Middle East and North Africa.* Princeton, N.J.: Princeton University Press.

Hammer, Ellen J. 1954. *The Struggle for Indochina.* Stanford, Cal.: Stanford University Press.

Hanna, Willard A. 1968. "The Mekong Project: The Enigma of Cambodia." *American Universities Field Staff Reports,* Southeast Asia Series 16 (September): 1-10.

Harbeson, John W. 1976. "Whither the Revolution?" *Africa Report* 21 (July-August): 48-50.

Harriman, James. 1977. "Party Grasps an Economic Lifeline." *Far Eastern Economic Review* (March 11): 12-14.

Harrington, Michael. 1972. *Socialism.* New York: Saturday Review Press.

Hayes, Grace P. and Paul Martell, eds. 1974. *World Military Leaders.* Loring, Va.: T. N. Dupuy Associates.

Hayter, Teresa. 1971. *Aid as Imperialism.* Baltimore: Penguin Books.

Heeger, Gerald A. 1977. "Politics in the Post-Military State: Some Reflections on the Pakistan Experience." *World Politics* 29 (January): 242-62.

Heilbroner, Robert. 1963. *The Great Ascent.* New York: W. W. Norton.

Herman, Margaret G. and Thomas W. Milburn. 1977. *A Psychological Examination of Political Leaders.* New York: Free Press.

Hibbs, Douglas A., Jr. 1973. *Mass Political Violence: A Cross-National Causal Analysis.* New York: John Wiley and Sons.

Hill, Frances. 1975. "Ujamaa: African Socialist Productionism in Tanzania." In *Socialism in the Third World.* Ed. by Helen Desfosses and Jacques Levesque. New York: Praeger Publishers.

Ho Chi Minh. 1957. "Instructions Given at the Meeting for Ideological Remolding of General and Field Officers (May 16, 1957)." In *On Revolution: Selected Writings 1920-56.* New York: Praeger Publishers.

Hobsbawm, E. J. 1973. *Revolutionaries: Contemporary Essays.* New York: Pantheon Books.

Hochman, Harold M. and C. Tait Ratcliffe. 1970. "Grant Aid or Credit Sales: A Dilemma of Military Assistance Planning." *Journal of Developing Areas* 4 (July): 461-76.

Hoffman, George W. and Fred Warner Neal. 1962. *Yugoslavia and the New Communism.* New York: Twentieth Century Fund.

Holcombe, John L. and Alan D. Berg. 1957. *MAP for Security: Military Assistance Programs of the United States.* Columbia, S.C.: University of South Carolina Bureau of Business and Economic Research.

Holsti, K. J. 1977. *International Politics.* Englewood Cliffs, N.J.: Prentice-Hall.

Hopkins, K. 1966. "Civil-Military Relations in Developing Countries." *British Journal of Sociology* 17 (June).

Horowitz, David. 1965. *The Free World Colossus.* New York: Hill and Wang.

_____. 1967. *From Yalta to Vietnam.* Baltimore: Penguin Books.

_____. 1969. *Empire and Revolution.* New York: Random House.

Horowitz, Irving Louis. 1967. "The Military Elites." In *Elites in Latin America.* Ed. by Seymour M. Lipset and Aldo Solari. New York: Oxford University Press.

_____. 1977. "From Dependency to Determinism: The New Structure of Latin American Militarism." *Journal of Political and Military Sociology* 5 (Fall): 217-38.

Horowitz, Irving Louis and Ellen Kay Trimberger. 1976. "State Power and Military Nationalism in Latin America." *Comparative Politics* 8 (January): 223-43.

Hovey, Harold A. 1965. *United States Military Assistance: A Study of Policies and Practices.* New York: Praeger Publishers.

Hughes, Anthony J. 1977. "Somalia's Socialist Road." *Africa Report* 22 (March-April): 41-49.

Huntington, Samuel P. 1965. "Political Development and Political Decay." *World Politics* 17 (April): 386-430.

_____. 1968. *Political Order in Changing Societies.* New Haven: Yale University Press.

Huntington, Samuel P. and Joan M. Nelson. 1976. *Participation in Developing Countries.* Cambridge, Mass.: Harvard University Press.

Hurewitz, J. C. 1969. *Middle Eastern Politics: The Military Dimension.* New York: Praeger Publishers.

Iskenderov, A. 1971. "The Army, Politics, and the People." *The Military and Modernization.* Ed. by Henry Bienen. Chicago: Aldine; 149–56.
Ismael, Tareky. 1975. "Socialism in Iraq." In *Socialism in the Third World.* Ed. by Helen Desfosses and Jacques Levesque. New York: Praeger Publishers.
Jackman, Robert W. 1976. "Politicians in Uniform?" *American Political Science Review* 70 (December): 1078–97.
Jacobs, Norman. 1966. *The Society of Development: Iran as an Asian Study.* New York: Praeger Publishers.
Jalee, Pierre. 1968. *The Pillage of the Third World.* New York: Monthly Review Press.
Janowitz, Morris. 1960. *The Professional Soldier.* New York: Free Press.
_____. 1964. *The Military in the Political Development of New Nations.* Chicago: University of Chicago Press.
_____. 1971. "Military Organization." *Handbook of Military Institutions.* Ed. by Roger W. Little. Beverly Hills, Cal.: Sage; 13–51.
_____. 1977. *Military Institutions and Coercion in the Developing Nations.* Chicago: University of Chicago Press.
Janowitz, Morris and Jacques Van Doorn, eds. 1971. *On Military Intervention.* Netherlands: Rotterdam University Press.
Jencks, Christopher. 1977. "Equality: Laissez-faire Economics and Repressive Politics." *Working Papers for a New Society* IV (Winter): 10–12.
Joffe, Ellis. 1965. *Party and Army: Professionalism and Political Control in the Chinese Officer Corps: 1949–1964.* Cambridge, Mass.: Harvard University Press.
Johnson, Dale. 1968–69. "The National and Progressive Bourgeoisie in Latin America." *Studies in Comparative International Development* 4 (4): 63–86.
_____. 1972. "Dependence and the International System." In *Dependence and Underdevelopment.* Ed. by James D. Cockcroft, Andre Gunder Frank and Dale L. Johnson. Garden City, N.Y.: Doubleday-Anchor.
Johnson, John J. 1964. *The Military and Society in Latin America.* Stanford, Cal.: Stanford University Press.
Jupp, James. 1977. "Democratic Socialism in the Tropics—The Case of Sri Lanka." Paper presented at 1977 Meeting of C.P.S.A., Fredericton, N.B. (June 9–11).
Kaba, Lasine. 1977. "Guinean Politics: A Critical Historical Overview." *Journal of Modern African Studies* 15 (1): 25–45.
Kahl, Joseph, ed. 1976. *Modernization, Exploitation and Dependency in Latin America.* New Brunswick, N.J.: Transaction Books.
Keefe, Eugene K. et al. 1971. *Area Handbook of Albania.* D.A. PAM 550–98. Washington, D.C.: U.S. Government Printing Office.
Kennedy, Gavin. 1974. *The Military in the Third World.* London: Duckworth.
_____. 1975. *The Economics of Defense.* Totowa, N.J.: Rowman & Littlefield.
Kim, Se-Jin. 1971. *The Politics of Military Revolution in Korea.* Chapel Hill, N.C.: University of North Carolina Press.
Kinross, Lord. 1978. *Ataturk.* New York: William Morrow.
Klare, Michael. 1972. *War without End.* New York: Alfred Knopf.
Kling, Merle. 1956. "Toward a Theory of Power and Political Instability in Latin America." *Western Political Quarterly* 9 (March).
_____. 1968. "Toward a Theory of Power and Political Instability in Latin America." In *Latin America: Reform or Revolution?* Ed. by James Petras and Maurice Zeitlin. New York: Fawcett.
Kolko, Gabriel. 1968. *The Politics of War.* New York: Random House.
_____. 1969. *The Roots of American Foreign Policy: An Analysis of Power and Purpose.* Boston: Beacon Press.
Kolkowicz, Roman. 1967. *The Soviet Military and the Communist Party.* Princeton, N.J.: Princeton University Press.

Kourvetaris, George A. and Betty A. Dobratz. 1972-73. *Social Origins and Political Orientations of Officer Corps in World Perspective.* Denver: University of Denver International Monograph Series in World Affairs, Vol. 10, Pt.D.

_____. George A. and Betty Dobratz, eds. 1977. *World Perspectives in the Sociology of the Military.* New Brunswick, N.J.: Transaction Books.

Krajacevic, Col. Alesksandar. 1968. "Certain Factors in the Defense of Yugoslavia." *Review of International Affairs* 19 (Sept. 20): 22-4.

Kraus, Jon. 1966. "The Men in Charge." *African Report* 11 (April): 16-20.

_____. 1976. "Socialism and Political Economy in Ghana." In *Socialism in the Third World.* Ed. by Helen Desfosses and Jacques Levesque. New York: Praeger Publishers.

Kurzman, Dan. 1965. *Santo Domingo: Revolt of the Damned.* New York: G. P. Putnam's Sons.

Krishnamurthy, S. 1977. "Political Stability under Military Regimes: The Burmese and the Indonesian Experiences." *India Quarterly* 33 (Oct.-Dec.): 391-400.

Laemmle, Philip. 1977. "Epidemiology of Domestic Military Intervention: Evaluation of Contagion as an Explanatory Concept." *Behavioral Science* 22 (September): 327-33.

LaFeber, Walter. 1963. *The New Empire.* Ithaca, N.Y.: Cornell University Press.

Laitin, David D. 1976. "The Political Economy of Military Rule in Somalia." *Journal of Modern African Studies* 14 (3): 449-68.

Lane, David. 1976. *The Socialist Industrial State.* Boulder, Colo.: Westview Press.

Lang, Kurt. 1972. *Military Institutions and the Sociology of War: A Review of the Literature with Annotated Bibliography.* Beverly Hills, Cal.: Sage.

LaPalombara, Joseph. 1969. "Macrotheories and Microapplications in Comparative Politics: A Widening Chasm." *Comparative Politics* 1 (October): 52-78.

Lappe, Frances Moore and Joe Collins. 1977. "World Recession Improves the Jamaican Diet." (May 25): 14.

Latin American Political Report. 1977. London (Jan. 14, 28): 15, 32.

Leca, Jean. 1975. "Algerian Socialism: Nationalism, Industrialism, and State Building." In *Socialism in the Third World.* Ed. by Helen Desfosses and Jacques Levesque. New York: Praeger Publishers.

Lee, J. M. 1969. *African Armies and Civil Order.* New York: Praeger Publishers.

Lee, William F. 1977. "Ethiopia: A Review of the Dergue." *African Report* 22 (March-April): 7-11.

Leifer, Michael. 1970. "Political Upheaval in Cambodia." *World Today* 26 (May): 179-88.

Leitenberg, Milton and Gabriel Sheffer, eds. 1979. *Great Power Intervention in the Middle East.* New York: Pergamon.

Lemarchand, Rene. 1976. "The CIA in Africa: How Central? How Intelligent?" *Journal of Modern African Studies* 14 (September): 401-26.

Lenczewski, George. 1975. "Socialism in Syria." In *Socialism in the Third World.* Ed. by Helen Desfosses and Jacques Levesque. New York: Praeger Publishers.

Lenin, V. I. 1918. "The State and Revolution." In *Handbook of Marxism.* New York: International Publishers, 1935; 722-59.

Lenski, Gerhard E. 1966. *Power and Privilege: A Theory of Social Satisfaction.* New York: McGraw-Hill.

LeoGrande, William M. 1978. "The Politics of Revolutionary Development: Civil-Military Relations in Cuba, 1959-1976." *Journal of Strategic Studies* I (December): 260-94.

Letelier, Orlando and Michael Moffitt. 1978. *The International Economic Order.* Washington, D.C.: IPS.

Levesque, Jacques. 1978. *The USSR and the Cuban Revolution.* New York: Praeger Publishers.

Levy, Marion J., Jr. 1971. "Armed Force Organizations." In *The Military and Modernization.* Ed. by Henry Bienen. Chicago: Aldine; 41-78.

Liddle, R. William. 1977. "Indonesia 1976: Challenges to Suharto's Authority." *Asian Survey* 17 (February): 95–106.

Lieuwen, Edwin. 1964. *Generals vs. Presidents*. New York: Praeger Publishers.

Lowenthal, Abraham F., ed. 1976. *Armies and Politics in Latin America*. New York: Holmes & Meier.

Luckham, R. 1971. *The Nigerian Military*. Cambridge: Cambridge University Press.

Luttwak, Edward. 1969. *Coup d'Etat: A Practical Handbook*. New York: Alfred Knopf.

_____. 1974. *The Political Uses of Seapower*. Baltimore, Md.: The Johns Hopkins University Press.

McFarland, Andrew P. 1969. *Power and Leadership in Pluralist Systems*. Stanford, Cal.: Stanford University Press.

McKinlay, R. D. and A. S. Cohan. 1976. *Performance and Instability in Military and Neo-Military Regime Systems*. American Political Science Review LXX (September): 850–64.

McLellan, David. 1971. *The Thought of Karl Marx: An Introduction*. New York: Harper & Row.

McQuarie, Donald. 1978. "Marx and the Method of Successive Approximations." *The Sociological Quarterly* 19 (Spring): 218–33.

MacEoin, Gary. 1974. *No Peaceful Way: Chile's Struggle for Dignity*. New York: Sheed and Ward.

Magdoff, Harry. 1969. *The Age of Imperialism*. New York: Monthly Review Press.

_____. 1978a. *Imperialism: From the Colonial Age to the Present*. New York: Monthly Review Press.

_____. 1978b. "Is There A Noncapitalist Road?" *Monthly Review* 30 (December): 1–7.

Malloy, James and Richard S. Thorn, eds. 1971. *Beyond the Revolution: Bolivia since 1952*. Pittsburgh, Pa.: University of Pittsburgh Press.

Marchetti, Victor and John D. Marks. 1974. *The CIA and the Cult of Intelligence*. New York: Alfred Knopf.

Marlowe, John. 1963. *Iran: A Short Political Guide*. London: Pall Mall Press.

Martin, Edwin W. 1977. "Burma in 1976: The Beginnings of Change." *Asian Survey* 17 (February): 155–59.

Martin, John Bartlow. 1966. *Overtaken by Events: The Dominican Crisis from the Fall of Trujillo to the Civil War*. Garden City, N.Y.: Doubleday.

Marxism. 1972. *Marxism-Leninism on War*. Moscow: Foreign Languages Publishing House.

Maynard, Harold W. 1978. "Views of the Indonesian and Philippine Military Elites." In *The Military and Security in the Third World: Domestic and International Impacts*. Ed. by Sheldon W. Simon. Boulder, Colo.: Westview Press.

Mazrui, Ali A. 1969. "Anti-Militarism and Political Militancy in Tanzania." In *The Military Profession and Military Regimes: Commitments and Conflicts*. Ed. by Jacques Van Doorn. The Hague: Mouton.

_____. 1978. *Political Values and the Educated Class in Africa*. Berkeley, Cal.: University of California Press.

Meghed, Horeya T. 1970. *Socialism and Nation Building in Africa: The Case of Mali, 1960–68*. Budapest: Academy of Sciences.

Melville, Thomas and Marjorie Melville. 1971. *Guatemala: The Politics of Land Ownership*. New York: Free Press.

MERIP. 1976. "Why Syria Invaded Lebanon." *MERIP Reports* (51): 9.

Merriam, John G. 1976. "Military Rule in Ethiopia." *Current History* 71 (November): 170–73, 183–84.

Middleton, Drew. 1970. "Thousands of Foreign Military Men Studying in U.S." *New York Times* (November 1): 18.

Miliband, Ralph. 1969. *The State in Capitalist Society.* New York: Basic Books.
_____. 1977. *Marxism and Politics.* New York: Oxford University Press.
Mittelman, James H. 1975. *Dependency and Civil-Military Relations.* Buffalo, N.Y.: SUNY – Council on International Studies, No. 67.
Mohri, Kenzo. 1979. "Marx and Underdevelopment." *Monthly Review* 30 (April): 32–42.
Monteforte Toledo, Mario. 1970. *La solucion militar a la Peruana: 1968-1970.* Mexico: UNAM.
Morray, J. P. 1962. *The Second Revolution in Cuba.* New York: Monthly Review Press.
Moore, Barrington. 1966. *Social Origins of Dictatorship and Democracy.* Boston: Beacon Press.
Moore, David W. and Thomas B. Trout. 1978. "Military Advancement: The Visibility Theory of Promotion." *American Political Science Review* 72 (June): 452–68.
Mueller, Claus. 1975. *The Politics of Communication: A Study in the Political Sociology of Language, Socialization and Legitimation.* New York: Oxford University Press.
Mylander, Maureen. 1974. *The Generals.* New York: Dial Press.
NACLA. 1974. "U.S. Counter-revolutionary Apparatus: The Chilean Offensive." *NACLA's Latin American and Empire Report* 8 (July-August): 1–39.
Needleman, Martin and Carol Needleman. 1969. "Marx and the Problem of Causation." *Science and Society* XXXIII (Summer-Fall 1969): 322–339.
Needler, Martin. 1963. *Anatomy of a Coup d'Etat: Ecuador, 1963.* Washington, D.C.: Institute for the Comparative Study of Political Systems.
_____. 1966. "Political Development and Military Intervention in Latin America." *American Political Science Review* 60 (September): 616–26.
_____. 1969. "The Latin American Military: Predatory Reactionaries or Modernizing Patriots?" *Journal of Inter-American Studies* 11 (April): 239–42.
Nelkin, D. 1967. "The Economic and Social Setting of Military Takeovers – Africa." *Journal of Asian and African Studies* 2 (July-October): 230–44.
Nirumand, Bahman. 1969. *Iran: The New Imperialism in Action.* New York: Monthly Review Press.
Nicasio. 1977. "Banana Exporters Unite against Monopolies." *Guardian* (May 11): 16.
Nkrumah, Kwame. 1969. *Dark Days in Ghana.* New York: International Publishers.
_____. 1973. *Revolutionary Path.* New York: International Publishers.
Nordlinger, Eric A. 1970. "Soldiers in Mufti: The Impact of Military Rule upon Economic and Social Change in the Non-Western States." *American Political Science Review* 64 (December): 1131–48.
_____. 1977. *Soldiers in Politics: Military Coups and Governments.* Englewood Cliffs, N.J.: Prentice-Hall.
North, Liisa. 1974. "The Military in Chilean Politics." Draft Paper Presented at Canadian Political Science Association. Reprinted in *Armies and Politics in Latin America.* Ed. by Abraham Lowenthal. New York: Holmes & Meier, 1976.
Nun, Jose. 1969. *Latin America: The Hegemonic Crisis and the Military Coup.* Berkeley, Cal.: University of California, Institutional Studies, Politics of Modernization Series, No. 7.
O'Connor, James. 1973. *The Fiscal Crisis of the State.* New York: St. Martin's Press.
Offe, Claus. 1972. "Advanced Capitalism and the Welfare state." *Politics and Society,* II (4).
Olorunsola, Victor A. 1977. *Soldiers and Power: The Development Performance of the Nigerian Military Regime.* Stanford, Cal.: Hoover Institution Press.
Otley, C. B. 1978. "Militarism and Militarization in the Public Schools, 1900–1972." *British Journal of Sociology* 29 (September): 321–39.
Ottaway, Marina. 1976. "Social Classes and Corporate Interests in the Ethiopian Revolution." *Journal of Modern African Studies* 14 (3): 469–86.

Packenham, R. A. 1966. "Political Development Doctrines in the American Foreign Aid Program." *World Politics* 18 (January): 194–235.

Paige, Glenn D. 1966. *The Korean People's Republic*. Hoover Institution. Stanford, Cal.: Stanford University Press.

Palmer, Ingrid. 1978. *The Indonesian Economy since 1966*. London: Frank Cass.

Palmer, Monte and William R. Thompson. 1978. *The Comparative Analysis of Politics*. Itasca, Ill.: F. E. Peacock.

Payer, Cheryl. 1974. *The Debt Trap: The International Monetary Fund and the Third World*. New York: Monthly Review Press.

_____. 1976. "Third World Debt Problems: The New Wave of Defaults." *Monthly Review* 28 (September): 1–22.

Perlmutter, Amos. 1969. "From Obscurity to Rule: The Syrian Army and the Baath Party." *Western Political Quarterly* 22 (December): 827–45.

_____. 1977. *The Military and Politics in Modern Times: On Professionals, Praetorians, and Revolutionary Soldiers*. New Haven: Yale University Press.

_____. 1977a. "Praetorianism: Prospect and Retrospect." Paper Presented at Joint Meeting of the Latin American Studies Association and the African Studies Association. Houston, Texas (November).

Petras, James. 1971. "Bolivia between Revolutions." *Monthly Review* 23 (June): 11–24.

_____. 1976. "Class and Politics in the Periphery and the Transition to Socialism." *Review of Radical Political Economics* 8 (2): 20–35.

_____. 1978. *Critical Perspectives on Imperialism and Social Class in the Third World*. New York: Monthly Review Press.

Petras, James and Morris Morley. 1975. *The United States and Chile*. New York: Monthly Review Press.

Philip, George. 1976. "The Soldier as Radical: The Peruvian Military Government, 1968–1975." *Journal of Latin American Studies* 8 (May): 29–51.

Pool, Ithiel de Sola. 1955. *Satellite Generals: A Study of Military Elites in the Soviet Sphere*. Hoover Institute Studies. Stanford, Cal.: Stanford University Press.

Porch, Douglas. 1977. *The Portuguese Armed Forces and the Revolution*. Stanford: Hoover Institution Press.

Porter, General Robert W., Jr., USA. 1968. "Address to the Pan American Society of the United States." New York, N.Y., March 26, 1968. Reprinted in U.S. Congress, House of Representatives, *Foreign Assistance Act of 1968, Hearings* before the Committee on Foreign Affairs. 90th Cong., 2nd Sess., 1204–5.

Portes, Alejandro. 1970. "Leftist Radicalism: Chile! A Test of Three Hypotheses." *Comparative Politics* 2 (January): 254–68.

Potash, Robert A. 1969. *The Army and Politics in Argentina*. Stanford, Cal.: Stanford University Press.

Poulantzas, Nicos. 1973. *Political Power and Social Classes*. London: New Left Books.

Powers, John J., Sr. 1968. "The Impact of U.S. Controls on Foreign Investment." *NACLA Newsletter*, II (November): 8–10. Address to the American Management Association.

Price, Robert M. 1971. "A Theoretical Approach to Military Rule in New States: Reference-Group Theory and the Ghanian Case." *World Politics* 23 (April): 399–430.

Putnam, R. D. 1967. "Toward Explaining Military Intervention in Latin American Politics." *World Politics* 20 (October): 83–110.

Pye, Lucien. 1962. "Armies in the Process of Political Modernization." *The Role of the Military in the Underdeveloped Countries*. Ed. by John J. Johnson. Princeton, N.J.: Princeton University Press.

Rabinovitch, J. 1973. *Syria under the Baath, 1963–66: The Army-Party Symbiosis*. New York: John Wiley and Sons.

Radosh, Ronald. 1969. *American Labor and United States Foreign Policy: The Cold War in the Unions from Gompers to Lovestone.* New York: Random House.

Rejai, Mostafa. 1973. *The Strategy of Political Revolution.* Garden City, N.Y.: Double-day-Anchor.

Rejai, Mostafa with Kay Phillips. 1979. *Leaders of Revolution.* Beverly Hills, Cal.: Sage.

Rhodes, Robert I., ed. 1970. *Imperialism and Underdevelopment.* New York: Monthly Review Press.

Riddleberger, Peter B. 1965. *Military Roles in Developing Countries: An Inventory of Past Research and Analysis.* Washington, D.C.: American University, Special Operations Research Office, AD 463188.

Ridout, Christine F. 1975. "Authority Patterns and the Afghan Coups of 1973." *Middle East Journal* 29 (Spring): 165–78.

Robbs, Peter. 1976. "Africa and the Indian Ocean." *Africa Report* 21 (May-June 1976): 41–45.

Rood, Leslie L. 1976. "Nationalisation and Indigenisation in Africa." *Journal of Modern African Studies* 14 (September): 427–48.

Rossoff, William. 1971. "Dissension in the Kingdom." In *Cambodia: The Widening War in Indochina.* Ed. by Jonathan S. Grant, Lawrence A. G. Moss, and Jonathan Unger. New York: Washington Square Press; 81–94.

Rupen, Robert A. 1966. *The Mongolian People's Republic.* Hoover Institution. Stanford, Cal.: Stanford University Press.

Russell, D. E. 1974. *Rebellion, Revolution and Armed Force: A Comparative Study of Fifteen Countries with Special Emphasis upon Cuba and South Africa.* New York: Academic Press.

Russett, Bruce M. 1970. *What Price Vigilance? The Burdens of National Defense.* New Haven: Yale University Press.

Salaman, G. and K. Thompson. 1978. "Class Culture and the Persistence of an Elite: The Case of Army Officer Selection." *British Sociological Review* (May): 283–304.

Sanger, Richard H. 1975. "Libya: Conclusions on an Unfinished Revolution." *Middle East Journal* 29 (Autumn): 409–17.

Sarkesian, Sam C. 1978. "A Political Perspective on Military Power in Developing Areas." In *The Military and Security in the Third World: Domestic and International Impacts.* Ed. by Sheldon W. Simon. Boulder, Colo.: Westview Press; 3–14.

Saxe-Fernandez, John. 1969. "The Central American Defense Council and Pax Americana." In *Latin American Radicalism: A Documentary Report on Left and Nationalist Movements.* Ed. by Irving Louis Horowitz, Josue de Castro and John Gerassi. New York: Random House.

_____. 1971. *Proyecciones Hemisfericas de la Pax Americana.* Lima: Instituto de Estudios Peruanos.

_____. 1974. *The Sociology of Terror.* Garden City, N.Y.: Doubleday-Anchor.

Schapiro, Leonard. 1956. "The Birth of the Red Army." In *The Red Army.* Ed. by B. H. Liddell Hart. New York: Harcourt, Brace; 24–32.

Schechter, Danny. 1977. "Michael Manley has a mandate for 'heavy manners.'" *Seven Days* 1 (Feb. 28): 24–5.

Schmitter, Philippe C. 1971. "Military Intervention, Political Competitiveness and Public Policy in Latin America: 1950–1967." In *On Military Intervention.* Ed. by Morris Janowitz and J. Van Doorn. Rotterdam: Rotterdam University Press.

_____. 1973. "Foreign Military Assistance, National Military Spending and Military Rule in Latin America." In *Military Rule in Latin America: Functions, Consequences and Perspectives.* Ed. by Philippe C. Schmitter. Beverly Hills, Cal.: Sage; 117–87.

_____, ed. 1973. *Military Rule in Latin America: Functions, Consequences and Perspectives.* Beverly Hills, Cal.: Sage.

Schneider, Ronald M. 1959. *Communism in Guatemala: 1944–1954.* New York: Praeger Publishers.

Schonfeld, William R. 1971. "The Focus of Political Socialization Research: An Evaluation." *World Politics* 23 (April): 544-557.

Scully, William L. and Frank Trager. 1979. "Burma 1978: The Thirtieth Year of Independence." *Asian Survey* XIX (February): 147-56.

Sellars, Robert C. 1968. *Reference Handbook of Armed Forces of the World*. Garden City, N.Y.: Robert C. Sellars and Associates.

Selover, William C. 1971. "U.S. Food for Peace Converted to Armament." *Christian Science Monitor* (January 8).

Shivji, Issa E. 1976. *Class Struggles in Tanzania*. New York: Monthly Review Press.

Silverstein, Josef. 1977. *Burma: Military Rule and the Politics of an Asian State*. Ithaca, N.Y.: Cornell University Press.

Sihanouk, Norodom. 1973. *My War With the CIA: The Memoirs of Prince Norodom Sihanouk*. New York: Pantheon Books.

Simon, Sheldon W., ed. 1978. *The Military and Security in the Third World: Domestic and International Impacts*. Boulder, Colo.: Westview Press.

Sinai, I. R. 1965. *The Challenge of Modernization*. New York: W. W. Norton.

Skidmore, Thomas E. 1967. *Politics in Brazil, 1930-1964: An Experiment in Democracy*. New York: Oxford University Press.

Sklar, R. L. 1976. "Postimperialism: A Class Analysis of Multinational Corporate Expansion." *Comparative Politics* 9 (October): 75-92.

Skocpol, Theda and Ellen Kay Trimberger. 1978. "Revolutions and the World Historical Development of Capitalism." In *Social Change in the Capitalist World Economy*. Ed. by Barbara Hockey Kaplan. Beverly Hills, Cal.: Sage.

Smith, Robert F. 1960. *The United States and Cuba: Business and Diplomacy 1917-1960*. New Haven: College and University Press.

Smith, Tony. 1975. "The Political and Economic Ambitions of Algerian Land Reform, 1962-1974." *The Middle East Journal* 29 (Summer): 259-78.

Sohn, Jae Souk. 1969. "Factionalism and Party Control of the Military in Communist North Korea." In *The Military Profession and Military Regimes: Commitments and Conflicts*. Ed. by Jacques Van Doorn. The Hague: Mouton; 269-94.

Stepan, Alfred. 1971. *The Military in Politics: Changing Patterns in Brazil*. Princeton, N.J.: Princeton University Press.

Stevens, Christopher. 1976. "The Soviet Union and Angola." *African Affairs* 75 (April): 137-41.

Stern, Richard. 1975. "Urban Policy and Performance in Kenya and Tanzania." *Journal of Modern African Studies* 13 (2): 267-94.

Sunkel, Osvaldo and Edmundo Fuenzalida. 1976. "An Interdisciplinary Research Programme on the Transnationalization of Capitalism and National Development." IDS (November): 3-8.

Survey. 1975. *The Far East and Australia: 1975-76. A Survey and Directory of Asia and the Pacific*. London: Europa Publications.

Szuprowicz, Bohdan. 1977. "The Role of the People's Liberation Army in the Chinese Economy and Foreign Affairs." *Military Review* 57 (December): 3-19.

Szymanski, Albert. 1976. "Dependence, Exploitation and Economic Growth." *Journal of Political and Military Sociology* 4 (Spring): 53-65.

Tannahill, R. Neal. 1976. "The Performance of Military Governments in South America." *Journal of Political and Military Sociology* 4 (Fall): 233-44.

Taylor, Charles L. 1977. "The Environment for Irregular Government Change." GPSA Journal 5 (Spring): 103-108.

Taylor, Charles L. and Michael C. Hudson. 1972. *World Handbook of Political and Social Indicators*. New Haven: Yale University Press.

Thompson, William R. 1973. *The Grievances of Military Coup-Makers*. Beverly Hills, Cal.: Sage.

_____. 1975. "Systematic Change and the Latin American Military Coup." *Comparative Political Studies* 7 (January): 441–59.

_____. 1976. "Organizational Cohesion and Military Coup Outcomes." *Comparative Political Studies* 9 (October): 255–76.

Ticktin, Hillel. 1976. "The Contradictions of Soviet Society and Professor Bettelheim." *Critique* 6 (Spring): 17–44.

Trimberger, Ellen K. 1977. *Revolution from Above: Military Bureaucrats in Japan, Turkey, Egypt, and Peru*. New Brunswick, N.J.: Transaction Books.

Tromp, H. W. 1971. "The Assessment of the Military Mind: A Critical Comment on Methodology." Ed. by M. R. Van Gils. In *The Perceived Role of the Military*. Rotterdam: Rotterdam University Press; 359–77.

Tucker, Robert C. 1969. *The Marxian Revolutionary Idea*. New York: W. W. Norton.

_____. 1970. In *Philosophers and Kings: Studies in Leadership*. Ed. by David Apter. New York: George Braziller.

_____. 1972. *The Marx-Engels Reader*. New York: W. W. Norton.

Tullis, F. LaMond. 1973. *Politics and Social Changes in Third World Countries*. New York: John Wiley and Sons.

Tun, M. C. 1977. "The Price of Treason." *Far Eastern Economic Review* 104 (March 4): 30.

_____. 1978. "Military Line Holds Firm." *Far Eastern Economic Review* 105 (January): 28.

United Nations. 1966–1974. *Demographic Yearbooks 1966–1974*. New York: United Nations.

_____. 1967. *Compendium of Social Statistics*. New York: United Nations.

_____. 1967–74. *Statistical Yearbooks. 1967–1974*. New York: United Nations.

United Nations Department of Economic and Social Affairs. 1972. *Disarmament and Development: Report of the Group of Experts on the Economic and Social Consequences of Disarmament*. New York: United Nations.

_____. 1974. *World Economic Survey, 1974*. Parts I and II. Mid-term Review and Appraisal of Progress in the Implementation of the International Development Strategy. New York: United Nations.

_____. 1974. *Statistical Yearbook*. New York: United Nations.

_____. 1975. *World Economic Survey, 1974*. Part I. Mid-term Review and Appraisal of Progress in the Implementation of the International Development Strategy. New York: United Nations.

_____. 1975. *Statistical Yearbook, 1975*. New York: United Nations.

_____. 1976. *Yearbook of National Accounts Statistics, 1975*. Vol. 3. New York: United Nations.

U.N. Secretary-General. 1974. *Permanent Sovereignty over Natural Resources*. (A/9716, Supplement to E/5425, 20 September 1974, Annex p.1) As cited by Rood.

U.S. Arms Control and Disarmament Agency. 1976. *World Military Expenditures and Arms Transfers: 1966–1975*. Washington, D.C.: U.S. Government Printing Office.

_____. 1979. *World Military Expenditures and Arms Transfers: 1968–1977*. Washington, D.C.: U.S. Arms Control and Disarmament Agency.

U.S. Army. 1968. *Area Handbook for Cambodia*. Washington, D.C.: U.S. Government Printing Office.

U.S. Army Signal Center and School. 1967. *Report of the Thirteenth Annual U.S. Army Human Factors Research and Development Conference*. October 25–27, 1967. Fort Monmouth, N.J.: U.S. Department of the Army.

U.S. Central Intelligence Agency. 1975. *Handbook of Economic Statistics*. Washington, D.C.: U.S. Central Intelligence Agency.

U.S. Congress. 1964. *Communist Takeover and Occupation of Bulgaria*. Reports of Select

Committee on Communist Aggression, House of Representatives. Report 2684, pt. 10.
_____. 1969. *Rockefeller Report on Latin America*. Hearings before the Subcommittee on Western Hemisphere Affairs of the Committee on Foreign Relations. 91st Congress (November 20).
_____. 1970. *Reports of the Special Study Mission to Latin America on Military Assistance Training and Developmental Television*. Submitted by C. J. Zablocki, J. G. Fulton and P. Findley to the Subcommittee on National Security Policy and Scientific Developments of the Committee on Foreign Affairs. 91st Congress (May 7).
_____. 1977. House of Representatives Foreign Assistance and Related Agencies Appropriations Hearings before a Subcommittee of the Committee on Appropriations. 94th Congress, 2nd. Session.
U.S. Department of Defense. 1970. *Military Assistance and Foreign Sales Facts: March 1970*. Washington, D.C.: Office of the Assistant Secretary of Defense for International Security Affairs.
_____. 1974. *Military Sales and Assistance Facts*. Washington, D.C.: Office of the Assistant Secretary of Defense.
Vagts, Alfred. 1959. *A History of Militarism*. New York: Free Press. Reissued in 1967.
Valdes, Nelson. 1976. "The Institutionalization of the Cuban Revolution." Cuban Studies.
Vali, Ferenc Albert. 1961. *Rift and Revolt in Hungary: Nationalism vs. Communism*. Cambridge, Mass.: Harvard University Press.
Vallance, Theodore R. and Charles D. Windle. 1962. "Cultural Engineering." *Military Review* 43 (December): 60-4.
Van Doorn, Jacques, ed. 1969. *The Military Profession and Military Regimes: Commitments and Conflicts*. The Hague: Mouton.
Van Gils, M. R., ed. 1971. *The Perceived Role of the Military*. Netherlands: Rotterdam University Press.
Vayrymen, Raimo. 1977. "Transnational Corporations and Arms Transfers." *Instant Research on Peace and Violence* 7 (3-4): 145-66.
Villaneuva, Victor. 1969. *¿ Nueva mentalidad militar en el Peru?* Lima: Libreria-Edit. Juan Mejia Baca.
Volman, Daniel. 1980. *A Continent Besieged: Foreign Military Activities in Africa since 1975*. Washington: Institute for Policy Studies.
Wallerstein, Immanuel. 1976. *The Modern World System: Capitalist Agriculture and the Origins of the World Economy in the Sixteenth Century*. New York: Academic Press.
Walton, Richard J. 1973. *Cold War and Counterrevolution: The Foreign Policy of John F. Kennedy*. Baltimore: Penguin Books.
Watson, Gayle Hudgens. 1977. "Our Monster in Brazil: It all Began with 'Brother Sam.'" *Nation* (January 15): 51-54.
Weaver, Jerry L. 1973. "Assessing the Impact of Military Rule." In *Alternative Approaches to Military Rule in Latin America: Functions, Consequences, and Perspectives*. Ed. by Philippe C. Schmitter. Beverly Hills, Cal.: Sage; 58-116.
Weinstein, James. 1968. *The Corporate Ideal in the Liberal State: 1900-1918*. Boston: Beacon Press.
Western Massachusetts ACAS. 1979. *U.S. Military Involvement in Southern Africa*. Boston: South End Press.
Welch, Claude E. 1970. *Soldier and State in Africa*. Evanston, Ill.: Northwestern University Press.
_____. 1976. *Civilian Control of the Military: Theory and Cases from Developing Countries*. Albany, N.Y.: State University of New York Press.
_____. 1977. "Warrior, Rebel, Guerrilla and Putschist: Four Aspects of Political Violence." *Journal of Asian and African Studies* 12 (June-October): 82-98.
_____. 1978. "Long-term Consequences of Military Rule: Breakdown and Extrication."

Journal of Strategic Studies I (September): 139–53.

Werlich, David P. 1977. "The Peruvian Revolution in Crisis." *Current History* (February): 61–81.

Whitehead, Laurence. 1972. "Bolivia Swings Right." *Current History* 62 (January): 86–90.

Wiarda, Howard J. 1969. *The Dominican Republic: Nation in Transition.* New York: Praeger Publishers.

Wilber, Donald N. 1958. *Iran: Past and Present.* Princeton, N.J.: Princeton University Press.

Williams, William A. 1962. *The Tragedy of American Diplomacy.* New York: Dell.

Wilson, A. Jeyaratnam. 1975. "Socialism in Sri Lanka." In *Socialism in the Third World.* Ed. by Helen Desfosses and Jacques Levesque. New York: Praeger Publishers.

Wise, David and Thomas B. Ross. 1964. *The Invisible Government.* New York: Random House.

Woddis, Jack. 1977. *Armies and Politics.* London: Lawrence and Wishart.

Wolf, Charles, Jr. 1965. *Military Assistance Programs.* Santa Monica, Cal.: Rand Corporation.

Wolpin, Miles D. 1972. *Cuban Foreign Policy and Chilean Politics.* Lexington, Mass.: D.C. Heath.

———. 1973. *Military Aid and Counterrevolution in the Third World.* Lexington, Mass.: D. C. Heath.

———. 1976. "Conservative Militarism and the Communist Military Subordination Model." *Social Praxis* 2 (Spring): 277–308.

———. 1977a. "Military Dependency and Technology Transfers vs. Third World Development." *Caribbean Quarterly* 23 (September).

———. 1977b. "Socialism and Civilian Supremacy vs. Militarism in the Third World: A Comparison of Development Costs and Benefits." Paper Presented to Canadian Political Science Association Meeting, Fredericton, N.B.

———. 1980. "Military Professionalism and Leftist Political Movements." Forthcoming.

———. 1981. "Military Radicalism in Latin America." *Journal of Inter-American Studies and World Affairs.*

Wright, Erik Olin. 1978. *Class, Crisis and the State.* London: New Left Books.

Wulf, Herbert. 1979. "Dependent Militarism in the Periphery and Possible Alternative Concepts." In *Arms Transfers in the Modern World.* Ed. by Stephanie G. Neuman and Robert E. Harkavy. New York: Praeger Publishers.

Zaveleta, Rene. 1972. "Bolivia: Military Nationalism and the Popular Assembly." *New Left Review* (73): 63–82.

Index